LIBRARY OF HEBREW BIBLE/
OLD TESTAMENT STUDIES

669

Formerly Journal for the Study of the Old Testament Supplement Series

Editors
Claudia V. Camp, Texas Christian University, USA
Andrew Mein, University of Durham, UK

Founding Editors
David J. A. Clines, Philip R. Davies and David M. Gunn

Editorial Board
Alan Cooper, Susan Gillingham, John Goldingay,
Norman K. Gottwald, James E. Harding, John Jarick, Carol Meyers,
Daniel L. Smith-Christopher, Francesca Stavrakopoulou,
James W. Watts

CHARACTERS AND CHARACTERIZATION IN THE BOOK OF SAMUEL

Edited by

Keith Bodner and Benjamin J. M. Johnson

LONDON • NEW YORK • OXFORD • NEW DELHI • SYDNEY

T&T CLARK
Bloomsbury Publishing Plc
50 Bedford Square, London, WC1B 3DP, UK
1385 Broadway, New York, NY 10018, USA
29 Earlsfort Terrace, Dublin 2, Ireland

BLOOMSBURY, T&T CLARK and the T&T Clark logo
are trademarks of Bloomsbury Publishing Plc

First published in Great Britain 2020
Paperback edition first published 2021

Volume Editors' Part of the Work © Keith Bodner and Benjamin J. M. Johnson, 2020
Each chapter © of Contributor

Keith Bodner, Benjamin J.M. Johnson, and contributors have asserted their right under the Copyright,
Designs and Patents Act, 1988, to be identified as Authors of this work.

All rights reserved. No part of this publication may be reproduced or
transmitted in any form or by any means, electronic or mechanical,
including photocopying, recording, or any information storage or retrieval
system, without prior permission in writing from the publishers.

Bloomsbury Publishing Plc does not have any control over, or responsibility for,
any third-party websites referred to or in this book. All internet addresses given
in this book were correct at the time of going to press. The author and publisher
regret any inconvenience caused if addresses have changed or sites have
ceased to exist, but can accept no responsibility for any such changes.

A catalogue record for this book is available from the British Library.

A catalog record for this book is available from the Library of Congress.

ISBN: HB: 978-0-5676-8086-0
PB: 978-0-5677-0205-0
ePDF: 978-0-5676-8087-7

Series: Library of Hebrew Bible/Old Testament Studies, ISSN 2513-8758, volume 669

Typeset by: Forthcoming Publications Ltd

To find out more about our authors and books visit
www.bloomsbury.com and sign up for our newsletters.

Contents

List of Contributors	ix
Preface	xi
List of Abbreviations	xv

Chapter 1
CHARACTER AS INTERPRETIVE CRUX IN THE BOOK OF SAMUEL
    Benjamin J. M. Johnson   1

Chapter 2
DESIRE DIVINE: POEMS—PILLARS—PIVOTS
    J. P. Fokkelman   14

Chapter 3
WORTHY TO BE PRAISED:
GOD AS A CHARACTER IN SAMUEL
    Stephen B. Chapman   25

Chapter 4
HANNAH: A WOMAN DEEPLY TROUBLED
    Jenni Williams   42

Chapter 5
ELI: A HIGH PRIEST THROWN UNDER THE WHEELS OF THE OX CART
    Marvin A. Sweeney   59

Chapter 6
ORTHODOX THEOLOGY, ULTERIOR MOTIVES
IN SAMUEL'S FAREWELL SPEECH?:
THE CHARACTERIZATION OF THE PROPHET IN 1 SAMUEL 12
    J. Richard Middleton   76

Chapter 7
FROM A HEAD ABOVE THE REST TO NO HEAD AT ALL:
TRANSFORMATIONS IN THE LIFE OF SAUL
    Paul S. Evans   101

Chapter 8
DAVID: KALEIDOSCOPE OF A KING
    Keith Bodner and Benjamin J. M. Johnson   121

Chapter 9
THE HEIR OF SAUL:
JONATHAN'S LIFE AND DEATH IN THEOLOGICAL PERSPECTIVE
    Diana Abernethy   139

Chapter 10
ANALOGIES BETWEEN MINOR CHARACTERS:
THE EXAMPLE OF MICHAL
    Jonathan Jacobs   157

Chapter 11
ABIGAIL: A WOMAN OF WISDOM AND DECISIVE ACTION
    Philip F. Esler   167

Chapter 12
JOAB'S COHERENCE AND INCOHERENCE:
CHARACTER AND CHARACTERIZATION
    Barbara Green   183

Chapter 13
KNOWING ABNER
    David Shepherd   205

Chapter 14
"A MAN OF SHAME":
RIDICULING SAUL'S SON, ISHBOSHETH
    Michael Avioz   226

Chapter 15
FOREIGNERS IN DAVID'S COURT
    David G. Firth   239

Chapter 16
ABSALOM: A WARRIOR FOR JUSTICE—
A LIFE STORY IN SEVEN STAGES
    Yairah Amit   255

Chapter 17
NATHAN: THE UNEXPECTED GIFT OF A PROPHET
    James E. Patrick   271

AFTERWORD   290

Bibliography   292
Index of References   309
Index of Authors   320

CONTRIBUTORS

Diana Abernethy, Assistant Professor of Religion (Old Testament), Huntingdon College

Yairah Amit, Professor of Bible, Tel-Aviv University

Michael Avioz, Associate Professor of Bible, Bar-Ilan University
Stephen B. Chapman, Associate Professor of Old Testament, Duke University

Philip F. Esler, Portland Chair in New Testament Studies, University of Gloucestershire

Paul S. Evans, Associate Professor of Old Testament, McMaster Divinity College

David G. Firth, Tutor in Old Testament, Trinity College Bristol

Jan P. Fokkelman, Associate Professor of Hebrew, retired, University of Leiden

Barbara Green, Professor of Biblical Studies, Graduate Theological Union

David M. Gunn, Professor Emeritus, Texas Christian University

Jonathan Jacobs, Associate Professor of Bible, Bar-Ilan University

Benjamin J. M. Johnson, Associate Professor of Biblical Studies, LeTourneau University

J. Richard Middleton, Professor of Biblical Worldview and Exegesis, Northeastern Seminary at Roberts Wesleyan College

James E. Patrick, Independent Scholar, Oxford University

David J. Shepherd, Lecturer in Hebrew Bible/Old Testament, School of Religion, Trinity College Dublin

Marvin A. Sweeney, Professor of Hebrew Bible, Claremont School of Theology

Jenni Williams, Tutor in Old Testament, Wycliffe Hall, Oxford

PREFACE

From Samuel to Saul, from Michal to Jonathan, from Abner to Joab, from Abigail to Bathsheba, from Absalom to David himself, the book of Samuel contains some of the most interesting and iconic characters in literature. David, for example, has been described as "the first human being in world literature."[1] However, even the most minor or most seemingly one-dimensional characters in the book of Samuel are often capable of surprising complexity. This volume is intended to recognize the significance of character and characterization in the book of Samuel by giving a range of scholars the space to reflect in depth on a number of key characters in this masterful narrative.

Recent studies in New Testament literature have begun to re-appreciate the role that characters play in that literature.[2] Given the rich presentation of characters in the book of Samuel we are hopeful that this volume will similarly highlight the importance of characters and characterization in Hebrew narrative.

Character and characterization have always been an important part of appreciating Hebrew narrative. Since Erich Auerbach argued that biblical narrative was "fraught with background" and that biblical characters were marked by "multilayeredness,"[3] most scholars offering literary analyses of biblical text have seen the importance and complexity of biblical characters. Robert Alter, for example highlighted the way that biblical narrative was artfully reticent in its characterization and suggested a "scale of means" with which the biblical authors offered their characterizations

---

1. Baruch Halpern, *David's Secret Demons: Messiah, Murderer, Traitor, King* (Grand Rapids: Eerdmans, 2001), 6.

2. See Christopher W. Skinner, ed., *Characters and Characterization in the Gospel of John*, LNTS 461 (New York: Bloomsbury T&T Clark, 2013); Christopher W. Skinner and Matthew Ryan Hauge, eds, *Character Studies and the Gospel of Mark*, LNTS 483 (London: Bloomsbury T&T Clark, 2014); and Frank Dicken and Julia Snyder, *Characters and Characterization in Luke-Acts*, LNTS 548 (New York: T&T Clark, 2016).

3. Erich Auerbach, "Odysseus' Scar," in *Mimesis: The Representation of Reality in Western Thought* (Princeton: Princeton University Press, 2003), 12–13.

from direct to indirect.⁴ Adele Berlin highlighted the different character types that can be found in biblical narrative, from type to agent to full-fledged character.⁵ Meir Sternberg offered an even more complex picture as he highlighted the surface-level characterization of a character that may be given in something like a characterizing epithet and the in-depth characterization that is only possible by appreciating the whole narrative.⁶

While there have been some advances and a considerable number of studies on the poetics of characterization in the literary guild, there has been a comparatively smaller body of research in biblical studies. Nonetheless, the volume of books and essays devoted to individual characters in biblical literature has been steadily on the rise, and this present project aims both to collate such recent studies and suggest other ways that the study of character might move forward.

One interesting factor in the study of characters in the book of Samuel is that whether one considers this book as part of the Deuteronomistic History, part of the Former Prophets, or part of some sort of Primary History, it is a narrative unit that is inherently connected to other literary units. For example, is it adequate to study the character of Joab without referencing his death which doesn't occur until 1 Kings 2? Or should Bathsheba's story be told without reference to her role in getting her son Solomon on the throne in 1 Kings?⁷ Thus this volume had to make decisions about whether characters should be considered in the book of Samuel or the book of Kings. Crossover characters such as Nathan, Bathsheba, Joab, and David, could be legitimately considered as part of Samuel and Kings. Luckily, this volume has a companion volume that is focused on characters and characterization in the book of Kings,⁸ and studies on characters such as Bathsheba can be found there.

---

4. Robert Alter, *The Art of Biblical Narrative* (New York: Basic Books, 1981), 114–30. The pagination for the Revised and Updated version is, *The Art of Biblical Narrative*, rev. ed. (New York: Basic Books. 2011), 143–62.

5. Adele Berlin, *Poetics and Interpretation of Biblical Narrative* (Sheffield: Almond, 1983), Chapter 2.

6. Meir Sternberg, *The Poetics of Biblical Narrative: Ideological Literature and the Drama of Reading* (Bloomington: Indiana University Press, 1985), esp. Chapters 9–10.

7. For helpful discussion of the "fuzzy edges" in biblical narrative, see Barbara Green, *David's Capacity for Compassion: A Literary-Hermeneutical Study of 1–2 Samuel*, LHBOTS 641 (London: Bloomsbury T&T Clark, 2017), esp. 33–8.

8. Keith Bodner and Benjamin J. M. Johnson, eds., *Characters and Characterization in the Book of Kings*, LHBOTS 670 (London: Bloomsbury T&T Clark, 2020).

The present volume, then, offers two general studies related to character in the book of Samuel and fourteen case studies on specific characters. Some studies are intentionally reading with the grain of the text, such as Stephen Chapman's study of the character of God. Others offer a reading that is attentive to the biblical narrative's presentation of character but also correct perceived misconceptions of standard views of some of these characters, such as Yairah Amit's attempt to soften the negative portrait of Absalom. Some of the contributions to this volume are complete studies that look at the entirety of the presentation of a character, such as Barbara Green's study of Joab or Paul Evans' study of Saul. Other studies are snapshots of the characterization of a given character in a particular pericope, such as J. Richard Middleton's study of Samuel in his speech in 1 Samuel 12. Other approaches are arguments are on offer. For example, Jenni Williams attempts to give Hannah more attention as a character in her own right rather than as the simple character type she is frequently considered to be. And David Gunn offers reflections on trends in study of the character of David over forty years after the publication of his monumental *Story of King David*.[9]

In short, this volume offers a kaleidoscope of studies of characters within the book of Samuel from different perspectives and different agendas. It is our hope that through this study, something of the significance, variety, and sheer enjoyment of these characters would come across to the reader and initiate more readings of these and other characters within the book of Samuel.

Keith Bodner
Benjamin J. M. Johnson
May 2018

---

9. David M. Gunn, *The Story of King David: Genre and Interpretation*, JSOTSup 6 (Sheffield: JSOT Press, 1978).

ABBREVIATIONS

AASF	Annales Academiae Scientiarum Fennicae
AB	Anchor Bible
ABD	David Noel Freedman, ed. *The Anchor Bible Dictionary.* 6 vols. Garden City: Doubleday, 1992
AIL	Ancient Israel and Its Literature
AJSR	*Association for Jewish Studies Review*
AOTC	Abingdon Old Testament Commentary
AOTC	Apollos Old Testament Commentary
AThANT	Abhandlungen zur Theologie des Alten und Neuen Testaments
BASOR	*Bulletin of the American Schools of Oriental Research*
BBR	*Bulletin of Biblical Research*
BETL	Bibliotheca Ephemeridum Theologicarum Lovaniensium
Bib	*Biblica*
BibInt	*Biblical Interpretation*
BibOr	*Biblica et Orientalia*
BKAT	Biblischer Kommentar, Altes Testament
BN	*Biblische Notizen*
BR	*Biblical Research*
BTS	Biblical Tools and Studies
BZAW	Beihefte zur Zeitschrift für die alttestamentliche Wissenschaft
CBQ	*Catholic Biblical Quarterly*
CBQMS	Catholic Biblical Quarterly Monograph Series
CTM	*Concordia Theological Monthly*
FAT	Forschungen zum Alten Testament
FOTL	Forms of Old Testament Literature
HBM	Hebrew Bible Monographs
HTS	Harvard Theological Studies
ICC	International Critical Commentary
JANES	*Journal of the Ancient Near Eastern Society*
JAOS	*Journal of the American Oriental Society*
JBL	*Journal of Biblical Literature*
JEOL	*Jaarbericht van het Vooraziatisch-Egyptisch Gezelschap (Genootschap) Ex oriente lux*
JESOT	*Journal of the Evangelical Study of the Old Testament*
JHS	*Journal of Hebrew Scriptures*
JNSL	*Journal of Northwest Semitic Languages*
JQR	*Jewish Quarterly Review*

JSNTSup	Journal for the Study of the New Testament Supplement Series
JSOT	*Journal for the Study of the Old Testament*
JSOTSup	Journal for the Study of the Old Testament Supplement Series
JSS	*Journal of Semitic Studies*
LHBOTS	Library of Hebrew Bible/Old Testament Series
NCBC	New Century Biblical Commentary
NIC	New International Commentary
OTL	Old Testament Library
SBLDS	Society of Biblical Literature Dissertation Series
SBR	Studies of the Bible and Its Reception
SJOT	*Scandinavian Journal of the Old Testament*
SJT	*Scottish Journal of Theology*
SSN	Studia Semitica Neerlandica
SOG	Story of God Commentary Series
ThZ	*Theologische Zeitschrift*
TOTC	Tyndale Old Testament Commentary
VT	*Vetus Testamentum*
VTSup	Vetus Testamentum Supplement Series
WBC	Word Biblical Commentary
ZAW	*Zeitschrift für die alttestamentliche Wissenschaft*

Chapter 1

CHARACTER AS INTERPRETIVE CRUX
IN THE BOOK OF SAMUEL

Benjamin J. M. Johnson

Introduction

In Aristotle's *Poetics* we read that character is a category that is subservient to the primary factor in narrative, namely plot. Aristotle writes:

> Necessarily then every tragedy has six constituent parts, and on these its quality depends. These are plot, character, diction, thought, spectacle, and song… [12] The most important of these is the arrangement of incidents [i.e., plot]… [13]…the incidents and the plot are the end at which tragedy aims, and in everything the end aimed at is of prime importance. [14] Moreover, you could not have a tragedy without action, but you can have one without character-study… [19] The plot then is the first principle and as it were the soul of tragedy: character comes second.[1]

Aristotle is explicitly interested in tragedy and it may be possible to argue that in the Greek tragedy, with the general worldview of humanity as subservient to fate, this may possibly hold true. However, it is probably not adequate as a general theory of narrative literature. As Seymour Chatman notes, "One could equally argue that character is supreme and plot derivative."[2] In fact, both are necessary. Chatman further asserts,

---

1. Aristotle, *The Poetics*, trans. W. Hamilton Fyfe, LCL 199 (Cambridge, MA: Harvard University Press, 1982), §9–19.
2. Seymour Chatman, *Story and Discourse: Narrative Structure in Fiction and Film* (Ithaca: Cornell University Press, 1978), 113.

"Stories only exist where both events and existents occur. There cannot be events without existents. And though it is true that a text can have existents without events ... no one would think of calling it a narrative."[3]

I want to go one step further in the following argument. First, characters in the book of Samuel resist easy classification, but, in fact, most characters from major to minor show some degree of ambiguity and complexity that the reader (and one assumes the original *hearers*) must wrestle with. Second and related, the understanding of any given character in the book of Samuel is often contingent upon one's assessment of other characters, which may have a degree of ambiguity themselves. Third and finally, one cannot really make sense of the narrative of 1–2 Samuel without making some assessment of an array of complex characters. Thus, characters become something of an interpretive crux in the book of Samuel.

Character and Hebrew Narrative: From Auerbach Onward[4]

One early argument for the fullness, complexity, and indeed potential ambiguity of characters in Hebrew narrative was Erich Auerbach's famous essay, "Odysseus' Scar."[5] For Auerbach, the style of Hebrew narrative, which left so much unexpressed, caused the narrative to remain mysterious and "fraught with background," to use his famous phrase. Reading biblical characters against characters from Homeric literature, Auerbach exclaims, "How fraught with background, in comparison, are characters like Saul and David! How entangled and stratified are such human relations as those between David and Absalom, between David and Joab!"[6] Some scholars have resisted this claim to "background" in biblical narrative which builds up the idea of mystery and ambiguity. Taking a more historical approach, James Kugel, for example, responds to Auerbach's thesis as follows:

> In a famous essay, Erich Auerbach once described biblical characters as "fraught with background." Certainly when they are compared to Odysseus this is true. But what makes them "characters" at all? As

---

3. Ibid.

4. For this section I found the following work helpful: James Adam Redfield, "Behind Auerbach's 'Background': Five Ways to Read What Biblical Narratives Don't Say," *AJSR* 39, no. 1 (2015): 121–50.

5. Eric Auerbach, "Odysseus' Scar," in *Mimesis: The Representation of Reality in Western Thought* (Princeton: Princeton University Press, 2003), 3–24.

6. Ibid., "Odysseus' Scar," 12.

I have suggested above, the Bible itself seems to treat them more as ancestors, and what happens to them is not so much in the category of adventures as of history—history in the particularly biblical sense of "present reality projected back to the time of causes." In that world, everything is significant because everything produces results going on through the present and into the future. The people of that world cannot marry or fight or go to sleep or leave home without producing results of national dimension. And so we (ancient Israelite) listeners hear the story as, yes, a tale about people like ourselves, but more precisely of ourselves in history, a tale which produces visible, verifiable results and in that sense is unarguably true, while literature is fiction. And so what need is there of narrative "foreground"? *All that we need to know is told to us by the text. I do not find that biblical "characters" are fraught with background so much as that they are, quite simply, blanks.*[7]

If biblical narrative is to be considered a work of literature, Kugel's position will not work. Sternberg, for example, argues that all narrative literature contains what he calls the universals of narrative; these include suspense, curiosity, and surprise.[8] In an earlier work he writes:

human nature being what it is, there is every reason to believe that people have always evinced curiosity when some desired information was withheld from them and felt suspense when somebody they liked was in mortal danger; and the tense excitement that characterizes the dramatized reactions of the Phaecian audience to Odysseus' account of his adventures strongly confirms this claim. There is similarly every reason to believe, and a great deal of evidence to support this belief, that Homer, like other storytellers ancient and modern, exploited and manipulated these primary narrative interests. The onus of proof to the contrary, therefore, obviously rests with the so-called historicists.[9]

Thus we must understand what kind of literature we are dealing with. In a substantial monograph, Robert Kawashima argues that what we have in biblical narrative is an innovation away from the epic tradition toward prose narrative, the very creation of which leads to a level of ambiguity and background. In fact, Kawashima writes, "One might say, then, that the

---

7. James Kugel, "On the Bible and Literary Criticism," *Prooftexts* 1, no. 3 (1981): 230. Emphasis mine.

8. See Meir Sternberg, "Universals of Narrative and Their Cognitivist Fortunes (I)," *Poetics Today* 24, no. 2 (2003): 297–395 (327–8); idem, "Universals of Narrative and Their Cognitive Fortunes (II)," *Poetics Today* 24, no. 3 (2003): 517–638 (517–18).

9. Meir Sternberg, *Expositional Modes and Temporal Ordering in Fiction* (Baltimore: Johns Hopkins University Press, 1978), 85.

biblical writer, by composing imaginative stories that derive from rather than determine character, invented literature."[10] This complexity is part and parcel of literary prose.[11]

The majority of studies on narrative criticism in the Hebrew Bible have followed the observations of Auerbach and found background and complexity in the characters in biblical narrative. The standard works on biblical narrative such as Alter,[12] Berlin,[13] Sternberg,[14] Bar-Efrat,[15] Gunn and Fewell,[16] Fokkelman,[17] and Amit[18] all tend to view biblical characters as potentially having background, complexity, and ambiguity. To highlight the complexity, ambiguity, and centrality of characters in the book of Samuel we will briefly look at two pericopes, each of which contains a character triangle that is more complex than may sometimes appear.

Before we begin to look at the reception and portrayal of biblical characters in the book of Samuel, it needs to be said that my concern is literary and thus I am concerned with the "final literary form" of the book of Samuel. The textual complexity of the book of Samuel requires scare quotes around "final literary form,"[19] but that issue is one for another time. Of course some of the complexity that I will discuss in this essay has been attributed to the textual history of the books of Samuel, whether that is John Van Seters's "David Saga"[20] or Timo Veijola's various pro-David or

---

10. Robert S. Kawashima, *Biblical Narrative and the Death of the Rhapsode* (Bloomington: Indiana University Press, 2004), 34.

11. See further Robert S. Kawashima, "Biblical Narrative and the Birth of Prose Literature," in *The Oxford Handbook of Biblical Narrative*, ed. Danna Nolan Fewell (Oxford: Oxford University Press, 2016), 51–60.

12. Robert Alter, *The Art of Biblical Narrative*, rev. ed. (New York: Basic Books, 2011).

13. Adele Berlin, *Poetics and Interpretation of Biblical Narrative* (Sheffield: Almond, 1983), Chapter 2.

14. Meir Sternberg, *The Poetics of Biblical Narrative: Ideological Literature and the Drama of Reading* (Bloomington: Indiana University Press. 1985).

15. Shimon Bar-Efrat, *Narrative Art in the Bible* (New York: T&T Clark, 2008).

16. David M. Gunn and Danna Nolan Fewell, *Narrative Art in the Hebrew Bible*, The Oxford Bible Series (Oxford: Oxford University Press, 1993), Chapter 3.

17. J. P. Fokkelman, *Reading Biblical Narrative: An Introductory Guide* (Louisville: Westminster John Knox, 1999).

18. Yairah Amit, *Reading Biblical Narratives: Literary Criticism and the Hebrew Bible* (Minneapolis: Fortress, 2001).

19. See e.g. Philippe Hugo and Adrian Schenker, eds, *Archaeology of the Books of Samuel: The Entangling of the Textual and Literary History* (Leiden: Brill, 2010).

20. See John Van Seters, *The Biblical Saga of King David* (Winona Lake: Eisenbrauns, 2009).

anti-monarchic sources.[21] However, historical conjectures on the reason for this complexity are not my concern. I am concerned with the product, not the process.

Character and Contingency: Two Character Triangles

The argument in this essay is that character is essential for interpreting the book of Samuel. The challenge in the book of Samuel is that the characters are often complex and ambiguous. In addition, the ambiguity and complexity of one character adds to the ambiguity and complexity of other characters. In other words, the characterization of one character is often contingent on other characters. In this section we will examine two pericopes which contain two character triangles that highlight this character contingency.

David, Nabal, and Abigail in 1 Samuel 25

Our first character triangle is David, Nabal, and Abigail in 1 Samuel 25.[22] It may seem odd to include Nabal and Abigail in a discussion of character complexity since they are two of the few characters who are given explicit direct characterization by the narrator in such a way that the reader anticipates their functioning as exaggerated character types. Indeed, this is how Adele Berlin describes them: "If Nabal is the proverbial 'fool,' then Abigail epitomizes the אשת חיל ('worthy woman')."[23] However, the narrative in 1 Samuel 25 contains gaps and ambiguities that leave some unanswered questions in relation to David, Nabal and Abigail. I highlight a few examples here.

First, we must decide whom we trust in this confrontation. Since the narrator does not make the exchange between David and Nabal clear in the first instance, the reader is left to make a judgment. In the exchange between Nabal and David's servants, David claims to have done Nabal a service in the wilderness of Carmel. Nabal, however, seems to deny that this has taken place. How are we to interpret this interchange? On the one hand, we do not have any obvious reason to be suspicious of David. On the other hand, it seems that it would have been easy for the narrator to

---

21. See T. Veijola, *Die ewige Dynastie: David und die Entstehung seiner Dynastie nach der deuteronomistischen Darstellung*, AASF Series B 193 (Helsinki: Suomalainen Tiedeakatemia, 1975).

22. For further reflection on these characters, see the contributions in the present volume by Keith Bodner and Benjamin Johnson, and Philip Esler, respectively.

23. Berlin, *Poetics and Interpretation*, 31.

inform us as to David's actions and it is easy to imagine a scenario where David is running a kind of protection racket. So, as Barbara Green notes, the question remains "is this the humble presentation of a bill, or is it an extortionate demand for payment which had better not be refused?"[24] The truth is that we cannot answer this question with certainty at this point in the story. We are forced to be at least a little bit sympathetic toward Nabal. In fact interpreters often see David's actions as more than a little nefarious in this pericope.[25] This decision flavors the whole interpretation of this event as Green notes, if David is extorting Nabal "the whole episode reads differently."[26]

As the story progresses one of Nabal's "young men" confirms David's perspective and states that David's men, "were very good to us, and we suffered no harm, and we never missed anything when we were in the fields" (1 Sam. 25:15).[27] On the one hand, we can probably take this as confirmation that Nabal is the bad guy in this story. As van Wolde notes, "The reader has it on unimpeachable authority and should be convinced by now of the truthfulness of David's words to Nabal."[28] However, since the young man is a character, it is no guarantee that we must trust him and not every interpreter does.[29] If we do accept this young man's testimony,[30] we are still left with a narrative that has forced us at least to entertain the possibility that David is nefarious in his dealings with Nabal.[31]

---

24. Barbara Green, "Enacting Imaginatively the Unthinkable: 1 Samuel 25 and the Story of Saul." *BibInt* 11 (2003): 12.

25. See, for example, Mark Biddle, "Ancestral Motifs in 1 Samuel 25: Intertextuality and Characterization," *JBL* 121 (2002): 637, who writes, "It is difficult to escape the conclusion that, in fact, the only threat to Nabal's flocks had been David himself. Surely, Nabal did not owe David payment for a theft not committed."

26. Barbara Green, *David's Capacity for Compassion: A Literary-Hermeneutical Study of 1–2 Samuel*, LHBOTS 641 (London: Bloomsbury T&T Clark, 2017), 105.

27. Unless otherwise noted biblical translations are from the NRSV.

28. Ellen van Wolde, "A Leader Led by a Lady: David and Abigail in 1 Samuel 25," *ZAW* 114 (2002): 360.

29. E.g. Green, *David's Capacity for Compassion*, 102 n. 88, suggests that the question of whether or not we can trust the words of this young man is undecidable.

30. I have argued that when we see "one of the young men" (אחד מהנערים) speak in the book of Samuel we ought to pay special attention because they are narratively significant and often speak significance beyond their own narrative perspectives. See Benjamin J. M. Johnson, "David Then and Now: Double-Voiced Discourse in 1 Samuel 16:14-23," *JSOT* 38 (2013): esp. 206.

31. On the fact that even closed gaps in a narrative force lingering doubt in the reader's mind see Jerome T. Walsh, *Old Testament Narrative: A Guide to Interpretation* (Louisville: Westminster John Knox, 2009), 76.

The question of whether or not David is justified in his outrage toward Nabal greatly affects the way the reader responds to David's murderous intent toward Nabal and his household (1 Sam. 25:21-22). Given his policy of refraining from harming Saul, who was actively seeking to harm him (see 1 Sam. 24:4-5; 26:9-11), we are probably likely to characterize David's intentions negatively. Indeed, many commentators see that it is precisely this revelation of David's "dark side" that is key to this pericope.[32] However, this revelation of David's dark side is complicated by the fact that it is possible, and indeed perhaps probable, that the narrative suggests that David has been wronged by Nabal. So we feel some sympathy for David, and this negative characterization is perhaps a bit softened.[33]

Discussion of David's intention toward Nabal leads us to Abigail. We have already noted that Abigail receives a level of direct characterization that may lead us to see her as a character type. However, we may perhaps speak of Abigail's direct characterization here as an example of what Meir Sternberg calls a "proleptic epithet" which may consist "in a partial revelation of a complex and otherwise opaque character (as when the narrator extols Solomon's wisdom but keeps his disastrous malleability hidden)."[34]

In much of the short story in which we meet Abigail she does appear to function something like an exaggerated character type. She is the antithesis of her husband Nabal. Where Nabal is described as "a hard man and an evildoer" (קשה ורע מעללים, 1 Sam. 25:3), Abigail is described as "intelligent and beautiful" (טובת־שכל ויפת, 1 Sam. 25:3). Where Nabal is the picture of the inhospitable, making David's servants wait (25:9), insulting David (25:10), and refusing any sort of provision (25:11), Abigail is depicted as the paragon of hospitality, hurrying to meet David (25:18), bringing substantial provisions as gifts (25:18), throwing herself at David's feet (25:23), and repeatedly referring to David as "my lord" and herself as "your handmaid" or "servant" (אמתך) (25:23-31). Where Nabal is depicted as completely clueless, getting drunk at a party while David plots his demise (1 Sam. 25:36), Abigail is depicted as nearly prophetic, understanding David as one who fights the Lord's battles (1 Sam. 25:28) and predicting the "sure house" (בית נאמן, 1 Sam. 25:28) that God will give David, anticipating the promise to David in 2 Samuel 7.

---

32. See, for example, Jon D. Levenson, "1 Samuel 25 as Literature and as History," *CBQ* 40 (1978): 23.

33. For a sympathetic reading of David's actions here in light of ancient Near Eastern parallels, see Daniel Bodi, "David as an 'Apiru in 1 Samuel 25," in *Abigail, Wife of David, and Other Ancient Oriental Women*, ed. Daniel Bodi (Sheffield: Sheffield Phoenix, 2013), esp. 52–7.

34. Sternberg, *Poetics of Biblical Narrative*, 328.

So in many ways she fits this character type. However, there are undercurrents of characterization that cause us to question such a simple reading of Abigail's character. First, Abigail's statement that "evil will not be found in you all your days" (25:28) must surely give us pause. As Bodner aptly puts it, "I assume she says this without blushing, but surely the reader cringes, since this staggering thesis will not be borne out in the text."[35] Second, her oath to "let your enemies and those who seek evil to my lord, be like Nabal" (v. 26b), causes a number of problems. While there are a number of options for what it may mean to be "like Nabal" it seems most plausible that what she means is dead. This would suggest that she is expressing her desire for Nabal's death,[36] or perhaps if we are interpreting her as "like a prophet" she could be anticipating Nabal's death,[37] or possibly, that she is planning Nabal's death![38] Finally, toward the end of her speech, she states "when the LORD does good to my lord, remember your handmaid" (25:31b), clearly signaling her own self-interest. All of this suggests that Abigail may be more than a simple character type. She is beautiful and intelligent. She is hospitable. She is apparently at least quasi-prophetic. But she is also a smooth-talker. She is also at least a little vindictive. She also has her own best interest in mind.

In recognizing the complexity of the portrayals of David, Nabal, and Abigail we can see that our perception of each character nuances our perceptions of the other. If Nabal is purely a harsh and cruel tyrant it is easier to be sympathetic toward David. However, if David is exercising a protection racket in which Nabal is a victim, then we can perhaps be a little sympathetic toward Nabal. If Abigail is purely a wise and valorous woman, then we read Nabal and David one way. If, however, she is at least a little ambitious, vindictive, and a bit of a smooth-talker, then perhaps we characterize David and Nabal another way. The narrative in 1 Samuel 25 may guide our perceptions of these characters to a certain degree, but a surprising range of characterizations of each of these characters is conceivable and there may be some truth to each perspective on these characters.

---

35. Bodner, *1 Samuel*, 267. Cf. also Green, "Enacting Imaginatively the Unthinkable," 16.

36. E.g. Bodner, *1 Samuel*, 267; David Jobling, *1 Samuel*, Berit Olam (Collegeville: Liturgical, 1998), 154.

37. E.g. van Wolde, "A Leader Led by a Lady," 362–3.

38. McKenzie, *King David*, 100. Cf. Berger, "Ruth and Inner-Biblical Allusion," 268–9.

David, Joab, and Abner in 2 Samuel 3

The second character triangle that we will look at is David, Joab and Abner in 2 Samuel 3.[39] The backdrop of this chapter is the events of the war between the house of Saul and the house of David in 2 Samuel 2. The most significant event that occurred in that chapter, for the purpose of our character assessment, was the killing of Joab's youngest brother, Asahel, by Abner (2 Sam. 2:18-23). The key question is whether or not Abner's killing of Asahel would incur any bloodguilt and give Joab the right to kill Abner to avenge his brother. On the one hand, Abner appears concerned about this (see 2 Sam. 2:22).[40] On the other hand, it seems unlikely that a killing in war would incur bloodguilt.[41] As Barbara Green notes, the decision on how to characterize this killing is not entirely straightforward since it appears not to take place at the actual battlefield. Green suggests that this is a place where the narrator "refuses clarity."[42] In this case, the possible ambiguity is significant since it influences how we perceive the rest of the action.

In ch. 3 the action turns away from the battlefield and toward political intrigue. In this chapter we see the characterization of Abner, Joab, and David intricately connected. The first scene that concerns us is the break between Saul's son Ishbosheth[43] and Abner. The context of this confrontation between these two Saulides is the steady rise of the house of David and the steady decline of the house of Saul (2 Sam. 3:1), coupled with the fact that "Abner was making himself strong in the house of Saul" (2 Sam. 3:6). It is in this context in which Ishbosheth apparently confronts Abner and asks him why he "went into the concubine of my father" (2 Sam. 3:7). Since we, the readers, only have Ishbosheth's accusation and Abner's denial, we are not in a clear position to judge the truth of the matter. Is Ishbosheth threatened by Abner and fabricating a charge against him? Is Abner scheming for a power grab within the house of Saul? We are left with the questions.

---

39. For further discussion of the complexity of these characters see the contributions on Joab and Abner in this volume by Barbara Green and David Shepherd, respectively.

40. Robert Alter, *The David Story: A Translation with Commentary of 1 and 2 Samuel* (New York: W.W. Norton & Co., 2000), 206, seems to suggest this possibility, but couches it in the language of honor.

41. So A. A. Anderson, *2 Samuel*, WBC 11 (Waco: Word, 1989), 44.

42. Green, *David's Capacity for Compassion*, 141 n. 5.

43. The NRSV reconstructs to Ishbaal. I will continue to use the name Ishbosheth.

After Ishbosheth's accusation Abner defects to David, offering to deliver all Israel over to David (2 Sam. 3:12). David accepts the offer (with the return of his Saulide bride, Michal, as the price), appears to accept Abner's terms (2 Sam. 3:20), and sends him off to rally Israel to his side (2 Sam. 3:21). Perhaps most significantly, he sends Abner off "in peace" (בשלם). Just as Abner leaves the scene, behold! (והנה), Joab returns to Hebron to find that Abner, the killer of his little brother, has been sent away "in peace" (בשלם). Joab's response is one of outrage. He confronts David, the king, claiming that Abner has obviously come to spy on David and his actions. For the second time we have an accusation that we are not truly able to discern. On the one hand, Abner does appear to work on David's behalf and so Joab's accusation may be false.[44] On the other hand, this is the second time that a character has accused Abner of something that we, the reader, cannot confirm. Both accusations, in fact, accuse Abner of inappropriate "coming into" (...בא אל, 3:7, 23). We cannot help but develop some level of suspicion for Abner's actions. So perhaps Joab is right. We cannot say for sure.

What unfolds after this is Joab's killing of Abner in such a manner that it recalls Abner's killing of Asahel, Joab's brother. The narrative is clear to mention that David doesn't know about any of this (3:26). The statement about David's lack of knowledge suggests to some that the narrator doth protest too much and thus suggests a Davidic cover-up.[45] This against-the-grain reading is possible, but what is perhaps more interesting is the question within the narrative world about what David *did* know. His old (and violent) general has a vendetta against his new general. What did David think was going to happen? Is he a powerless dupe or is he, perhaps deviously, creating a situation that may have predictable results?

The point of tracing the interactions of Abner, Joab, and David is to highlight the variability of interpretations of their actions and motivations and to highlight how interconnected they are. We know Joab has reason to want Abner dead because of his brother. However, is he wrong about Abner or is Abner really a threat to David? We are not sure. Are Ishbosheth's and in turn Joab's suspicions about Abner justified? It is hard to say, both Ishbosheth and Joab have reason to feel threatened by Abner. Turning to David we may ask: is he a dupe or is he devious? Is he powerless to stop the machinations of Abner and Joab or is he playing a more subtle game and getting what he can out of each character's motivations? Each decision about each character is to a certain degree dependent

---

44. So David G. Firth, *1 & 2 Samuel*, AOTC (Downers Grove: IVP, 2009), 350.

45. James C. VanderKam, "Davidic Complicity in the Deaths of Abner and Eshbaal: A Historical and Redactional Study," *JBL* 99, no. 4 (1980): 533.

on decisions about another case in this instance. If the narrative is thus so fraught with motivational background, can we ever fill in the gaps? The answer is probably: only to limited degrees of certainty.

Character as Complicated Crux

When it comes to interpreting the book of Samuel, what do we think this book is about? This question resists an easy answer. Sometimes the book of Samuel is seen as largely apologetic, defending David and his heirs. Sometimes the book of Samuel is seen as a largely negative account of David and his dynasty. More often, perhaps, it is recognized that both positive and negative elements are present in the book of Samuel. Scholars often speak of a positive History of David's Rise (roughly 1 Sam. 16 to 2 Sam. 5) and a more negative Court History or Succession Narrative (roughly 2 Sam. 9 to 20).[46] Others resist this simple demarcation of the Samuel text and suggest more complex history and intention. A recent example can be seen in Van Seters's study of Samuel in which he suggests that the original deuteronomistic telling of David's story was supplemented and subverted by a David Saga that was woven throughout the text.[47] The analysis offered here suggests the complexity goes even further. As Alter notes in the introduction to his commentary on the David story, "Biblical scholarship by and large has badly underread this book by imagining that ideological strands can be identified like so many varieties of potatoes and understood as simple expressions of advocacy."[48] Instead, in this study we have seen that in any given scene, assessment of a character's motivation and characterization was complicated and contingent on decisions on other character motivations and characterizations.

So what do we make of all of this complexity? All this ambiguity? All this background? For Auerbach, the complexity and "background" were a result of the complexity of the "vertical connection" between God and these characters. He writes:

---

46. For a recent discussion of these classic "sources" in the Samuel narrative see the recent study of the Deuteronomistic History by Brian Neil Peterson, *The Authors of the Deuteronomistic History: Locating a Tradition in Ancient Israel* (Minneapolis: Fortress, 2014).

47. John Van Seters, *The Biblical Saga of King David* (Winona Lake: Eisenbrauns, 2009). Van Seters sees the following texts as this later David Saga: 1 Sam. 17:1–18:4, 6a; 19:18–21:10[9]; 22:6-23; 23:6-14, 19-24a; 25:1–28:2; 29:1–30:31; 2 Sam. 1:1aβb, 5-10, 13-16; 2:2aβb; 2:4–4:12; 5:3a, (4), 5, 13-16; 6:1, 3b-4, 6-14, 20-23; 8:16-18; 9:1–20:26; and 1 Kgs 1:1-52; 2:5-9, 13-46 (Van Seters, *Biblical Saga*, 362–3).

48. Alter, *The David Story*, xiv.

God chose and formed these men [and, I would add, women] to the end of embodying his essence and will—yet choice and formation do not coincide, for the latter proceeds gradually, historically, during the earthly life of [the one] upon whom the choice has fallen. How the process is accomplished, what terrible trials such a formation inflicts, can be seen from our story of Abraham's sacrifice. Herein lies the reason why the great figures of the Old Testament are so much more fully developed, so much more fraught with their own biographical past, so much more distinct as individuals, than are the Homeric heroes.[49]

So one answer to the question of this complexity can be the concept of character arc or character formation. We might understand this literature as having a more nuanced understanding of the human journey, in terms of growth, formation, etc. And we might understand this literature as having more to say about the complex nature of human and divine relationship.

For Sternberg, this ambiguity and the gaps in our knowledge that this "background" creates, make for a story that invites the reader in. To quote James Redfield's helpful assessment of Sternberg:

Sternberg's contribution is clear. Rather than a reader whose response is limited from the outset by fixed generic features of the narrative, Sternberg theorizes and tests the biblical text against an active reader—a reader who constantly constructs and reconstructs new versions of a protean story from the scraps of information and rapidly changing plot that the author and the narrator have chosen to give him... Still more importantly, Sternberg's theory includes internal criteria for verifying its application on a case-by-case basis. We can ask, *How would I, the reader, close a gap at this point in the narrative, on the basis of the information I have, in order to fulfill my primary narrative interests?*"[50]

To these observations, it might also be helpful to reflect on an analogous study in the Gospel of John. The Gospel of John has been the object of much literary study, especially as it relates to character.[51] While some studies tended to see characters in the Gospel of John as representative (e.g. Nathaniel as representative of a "true Israelite") or as character types (e.g. Nicodemus as a type of misunderstanding), some recent studies have seen much more complexity and ambiguity in the characters in John's

---

49. Auerbach, "Odysseus' Scar," 17.
50. Redfield, "Behind Auerbach's 'Background,'" 137 (italics original).
51. E.g. Christopher Skinner, ed., *Characters and Characterization in the Gospel of John*, LNTS 461 (London: T&T Clark, 2013), and Steven A. Hunt, D. Francois Tolmie, and Ruben Zimmerman, eds., *Character Studies in the Fourth Gospel: Narrative Approaches to Seventy Figures in John*, WUNT 314 (Tubingen: Mohr Siebeck, 2013).

Gospel. These recent studies have suggested that perhaps the character complexity highlights something true about the vision of the life of faith and encounter with Jesus. So Colleen Conway writes:

> How does a Gospel speak through ambiguity? What I have come to conclude is that even in this dualistic Gospel, the construction of the characters gives implicit recognition of what actually constitutes a life of faith, whether in the first or twenty-first century... Perhaps there is a continuum [of faith]...found within individual characters, and as one moves through the narrative their positions seem always in motion.[52]

Or as Alicia Myers writes, "perhaps this ambiguity can encourage even contemporary disciples to remain with Jesus in spite of their own misunderstandings and to give grace to those around them who likewise struggle to live a life of faithfulness and trust."[53] The thing that Sternberg has in common with these Johannine scholars is the view that the ambiguity and the complexity in the narrative is somewhat invitational and unfinalizable.

Perhaps, then, this character ambiguity invites us to see biblical narrative as in some sense an open text, to use Umberto Eco's terminology.[54] Perhaps the biblical narrative is not as simplistically ideological or moralistic as we might assume. Perhaps we ought to look at this narrative as less of an apology and more of an inquiry. Perhaps we ought to see it as an invitation to experience this complex narrative world. It is a narrative world that invites us to explore the complexity of human persons, the complexity of human relationships, and the complexity of divine–human relationships. It is a narrative world where one cannot understand David without Saul, or Saul without David, or David without Joab, or Joab without David, or Absalom without David, or David without Absalom, or Michal without David, or David without Michal or any of these without God. It is a narrative world that invites us into its complexity and invites us to see in it our own complicated world and our own complex web of interrelationships. The narrative that we find remains to a degree unfinalizable, but our assessment and indeed our relationship with these characters stands as something of an interpretive crux of the narrative world we find ourselves in.

---

52. Colleen M. Conway, "Speaking through Ambiguity: Minor Characters in the Fourth Gospel," *BibInt* 10, no. 3 (2002): 340.

53. Alicia D. Myers, "The Ambiguous Character of Johannine Characterization An Overview of Recent Contributions and a Proposal," *Perspectives in Religious Studies* 39, no. 3 (2012): 297.

54. See Umberto Eco, *The Open Work* (Cambridge, MA: Harvard University Press, 1989).

Chapter 2

Desire Divine:
Poems—Pillars—Pivots

J. P. Fokkelman

Introduction

The books of Samuel (including 1 Kgs 1–2) open with a young woman from the people who longs for a child, and end with a chapter in which an old woman, the queen-mother, is the center. Hannah's desire looks forward to new life; Bathsheba's desire will end in the death of her son's competitor. This frame around the huge composition becomes compelling because of the keyword for "to ask, to desire," the root *sh'l*, that permeates both chapters—a feature that deserves closer attention.

The cohesion of the almost sixty chapters is next guaranteed by powerful pillars from a different language register than that of the narrative prose. These are three poems, which shore up beginning, middle and end: (a) Hannah's Song, (b) David's lament for Jonathan, and (c) King David's great Song of Thanksgiving in 2 Samuel 22. Each of these poems turns around a pivot of thematic importance: in (a) and (c) this is life and death, in b only death as exclusive cause and subject.

On the basis of my earlier studies in the books of Samuel I will here discuss the topics of poems, pivots, and pillars.[1] My analysis will also

---

1. The four volumes of my *Narrative Art and Poetry in the Books of Samuel (NAPS)* published as *Vol. 1, King David,* SSN 22 (Assen: Van Gorcum, 1981); *Vol. 2, The Crossing Fates,* SSN 23 (Assen: Van Gorcum, 1986); *Vol. 3, Throne and City,* SSN 27 (Assen: Van Gorcum, 1990); and *Vol. 4, Vow and Desire,* SSN 31 (Assen: Van Gorcum, 1993). An extended version of my lecture at an international Samuel

be supported by numerical data. For my tetralogy *Major Poems of the Hebrew Bible* I counted (without intending to torment my readers) the syllables of almost 200 poems in the original, i.e., pre-Masoretic, Hebrew and found that the numbers 7, 8 and 9 are normative for the poet: they are always crucial to the verse structure.² In the following there will be a modicum of numerical data, but I trust that for readers of the books of Samuel these will be a useful addition to my argument.

Why include an analysis of the cohesion of the composition of the books of Samuel in a volume on characters and characterization? As I have said in my manual, *Reading Biblical Narratives*, "characters only live inside the story; they are part of that world that by virtue of a string of language signs is said to have existed then and there. They are themselves language signs."³ By understanding the compositional house in which they live, we are better situated to understand the characters themselves.

Cohesion and the Power of Construction

The story of Hannah and her Song are of fundamental importance for the whole of 1–2 Samuel. The first half of the prose narrative (1 Sam. 1:1-13) is mainly narrator's text and preparation; in contrast, the second half (vv. 14-26) contains a lot of embedded speech. The priest Eli of the temple in Shiloh has the first word, which immediately shows him as a none too bright character. It is painful to read how he misinterprets the silent prayer of the tormented woman. Hannah defends herself adequately in vv. 15-16, after which Eli comes round and pronounces the wish *welohe yisra'el yitten 'et shelatek ᵃsher sha'alt me'immo!* (v. 17b). Those words make an impression; when, years later, Hannah again visits the temple, this time with her young child, it is her turn to explain to the priest: *wayyitten*

---

conference in Nijmegen (March 2006) has been published as "The Samuel Composition as a Book of Life and Death: Structural, Generic and Numerical Forms of Perfection," in *For and Against David: Story and History in the Books of Samuel*, ed. A. G. Auld and E. Eynikel, BETL 232 (Leuven: Peeters, 2010), 15–46.

Classical poetry was the topic of my *Major Poems of the Hebrew Bible*, 4 vols, SSN 37, 41, 43, 47 (Assen: van Gorcum, 1981–96). Here, almost 200 poems are discussed.

2. The creation story in Gen. 1 covers the working week, which is reflected in the arrangement of its paragraphs according to the 6 + 1 structure. The seventh paragraph is devoted to the climax: the sabbath. It comes at the beginning of Gen. 2, i.e., in the wrong place. We may safely call that a decapitation.

3. J. P. Fokkelman, *Reading Biblical Narrative: An Introductory Guide* (Louisville: Westminster John Knox, 1999), 63.

Yhwh li 'et sh^e'elat $^{\prime a}$sher sha'alti me'immo (v. 27b)—an unmissable introduction of the keyword "to wish."

Immediately after this—Hannah has not finished yet—the keyword *sh'l* reaches the number of seven occurrences in the two clauses of an exceptional verse:

> w^{e}gam 'anoki hish'iltíhu laYhwh:
> kol hayyamim $^{\prime a}$sher chay hu sha'ul laYhwh.

The significance of this statement cannot be underestimated.[4] I will try to support this claim with seven arguments:

1. *hish'iltíhu* is exceptional, because it is the only Hiphil form in the Bible of an otherwise well-known root;
2. the full form of the first person singular pronoun "I" with its three long vowels, which however is grammatically redundant (the verb is already a conjugated form);
3. the underlining of the sentence core via *gam*, a form of emphasis that lends grandeur to the occasion;
4. the performative character of the predicate (perfect) of Hannah's statement (and which together with the JPS I translate as "I hereby lend him to the Lord")…
5. …also lends an official and binding character to the content;
6. the fact that the lines have monorhyme (God's proper name) enables us to scan them as a tricolon (4 + 3 + 3 stresses): as a full poetic line with *parallelismus membrorum*;
7. the passive participle has a huge echo, as it touches the heart of all themes throughout Samuel, with an unexpected subversive power.

Deploying the Hiphil is an original thought, and it is quite possible that this causative conjugation was chosen specifically for this situation and context. In this way Hannah causes a radical reversal. During long years of humiliation she herself was the asking party, but now that her greatest desire has been realized she reverses the relationship: she puts God at the receiving end and she herself becomes the gracious giver. Very assertive!

The author himself is also original and radical: he has raised a disconcerting question, a fundamental question that permeates the whole of 1 Samuel and characterizes the tragedy of the first king: *who really is*

---

4. For the small correction (to *chay*) of the Masoretic text, see the critical apparatus of the *BHS*, which refers to two Mss, and to the readings in three *Versiones Antiquae*.

God's desired one? Samuel or Saul? Hannah's Samuel, when he has grown up and has been trained in the temple at Shiloh? Or the son of Kish, who will be anointed and instructed by none other than Samuel in his function as prophet? How can Saul wipe out Samuel's lead? A large part of 1 Samuel is blighted by the contacts, increasingly more like clashes, between prophet and king.

The weight of ch. 1 is also underlined by numerical means. In the preparatory half (vv. 1-13) God's proper name, *Yhwh*, appears *seven* times, in the half occupied by the dialogue *eight* times, and in Hannah's Song the Name appears *nine* times. Add to this the articulation of the first story: actually, the poem, as the climax, is part of it; the traditional division into chapters has gone wrong here. In the same way as the Creation story, in Genesis 1, has been decapitated because the paragraph dealing with the seventh day, the Sabbath, which has been placed at the beginning of ch. 2, the opening of 1 Samuel has been truncated. The correct proportions are: the narrative prose consists of seven sequences, and is given a climax in verse—the poem is the eighth sequence.[5]

This uncovers an important parallelism one textual level higher. The positive story of the infertile woman who becomes a mother and sings is followed by the negative story of the corruption in Shiloh, at the temple where Eli is a priest. Both texts end in a specific form of direct speech. As ch. 1 is crowned by Hannah's hymn (2:1-10), so does the account in the next chapter finish with a huge prophecy of doom (such as is hardly found in prose) against Eli's family (2:27-36).

We find the central normative figure 8 in 1 Samuel 16, in the "discovery" of David: the narrator purposely wrongfoots the reader beforehand by confronting Samuel with "Jesse and his *seven* sons" upon his arrival in Bethlehem. The number 8 also works at a much higher textual level, that of the 15 acts that constitute the entire composition (including 1 Kgs 1–2): Act VIII (i.e., chs. 27–31 plus 2 Sam. 1) is its center. This eighth section contains the climax of 1 Samuel, and recounts the death of the first king in three ways, in three different literary units.[6] What is more, a sizeable and subtle synchronism has been constructed here that, once we have

---

5. The seven sequences in 1 Sam. 1 are: vv. 1-2/3-8/9-11/12-18/19-20/21-23/24-28; see *Vow and Desire* (= *NAPS, vol. 4*), 4, and the corresponding analysis.

6. In ch. 31 the author first presents the authoritative account of Saul's defeat on Mount Gilboa, then the Amalekite messenger tells his heavily manipulated story to David in 2 Sam. 1, and following that David speaks/sings his lyrical reaction in the Lament.

Note: 2 Sam. 1 is another example of a wrong arrangement. This chapter is actually the ending of the *first* book of Samuel, as it is the climax of Act VIII.

noticed it and done our calculations, tells us that Saul's death in battle takes place on exactly the same day as David's victory in the South over the Amalekites.[7]

Poems: Pillars and Pivots

The whole of the composition 1–2 Samuel is supported by three pillars: Hannah's Song, David's Lament, and David's great Song of Thanksgiving in 2 Samuel 22. These poems deserve being treated as a threesome, because of their respective pivots (more about these below), and because of the relationship between the endings of the first and last songs—in both cases a wish, a "pro-king" strophe.

The bicolic poem in 1 Samuel 2 also contains one tricolon, so that the total number of cola is an odd number: 35. This means that one colon is the exact center, no. 18 (v. 6a):

yhwh memit um^{e}chayyeh.

This is the first half of a verse of exceptional content and shape. The deity's proper name comes first, as the subject of no fewer than four verbal predicates. These are two times two causative participles, filling out the verse, and each pair presents an opposition. The most far-reaching comes first and speaks of life and death—or rather, death and life. It falls to us, as adequate interpreters to recognize this order as strange or uncommon, and then explain it.

This eighteenth colon is the first of a long chain that stretches through all of 1–2 Samuel (23 occurrences linking life and death) and hence is of great thematic weight.[8] The middle of 23 is 12 (a prestigious number), and the twelfth instance of life-and-death comes in the middle of David's Lament, which itself forms the center of the entire Samuel composition.

The rhythm of the poetic lines is determined by the frequent occurrence of pairs: two words that sometimes make up a short colon, sometimes form half a colon. Verse 23 in 2 Samuel 1 consists of nothing but pairs, but combines these again into longer pairs (v. 23a), after which v. 23b consists of two short clauses of two words each:

---

7. The chronological table of Act VIII can be found on p. 594 of *The Crossing Fates* (= *NAPS*, vol. 2). It can also be found on p. 126 of my article "Structural Reading on the Fracture between Synchrony and Diachrony," *JEOL* 30 (1987–88): 123–36.

8. The chain of life-and-death combinations is 1 Sam. 2:6; 14:39, 45; 19:6; 20:3, 14, 31; 26:10, 16; 28:9-10; 2 Sam. 1:10, 23; 4:9-10; 8:2; 12:5, 18, 21, 22-23; 15:21; 18:14-15; 19:7; 20:3; 1 Kgs 2:24.

Sha'ul wihonatan	*hanne'ehabim wehanne'imim*
bechayyehem ubemotam	*lo nifradu* (v. 23a)
minnesharim qallu	*me'arayot gaberu* (v. 23b)

I note that v. 23a is exceptional: this center of the poem is one very long sentence, of which subject and predicate form head and tail. In between there are complements that are not indispensable; it is these that are responsible for the extraordinary length of the sentence. In this way the appearance of the predicate has been put off as long as possible. Next, we note how the second half starts, and find that the phrase "in life and death," in a poem that nowhere mentions the deity, has the normal word order and so is an inversion of Hannah's middle colon. Life and death usually form an incompatible duo, but their antithesis is here attacked and overcome by the flanking cola: after a delay of three cola the predicate "not parted" is a litotes that defines the unity of father and son and makes it immune to death.

The third pillar of the long composition is 2 Samuel 22. Its text is rather frayed,[9] but we are in luck: this long poem returns in the Psalter as Psalm 18 and in good condition, so that is the version I would like to look at in more detail.

Psalm 18 is an extremely long poem. The complete text has *nine* hundred syllables in *nine* stanzas, with ninety-nine syllables filling up stanza *nine*; the three names for God that the poet uses (*El*, *Elohay* and *Yhwh*) together have *nine* occurrences in each of the three sections.[10] The central section is about integrity (keyword **tmm*), and its middle strophe is strophe 13, consisting of the bicolic vv. 26-27. Each of its four cola contains 13 syllables, and the entire strophe consists of 13 words. They say the following:

v. 26 *'im chasid titchassad*	*'im gebar tamim tittammam*
v. 27 *'im nabar titbarar*	*we'im 'iqqesh titpattal*

It is immediately clear that practically every single aspect here is unique: the anaphoras, the repeated roots, the choice of words, and the ad hoc use of the Hithpael form an extreme ensemble. This strophic unit is the apex

---

9. However, I have extensively discussed 2 Sam. 22 in *Throne and City* (= *NAPS, vol. 3*), Chapter 8.

10. Psalm 18 has been discussed in detail in my *Major Poems, vol. 3*; all data can be found in Chapter 2, pp. 26–38. The psalm is chock full of (numerical) symmetries and other forms of balance.

of an argument about integrity in which God (here in the second person, addressed by David) exactly mirrors the behavior or moral quality shown by human beings—a view that deserves generous attention.

The four strophes that constitute the center of Psalm 18, vv. 21-29, are flanked by wars: in vv. 5-7 and 17-20 a war that gets David in such a tight spot that only a spectacular theophany can save him (vv. 8-20); in contrast, the war for which David is being trained by God himself, so that he will come out victorious (vv. 30-46). In this way, the heart of the matter, integrity, is framed by a big "minus" and a big "plus," namely, defeat versus victory. This song of thanksgiving by the warrior David is the compositional answer to the lament in the center of the Samuel books.

Life and Death

In the center of the long composition, in the eighth of 15 acts (1 Sam. 27–31 plus 2 Sam. 1), the three units devoted to the catastrophe on Mount Gilboa draw particular attention. In the run-up an ominous story stands out. On the eve of the battle King Saul pays a visit that normally would be subject to heavy taboos: he seeks the advice of a necromancer. She is a professional, and given the way she handles the client who in vain tries to remain anonymous she deserves a certificate as a psychotherapist, but she cannot fob him off with fine talk. Saul finds what he was looking for: the announcement of his end. This sets the tone for the entire act.

The relationship between a writer and his characters is like that between a puppeteer and his marionettes: in his *persona* as narrator the writer is boss. For ch. 31 this means that the narrator's story contains the facts of the war. Thus, in 2 Samuel 1 neither we nor David are fooled by the story of the Amalekite messenger, who after a march at top speed in the South reports to David to bring...*fake news* to the new Number 1.

The way the messenger recounts the last conversation with Saul makes for breathtaking reading. According to the Amalekite, Saul asked him to deliver the *coup the grâce*, and he did. However, from ch. 31 we already know that Saul's arms bearer had refused the exact same request. This raises two pressing questions: What is the connection? And why does David not fall for the Amalekite's story?

On the basis of ch. 31 the reader will have to assume that the Amalekite overheard the dialogue between the king and his aide, and out of self-interest creatively rewrote the story with himself in the lead. David, however, reacts by executing the man. I think that for a correct explanation of this surprising sentence we will have to think in terms of judicial procedures.

David's confrontation with the mercenary (was he hired by the troops?) represents a clash between two legal principles. The Amalekite will argue: exactly *because* I am "only a *ger*" (i.e., not an Israelite) I was entitled to accede to Saul's request and kill him. David can turn this completely around and say: exactly because you are a "hired laborer," a foreigner, you are *not* allowed to lay hands on the king. We note that of all people it is David who in chs. 24 and 26 explicitly recorded that the king of Israel is inviolable, because his office (he is the Lord's anointed) is holy. Soon afterwards we learn from David himself that he immediately had a dark suspicion that something was not right in the messenger's story: the man was undoubtedly after a generous reward, as David explains later, in 2 Sam. 4:10.

Elsewhere I have characterized the composition of the books of Samuel as *The Book of Life and Death*.[11] The series of 23 places where the roots *ch-y-y* and *m-w-t* occur together is not the only foundation for such a title; let me look a little bit further.

The root for "life" occurs 33 times in 1 Samuel 1 through 2 Samuel 1, and 32 times in 2 Samuel 2 through 1 Kings 2. This means that the middle form of the series of 65 occurrences is no. 33. The root for "death" and "dying" occurs 15 times in 1 Kings 1–2, but has a striking distribution over 1 and 2 Samuel: 74 + 74 times.

Where is the 33rd "life," and where the 74th form of *mwt*? They occur together(!), and it will not surprise the reader that this route, too, takes us to the sentence that is the middle of David's *qina* and stands out by its length (2 Sam. 1:23). As said before, "life" and "death" together are the word pair that forms what is called an inverted quotation of the word pair *memit um^{e}chayyeh*, which occupies the exact middle colon of Hannah's Psalm.

God is very much present in Hannah's Song, but not in David's lament. However, there is a remarkable series of places that include him in the contrast of life and death. It regularly happens that someone wishes someone else dead, and makes very clear how serious he—it is always a man—is. In those cases the usual form of the oath is *chay Yhwh*. Occasionally an oath ensures exactly the opposite; this happens eleven times in 1 Samuel, and another four times in 2 Samuel through Kings 2.[12]

---

11. See Fokkelman, "The Samuel Composition as a Book of Life and Death."

12. Oaths in favor of, or against, death, containing *chay* (or *che*) *yhwh*: in 1 Sam. 14:39, 45; 19:6; 20:3, 21, 31; 25:26, 34; 26:10, 16; 28:9-10; and 29:6. In 2 Samuel four times: 12:5; 15:21(×2), and 1 Kgs 2:24. Cf. also the combinations of life and death (without oath) in 2 Sam. 1:10, 23a. Oaths in 2 Samuel: in 12:5; 15:21(×2), and 1 Kgs 2:24.

In this respect we, for instance, remember the father who wishes death upon his charismatic son (Saul contra Jonathan, in 1 Sam. 14:39); the troops who do not agree (v. 45); the king who recognizes David's innocence (1 Sam. 19:6) but nevertheless wishes him dead one chapter further down (*mwt* appears seven times!); or 26:10 and 16. With so many Israelites fixated upon life and death and apparently convinced they have to choose one side or the other, it is a relief to find one heathen, a Philistine of all people, who goes beyond the black-and-white attitudes and is given the space to do that by the author. This is the officer Ittai, who in the hour of David's greatest danger shows his loyalty to his king, in a formal oath containing an inversion (here shown in roman) which as a mirroring ab-b'a' figure expresses fidelity:

Chay yhwh w^{e}che '^{a}doni hammelek !!
    ki bimqom '^{a}sher yihyeh-sham '^{a}doni hammelek
        'im l^{e}mawet 'im l^{e}chayyim
    ki sham   yihyeh 'abdeka (2 Sam. 15:18-22)

Now to the end of the composition. 1 Kings 1 gives a detailed account of a breathtaking contest. A difference of mere minutes (who gets to David first and receives his blessing?) decides on life and death. There are two factions full of prominent figures, competing for the throne: who will succeed David, Solomon or Adonijah? The latter, being the loser, is stupid enough to then ask the winner's mother for a special intervention. The account of Bathsheba's audience with the king occupies the middle of 1 Kings 2 and is characterized by seven occurrences of the root *sh'l*. The queen-mother plays along, whilst knowing very well that the outcome will be fatal. The chain of seven times "ask/asking" has been arranged as 6 + 1, because the seventh occurrence of the root (in 1 Kgs 2:22) is a veritable explosion that costs Adonijah his life: Solomon bursts out: "you might as well ask for the throne!" Literally, the text says "the kingship." At the author–reader interface this climax means that at the end of the huge composition Solomon states what was at stake in the whole of 2 Samuel (including 1 Kgs 1–2): the throne.

There is one figure that overrules the sacred number 7: the number 8, the central normative figure in biblical poetry. This decisive number now marks the actual start of the books of Kings, because in 1 Kings 3

In 2 Sam. 12, the story of David's dying child, the vocabulary occurs frequently: five times life and five times death, in vv. 5-23.

the keyword *sh'l* occurs eight times, in favor of Solomon and in honor of Wisdom. This happens in vv. 5-13. In Gibeon God appears to Solomon in a dream, and says "*Ask*, what shall I grant you?" Solomon's elegant answer ends in the request for 'a hearing heart' (JPS: "an understanding mind"). Verses 10-13 deliver God's decision; and yes, the eighth occurrence of the keyword is clue and climax:

> The LORD was pleased that Solomon had *asked* for this. And God said to him, "Because you *asked* for this—you did not *ask* for long life; you did not *ask* for riches, you did not *ask* for the life of your enemies, but you *asked* for discernment in dispensing justice—I now do as you have spoken. (…) And I also grant you what you did not *ask* for—both riches and glory all your life—the like of which no king has ever had."

I have shown in this essay some aspects of the poems, pivots, and pillars which give structural coherence to the Samuel composition. It is this structure in which all the characters of this great narrative are embedded. It is the backdrop against which they speak and act and play out their great drama. The better we understand this frame, the better equipped we are to engage with the characters therein.[13]

The material in 1–2 Samuel is based on two squares. Here first the small square representing the structure of Act VIII:

Saul's death predicted, he failed against the Amalekites		Saul and his sons die against the Philistines
	Endor/Gilboa	
1 Sam. 28		1 Sam. 31
1 Sam. 27/29		1 Sam. 30/2 Sam. 1
	Ziklag	
David vassal of The Philistines		David kills the Amalekite(s)

The large square places Acts III and IV (in 1 Samuel) opposite Acts X and XI (in 2 Samuel):

---

13. See further on the relationship between characters and narrators and the text at large in my *Reading Biblical Narrative*, esp. Chapters 4–5.

The deity positive ACT III God designates Saul twice as king, the Spirit invades him twice, his finest hour: he defeats Ammon	The deity negative ACT IV Saul fails against the Philistines and Amalekites; two oracles cancel his dynasty and his office via Samuel
prophet: Samuel	prophet: Nathan
ACT X David subdues the Philistines definitively; via Nathan: a lasting dynasty	ACT XI war with Ammon is framework and stage of oracle David's fall; double oracle of doom via Nathan

Chapter 3

WORTHY TO BE PRAISED:
GOD AS A CHARACTER IN SAMUEL

Stephen B. Chapman

Meir Sternberg has described biblical narrative as representing "a rhetoric of glorification."[1] For Sternberg, the Bible's "drama of reading" is resolutely epistemological rather than existential, concerned above all with knowledge rather than mortality. Many of its narratives feature the senses, primarily seeing and hearing.[2] Its characters often seek fuller understanding, even as they wrestle with partial information and conflicting perceptions, reports, and instructions. "Knowing the Lord" is frequently an explicit motif and goal.

Nor does this epistemological drama transpire only within biblical narratives. The Bible employs a variety of rhetorical techniques to interrogate the knowledge and knowledge-making ability of its reader "in and through the reading experience," especially by using a "ubiquity of gaps" to "expose us to our own ignorance" and "challenge us to repair the omissions by our native wit."[3] Even though the Bible is "ideological literature,"[4] it "habitually generates ambivalence"[5] in order to communicate what Sternberg terms "the perspectival gulf between God

1. Meir Sternberg, *The Poetics of Biblical Narrative: Ideological Literature and the Drama of Reading*, Indiana Studies in Biblical Literature (Bloomington: Indiana University Press, 1985), 91.
2. Ibid., 47.
3. Ibid., 46–7.
4. Ibid., 37.
5. Ibid., 38.

and man"⁶ and "the cognitive antithesis between God and humanity."⁷ Sternberg frames this "epistemological novelty" theoretically and historically as the result of Israel's "monotheistic article of faith."⁸ In contrast to other ancient worldviews, Israel believed that "God is omniscient, man limited, and the boundary impassable."⁹

Sternberg explains the omniscient narrator of biblical narrative on this same basis:

> The Homeric narrator stands above the gods, varying their access to knowledge to suit his own requirements. The biblical narrator and God are not only analogues, nor does God's informational privilege only look far more impressive than the narrator's derivative or second-order authority. The very choice to devise an omniscient narrator serves the purpose of staging and glorifying an omniscient God.[10]

Yet for Sternberg the omniscient narrator's role is ultimately circumscribed. This narrator possesses informational access to words he did not personally hear and deeds he did not himself observe, allowing him freedom over time and space.[11] He can offer editorial comments within the narrative that he is relating. But unlike some modern uses of an omniscient narrator, the biblical narrator is not granted a personality and does not assert his compositional role directly.[12] Even with regard to this "omniscient" narrator, no one is allowed to equal or challenge God's epistemological priority.[13] There is a steady modesty to the narrator's role in biblical narrative, since his handiwork and commentary are finally designed to serve the "art of ambiguity."[14] The narrator apparently has "access to the whole truth within the discourse," but he uses this access

---

6. Ibid., 92.
7. Ibid., 46.
8. Ibid., 12.
9. Ibid., 46.
10. Ibid., 89.
11. Ibid., 84.
12. Ibid., 119.
13. According to Sternberg (ibid., 323), this epistemological priority is evident in how God is not characterized in the same fashion as other narrative figures. For example, God is often depicted as "off-stage." Sternberg also insists that, unlike human characters, God's character does not change or develop in biblical narrative: "God's mode of action shifts from one moment to another, yet his nature remains static; while human personality…may itself develop or crystallize under pressure" (ibid., 324).
14. Ibid., 122.

selectively and creatively in order to "bring home God's unique privilege within the world."[15]

If Sternberg is right, then two interpretive corollaries emerge. First, an interpreter of biblical narrative must not only note the content provided by the narrative but also observe the placement of that content and its mode of presentation within the larger narratival strategy. Is information provided to clarify or obscure? Is it straightforward or ironic? Does it reflect a subjective impression, even when reported by the narrator? Or is it "objective" in the sense of revealing the narrative's own point of view? Information necessary for understanding and evaluating a narrative feature may also be withheld at first. Biblical narrative characteristically employs "retrospective or last minute clarification" in order to sort out the multiple interpretive possibilities that have arisen in the course of a reading, fully enlightening the reader only after the fact.[16] Daringly, biblical narrative may even create a false impression to then reveal the truth with heightened drama and enhanced significance.[17]

Second, Sternberg's account of biblical narrative as a drama of reading intended to exalt God's epistemological privilege means that in the end the entirety of the narrative serves to characterize God within that narrative—and, for biblical narrative's implied reader, outside the narrative as well. The narrator in particular serves as a proxy for God, a reminder within the narrative that there can be an intelligence unbound by normal constraints of time and space. The narrator's intersubjective knowledge of the internal thoughts and emotions of narrative characters is a consistent pointer to the surpassing knowledge of God, which must be similar, only more so. In biblical narrative, the "extra-ordinary" knowledge of the narrator is not a marker of fictionality for the implied reader but a gesture toward the fullness of divine knowing (cf. 2 Sam. 14:20). These two corollaries—the strategic deployment of narrative information and the theocentric cast of the narrative as a whole—are thus crucial for any investigation of God's literary portrait in Samuel.

David Gunn and Marti Steussy have already done important work on this topic.[18] However, their work has not taken sufficient account of

---

15. Ibid., 93. Sternberg explains this narratorial access historically as a prophetic conception grounded in the idea of divine inspiration (ibid., 32–5).

16. Ibid., 55; cf. 99: "initial blurring and retrospective lucidity."

17. Ibid., 56.

18. David M. Gunn, *The Story of King David: Genre and Interpretation*, JSOTSup 6 (Sheffield: JSOT Press, 1978); idem, *The Fate of King Saul: An Interpretation of a Biblical Story*, JSOTSup 14 (Sheffield: JSOT Press, 1980); Marti J. Steussy, "The Problematic God of Samuel," in *Shall Not the Judge of All the Earth Do What Is*

the close relationship between the biblical narrator and the character of God, nor of the distinctive drama of reading represented by the Samuel narrative.[19] In her initial essay Steussy offered helpful ground-clearing and tabulating exercises for such a task, making lists of references in the narrative to (1) God's inner life, (2) God's actions, (3) God's speech, and (4) speech about God. In her discussion of the individual references at issue, she offered contextualizing comments but largely read them as isolated items of evidence apart from their narrative sequence or context.[20] Her conclusion, that the "dark" portrait of God in Samuel may

Right? Studies on the Nature of God in Tribute to James L. Crenshaw, ed. David Penchansky and Paul L. Redditt (Winona Lake: Eisenbrauns, 2000), 127–61; eadem, *Samuel and His God*, Studies on Personalities of the Old Testament (Columbia: University of South Carolina Press, 2010).

19. Indeed, David Gunn, "Right Reading: Reliable and Omniscient Narrator, Omniscient God, and Foolproof Composition in the Hebrew Bible," in *The Bible in Three Dimensions: Essays in Celebration of Forty Years of Biblical Studies in the University of Sheffield*, ed. David J. A. Clines, Stephen E. Fowl, and Stanley E. Porter, JSOTSup 87 (Sheffield: Sheffield Academic, 1990), 53–64, has usefully challenged Sternberg's account of an omniscient narrator by detailing a number of exceptions to the biblical narrator's omniscience. However, Gunn's failure to see how Sternberg also limits the omniscient narrator means that his criticism misfires. Sternberg would be the first to say that his narrator is not perfectly omniscient and that the narrative's dramatization of God's omniscience may not survive logical analysis. The matter is not one of logic but rhetoric. Biblical narrative is directed toward an implied audience of believers. "And whether or not interpreters share this belief, they cannot make proper sense of the narrative unless they take the narrator's own omniscience as an institutional fact and his demonstration of God's omniscience as a [sic] informing principle" (Sternberg, *Poetics*, 90). Gunn, "Right Reading," 60, does not think that even God is depicted as omniscient in biblical narrative. By contrast, Michael Carasik, "The Limits of Omniscience," *JBL* 119 (2000): 221–32, concedes that some biblical narratives present God as omniscient, although he too quarrels with the idea that the Old Testament as a whole does.

20. E.g., in her exploration of God's inner life ("Problematic God," 130–1), Steussy begins by viewing 1 Sam. 2:25 and 2 Sam. 17:14 together, despite the fact that they are far removed from each other in the narrative. This kind of approach results in quantitative judgments, such as God's "feelings and motives are more often negative than positive" (ibid., 130). The advantage of such an approach comes from its reorganization of narrative data within another explanatory framework. That alternative framework may illuminate a familiar story from a different angle of vision. But narrative information will always be lost through such a procedure as well. Figures are not merely characterized at discrete narrative moments, they are rendered by a narrative as a whole. This problem is evident, for example, in Steussy's methodological decision (ibid., 133) not to include in her list of God's actions any references to

be an intentional problematization designed to subvert human claims to divine authority, especially the pretensions of monarchy,[21] could be taken as complementary to Sternberg's epistemological approach to biblical narrative. But Steussy's fundamental complaint is that in Samuel "God is more inclined to anger than love,"[22] an objection relying on an imported criterion: namely, that God should be loving, and that love is the right standard to use in evaluating God's actions and speech in the Samuel narrative.

The same criterion appears in Steussy's 2010 book, *Samuel and His God*.[23] In this expanded treatment of the topic, Steussy moves through what are more or less the same lists of words and actions, but this time in narrative order and with more detailed literary evaluation.[24] She further supplements her discussion with an entire chapter titled "A Sequential Reading of Samuel," with an eye toward how Samuel and God figure throughout the narrative.[25] In this reading she attends to the presence of dramatic irony and artful gaps more than before, citing Sternberg for support.[26] Yet Steussy sometimes explains away unsavory aspects of God's character by historicizing them: e.g., "When the writers portray [the] LORD as angry at the disrespectful behavior of Eli's sons or unable to forget wrongs done by Amalek generations earlier, they describe a God who shares their own cultural sensibilities."[27] This explanation of the biblical writers as sometimes possessing an antique and unenlightened view of God operates with the developmental "husk-kernel" hermeneutic at home in liberal Protestant theology. The interpretive goal is to trim away the objectionable premodern trappings of the Bible in order to identify its abiding valuable core.

God as being present at certain events, since "being present" is not an action. Not only could "being present" in fact be conceived as an action, an explicit notice by the narrator that God was "present" at a particular moment or "with" a specific character is valuable information about the nature of that event or character as well as about the character of God.

21. Ibid., 157–9.
22. Ibid., 148; cf. 157, 159.
23. Steussy, *Samuel*, 48: "Both Judaism and Christianity, as we know them, speak of God as loving. God is also generally depicted as concerned with the personal lives of individuals."
24. Ibid., 48–72.
25. Ibid., 73–94.
26. Ibid., 74 n. 5. She also cites Gunn's critique of Sternberg but does so without comment.
27. Ibid., 98.

Steussy still considers the God of Samuel "inscrutable and dangerous," but now she suggests that this is the case because the early framers of the Samuel narrative wanted people to "understand why they need prophets and need to listen to them."[28] She believes that the writers of Samuel thought "simple obedience would solve everything," and that they perceived God as "a partisan warrior who will champion our cause as long as we repay the favor with obedience and flattery."[29] Steussy suggests that "[if] you interpret everything that happens as a direct reflection of divine will" (as, she implies, occurs in Samuel), the result is "[a] God who is not particularly loving or lovable and who is not a champion of the oppressed," a God "for whom 'might makes right.'"[30] She worries out loud that this sort of God is too liable to abuse, especially in the hands of "those who claim to speak for such a God,"[31] and she declares that she herself refuses to submit to the God of Samuel.

The Start of the Story

A contrasting approach may be charted by attending more closely to the introduction to the Samuel narrative in 1 Samuel 1, Hannah's story. Steussy alleges that "casual readers" are sometimes taken in by the idea that God has compassion for Hannah. As Steussy points out, the first action attributed to God in 1 Samuel is the closing of Hannah's womb (1:5-6). Although the narrative proceeds to detail how God intervenes on Hannah's behalf, "remembering" her (1:19) and giving her a child, Steussy insists that God is then only solving a problem that was of God's own making. She notes as well that God's gift of this child is tempered, if not negated, by Hannah's subsequent loss of the child to priestly service.[32] In handling the material, Steussy is clearly concerned to undercut what she considers to be a common perception that this introductory narrative depicts a God who can "care for and intervene on behalf of ordinary individuals." Even so, Steussy acknowledges how the story "does elicit concern for Hannah" and that God's "response to her allows the conclusion that [God] is interested in not only the great and mighty, but also the needy."[33]

---

28. Ibid., 99.
29. Ibid., 100.
30. Ibid., 101.
31. Ibid., 101.
32. Steussy, "Problematic God," 134.
33. Steussy, *Samuel*, 50–1.

If this introductory chapter has often been perceived to tell of a God who cares for ordinary people, that perception is better regarded not as a superficial impression of casual readers but as the successful result of an effective rhetorical strategy. Whether or not it may have been conventional to stress the modest origins of great men, the introduction to the Samuel narrative is remarkable for its attention to the personal struggles of a female character,[34] as well as for its misdirection. It is after all not David's birth or even Saul's that is being recounted. The present form of the narrative teases the reader in this regard, referring to Samuel with Hebrew terms reflective of and even identical to Saul's name (1:20, 27-28). A basic question for the reader throughout the introductory chapter is what *this* has to do with *that*. And yet the fact that these events are the subject of the Samuel narrative at its outset suggests their importance is greater than it seems at first glance. The narrative implies a deeper purposiveness to the events it reports, even as it avoids offering explicit links to the larger situation in which Israel finds itself. There are no introductory cues such as "In those days there was no king in Israel" (Judg. 18:1; 19:1), although the reference in 1 Sam. 1:1 to "the hill country of Ephraim" does recall Judg. 17:1 and 19:1. The story about Hannah and Elkanah could easily be the introduction to yet another story about a judge, and its nazirite motifs (1:11, 22) reinforce that possibility.

Set within this account of a rural family conflict, however, is another story about Hannah's visit to Shiloh and her vow to the Lord. Here the narrative contrasts Hannah's uncommon devotion with Eli's lack of perception (1:10, 12-16). Hannah prays directly to this deity, something the narrative emphasizes repeatedly (1:10-12, 15, 20, 26-28), and she is granted her petition despite Eli's cynical misinterpretation of her piety. Both Eli and the Lord are apparently swayed by the highly emotional nature of Hannah's appeal (1:17).

Steussy criticizes the transactional character of God's response to Hannah, as if God is "someone whose favor can be won by gifts."[35] In fact, the narrative pushes beyond the adequacy of a transactional view by focusing on the subjective dimension of Hannah's plea. What inclines Eli and God to respond favorably is not so much the content of Hannah's vow but the fervor of her presentation.[36] Eli's lack of perception similarly

---

34. See further Carol Meyers, "The Hannah Narrative in Feminist Perspective," in *"Go to the Land I Will Show You": Studies in Honor of Dwight W. Young*, ed. Joseph E. Coleson and Victor H. Matthews (Winona Lake: Eisenbrauns, 1996), 117–26.

35. Steussy, *Samuel*, 51.

36. In this regard the narrative calls to mind the Parable of the Importunate Widow in Lk. 18:1-8.

subverts a customary understanding of ritual practice by depicting the religious professional as less pious than a non-professional, and a woman at that. Eli does recognize Hannah's deep faith in the end, and he is the one to confirm that God will grant her petition. This introductory narrative does not condemn Eli or the priesthood or temples. They all have their place in this narrative world. But they are already revealed to be insufficient guarantees of divine favor and action. The God of this narrative world uses them but is not restricted to them. Rather than being moved to action exclusively by a gift or vow, this God is attentive to personal distress, and not only among the highborn but the lowly (cf. 1 Sam. 2:7-8). Nor is this attentive God merely a personal or family deity but, as Eli states, "the God of Israel" (1:17).

Nevertheless, the rhetoric of divine compassion is absent from this narrative, a confirmation that criticism of God as insufficiently loving functions at too great a distance from the terms of the narrative itself. Rather than foregrounding the love of God, this introduction emphasizes God's *responsiveness*.[37] Hannah directs her petition to God and God intervenes. The reason why God responds is left unstated, but the implication is that Hannah's unconventional appeal to God has made a difference. So God as a character in this narrative is a presence inhabiting sacred precincts and considering petitions. Yet although this God resides at a temple, the objects of divine concern extend beyond the boundaries of the sacred into the mundane. Indeed, the earlier references to how God had closed Hannah's womb (1:5-6) take on a different resonance when considered in this light. The attribution of this phenomenon to God signals a deity who is present and active in families and women's lives rather than only at temples and among the priesthood.[38]

As Steussy rightly notes, such language may also reflect an ancient tendency to ascribe natural phenomena to God (cf. Amos 3:6b) and therefore may not be intended as a description of God's direct intervention in the same way as other divine acts in the narrative.[39] Yet any degree of

---

37. God's responsiveness is underscored by use of the verbal root *š'l* at the conclusion of the initial narrative (1 Sam. 1:27-28).

38. Moreover, the closing of Hannah's womb is not necessarily to be understood as an arbitrary and unfair imposition. Cf. John Goldingay, *Biblical Theology: The God of the Christian Scriptures* (Downers Grove: IVP Academic, 2016), 45: "God may make infertility or blindness happen as a chastisement, or as an experience into which he intends to intervene in order to achieve something." Cf. Deut. 8:16, "to humble you and test you, and in the end to do you good."

39. Steussy, *Samuel*, 51–2.

divine involvement within the family signals a belief in a deity whose activity is interwoven within the basic functions of human life. Between the lines sketched by this introductory narrative there emerges a God who is alert and interactive, unconfined by conventional religious practice, and autonomous. Neither the characters nor the narrator presume to tell us why God does the things God does; we only see that God does them.

This withholding of information is part of the rhetorical strategy of the narrative. Its purpose is precisely to pose the rationale for God's actions as a presenting question. Hannah herself provides a provisional answer in her subsequent song (1 Sam. 2:1-10). God is "a God of knowledge," by whom "actions are weighed" (2:3), who "brings death and life" (2:6), but who "will guard the feet of his faithful" (2:9). The Lord will "shatter his foes" and "vindicate [$\sqrt{dyn}$] to the ends of the earth" (2:10).[40] Now the nature of God's responsiveness becomes clearer. God's work of measuring actions is done for the purpose of *vindication*: the protection of the lowly and disadvantaged, as well as the preservation of God's people in confrontation with those who threaten them. Hannah's experience of this God issues forth naturally in praise, just as David will praise God at the conclusion of the Samuel narrative (2 Sam. 22).[41]

The biblical narrator points in the direction of God's surpassing knowledge by knowing more than any one person could know about the events related in the narrative. When the Samuel story begins, it is conceivable that the narrator might be personally acquainted with Elkanah, Hannah, and Peninnah. Most of the actions and speech within this narrative concern outward appearance. The reader is told what characters do and say. Some additional items of information, such as the knowledge that Hannah's childlessness is a consequence of divine action, could in turn be deductions made from external actions and public speech. Yet as the introductory narrative proceeds it is increasingly clear that the narrator's

---

40. Biblical translations here and elsewhere are my own.

41. The hermeneutical importance of the two framing poems in 1 Sam. 2 and 2 Sam. 22, one at the beginning and one at the end of Samuel, was emphasized by Brevard S. Childs, *Introduction to the Old Testament as Scripture* (Philadelphia: Fortress, 1979), 273–8. Walter Brueggemann concurs in "1 Samuel 1: A Sense of a Beginning," *ZAW* 102 (1990): 33–48, while making the same point about the significance of Samuel's introductory and concluding narratives. Randall C. Bailey, "The Redemption of YHWH: A Literary Critical Function of the Songs of Hannah and David," *BibInt* 3 (1995): 213–31, reads the two songs as exilic additions intended to provide orthodox reassurance to displaced Jews worried that their God might be just as capricious as the God depicted in the remainder of the Samuel narrative.

knowledge has not come exclusively from personal observation but from a privileged vantage point, especially when the narrator knows what Eli is thinking (1:13). What the narrator knows and how he knows it already register with the reader as important interpretive questions. The narrator's shaping of the narrative is also demonstrated in small flourishes, such as his use of the expression *dibbēr 'al lēb* in 1:13 as a description for Hannah's emotional prayer. The Hebrew idiom connotes consolation (lit., "speaking to the heart"), not merely internal discourse (NRSV: "silently"), and only in this single instance of the biblical phrase are the speaker and addressee the same person.[42] In this fashion the narrator subtly critiques Eli for not providing comfort while affirming Hannah's initiative.

In due course the narrative will present multiple cases in which the narrator somehow knows the internal thoughts of other characters, including God.[43] The narrator will also withhold information from the reader, as when a previous word of the Lord to Samuel concerning Saul is revealed in flashback-fashion midstream in the story about Saul's search for the lost donkeys of Kish (1 Sam. 9:15-16). The purpose of this rhetorical peekaboo is to remind readers of God's even greater knowledge and far-reaching work of vindication. The God of Samuel is neither complaisant nor rigidly predictable. Within this narrative world, God is nevertheless "worthy to be praised" (*mĕhullāl*, 2 Sam. 22:4) because this God delivers God's people from its enemies. For this narrative, that is more important than love.[44]

The Anachronism of Moralism

Perhaps the greatest obstacle to a description of God in Samuel as praiseworthy occurs in 1 Samuel 15, a narrative in which God directs Saul to slaughter all of the Amalekites, including non-combatants (i.e., women, children, animals), and then condemns Saul for not killing Agag, the Amalekite king, and some of the Amalekite livestock. There is no getting

---

42. J. Gerald Janzen, "Prayer and/as Self-Address: The Case of Hannah," in *A God So Near: Essays on Old Testament Theology in Honor of Patrick D. Miller*, ed. Brent A. Strawn and Nancy R. Bowen (Winona Lake: Eisenbrauns, 2003), 113–27 (125).

43. The narrator knows what David says to himself (1 Sam. 27:1), what Michal feels (2 Sam. 6:16), and what displeases God (2 Sam. 11:27b).

44. Even when "love" does appear as an explicit motif in the biblical tradition, its sense is often more like "faithfulness" or "loyalty" than simple affection—although it also retains an emotional valence. See Jacqueline E. Lapsley, "Feeling Our Way: Love for God in Deuteronomy," *CBQ* 65 (2003): 350–69.

around the fact that this horrific directive is presented as coming from God.[45] Indeed, it only intensifies a motif of divine judgment heard within the narrative from its start.[46]

After all, God had closed Hannah's womb (1 Sam. 1:5). God is described as wanting to kill Eli's disobedient sons (1 Sam. 2:25). God's harsh verdict against Eli and his family is announced by a prophetic man of God (1 Sam. 2:31-34), a judgment explicitly reversing an earlier divine promise. This reversal is not depicted as capricious; a retributive principle is articulated: "for those who honor me I will honor, and those who despise me shall be treated with contempt" (1 Sam. 2:30; cf. 3:11-14).[47] Even so, gifts from God evidently do not always turn out to be good ones in this narrative world. When the people eventually request a king, God treats the request as their rejection of him (1 Sam. 8:7), but grants it anyway as a negative lesson to be learned in the future (as implied by Samuel's speech in 1 Sam. 8:10-18). God kills Nabal (1 Sam. 25:38) and Uzzah (2 Sam. 6:7). These killings are attributed directly to God, using the language of personal agency, and without clearly articulated justifications.[48]

The narrative in 1 Samuel 15 exemplifies this troubling aspect of God's portrait. The initial command reads: "Now go and attack Amalek, and utterly destroy all that they have. Do not spare them but kill both man and woman, child and infant, ox and sheep, camel and donkey" (15:3). Saul attacks as ordered. However, he does not kill King Agag and "the best of the sheep and the cattle and the fatlings and the lambs, and all that had value" (15:8-9). Contrary to the divine directive, Saul and the people

---

45. The prophet Samuel introduces his instructions with the standard prophetic speech formula "Thus says the Lord of hosts." As observed in J. Richard Middleton, "Samuel Agonistes: A Conflicted Prophet's Resistance to God and Contribution to the Failure of Israel's First King," in *Prophets, Prophecy, and Ancient Israelite Historiography*, ed. Mark J. Boda and Lissa M. Wray Beal (Winona Lake: Eisenbrauns, 2013), 69–91, use of this kind of formula by a character in biblical narrative is not a sufficient guarantee that God is the true source of an accompanying oracle (cf. Hananiah in Jer. 28:2, 10). However, God's subsequent judgment that Saul "has not carried out my words" (1 Sam. 15:11) reinforces the presumption that Samuel's oracle had a divine origin. On this point, see further Benjamin J. M. Johnson, "Characterizing Chiastic Contradiction: Literary Structure, Divine Repentance, and Dialogical Biblical Theology in 1 Samuel 15:10-35," in *Theology of the Hebrew Bible*. Vol. 1, *Methodological Studies*, ed. Marvin A. Sweeney (Atlanta: SBL, 2019), 185–211.

46. On the following, cf. Bailey, "Redemption," 228.

47. Contra K. L. Noll, "Is There a Text in This Tradition? Readers' Response and the Taming of Samuel's God," *JSOT* 83 (1999): 31–51.

48. Bailey, "Redemption," 230.

destroy only what is "despised and worthless" (15:9). Samuel then arrives on the scene to condemn Saul, who initially offers excuses but eventually admits his failure (while continuing to blame the people, 15:24). Yet Samuel imposes a divine judgment on Saul: the loss of his kingship and dynasty (15:26-28, building on the similar narrative of divine judgment against Saul in 1 Sam. 13:8-15). Samuel insists on killing Agag himself (15:32-33).[49] The scandal of this narrative is thus its repudiation of mercy as well as its imputation of genocidal slaughter to God.

Interpretation of 1 Samuel 15 usually becomes captive to the moralism of the theological right or theological left. Both are equally unappealing. Right-wing moralists seek to sidestep the interpretive difficulty of the passage by deciding in advance that whatever God is said to do must be right, at least within the specific historical context suggested by the text.[50] Because the literary character of God is held to be identical to that of the real God, there must be valid historical reasons for the seemingly offensive things that God does as a biblical character, even if those reasons ultimately come from historical speculation rather than from explicit information provided in the narrative.[51] This sort of interpretive argument can be faulted for blaming the victims.[52]

---

49. The verb often translated "hew in pieces" is obscure and uncertain, occurring only here in the Hebrew Bible. The context nevertheless implies that Agag is killed.

50. E.g., Paul Copan and Matthew Flannagan, *Did God Really Command Genocide? Coming to Terms with the Justice of God* (Grand Rapids: Baker Books, 2014), 169: "Because God is necessarily good, he would have a very good reason for commanding the killing of the Canaanites in utterly unique circumstances." As this statement suggests, their argument relies on the possibility of time-bound divine commands in the Bible, which they define as "given to a particular person for a particular occasion and not to be understood as general commands issued to all people everywhere" (ibid., 54). In this fashion they attempt to create space for certain divine commands to have been real and just in the past but no longer in force in the present. There are obviously complex questions pertaining to the relationship between the historical situation as such and the historical situation as it is depicted in the narrative.

51. E.g., Copan and Flannagan, *Genocide*, 227: "But the biblical narrative shows that for nearly a millennium—from the Red Sea crossing (fourteenth/thirteenth century BCE) to Haman the Agagite's attempt to wipe out the Jews under Ahasuerus in Persia (fifth century BCE)—the Amalekites were unrelenting in their hostility toward Israel." In support of this sweeping historical claim, they merely cite scattered biblical texts (Judg. 3:13; 6:3-5, 33; 7:12; 10:12; 1 Sam. 15; 27; 30; 1 Chron. 4:43; Est. 3:1).

52. See Copan and Flannagan, *Genocide*, 224–7. They note that the Amalekites were previously said to have "plundered" Israel (1 Sam. 14:48), are characterized as "sinners" by Samuel (15:18), and that Agag is described as having "made women

Left-wing moralists determine in advance what "good" is, often reaching conclusions about what God could or could not have done based upon this prior presupposition.[53] When Martin Buber writes, "Nothing can make me believe in a God who punishes Saul because he has not murdered his enemy," Buber's humanism and moral probity are deeply moving. But when Richard Rohr says, "If you see God operating at a lesser level[54] than the best person you know, then the text is not authentic revelation,"[55] the moral concern has become incoherent, muddling narrative and history, and combining the result with lousy theology.[56] Eric Seibert has attempted to clarify this mode of critique by delineating more sharply between what he terms "the textual God" and "the actual God."[57] He does not want to accept the further conclusion of some interpreters that biblical narratives about God are unreliable accounts of God's actual nature. Yet Seibert does want to evaluate the characteristics of the textual God by what can be "judged to accurately reflect" the character of the actual God, and he is "ready and willing to reject those aspects of the textual God that do not correspond to the actual God."[58] Such interpretations often appear eager to assume the worst about God's literary portrait in order to underline the contrast between that portrait and a supposedly

---

childless" by his sword (15:33)—the point being that Agag and the Amalekites got what they had coming. Reading 1 Sam. 15 together with Exod. 17:8-16 and Deut. 25:17-19 heightens the sense of Amalekite perfidy, even though the precise manner of the Amalekites' prior offense against Israel remains obscure. While an earlier incident is cited, there is no implication in 1 Sam. 15 that killing Amalekites is required on the basis of a long-standing divine injunction. What is at stake for Saul is whether he will be obedient to this present command from God, here and now, as God's contemporary word.

53. As Copan and Flannagan, *Genocide*, 169, frame the position contrary to their own: "God couldn't command the killing of the Canaanites because he is necessarily good."

54. Martin Buber, "Autobiographical Fragments," in *The Philosophy of Martin Buber*, ed. Paul Arthur Schilpp and Maurice Friedman (La Salle: Open Court, 1967), 32.

55. As cited approvingly in John M. Buchanan, "Editor's Desk: The Bible's Violent God," *Christian Century* (April 17, 2013): 3.

56. For an articulation of what is problematic with this kind of view, as well as a pointer in the direction of an alternative theological construal, see D. Stephen Long, "God Is Not Nice," in *God Is Not...Religious, Nice, "One of Us," an American, a Capitalist*, ed. D. Brent Laytham (Grand Rapids: Brazos, 2004), 39–54.

57. Eric Seibert, *Disturbing Divine Behavior: Troubling Old Testament Images of God* (Minneapolis: Fortress, 2009), 169–81.

58. Ibid., 181.

more attractive account of God derived from somewhere else. Of course, obtaining non-textually mediated knowledge of "the actual God" is its own sort of slippery business.

What both of these contemporary approaches have in common is a preoccupation with modern morality, a morality that stands at too great a distance, both in the nature of its ethical concerns and its scrupulous desire for complete consistency, from the literary contours of biblical narrative.[59] To isolate the moral issue of genocide in a reading of 1 Samuel 15 is to miss the forest for the trees. In stipulating the complete destruction of the Amalekites, Samuel's oracle is not imposing a new and unprecedented practice in warfare. Destruction of booty, including the killing of captives, was a recognized military procedure in the ancient Near East.[60] The ban on spoil (*ḥērem*) was a means of eliminating self-interest on the part of the combatants, who would have normally received captured goods and/or slaves as compensation. The rationale for killing captives and destroying captured goods was to devote them exclusively to a deity.[61]

These practices are not understood in 1 Samuel 15 as an exceptional expression of vengeance or bloodthirsty abandon. To treat them so will obscure the tightly constructed nature of the narrative, which turns on Saul's fitness for the kingship, in particular whether Saul will

---

59. Cf. John H. Walton and J. Harvey Walton, *The Lost World of the Israelite Conquest: Covenant, Retribution, and the Fate of the Canaanites* (Downers Grove: IVP Academic, 2017): "Both critics and apologists generally assume that the Bible's purpose—the reason behind God's revelation—was to teach the Israelites and thereby also teach future readers of the documents how to be good. Apologists try to argue that what the Bible portrays as goodness really is good, while critics argue that what the Bible portrays as goodness really is horrible. Both of these arguments are misguided for the same reasons. God's revelation was not written to teach the Israelites how to be good, and it was not written to teach us how to be good, either." While I have sympathy with this statement, I also think it goes too far. There is in fact a moral sensibility evident in the Bible's narratives, laws, and oracles, and this sensibility is not merely equivalent to ancient Near Eastern custom, although there is considerable overlap. My point is instead that biblical narratives like Samuel do not have moral pedagogy as their direct or primary goal.

60. Not all would agree. For further discussion, see Stephen B. Chapman, "Martial Memory, Peaceable Vision: Divine War in the Old Testament," in *Holy War in the Bible: Christian Morality and an Old Testament Problem*, ed. Heath A. Thomas, Jeremy Evans, and Paul Copan (Downers Grove: IVP Academic, 2013), 47–67, and Walton and Walton, *Lost World*, 195–211.

61. Richard D. Nelson, "*Ḥērem* and the Deuteronomic Social Conscience," in *Deuteronomy and Deuteronomic Literature*, ed. M. Vervenne and J. Lust, BETL 133 (Leuven: Leuven University Press, 1997), 36–54.

acknowledge God's overlordship (as set forth programmatically in 1 Sam. 12:14-15, with its stress on the need for a king to "heed" [šmʻ] God's voice; cf. 15:2, 22). The narrative in 1 Samuel 15 is not a treatise on the ethics of warfare. It is a story about Saul's inability to follow God's instructions. He is told to fight the Amalekites and relinquish everything he captures. He does not do so.

More to the point, Saul reveals himself in the course of the narrative either not to understand how this destruction is an expression of devotion to the deity (he twice tells Samuel that he kept some of the spoil so he could offer it to God instead, 15:15, 20-21) or to understand the theory but be playing fast and loose with its implementation out of self-interest. There is no suggestion at all that Saul is motivated by humanitarian concerns. Moreover, God's rejection of Saul and his dynasty (15:26, 28) needs to be viewed in light of the deep ambivalence about kingship throughout the Samuel narrative. While kingship is perceived as a source for good (if wielded well), it is also sure to bring about bad things over time. Crucial therefore will be a king's continued reliance on God, who is Israel's true king (cf. Judg. 8:23; 1 Sam. 8:7; Ps. 93:1; Isa. 6:5; Zeph. 3:15b). Saul's failing in 1 Samuel 15 is not an accidental misinterpretation of his instructions or a one-time strategic miscalculation but a paradigmatic flaw in his character that rules him out as a suitable monarch.

The more challenging interpretive question is not why God rejects Saul but why God chose Saul in the first place—how could God have been so wrong about Saul and why is God unwilling or unable to fix him? From the outset of the misadventure of Saul, God seems inclined to honor the will of the people. Given that any human king entails a rejection of God's kingship, God nonetheless directs Samuel to "listen to the voice of the people" (1 Sam. 8:7, 9, 22) with regard to their new monarch's selection. To be sure, other portions of the narrative suggest a more direct role for God in the choosing of Saul (9:16-17). Even so, Saul is cumulatively characterized as "Israel's desire" (9:20) more than God's. There may even be an implication in the narrative that God did attempt to fix Saul by leading him to Samuel (ch. 9), directing him through a series of educative sign-acts (10:1-8), giving him "another heart" (10:9), bestowing on him an ecstatic experience with a band of prophets (10:10-13), and imparting divine spirit to him (11:6). None of it appears to work, however, and so God decides to reject Saul in favor of "a man after [God's] own heart" (13:14).

Beginning in 1 Samuel 13, the narrative hints that God may no longer be quite as willing to let the people choose their own king. Perhaps the stakes are just too great. The narrative's attitude toward the monarchy remains one of ambivalence, but in light of the Saul debacle God becomes more "hands on" in the selection process—a new stance dramatized with David in 1 Samuel 16. Here again the feature of God's literary portrait which comes into the foreground is divine responsiveness. On the one hand, there is no real suggestion in the narrative that God is learning and developing over time. Sternberg seems right about that. On the other hand, God is not static either and does not act in a woodenly consistent manner. God appears entirely able to adopt a new course of action even when it alters or contradicts a previous one. So God is not unchanging in the sense that even Samuel imagines (1 Sam. 15:29). The narrative explicitly credits God with regretting his earlier endorsement of Saul (1 Sam. 15:10-11a, 35b).[62] Yet the narrative does not consider God to be unreliable. God's changeability does not arise out of an arbitrary effort to dodge divine responsibility or stymie human discernment but from a willingness to adopt the best course of action for Israel's well-being and success.[63]

Quite a Character

In many respects God functions literarily in Samuel as one character among the rest. God often speaks and acts in the narrative as other characters do. Other characters refer to God and speak to God as they would to another person. This dimension of God's characterization remains underdeveloped in Sternberg's treatment. Yet, as Sternberg rightly insists, God also knows more and does more than other characters in the narrative can manage. An apprehension of immense power accompanies God's literary profile, an ominous sense that this God-character represents the ultimate authority in the narrative's unfolding story. However, this character's power never obliterates human freedom and responsibility within the narrative's world. Indeed, God seems surprisingly disposed to let the Israelites make important decisions for themselves. The reticence of God in the second half of 1 Samuel highlights this point. By that time Saul has been rejected and David chosen, but Saul still rules from his throne, David is on the run, and God apparently lets things ride rather than forcing a resolution.

---

62. See Yairah Amit, "'The Glory of Israel Does Not Deceive or Change his Mind': On the Reliability of Narrator and Speakers in Biblical Narrative," *Prooftexts* 12 (1992): 201–12.

63. For another effort to read 1 Sam. 15 as combining a view of God as both dynamic and reliable, see Johnson, "Chiastic Contradiction." Cf. Hans Wilhelm Hertzberg, *I & II Samuel: A Commentary* (Philadelphia: Westminster, 1964), 126: "God is not slavishly bound by his own decisions, but is almighty to such an extent that he is Lord even of them."

So it is basic to God's portrait in Samuel that God is characterized as simultaneously both like and unlike the other characters. Rather than trying to choose between standard literary designations for God's character such as "flat" (one-dimensional) or "rounded" (three-dimensional),[64] it is preferable to think of God's characterization as episodic or punctuated. God's character cannot be entirely encompassed within the limits of literary characterization. God can only be characterized partially, in flashes and hints, and the uneven nature of God's characterization is its most crucial aspect. God *is* a sort of person in Samuel, but without what might be termed a personality. God's personal nature is established through fragmentary analogies and abbreviated moments of encounter. God can be present or "with" other characters in a decisive and trustworthy manner, but God can also be distant from and even opposed to them. The narrative plays a tricky game, suggesting on the one hand the possibility of the most intimate kind of interaction between other characters and this literary deity, while at the same time ensuring that the deity is never fully reduced to human form, never literarily captured or tamed.

God is even understood to work in and through other narrative characters, as is seen most radically in God's strategic use of Hushai's bad counsel (2 Sam. 17:14). God somehow disposes Absalom and his men to favor Hushai's counsel over Ahithophel's wiser advice, so that they bring destruction upon themselves. This kind of "double causality"[65]—God and humans working mysteriously in tandem—means that there is finally no absolute distinction between God and other characters in the Samuel narrative, just as there is no absolute distinction between God and the narrator. Just because God is literarily off-stage or not explicitly portrayed in a narrative episode does not mean that the narrative considers God absent or uninvolved. The narrative is *all* about God, all the way along.

Modern readers will vary in their response to God's characterization in Samuel, and whether they consider such a portrait of God to be praiseworthy. The burden of this essay has been to insist that for the Samuel narrative itself God is a praiseworthy literary character. From the perspective of this particular narrative, the God of Israel, at turns both tender and terrifying, is deserving of thanks and praise. Modern readers certainly have a responsibility to evaluate that portrait of God, but they will only be able to assess it adequately when they first see it for what it is.

---

64. This influential distinction was advanced by E. M. Forster, *Aspects of the Novel* (London: Edwin Arnold, 1949), 65–75. Cf. Shimon Bar-Efrat, *Narrative Art in the Bible* (New York: T&T Clark, 2004), 90.

65. Bar-Efrat, *Narrative Art*, 28.

Chapter 4

Hannah: A Woman Deeply Troubled

Jenni Williams

> I think that many confuse "applicability" with "allegory"; but the one resides in the freedom of the reader, and the other in the purposed domination of the author.[1]

Introduction

Professor Tolkien's quotation above deals with the question of power in the hermeneutical process. He is wary of allegory as a way that an author provides only one hermeneutical lens through which a reader may interpret what a story is "really" about. In this chapter I want to explore a very common way of reading characters which I will argue may cause the opposite problem: the impoverishing domination of the reader. I will argue that whilst "typology" has much to offer in understanding the dynamic of a text, it has reductionist tendencies which can cause us to miss out of the richness of biblical character.

The Tolkien quotation reminds us that narrative constructions such as allegory or typology are not "innocent" strategies. When a character is marked as estimable by the author or constructed according to a series of traits which the author knows the reader will consider desirable, this may coerce the reader into identifications. These identifications can be either

---

1. J. R. R. Tolkien, "Foreword to the Second Edition," in *The Lord of the Rings*, 50th Anniversary Edition (New York: Houghton Mifflin, 2004), xxiv.

idealistic or realistic, but if idealistic they may impact on and even modify the reader's behavior or worldview according to a desired good of the author, which may not be necessarily in the best interests of the reader.[2] But equally, "types" identified by the reader may achieve exactly the same power imbalance.

Part of the problem, as I will argue below, is that the degree to which typology and associated devices such as allusion can be identified in a biblical text is as great or less as the eye of the reader beholds.

Identifying the "Type"

Typology is one of a series of associative devices by which a reader may experience a story as inviting them to think of something else. It belongs thus in the category of allegory, metaphor, quotation, and allusion. All of these associative devices are designed to connect two things in the reader's mind. Many characters in the Old Testament have been identified through the centuries of interpretation as "types" of one kind or another. Thus we may say that when a character breaks into a psalm, and a psalm containing a clear anachronism at that (1 Sam. 2:1-10), the author somehow intends the reader to understand the character as having some qualities desirable of emulation by an implied worshipping community. This is commonly interpreted to indicate a "type": that a scene or person represents another. I want to suggest that the identification and interpretation of "type" is not always the "purposed domination of the author" but rather lies within "the freedom of the reader," and this is not always a good thing, since readers, no less than authors, may use their freedom to good or bad ends. Hannah is often identified as a "type" of the barren woman or the heroic mother or similar ideas. She is held to be an upholder of patriarchy as she cannot value herself until she's done the "woman's job" of providing sons. Some of these aspects are explored below. And we can certainly say that Hannah does indeed live in a patriarchal world and does indeed long for a child. But there is a huge loss if we reduce her merely to these aspects. The identification of a "type" of Israel is relatively straightforward if the only thing this character does is sing a Psalm. But what happens when the character is saying and doing other things? What if they engage with other people, if they have a burning desire, if they make statements about

---

2. A perfect example of this can be seen in the film "The Jane Austen Book Club" where one of the characters is debating a dubious moral decision based on the behavior of a character in a Jane Austen novel. "What is this, a rule book now?" asks one character. "We could do worse," says another.

themselves and their emotional state is described? Where a character is more than a mere cypher, understanding what the type is and how the author intended it to be interpreted becomes a very difficult enterprise. This section will demonstrate this difficulty. Moreover, the very employment of typology may, from a narratologist's and indeed any reader's point of view, impoverish the character to the detriment of the whole reading experience.

This initial premise that "typing" is a readerly construct may seem a strange one. But consider the difficulties of the typing method when it is ascribed to the author. In order to consider Hannah as type in this approach we need first to identify authorial strategies which lead us to detect typing before we can interpret the intentionality behind the type. But, as Alter observes,[3] the conventions of typing are only rarely explicit and certainly in ancient Israel are not codified but rather: "an elaborate set of tacit agreements between artist and audience about the ordering of the art work is at all times the enabling context in which the complex communication of art occurs."[4]

Alter further notes the challenge of identifying macro conventions because of the lack of Hebrew literature available to us as well as the sheer distance of cultural time between the modern reader and the ancient writer which prevents perceptions of conventionality.[5] In essence, Alter identifies the major problem for the modern reader looking to identify type-scenes or types: it can be relatively straightforward to "sense" a typing strategy but no one can exactly identify or quantify it, far less explain its intent in any definitive way.

Moreover, sometimes modern narratological dissatisfactions can lead to the dismissal or reduction of a character to a "type." We may identify a character as a "type" because they appear undeveloped, one-dimensional, or wooden in the reader's eyes. From this we infer or impose authorial intention. For example, in feminist analysis emphasis is often placed on the fact that the women disappear after their function in the narrative has been fulfilled. In other words, an imposed readerly sense of satisfaction or closure is perceived absent and from that absence an intentionality is inferred. This kind of inference can only happen because we cannot say for sure what were the narrative conventions in ancient Israel.

---

3. Robert Alter, *The Art of Biblical Narrative* (New York: Basic Books, 1981), 47.

4. Whilst Alter primarily concerns himself with literary type-scenes, his observations work equally well with a literary type figure or a theological type.

5. Alter, *Biblical Narrative*, 47.

The problem with this idea is that it is not just female characters to whom this happens:

> Since biblical narrative characteristically catches its protagonists only at the critical and revealing points in their lives, the biblical type-scene occurs, not in the rituals of daily existence but at the crucial junctures in the lives of the heroes, from conception and birth to betrothal to deathbed.[6]

The mere ascription and reduction to type in the basis of some perceived form of inadequacy or bias on the author's part is ultimately unsatisfactory, unless we can prove that the author does this consistently to one particular group.

Nevertheless, Alter argues it is possible to discern type-scenes to a certain extent because of the fact of the repetition of a basic idea. In the case of the character we are examining in this chapter, we may identify the rivalry between two wives, one of whom is barren, as an often repeated biblical shape, preceding the birth of someone significant who is only born because of an explicitly stated intervention by the Lord. But again, reader's inference plays a key part: shall Hannah be the hero or, following Brenner, the "hero's mother"? Is her only importance as the one who achieves the miraculous child, hence "hero's mother," or do her actions merit her being given the title "hero" in her own right?

1. *"Typing" Hannah*

So with these questions in mind we will explore three approaches to "typing" the character of Hannah.

1a. *Hannah as Literary Type*

As a good example of how literary typing is approached, we will consider Athalya Brenner's outstanding literary-feminist work *The Israelite Woman*. We must first say that different authors who examine Hannah as part of a type or type-scene identify slightly different elements,[7] but Brenner argues that this type can display the following characteristics: the "mother-to-be" is infertile until a relatively advanced age; she receives a divine promise to assure her that her situation will be rescued; she competes with some form of co-wife by whom she is humiliated and who

---

6. Ibid., 51.
7. See, for example, James G. Williams, "The Beautiful and the Barren: Conventions in Biblical Type-Scenes," *JSOT* 5 (1980): 48–55.

has some form of lower status (in this case, in her husband's regard). This conflict escalates until the family is consumed by it; the women cannot cooperate with each other unless some external danger threatens them; the birth of the son is the "true heir"; the fulfilment of the promise and his birth bring "at least a semblance of security" to the mother.[8]

Immediately, though, we can see some variations in the Hannah story. As we shall see, she does not compete, indeed refuses to compete. She is silent in the face of Peninnah's provocation, and this silence becomes an act of resistance to the type: Hannah will not join in the conflict and so the family is not consumed. We shall see that she contrasts with Rachel who reproaches Jacob about her infertility[9] and then begs Leah for help. Hannah does not follow Rachel's paradigm, hoping for a cure in mandrakes, or Leah's hoping for more sex. Nor does she follow Sarai's approach of surrogacy. Although both Sarai and Rachel are given a child miraculously, neither character appears to expect it. In Sarai's case we may consider this understandable since the promise is to Abram (not Sarai) until Genesis 17,[10] which is the point at which the miracle son's matriline is fully articulated and by then the Hagar episode has happened. It is perhaps also understandable in Rachel's case since she has had no promise. However that may be, both these women resort to human efforts whilst Hannah turns to the divine. If Eli's pronouncement at 1 Sam. 1:17 is a prophecy or a guarantee of divine blessing,[11] the birth announcement we would expect from this type-scene is stunningly inexplicit. Here is an obvious place where it should be, pronounced by a priest of the Lord no less, but Hannah's refusal to share her trouble blocks any such announcement, as we will explore below. Nevertheless, Hannah apparently is content to rest on the promise/prophecy and takes no further action. Moreover, as we will observe, the conflict between the women is decidedly one-sided: Peninnah seeks conflict but Hannah refuses to engage with it.

In sum we may observe that literary types are constructed, as we have seen, by comparing characters who find themselves in similar situations or who act in comparable ways. These situations somehow become perennialized: the age-old problem of this or that. Now there is nothing wrong

---

8. Athalya Brenner, *The Israelite Woman: Social Role and Literary Type in Biblical Narrative* (Sheffield: JSOT Press, 1985), 95.
9. Rachel's approach to human (rather than divine) sources of help are criticized directly by Jacob (Gen. 30:1).
10. Later both in narrative sequence and in probable dating.
11. This depends on how we read the imperfect here.

with this way of working of course. Stories do perennialize: if they dealt only with the unique without referentiality they would become inaccessible. Literary theory looks for patterns and commonalities and by doing so identifies ways in which stories can be understood on a broader stage. Without this, the experience of reading would be terribly impoverished. It is a sound, even necessary, approach, always provided that the perennial problem does not become the driver for interpretation. So in this case, Hannah shares a problem with Sarai, Rachel, Manoah's wife, and others. But if we (a) limit our view of her to this one problem or (b) allow the type to constrain us so that we miss valuable aspects of the character, the reading experience is impoverished. In writing that last sentence, I originally wrote "valuable anomalies," and this exactly illustrates the problem: commonalities too easily become norms, uniformities, and finally hermeneutical keys.

Moreover, as we considered briefly above, the attribution of typing may also lead to identifying authorial intent across *all* examples of the type. There is a risk which arises when the idea of types and type-scenes is considered in consequence to be intrinsically inimical, an authorial strategy designed to oppress or control. The typicality of two women arguing over one man when one woman is fertile and the other is not, and the conflict between them, can be inferred to be the author's "typical" comment. Brenner uses this type to infer male comment about female behavior: that women cannot cooperate, that they allow personal ambition to supersede "greater values":[12]

> Here we might stop, chuckle and murmur: There is very little that is new under the sun. Traditional opinions and conventions change very slowly. The characterization of the female as a battle-axe who is unable to get along with other women, especially where her menfolk (lovers, husbands, sons) are concerned, is as commonplace today as in the book of Genesis.[13]

Brenner is arguing that unless the type is identified and resisted, the author and the reader are forced into some dubious collusion regarding what women are like. A type can either be inferred as the author's intent to set a character up as a suitable type to emulate or a negative type to warn the reader against emulating. But it is the identification of the type which can drive this interpretation. If we separated Hannah from Rachel and Sarai, would that still be the intent we would perceive in her story?

---

12. Brenner, *Israelite Woman*, 95.
13. Ibid., 96.

1b. *Hannah as Israel: Theological Type*

To identify Hannah as a theological type presents several possibilities. One of the simplest ways in which an author can identify a character as somehow typing the nation is if the character does something which the nation typically does. So in the story of Hannah, the obvious character construction of type featured is simply that, like Israel in times of trouble and joy, she sings psalms. We may immediately note that Hannah is constructed as one who at first only speaks to God about her trouble but, after the encounter, is willing to recount his mighty deeds to others. Firth observes that the book of 1 Samuel begins and ends in worship.[14] Looked at from a structural or plot-based perspective, in her trouble Hannah sings a lament and then sings a psalm of thanksgiving and rejoicing after the resolution of her trouble, which is exactly the pattern we would expect to convey an understanding of YHWH as one who intervenes for the one who cries out to him. Psalms of lament may contain protestations of innocence or an utterance of confession. Whilst a protestation of innocence is not in Hannah's lament, her retort to Eli proclaims her as innocent petitioner needing YHWH's help. The psalm in ch. 2 is clearly anachronistic with its reference to the king, but this merely reinforces the intentionality of its use. The pre-exilic psalms often supplicate for the strengthening and safety of the king. So Hannah in her rejoicing is the epitome of Israel vindicated.

There are other ways in which Hannah may be said to type the nation, within the very action of her narrative. To begin with, the action in her story happens at a time of festival, but in a time of plenty Hannah hungers. Surrounded by those who are against her (Peninnah), for reasons of jealousy and those who are indifferent to her pain (Elkanah, Eli), she represents Israel among the nations.

Some scholars have turned to questions of structure in the books of Samuel as a way of identifying a type. One approach to this is that the function of Hannah is as theological corrective: Bailey argues that, in combination with the Song of David at 2 Sam. 22:1-51, the Song of Hannah's literary function is to reset in a "theologically orthodox picture" the character of YHWH, whose character appears ethically more complex elsewhere in the book.[15] Thus the function of Hannah as character is structurally related to the book which her story begins.

---

14. David G. Firth, *1&2 Samuel: A Kingdom Comes* (London: T&T Clark, 2017), 26–7.

15. Randall C. Bailey, "The Redemption of YHWH: A Literary Critical Function of the Songs of Hannah and David," *BibInt* 3, no. 2 (1995): 231.

Jero[16] finds Hannah's story types Israel's request for a king, thus connecting it in a different way to the rest of Samuel. He adduces the linguistic significance of the wordplay on *šā'ûl* ("ask") in vv. 27-28 and the Song's allusion to the king.[17] He also identifies structural parallels:

Hannah has no child	Israel has no king
Hannah wants a child	Israel wants a king (1 Sam. 8:5)
Hannah's rival has many	Israel's rival (Philistines [*sic*]) has 5 kings
Hannah's rival harasses her	Philistine conflict (1 Sam. 4–7)
Hannah's husband loves her uniquely / gives her a special portion	Israel is YHWH's people (1 Sam. 2:29)
Hannah's husband is better than 10	Israel needs no king because YHWH is king (1 Sam. 8:7)
YHWH grants her request	YHWH tells Samuel to hear their request (1 Sam. 8:7)
Hannah receives what she "asked for"	Israel receives what they ask for: Saul

Jero gives attention to questions of story detail, where the author has included aspects without which the plot could still go forward, as, for example, the attitudes of Eli and Elkanah: the latter articulating an unnecessary request in the light of his own love and the former initially scorning then supporting the request.[18] These, he argues, typify attitudes to kingship expressed elsewhere in the books of Samuel.

All of these perspectives are valuable in that they offer a more narratological sense of connection with the rest of the book in a way commentators have not always managed. Some scholars have simply reduced Hannah's story to the birth of Samuel, and this shows how easy it is to be unable to allow an apparently contiguous episode fully to be part of a broader narrative without some form of interpretative or associative process. Therefore, to understand how Hannah (as opposed to the medium by which Samuel comes to be) can be part of what the book is saying can only be welcome. It pays appropriate attention to the ancient author as intentional storyteller. It gives perspective on the story in terms of its belonging to what is essentially a book about Israelite kingship and its origins.

---

16. Christopher Jero, "Mother-Child Narratives and the Kingdom of God: Authorial Use of Typology as an Interpretive Device in Samuel-Kings," *BBR* 25, no. 2 (2015): 159.

17. Jero's point is complicated by his use of the term "Messiah," but the basic point remains.

18. Jero, "Mother-Child," 158.

That said, this approach, for all its usefulness, is not without problems if not set within a reasonable boundary. Jero goes on to observe, "Everything in the Hannah narrative—its details, structure, emphases, and even its curious twists—all work together to create a situation that mirrors that of Israel in desiring a king."[19]

This is where typing becomes a limitation, for now *everything* about Hannah must be subsumed in the type. This, I want to argue, is what makes readerly constructions of type impoverishing. This denies the author the freedom to write good narrative under the driving imperative of writing structurally coherent narrative. What I am trying to say is this: that a story is included and constructed so as to connect with a broader theme of a book does not, and should not, preclude details which make it unique and valuable in and of itself.

A more nuanced approach is taken by Polzin, who argues:

> ...the voices we hear in chapter 1, those of the narrator and the characters, take on a dual accent that reverberates backward and forward on the question of kingship in Israel. The expository material in verses 1-8 deepens in significance both as a depiction of Israel before the establishment of monarchy and as background material about Elkanah's family life before the birth of Samuel.[20]

In this approach, space is made both for an understanding of an editor who can use a shorter story to pre-figure a larger narrative without sacrificing the intrinsic value of the story in itself.

1c. *Hannah as "the Poor": Sociological Type*

Esler approaches the typing of Hannah from a sociological perspective: he argues that there has been from the beginning of the book a narrative set up between the righteous non-elite and the unjust elite. He notes the mention of the two worthless sons of Eli at the beginning of the story. This inclusion has no particular significance for the Hannah narrative and, therefore, coupled with the fact that Hannah does not fully disappear from the scene until after their worthlessness has been revealed (1 Sam. 2:12-17), he argues its inclusion must be part of indicating Hannah has a role in the larger narrative. He bases this role on examining the power relationships in Hannah's life and comparing them to perspectives from sociological studies among polygynous families.

---

19. Ibid., 161.
20. Robert Polzin, *Samuel and the Deuteronomist: A Literary Study of the Deuteronomistic History, Part 2: 1 Samuel* (Bloomington: Indiana University Press, 1993), 26.

Esler emphasizes the rivalry between Hannah and Peninnah and considers that Peninnah challenges Hannah when the portions of food are doled out exactly because it is a public space and therefore a place better to humiliate her.[21] He argues that Hannah's psalm of rejoicing reflects exactly the same attitude as Peninnah's, now that roles have been reversed.[22] He notes the clear gap in social status between Hannah and Eli, since she addresses him as "my lord" and refers to herself as "your servant." Esler quotes Bourke's description of Hannah as one of the lowly whom YHWH loves.[23]

Esler also appeals to the second psalm and its widening view about the triumph through God of the "non-elite."[24]

"Thus Hannah carries her message beyond the domestic realm to society at large, where there are pronounced differentials of wealth and status, which the oppressed long to see overturned."[25] As we have seen, he argues that this relates to those who have power and those who do not and their worth. "Hannah is actually setting the standard against which the sons of Eli will be judged."[26] This approach, no less than the others outlined above, has great value in identifying the multifarious ways in which the author has connected this story to the rest of the book, and giving these strategies due credit.

2. The Limitations of Typing

2a. The Non-existence of the Type

All this said, there are elements within type or type-scenes which can be identified by their particularity, their insistent nature, or their unexpectedness. Both literary type and theological type are constructs: they do not exist of themselves. Literary type is in essence a composite of characters who happen to find themselves in similar situations, as Alter argues. As such the "hero's mother" type is wholly artificial: a composite of characteristics and circumstances taken from Hannah, Sarah, Leah, and Rachel. As such, no one character will display all her characteristics or reactions: she will change and flex according to her intrinsic plot, and each plot will have its own concerns from its narrative context. But here

---

21. Philip Esler, *Sex, Wives, and Warriors: Reading Old Testament Narrative with Its Ancient Audience* (Eugene: Cascade, 2011), 127.
22. Ibid., 128.
23. Ibid., 130.
24. Ibid., 134.
25. Ibid.
26. Ibid., 136.

is exactly the interest: why is it, for example, that while Rachel and Hannah follow almost the same life situation (fertile rival, husband who does not understand) they should be constructed so differently? Rachel speaks and interacts with people only, Hannah reserves her words for the Lord and her actions also. It is this variation which may lead us to understand Hannah as more than "hero's mother" type and as "Israel" type. As Sternberg observes:

> Analogy is an essentially spatial pattern, composed of at least two elements (two characters, events, strands of action, etc.) between which there is at least one point of similarity and one of dissimilarity: the similarity affords the basis for the spatial linkage [between two texts] and confrontation of the analogical elements, whereas the dissimilarity makes for their mutual illumination, qualification, or simply concretization.[27]

Williams observes that these changes and flexes are the tension between working within a convention and bringing something new to it:

> The typic scene is a convention of story telling. Like conventions in painting and iconography, it has fixed elements that constrain the artist to work within them. For the artist there is a social necessity to offer the continuity of the long standing convention that the audience expects. The challenge to creativity is to achieve new meaning by dropping or adding an element here and there (too much dropping or adding would ruin the continuity), to effect different nuances, or to mold variations on the traditional elements.[28]

In my view, the point at which the type becomes most valuable is when it breaks down. As such, one of the type's great contributions to narratology is essentially apophatic. When a character flexes away from the constructed type, something is to be inferred about authorial intent. The type cannot be said to be subjective, but neither is it objective and it must be sacrificed to gain the full richness of what the story can offer.

As long as the literary theorist recognizes both the necessity and value of this abnegation, discussion of type remains valuable: the interpreter has, so to speak, nothing to lose since the type is a nothing by which some things are measured rather than a controlling interpretative device. Once an interpreter loses their critical distance from their treasured type, all this changes. The type dictates the interpretation of the character, and the richness and depth of a literary portrait is lost.

27. Meir Sternberg, *The Poetics of Biblical Narrative: Ideological Literature and the Drama of Reading* (Bloomington: Indiana University Press, 1985), 365.
28. Williams, "The Beautiful and the Barren," 40.

2b. *What Type of Type?*

As we have observed, theological typing is valuable because it entails observing the book of Samuel as a whole and asking what part the stories within it contribute to the whole. Yet immediately the issue presents itself: *which* Israel is Hannah? The perfect, ideal, faithful Israel who turns to the Lord in tribulation and is vindicated? Or the real, flawed Israel who faithlessly demands a king? Jero's observations lean inevitably towards the second because of his intention to see how the opening of 1 Samuel reflects a greater theme in the book: the monarchy. But this must inevitably lead to a back-read of Hannah that her infertility is somehow a sanction. This is a widespread understanding among scholars of infertility in the Old Testament, but I contend it is ultimately unsatisfactory and requires that we background aspects of Hannah's story, such as the lack of a confession in her lament and her assertion that she is *not* a worthless woman, which sounds similar to a psalmic protestation of innocence. It is true that the narrator notes that her barrenness comes from YHWH himself (1:5), but this is best understood as a statement of YHWH's sovereignty over life if we are to pay attention to the portrait of Hannah we are offered. Moreover, in the end, should we see Hannah's story as beginning the story of the desire for monarchy or as the beginning of the story of why the monarchy went wrong? I would argue the latter is more consistent with the view of the Deuteronomistic Historians. In that case Hannah as one who ignores human help and seeks the divine will is rather what Israel should have done (at least according to 1 Sam. 8) and didn't do. This might lead us to questions of editorial layers in view of the second psalm. But what it illustrates is that the theological type is no more an all-embracing way to understand Hannah than the literary type was.

Esler's type too reveals limitations. That Eli has a higher social status than Hannah may be reasonably accepted, but Esler fails to bring into clear focus exactly how extraordinary is her verbal resistance in this situation because he is working with a type of the lowly whom YHWH lifts up. This almost equates to "victims" who are rescued, and thus backgrounds the element of self-rescue and theological acuity in Hannah.

3. *Hannah: A Woman Deeply Troubled*

Finally, then, what if we were to read Hannah simply for Hannah and then see how she interacts with all the types above? The story of Hannah is narratologically complex, revealing multiple interweavings at the level of character and in particular, speech. This section will use the character/plot/language lenses.

Linguistically, the story is set up by structural antithetical pairs and antithetical parallelisms. The first and second pieces of information given about Hannah are phrased in this way:

> He had two wives; the name of the one was Hannah//the name of the other was Peninnah. Peninnah had children//Hannah had no children. (1 Sam. 1:2)

From the outset, therefore, Hannah is placed in an inextricable connection and opposition with Peninnah, and from this inextricability and contrast comes at least part of the tension of the narrative. Two women, one man. In this beginning, the function of Peninnah's character is to represent the fertile, the fortunate, and their mocking of the infertile, the unfortunate.

The time setting of the story sets up a further antithetical pair related to fullness and emptiness. The action takes place at a time of festival when there is fullness and yet Hannah cannot eat: she is emptied by her distress at Peninnah's bullying. This antithesis is played out in speech also: Elkanah goes to some trouble to make Hannah full in 1 Sam. 1:5 and is dismayed at her resistance to his conveyed, even imposed, fullness. His efforts to keep Hannah content and Peninnah's efforts to distress her are both underpinned by the underlying cause:

> To Hannah he gave a double portion because he loved her though the Lord had closed her womb//Her rival used to provoke her severely, to irritate her, because the LORD had closed her womb. (1 Sam. 1:5-6)

Elkanah's speech reveals his anxiety about Hannah's state of mind and, as Amit[29] has pointed out, his anxiety is not necessarily generous. Although she is empty (the Lord has closed her womb) he wants her to be filled by *her* love for *him*. Although he tries to fill her by his love and regard expressed through food portions, it is her love which he considers should sate her, not his.

> Her husband Elkanah said to her, "Hannah, why do you weep? Why do you not eat? Why is your heart sad? Am I not more to you than ten sons?" (1 Sam. 1:8)

The function of Elkanah's character and utterances, which are developed into speech in a way Peninnah is not, serves to emphasize the fullness of

---

29. Yairah Amit, "'Am I Not More Devoted to You than Ten Sons?' (1 Samuel 1.8): Male and Female Interpretations," in *A Feminist Companion to Samuel and Kings*, ed. Athalya Brenner (Sheffield: Sheffield Academic, 1994), 75.

celebration against the emptiness of lament. Miller[30] notes that lament is sung by people who feel alone, and this is part of Hannah's trouble. We may observe that Elkanah, whilst trying to help, simply emphasizes Hannah's aloneness.

Both Elkanah and Peninnah represent the apparently inextricable, as we have seen. Hannah's aloneness is in her experience of pain and hence her emotional experience: relationally or even publicly she is bound to the co-wife who provided the family's children as surely as she is bound to the husband whose wife she is. Yet, Hannah does not respond either to Peninnah's mocking or Elkanah's rather petulant reassurances. Her silence in the narrative is hugely significant. It allows the author to portray her as someone who knows her own aloneness in this family and then to show that this is not the place where she needs to deal with her problem: unlike Rachel who reproached Jacob (Gen. 30:1) and begged Leah for help (Gen. 30:14), Hannah's first speech will be to God.

1 Samuel 1:9 marks a deep narrative shift as Hannah extricates herself from this apparently inextricable situation: she leaves their scene of "fullness" and moves to the sanctuary, and this spatial shift represents shaking herself free from the fertility and fullness which has bowed her down. The narrative certainly seems to imply that she was in a liminal space, since Eli is at the doorpost and can see her. But it is apparently not a time when some kind of cultic activity is taking place: Hannah's aloneness is emphasized by approaching an apparently empty sanctuary. Hannah is not fully in the festival. Moreover she is being watched, inimically. Even the lonely space is made conditional for her by human contact. The shift in narrative is both spatial and speech focused. Hannah's lack of audible speech is taken by Eli as incoherent (because drunken) speech, hence somehow invalid speech. But this challenge will bring about the change in how Hannah interacts with people. She has gone from silence at home to silent prayer in the sanctuary to audible speech to justify herself: something she never did for her husband or her co-wife. When finally she engages in speech with human beings she defends herself vigorously (1 Sam. 1:16-17). Within her utterance is an often-observed narrative irony: Hannah defends herself against being a daughter of Belial, which is exactly what Eli's sons prove to be when they engage with the holy space (1 Sam. 2:12). The holy space is not conditional for them, nor do other humans prevent their being part of festival, yet they betray the holy space. Hannah, whose right to it is questioned, uses it appropriately.

---

30. Patrick D. Miller, *The Way of the Lord: Essays in Old Testament Theology* (Grand Rapids: Eerdmans, 2007), 205.

As such Eli is the epitome of a fool: he cannot tell the faithful from the faithless. The malign presence of Eli acts as an inclusion around Hannah's psalm of lament: first he is there guarding the sanctuary then he challenges the petitioner's worthiness. Moreover, his words mock the petitioner's hope: her heartfelt lament is reduced to drunken chatter. Eli becomes the "enemy" of the psalms, the one who mocks, who prevents.

Hannah's reply also illustrates and reinforces something we have already noted: the startling silences and reticences in her speech and the power they have. Hannah did not speak to Peninnah or to Elkanah and her first speech is to the Lord. But now, faced with the Lord's priest, although she is more than happy to defend herself, even to Eli she does not reveal the nature of what is causing her pain. This might at first appear puzzling: what can be gained by having the character withhold this information when the reader already knows what she wants? This reticence with Eli reinforces the first reticence with Elkanah and Peninnah and makes clearer the intentionality of the withholding in Hannah's speech. It develops further as Hannah's initial explanation about "great anxiety and vexation" is met by Eli's blessing (or prophecy) that YHWH should grant what she asks, without further details. This at first seems further to complicate the issue: if it is a prophecy Eli pronounces, just what is he prophesying? But it is thus that the reader is prevented from interpreting Hannah as victim in the face of Peninnah and Elkanah's words: she withholds her complaint until she comes to the holy space, even as the help she seeks to receive is YHWH's not her husband's. In the same way she withholds from Eli because it isn't his help she seeks, either. The extent to which she speaks to Eli is only to defend her right to an encounter with YHWH.

Later, Hannah will willingly share what her trouble has been when she returns with Samuel years later (1:26), but for the moment we notice how not only the nature of her trouble but also the psalmic form (1 Sam. 1:11) is nowhere else part of Hannah's speech with human beings.

The reply to Eli makes him shift his attitude and he pronounces a blessing or perhaps a prophecy that Hannah should/will receive what she has asked for. This encounter (with God or with his spokesman?) closes the episode and Hannah returns to the situation she left. However, something at home has changed in the light of the encounter: Hannah can eat and drink with her husband. Fullness is now something Hannah can bear (1 Sam. 1:18), both in the sense of the food of festival and also the company of her husband: his clumsy attempts to comfort her either now have no impact on her or can be re-situated in her broader security. She returns with Elkanah to the holy space (1 Sam. 1:19). Whether this is at a time of service or not, Hannah is now in the holy space with others, not alone. It remains significant that her right to be there is acknowledged without her husband in 1 Sam. 1:17. The scene changes briefly to Ramah for a classic birth formula: sex, the Lord's "remembering," birth, theophoric paronomasia. The sheer brevity of such a huge amount of event packed into two sentences suggests this is a literary formula.

The birth of the child and the theophoric name adds to the insistence of Hannah's focus on YHWH as the source of her help: without Elkanah, she names the child for her experience at the sanctuary. Then occurs a reversal of the tensions of festival which opened the episode: Hannah came and was sad, now she does not come and is happy. Moreover, these are Hannah's first words to her husband and they are all about her interaction with YHWH, recalling the vow she made and re-iterating her own agency:

> But Hannah did not go up, for she said to her husband, "As soon as the child is weaned, *I* will bring him, that he may appear in the presence of the LORD, and remain there forever; *I* will offer him as a nazirite for all time." (1 Sam. 1:22, emphasis mine[31])

Elkanah too sees things differently: his disapproval of his wife's refusal to engage in festival has now transmuted into acceptance that her *not* engaging with festival is some kind of prophetic act:

> Her husband Elkanah said to her, "Do what seems best to you, wait until you have weaned him; only—may the LORD establish his word." (1 Sam. 1:23)[32]

Commentators often seem to assume that a woman with an infant would not make this kind of journey but this seems unlikely, and from the narrative's point of view her not coming is not a sidelight: it is somehow accomplishing the prophecy.

When Hannah does go to Shiloh, she re-iterates the story for Eli, this time telling him what she prayed for, and she devotes Samuel to the Lord. Quite why on earth she would leave her child with a man who can't tell the difference between prayer and drunken gibberish is not clear but a promise is a promise. So good does Hannah feel about this that a second psalm, this time a psalm of praise, is put in her mouth by the author. The character is cast here not as a mother ruefully leaving her child but as a

---

31. This last phrase is not present in MT or LXX.
32. There is not space here to consider the puzzle of Elkanah's vow in v. 23: Ruth Fidler, "A Wife's Vow—the Husband's Woe? The Case of Hannah and Elkanah," *ZAW* 118 (2006): 374–88, provides a comprehensive consideration.

triumphant worshipper who has received favor. Hannah who had nothing to say to Peninnah's meanness and Elkanah's emotional blackmail, has become supremely confident.

Two vignettes remain: one the poignant story of Hannah's making Samuel a robe and bringing it every year: presumably a mark of his growing bigger even when she does not see him growing; the second apparently a response to her vow as a "firstfruits" mechanism:[33] Hannah who fulfilled her vow has indeed borne children, albeit not the seven of her psalm (1 Sam. 2:5).

Conclusion

Even this very short survey is enough to show why the story of Hannah has lent itself to so many typological inferences: its use of significant themes, including the establishment of the Israelite monarchy, the preoccupation of the Deuteronomistic Historian, the intensity of its utterances, and its use of psalms. It is both appropriate and enriching to read into it more than just the story of the birth of a significant figure. Moreover, it is impoverishing to read an episode in isolation, and many of the typological inferences we were examining enrich the story of Hannah and identify the impact of the rest of the book on her story. In the end, "types" are important and valuable as a way of seizing hold of what a story is trying to do. The possible cost is when they are allowed to detract from the character by their generalizing tendency. The text's focus on the character is lost: because the character could function to mean almost anything, it comes to mean nothing. The story of Hannah is the story of someone in need, someone victimized but someone with courage and a deeply grounded sense of theological truths. Much of this is the story of others in the Old Testament. But it is also uniquely hers.

---

33. Jo Ann Hackett, "1 and 2 Samuel" in *The Women's Bible Commentary*, ed. C. A. Newsom, S. H. Ringe, and J. E. Lapsley (Louisville: Westminster John Knox, 1998), 95.

Chapter 5

ELI: A HIGH PRIEST THROWN UNDER THE
WHEELS OF THE OX CART

Marvin A. Sweeney

I

One of the major scholarly issues in the modern, critical study of the book of Samuel is the differentiation between those who call for largely diachronic historical study of the book and those who call for largely synchronic literary study. Historical scholars, such as McCarter, McKenzie, Halpern, Tsumura, Dietrich, Auld, and Wright, emphasize Samuel's historicity, historical context, compositional history, and textual character,[1] whereas literary scholars, such as Fokkelman, Polzin, Alter, Sternberg, Gunn, and Noll, emphasize its narrative formulation, plot development, and characterization.[2] Others, such as Campbell, present

1. P. Kyle McCarter, Jr., *1 Samuel*, AB 8 (Garden City: Doubleday, 1980); idem, *2 Samuel*, AB 9 (Garden City, 1984); Steven L. McKenzie, *King David: A Biography* (Oxford: Oxford University Press, 2002); Baruch Halpern, *David's Secret Demons: Messiah, Murderer, Traitor, King* (Grand Rapids: Eerdmans, 2003); David Tsumura, *The First Book of Samuel*, NICOT (Grand Rapids: Eerdmans, 2007); W. Dietrich, *Samuel*, BKAT VIII/1-4 (Neukirchen-Vluyn: Neukirchener Verlag, 2003–2007); A. Graeme Auld, *1 and 2 Samuel: A Commentary*, OTL (Louisville: Westminster John Knox, 2008); Jacob L. Wright, *David, King of Israel, and Caleb in Biblical Memory* (Cambridge: Cambridge University Press, 2014).
2. David M. Gunn, *The Story of King David: Genre and Interpretation* (Sheffield: JSOT Press, 1978); Meir Sternberg, *The Poetics of Biblical Narrative: Ideological Literature and the Drama of Reading* (Bloomington: Indiana University Press, 1987); Jan Fokkelman, *Narrative Art and Poetry in the Books of Samuel: Vow and Desire*,

a synchronic analysis of the book of Samuel even though the analysis is rooted in deep engagement with diachronic scholarship.[3] Frolov combines a detailed formal analysis with valuable insights concerning characterization and plot development.[4] Although the diachronic and synchronic concerns can intersect at times, they remain largely independent of each other in most scholarly discourse, particularly in an environment when so many are anxious to deny or downplay the early history of the Israelite monarchy as an ideological or theological construction based in the interests of later historical periods. These interests range from ancient times, such as the late monarchy, the Persian period, or the Hellenistic period, through modern times and concerns, such as those of contemporary American evangelicalism or modern Jewish Zionism.[5]

But such differentiation is unnecessary and in the end, counterproductive. History is known to modern interpreters in large measure through the works of writers who constantly display their ideological or theological perspectives in the written works that they produce. We may consider the contemporary assessment of Abraham Lincoln, arguably one of the greatest of the American presidents. Lincoln's reputation is based especially on his role in freeing African and African-descended slaves in the southern United States and on defending the Union during the American Civil War. But Lincoln was pilloried in the American press—both North and South—during the war, both because of doubts about his background as an unknown and self-educated lawyer from what was then the Illinois frontier and because of the staggering casualties and destruction caused by waging a war with modern lethal weapons and outdated military tactics.[6]

SSN 31 (Assen: Van Gorcum, 1993); Robert Polzin, *Samuel and the Deuteronomist: A Literary Study of the Deuteronomistic History: Part II: Samuel* (Bloomington: Indiana University Press, 1993); K. L. Noll, *The Faces of David* (Sheffield: Sheffield Academic, 1997); Robert Alter, *The David Story: Translation with Commentary of 1 and 2 Samuel* (New York: Norton, 2000). Although one might expect character and plot analysis from David Jobling, *1 Samuel*, Berit Olam (Collegeville: Liturgical, 1998), his analysis focuses primarily on governmental issues.

3. Antony F. Campbell, S.J., *1 Samuel*, FOTL 7 (Grand Rapids: Eerdmans, 2003); idem, *2 Samuel*, FOTL 8 (Grand Rapids: Eerdmans, 2005).

4. Serge Frolov, *The Turn of the Cycle: 1 Samuel 1–8 in Synchronic and Diachronic Perspectives*, BZAW 342 (Berlin: de Gruyter, 2004).

5. See, e.g., Joel Baden, *King David: The Real Life of an Invented Hero* (San Francisco: Harper One, 2013).

6. For an up-to-date biography of Lincoln, see David Herbert Donald, *Lincoln* (New York: Simon & Schuster, 1996).

Even one of Lincoln's generals, George B. McClellan, ran against him as a Democratic candidate in the 1864 Presidential election in a bid to end the war by a negotiated settlement. Indeed, McClellan nearly won the election. But we must also recognize the role played by other factors, especially Lincoln's assassination shortly following Lee's surrender at Appomattox and William H. Herndon's biographical portrayal of Lincoln, which facilitated the idolization of the sixteenth president. Although Herndon, Lincoln's friend and law-partner from Springfield, Illinois, sought to portray Lincoln as a man, his adulatory approach to Lincoln did much to create the image of Lincoln as a great man and American hero who overcame adversity to abolish slavery and to save the United States from dissolution.[7] Much of Herndon's account is anecdotal and the product of his own very favorable and biased view of Lincoln, but it nevertheless gives perspective on one of the most important leaders in American history. An analogous laudatory account of David's rise to power appears in 1 Samuel 16–2 Samuel 8, in which David seemingly does no wrong, but readers must also note a highly critical account of David's actions in 2 Samuel 9–24, in which David emerges as an incredibly flawed character. In each case, the general biases of the narrative (and narrator) toward David are clear even as they include clues for a much more nuanced account.

Most interpreters recognize that Samuel is a book about David. But Samuel is a book that presents a very biased account of David's life and rise to power as well as the lives of those who played key roles in his life, his rise to power, and the exercise of that power throughout his reign. The book of Samuel begins with a portrayal of Eli, the high priest of the Shiloh sanctuary, who would take in young Samuel ben Elkanah and raise him to become a priest, prophet, judge, and military leader of Israel—much on the model of Moses. Samuel would facilitate the transition of Israelite leadership from Judge to King and therefore pave the way for the foundation of the ruling house of David in ancient Israel and Judah.

The presentation of Eli is biased, because David's rise to power also entails the rise of his youngest son, Solomon, who actually founds the dynasty and redefines Israel's presiding priesthood from the house of Eli and his descendant, Abiathar, to the house of Zadok, which would preside in the Jerusalem Temple throughout the duration of Davidic rule. 1 Samuel 1–3; 4 characterizes Eli as an incompetent priest, who is not fit to preside in YHWH's holy sanctuary and who loses his life and

---

7. William H. Herndon and Jesse W. Weik, *Herndon's Lincoln: The True Story of a Great Life* (Chicago: Belford, Clarke & Co., 1889).

the right of his family to serve as Israel's priesthood because of his own alleged incompetence. 1 Samuel 1–3; 4 therefore anticipate the account of Solomon's expulsion of Abiathar as high priest in Jerusalem in favor of Zadok, all on the advice of David shortly before his death as portrayed in 1 Kings 1–2. Indeed, the account of Solomon's expulsion of Abiathar in favor of Zadok appears to drive the placement of the Eli narratives at the beginning of the book of Samuel; to a certain extent, this account also drives the composition and presentation of the Eli narratives.

The balance of this paper therefore focuses on the characterization of Eli as a means to justify the removal of his family from the high priesthood and its replacement by the house of Zadok at the outset of the reign of King Solomon ben David. 1 Samuel 1–3; 4 characterize Eli as an incompetent priest and father whose priestly line must be pushed aside to ensure a secure future for Israel. It focuses on four major episodes, including the portrayal of Eli as an incompetent priest who does not recognize a woman at prayer in 1 Samuel 1; an incompetent father who cannot properly discipline his sons in 1 Samuel 2; an incompetent priest once again who cannot recognize the visionary experience of YHWH by Samuel before the Ark of the Covenant in 1 Samuel 3; and as an incompetent and even blind father once again who does not recognize the coming demise of his sons and his people when they carry to Ark into battle against the Philistines based on their belief that YHWH would protect them in 1 Samuel 4. Eli's characterization provides background for the massacre of his priestly line by Saul in 1 Samuel 22 and the expulsion of his presumed descendant, Abiathar, from Jerusalem by Solomon in 1 Kings 2.

II

Campbell identifies 1 Samuel 1–16 as the first major sub-unit of the book of Samuel concerned with the preparations for David's emergence as the king to be.[8] Within that text, 1 Sam. 1:1–4:1a constitutes a sub-unit that takes up the preparations for David's emergence by focusing on the arrival of Samuel on the national scene.[9] 1 Samuel 1:1–2:11 then concentrates on the origins of Samuel.[10]

1 Samuel's characterization of major figures in the narrative lacks any attempt to identify the major priestly characters of the narrative, such as Samuel and his father, Elkanah, and Eli himself, as Levites as might be

---

8. Campbell, *1 Samuel*, 23–33.
9. Ibid., 34–59.
10. Ibid., 34–46.

found in Chronicles (e.g., 1 Chron. 9). Samuel was apparently written in a time or socio-political context prior to that of Chronicles, i.e., during the early periods of the Northern Kingdom of Israel, which apparently made use of non-Levitical priests.[11] But when considered from a synchronic perspective, the absence of full Levitical identification of these characters suggests to later readers that something is lacking in their characters that would therefore justify the replacement of the priestly house of Eli with the priestly house of Zadok.

1 Samuel 1 begins with the identification of Samuel's father as Elkanah ben Jeroham ben Elihu ben Tohu ben Zuph, an Ephraimite from Ramathaim of the Zuphites. Samuel is therefore not a Levite. His mother is Hannah, who is one of Elkanah's two wives, the other being Peninnah. Although Peninnah had children, Hannah did not, and this circumstance sets the stage for the birth of Samuel, who would be instrumental in founding the early Israelite monarchic houses of Saul and David. The inability of Hannah to bear children signals a typical motif in early Israelite literature, viz., the birth of a major figure in Israel's history to a woman who remained barren even as a rival bore children to her husband. Hannah must deal with taunting by Elkanah's other wife, Peninnah. Other examples of such maternal wifely rivalry include Hagar's bearing a son to Abraham while Sarah remained barren until eventually she gave birth to Isaac, the heir to the covenant (see Gen. 16; 21); Leah's bearing sons to Jacob until such time as the barren Rachel gave birth to Joseph, the father of Ephraim and Manasseh, the ancestors of the two key tribes of the Northern Kingdom of Israel, and later to Benjamin, the ancestor of Saul, Israel's first king (see Gen. 31; 35).

Elkanah's identity as an Ephraimite proves to be troublesome insofar as Samuel will be raised to serve as a priest. Although 1 Chron. 6:1-15 includes Elkanah, Samuel, and Samuel's sons in the Levitical genealogy, Samuel appears to be an example of a non-Levitical firstborn son (to the mother), who is dedicated to priestly service in Israelite sanctuaries, apparently a typical practice in northern Israel;[12] indeed YHWH tells

---

11. Marvin A. Sweeney, "Israelite and Judean Religions," in *The Cambridge History of Religions in the Ancient World*. Vol. 1, *From the Bronze Age through the Hellenistic Age*, ed. M. Salzman and M. A. Sweeney (Cambridge: Cambridge University Press, 2013), 151–73.

12. Cf. Gary N. Knoppers, *1 Chronicles 1–9*, AB 12 (New York: Doubleday, 2003), 421; Ralph Klein, *1 Chronicles*, Hermeneia (Minneapolis: Fortress, 2006), 182; Sara Japhet, *1 and 2 Chronicles: A Commentary*, OTL (Louisville: Westminster John Knox, 1993), 155–6.

Moses in Numbers 3 and 8 that the Levites will ultimately replace the firstborn sons of Israel as the priestly tribe.[13] Although Samuel may have become a priest historically by virtue of his status as a firstborn son of his mother sent to Shiloh for training, the larger canonical context would understand him as a priest of the line of Aaron. But Samuel does not share this understanding.

Eli is the high priest of the Shiloh Temple, although the text of Samuel provides no genealogy for him. Based on Chronicles, he is apparently understood to be a descendant of Aaron through Aaron's son Ithamar. This identification is established through Abiathar, who is identified as the son of Ahimelech and grandson of Ahitub in 1 Sam. 22:20. Ahitub is identified as the brother of Ichabod, the son of Phineas and therefore the grandson of Eli in 1 Sam. 14:3, and Ahimelech is identified as among the sons of Ithamar in 1 Chron. 24:1-3. These identities might have been constructed by the Chronicler, and so the identity of Eli as a descendant of Aaron through Aaron's son, Ithamar, may not be historical. Nevertheless, in the larger context of the biblical canon, they would have been understood as a legitimate characterization of Eli as a high priest of the line of Aaron at Shiloh.

The lack of a Levitical genealogy for Eli (and Samuel) may raise questions concerning their fitness to serve as priests in the view of later readers who would expect Israel's early priests to be Levites. But regardless of the question of Levitical genealogy, the presentation of Eli's actions in relation to Hannah in 1 Sam. 1:1–2:11 makes it clear that Eli is an incompetent priest and therefore not fit to hold the office of High Priest of the Shiloh sanctuary of early Israel.

The first episode of the narrative in 1 Sam. 1:1–2:11 asserts that Elkanah's wife, Hannah, is in distress because of her failure to bear a child. Insofar as Elkanah has another wife, Peninnah, who bears him many children, the text emphasizes Peninnah's taunting of Hannah as a major factor in her misery. Indeed, Hammurabi's law code and the narratives in Gen. 16; 29-30 stipulate that a wife who does not bear children may be divorced, but the wife may protect herself by providing her husband with

---

13. Marvin A. Sweeney, "Samuel's Institutional Identity in the Deuteronomistic History," *Constructs of Prophecy in the Former and Latter Prophets and Other Texts*, ed. L. L. Grabbe and M. Nissinen, ANEM 4 (Atlanta: SBL, 2011), 165–74; cf. idem, "Prophets and Priests in the Deuteronomistic History: Elijah and Elisha," in *Israelite Prophecy and the Deuteronomistic History: Portrait, Reality, and the Formation of History*, ed. M. R. Jacobs and R. F. Person, Jr., AIL 14 (Atlanta: SBL, 2013), 35–49.

a maid servant with whom he may have children that would be considered legally the children of his wife.[14] Sarah's provision of Hagar to Abraham (Gen. 16; 21) and Rachel's and Leah's provision of Bilhah and Zilpah to Jacob (Gen. 29–30) constitute examples of such practice.

Hannah makes no move to provide Elkanah with a maid servant, but instead she concentrates on appeals to YHWH every year when she and her family travel to Shiloh to attend the annual observance of a sacrifice. The text does not specify which sacrifice this might be; Sukkot, Pesach, Shavuot are all possibilities, but no specific observance is named. The narrative maintains that because of Peninnah's taunting of her at the festival one year, she was so upset that she would not eat or drink at the festival meal. She wept and prayed to YHWH to give her a son in the presence of Eli, who was sitting in his customary place by the entrance to the Shiloh sanctuary. Eli watched as she prayed and saw that her lips moved but no sound emerged from her mouth. As a result of his observations, Eli concluded that Hannah was drunk, so he reprimanded her, demanding to know how long she intended to engage in drunken behavior and that she cease her drinking immediately. Hannah responded by denying Eli's accusations, insisting that she had no wine nor had she drunk anything alcoholic, but stated instead that she was in distress and pouring out her heart to YHWH. Upon hearing Hannah's response, Eli pronounced a blessing over her, and told her to go in peace. Hannah's dismay was gone, and she returned home to become pregnant by her husband. She vowed to send her baby son, Samuel, to be raised as a priest once he was weaned, thereby illustrating a common Israelite practice of dedicating the firstborn son of a woman for service as a priest in YHWH's sanctuary as stipulated in Exod. 34:19-20.[15] Upon weaning young Samuel, Hannah did as she had vowed and took Samuel to Shiloh together with the appropriate offerings to have her young son raised at the sanctuary to become a priest in Israel. The passage concludes with Hannah's song of praise to YHWH, and a brief notice that she and her family returned home.

---

14. For Hammurabi's law code, see James B. Pritchard, *Ancient Near Eastern Texts Relating to the Old Testament* (Princeton: Princeton University Press, 1969), 163–80, secs., 144–7. For treatment of Gen. 16; 29–30 in relation to the practice of providing a handmaiden to bear children on behalf of the wife, see Ephraim A. Speiser, *Genesis*, AB 1 (Garden City: Doubleday, 1964), 116–21, 224–33.

15. For discussion of the Israelite practice of using firstborn sons as priests, see Sweeney, "Samuel's Institutional Identity"; idem, *The Pentateuch*, CBS (Nashville: Abingdon, 2017), 40–1, 77–9, 84.

The narrative concerning Eli's encounter with Hannah at Shiloh is a remarkable window revealing the character of Eli, the high priest at Shiloh. As high priest, Eli would supervise the sanctity and activities of the Shiloh sanctuary and all that takes place within it. Eli would preside over the sacrifices offered at the Shiloh sanctuary and all affairs of holiness that would take place within. It is noteworthy that although ancient Israelite sacrifice functions as the central event of Israelite worship, that sacrifice is always accompanied by prayers to YHWH. The account of Solomon's speech before the nation at the dedication of the Jerusalem Temple in 1 Kings 8 is an illustration of this principle. But Eli is the high priest. He would be expected to understand something about prayer, and so it is remarkable that he does not recognize the fact that Hannah is praying and concludes instead that she is drunk. It is not unheard of that people might drink to excess at Israelite festivals, but a high priest might be expected to recognize prayer when he sees it; it is not so hard to realize that many might pray silently to themselves in the sanctuary.

The narrative suggests that Eli is not so familiar with prayer, but he does seem to know something of drunkenness. Such a portrayal might prompt readers to consider that Eli has more familiarity with drunkenness rather than prayer, and thus lead them to conclude that Eli is an incompetent high priest.

III

Campbell identifies 1 Sam. 2:12-26, which portrays the contrasting behavior of Samuel and the Elides, as the second major sub-unit of chs. 1–3.[16] His conclusions must be modified, however, insofar as 2:27-36, which presents the condemnation of the house of Eli by an anonymous Man of G-d, must be included in the sub-unit as well. 1 Samuel 2:27-36 is linked syntactically to 2:12-26 by a *waw*-consecutive verbal formation, *wayyābô'*, "and he (the Man of G-d) came," which indicates that this segment presents a consequence of the improper behavior of the Elides as presented in the preceding text. By contrast, 2:12-26 begins with a conjunctive noun formation, *ûbĕnê 'ēlî*, "and the sons of Eli," which indicates a break in the narrative action and the introduction of a new topic. Likewise, 3:1 begins with a similar conjunctive noun formation, *wĕhanna'ar šĕmû'ēl*, "and the boy, Samuel," which indicates another break in narrative sequence and the introduction of a new topic. 1 Samuel 2:18 begins with the conjunctive noun formation, *ûšmû'ēl*, "and Samuel," which introduces a segment concerned with Samuel, and 2:22 begins with

---

16. Campbell, *1 Samuel*, 46–51.

another conjunctive noun formation, *wĕʿēlî*, "and Eli," which introduces the segment in 2:12-36 concerned with the condemnation of Eli's house. Thus, the sub-units should include 2:12-17, which focuses on the behavior of Eli's sons; 2:18-21, which focuses on the behavior of Samuel; 2:22-36, which focuses on the condemnation of the house of Eli, and 1 Sam. 3:1–4:1, which focuses on Samuel's visionary experience of YHWH. For the present, discussion will focus on 2:12-17; 2:18-21; and 2:22-36, which work together to portray the inadequacies and condemnation of the house of Eli. Overall, the inadequacies of Eli's sons point to the inadequacies of Eli himself and therefore to his characterization as an incompetent priest in need of replacement.

1 Samuel 2:12-17 focuses on the unacceptable behavior of Eli's sons, Hophni and Phineas, in their capacities as priests of the house of Eli at the Israelite sanctuary at Shiloh. They are accused of a number of abuses in their exercise of priestly office. They are accused of not knowing YHWH, which serves as a general statement concerning their inadequate characters. Specific charges include taking unauthorized portions of the people's meat offerings from the boiling pots; taking uncooked meat from the people's offerings even before the meat was burned on the altar; and threatening to take meat from the offerings by force in cases when the people would object at this abusive behavior. Altogether, the text indicates that such behavior constitutes abuse of their holy office that is entirely unacceptable for a priest dedicated to the holy service of YHWH's sanctuary. Although Eli may appear quite aged in this text and potentially exercises little influence over the actions of his sons, he is nevertheless their father and, as high priest, also their mentor. Eli is therefore responsible for their upbringing and understanding of their roles as priests in ancient Israel.

1 Samuel 2:17-21 focuses on little Samuel. The passage says little concerning Samuel's behavior since he is simply a small boy acting as an attendant for the priests. Rather, it focuses on Hannah's love for her son, insofar as she makes him a little tunic each year and brings it to him at the time of the annual sacrifice. As a result, Eli would bless Elkanah and his family so that YHWH would take note of Hannah and grant her five more children, viz., three boys and two daughters. Such blessing from YHWH indicates YHWH's satisfaction with Samuel, Hannah, and the rest of the family. In the current literary context, it presents a contrast between Samuel and the sons of Eli.

1 Samuel 2:22-36 begins with a portrayal of Eli's unsuccessful attempts to discipline his sons in vv. 22-26 as a prelude to the account of the condemnation of Eli's house by the anonymous Man of G-d. Verses 22-26 state that Eli was very old when he heard about the conduct of his sons.

The statement includes a reference to all that they had done, which looks back to the previously stated account of their excesses in vv. 12-17, but the account adds that Hophni and Phineas were laying with the women who served in the sanctuary. First, it is noteworthy that women served in northern Israelite sanctuaries, but it is unlikely that they were serving as cultic prostitutes or the like as some biblical texts allege. Indeed, there is evidence that women played a role in the activities of northern Israelite sanctuaries, although they appear to play no major role in southern Judean sanctuaries.[17] Second, the charge that Hophni and Phineas were laying with them entails improper conduct as the women would presumably be married to other men and priests are to marry women who are virgins or widows of other priests. Eli reprimands his sons in 1 Sam. 2:23-25 by declaring that a wrong done to another man could be forgiven, but that wrong done to G-d can presumably not be forgiven, according to Eli's statement. The latter postulate is not true, as demonstrated by YHWH's forgiveness of David for his adultery with Bath Sheba and his role in the murder of Uriah the Hittite, even though the sins were against both the human characters and against YHWH (2 Sam. 12:20-25; 1 Kgs 15:5; cf. Lev. 4, which prescribes the sin offering which accompanies repentance for violating in error the commandments of YHWH), indicating once again that the aging Eli is incompetent as a priest. But he also proves incapable of controlling his sons, who refuse to listen to him and continue in their abusive behavior. Altogether, these verses demonstrate that Eli is an incompetent father as well as an incompetent priest. Insofar as it is his duty to instruct his sons correctly in their obligations as holy priests of YHWH, he is once again characterized as an incompetent priest who is not fit to serve in YHWH's holy sanctuary.

1 Samuel 2:27-36 then follows with an account of a prophetic judgment speech against the priestly house of Eli delivered by an anonymous Man of G-d to Eli himself.[18] Campbell considers this text to be part of an early

---

17. For discussion of this point, see M. A. Sweeney, "Israelite and Judean Religions," in Salzman and Sweeney, eds, *The Cambridge History of Religions in the Ancient World*, 1:151–73, esp. 169–70.

18. See esp., Campbell, *1 Samuel*, 51–9; cf. idem, *Of Prophets and Kings: A Late-Ninth Century Document (1 Samuel 1–2 Kings 10)*, CBQMS 17 (Washington, DC: Catholic University of America, 1986); Antony F. Campbell, S.J., and Mark A. O'Brien, *Unfolding the Deuteronomistic History: Origins, Upgrades, Present Text* (Minneapolis: Fortress, 2000), 24–32; for a revision of the prophetic record hypothesis to a proposal for the Jehu dynastic history, see Marvin A. Sweeney, *1 and 2 Kings: A Commentary*, OTL (Louisville: Westminster John Knox, 2007), 26–30.

prophetic record, a northern Israelite document written in the late ninth century BCE as a prophetic critique of the early Israelite monarchies. The use of the title "Man of G-d" for the prophet is a typical designation within Campbell's proposed prophetic record, insofar as it is also used for the prophets, Elijah and Elisha, whose narratives in 1 Kings 17–2 Kings 13 also appear as part of the prophetic record. In the present form of the text, this passage anticipates the account of Solomon's expulsion of the high priest Abiathar, the major surviving member of the priestly house of Eli, and his replacement by Zadok, the founder of the priestly house of Zadok, in 1 Kings 2. The account itself presents the major elements of prophetic judgment speech form, including the account of the reproach or grounds for punishment in vv. 27-29 and the announcement of punishment in vv. 30-36. The grounds for punishment in vv. 27-29, introduced by the prophetic messenger formula in v. 27b, are the previously reported abuses of the sacrificial offerings made by the people in the Shiloh sanctuary. The announcement of punishment, introduced by the particle *lākēn*, "therefore," and the oracular formula, "utterance of YHWH, G-d of Israel," announces YHWH's intention to replace the priestly house of Eli with another unnamed priestly house, leaving the house of Eli to beg for holy work from the so-called "faithful priest," who will serve in the place of the house of Eli before YHWH's anointed king.

This narrative concerning the condemnation of the house of Eli also serves as a means to characterize Eli himself. One of the responsibilities of the priesthood in ancient Israel and Judah is to instruct the people concerning what is holy and profane and what is clean and unclean. Although this principle is articulated in Lev. 10:10-11, which most interpreters view as a late-Priestly stratum text, it nevertheless expresses the expectations of the duties of the priesthood throughout the entire history of ancient Israel and Judah. As the preceding narratives make clear, Eli's sons abuse their priestly offices, which entails that they do not carry out their task of instructing the people in holy matters properly. Their abusive behavior therefore entails the failure of Eli, their father as well as the senior priest in charge of the Shiloh sanctuary, to instruct his own sons in such holy matters, much less the people. Although the narrative portrays him as a father who attempts to instruct his sons properly, they ignore him, perhaps because of his advanced age. Nevertheless, Eli fails to carry out the training of his own sons as one of the basic expectations of the priesthood. The narrative therefore portrays him as an incompetent priest and an incompetent father. Such characterization thereby justifies the replacement of his priestly house in the larger narrative ranging from 1 Samuel 1–3 through 1 Kings 1–2.

IV

Although Campbell groups 1 Sam. 3:1–4:1a with the preceding narratives in his assessment of the formal structure of 1 Samuel 1–3,[19] the introductory conjunctive noun clause, *wĕhanna'ar šĕmû'ēl*, "and the lad, Samuel," instead of a *waw*-consecutive clause, indicates that this narrative is a discrete structural sub-unit rather than a sequential sub-unit within the larger formal structure of the text. It concludes with 1 Sam. 3:19–4:1a, which narrates how Samuel grew up to become a trustworthy prophet to YHWH, how YHWH continued to appear at Shiloh, and how the word of YHWH continued to come to Samuel. The account of the capture of the Ark of G-d beginning 1 Sam. 4:1b begins another narrative within the larger formal structure of the book of Samuel.

1 Samuel 3:1–4:1a is formulated as a vision account concerning young Samuel's first visionary encounter with YHWH.[20] As a result of this encounter, Samuel become a prophet of G-d, but in the context of priestly identity and practice in the Northern Kingdom of Israel, he also would have become a priest at the Shiloh sanctuary due to his status as a firstborn son of his mother and his training under the tutelage of Eli. The narrative is silent about his priestly status at this point, but later narratives, such as 1 Samuel 13–14 concerning the war with the Philistines, make it clear that Samuel serves as a priest who would offer sacrifice to YHWH. Although Samuel becomes a prophet as a result of his encounter with YHWH in 1 Sam. 3:1–4:1a, scholars do not classify this text as a prophetic call narrative because it does not include the classic elements of the genre.

1 Samuel nevertheless must be recognized as a vision account. It is noteworthy that Samuel encounters YHWH while sleeping in the sanctuary near the Ark of G-d. This would suggest that the setting for the vision is in the Holy of Holies of the Shiloh sanctuary where the Ark of G-d would presumably reside. Such a setting suggests that Samuel's visionary experience would serve as the means by which he was consecrated as a priest in ancient Israel, recognizing that firstborn sons were also eligible to serve as priests during the early years of the Northern Kingdom of Israel even though such practice does not appear to be recognized in Judah. It is also noteworthy that Samuel's vision of YHWH

---

19. Campbell, *1 Samuel*, 34–6, 51–9.
20. See esp. Robert Karl Gnuse, *The Dream Theophany of Samuel: Its Structure in Relation to Ancient Near Eastern Dreams and its Theological Significance* (Lanham: University Press of America, 1984).

begins with audial elements as YHWH initially speaks to Samuel in vv. 3-9, and only appears visually to Samuel in v. 10 where YHWH stands in the sanctuary and calls to Samuel once again. Interpreters must recognize that the Hebrew verb, *ḥzh*, "to envision," which does not appear in this narrative, is generally translated in visual terms, but the verb nevertheless entails audial experience as well. In general, the verb is best translated as "to perceive" or something analogous that would convey both visual and auditory experience.[21] Such a visionary experience would be typical of the ordination of priests in ancient Israel and Judah. Exodus 29, Leviticus 8, and Numbers 8 all portray the ordination of priests and Levites in ancient Israel. In all cases, prospective priests and Levites are incubated in the Temple before the Ark of the Covenant for a period of seven days, presumably during the festival of Sukkot when the Temple altar is typically dedicated. During the period of their incubation before the Ark, prospective priests or Levites presumably have some visionary experience of YHWH. At the conclusion of their seven-day incubation, they are then qualified to serve as priests in YHWH's Temple and to make the offerings to YHWH required on the various festivals and observances of the ancient Israelite (or Judean) holy calendar.

1 Samuel 3:1–4:1a is also formulated to characterize Eli and to demonstrate once again his incompetence to serve as the high priest of the Shiloh sanctuary. It therefore serves the literary purpose to anticipate Solomon's expulsion of Abiathar and his replacement by Zadok in 1 Kings 2. In depicting Samuel's inaugural visionary experience of YHWH, 1 Sam. 3:1–4:1 deliberately portrays Eli's initial inability to recognize that YHWH was speaking with young Samuel. Indeed, at the outset of the narrative in 1 Sam. 3:2, the text emphasizes Eli's failing eyesight as a means to introduce him as a character in the narrative who is unable to see. That notice serves as background for the following events in which Eli will fail to see that YHWH is attempting to communicate with Samuel. As young Samuel sleeps in the sanctuary before the Ark of G-d, he hears a voice calling to him, "Samuel! Samuel!" Thinking that it is Eli, who is sleeping elsewhere in his usual place, who calls him, he awakens Eli to see what he wants. Eli responds by rebuking Samuel for waking him and sends him back to bed. YHWH makes two more attempts to call Samuel with similar results. It is only with YHWH's third attempt to call Samuel that Eli finally recognizes what is actually happening, viz., YHWH is

---

21. A. Jepsen, "*ḥāzâ*," in *Theological Dictionary of the Old Testament*, ed. G. J. Botterweck and H. Ringgren (Grand Rapids: Eerdmans, 1980), 4:280–90.

attempting to call Samuel. Eli instructs Samuel to go back to bed, and if he hears YHWH once again, he is to respond, "Speak, YHWH," in answer to YHWH's call. Samuel does so, and YHWH then tells young Samuel about the divine plans to punish the house of Eli as earlier reported by the anonymous Man of G-d. Samuel later reported YHWH's words at Eli's insistence. Although the narrative does not specify that Samuel became a prophet or a priest as a result of this experience, it is clear that this is precisely what happened.

From the foregoing, it should be clear that 1 Sam. 3:1–4:1 portrays Eli as an incompetent priest. It is the duty of the priesthood to recognize the presence of YHWH and to communicate that presence and the appropriate response to YHWH's presence to the people of Israel at large. And yet here, the narrative makes it clear that it takes some three attempts by YHWH to communicate with Samuel before Eli finally recognizes that Samuel is experiencing a vision of YHWH's holy presence. Such a failure to recognize a revelation or vision of YHWH at the outset of the experience would serve as convincing evidence that Eli is incompetent and therefore unqualified to serve as high priest of the Shiloh sanctuary.[22] As a result, 1 Sam. 3:1–4:1 provides further justification for Solomon's removal of the house of Eli and its replacement by the priestly house of Zadok at the outset of Solomon's reign as related in 1 Kings 2.

V

The next and last episode in which readers see Eli is 1 Sam. 4:1b-22 in which the Philistines defeat Israel in battle at Aphek along the border between the hill country of Israel and the coastal plain dominated by the Philistines. As a result of the battle, Eli's sons, Hophni and Phineas, are killed, the Ark of G-d is captured by the Philistines, Eli drops dead when he hears the bad news, and Phineas's wife dies while giving birth to a son named Ichabod, "No Glory," when she hears the news of the death of her husband and her father-in-law.

---

22. Moberly argues that it is Eli who ultimately recognizes that YHWH is calling Samuel, thereby enabling Samuel to recognize YHWH's call as well (R. W. L. Moberly, "To Hear the Master's Voice: Revelation and Spiritual Discernment in the Call of Samuel," *SJT* 48, no. 4 [1995]: 443–68). Nevertheless, Eli's failure to recognize YHWH's call from the outset raises questions concerning his competence as high priest as he is aging and therefore slow to respond to even when confronted by the presence of YHWH.

Interpreters normally consider 1 Samuel 4 to be the introductory episode of the so-called "Ark Narrative" in 1 Samuel 4–6; 2 Samuel 6, which recounts the journeys of the Ark of the Covenant from the time when it is captured in battle by the Philistines, paraded around the Philistine cities, placed in Kiryat Jearim when it proves to be too dangerous to Philistine temples and gods, and finally is brought by David to Jerusalem to serve as the central shrine for all Israel. Initially identified by Leonhard Rost as a discrete diachronic element in the book of Samuel, Campbell places it in the early history of Israel as a narrative that anticipates the rise of the house of David in Jerusalem and later sees it as a synchronic literary element of Samuel.[23]

1 Samuel 4:1b-22 is formulated as an account of Israel's loss in battle to the Philistines at Aphek, located to the west of the territory of Benjamin along the juncture of the Israelite hill country and the Philistine coastal plain. The battle was apparently fought as Israel and Philistia fought for control of the land of Canaan. Israel's loss at Aphek meant that the Philistines gained an important toehold in their struggle to surround the Israelite hill country, contain and dominate Israel, and thereby ensure that Israel could not threaten Philistia or interfere with its activities. Within the larger Samuel narrative, 1 Samuel 4 sets the stage for the rise of the Israelite monarchies, particularly the house of David which makes Jerusalem Israel's capital and holy city, and it also anticipates Solomon's expulsion of Abiathar of the house of Eli and his replacement by Zadok, the founder of the house of Zadok.

The action of the narrative begins with an initial engagement between the Israelites and the Philistines at Aphek in which the Israelites are defeated. In order to regain the initiative, they decide to bring the Ark of G-d, carried by Eli's sons, Hophni and Phineas, to the battle. When the Philistines see the Ark, they believe themselves to be hopelessly outmatched due to the presence of YHWH. They therefore resolve to renew their efforts in battle since they believe themselves to be doomed, and they end up killing Hophni and Phineas, capturing the Ark of G-d, and defeating the Israelites. In the aftermath of the defeat, a Benjaminite man flees to Shiloh where he finds the aged Eli sitting in his customary seat. Eli is described as an old man of ninety-eight whose eyesight is failing as he ages. Indeed, Eli's blindness has been mentioned before, and

---

23. Leonhard Rost, *The Succession to the Throne of David* (Sheffield: Almond, 1982; German original, 1926); Antony F. Campbell, S.J., *The Ark Narrative (1 Sam 4–6; 2 Sam 6): A Form-Critical and Traditio-Historical Study*, SBLDS 16 (Missoula, MT: Scholars Press, 1975); idem, *1 Samuel*, 60–70.

it emphasizes that our priest cannot even see anymore. When he asks for news about the battle, the Benjaminite informs him of Israel's defeat, the deaths of his sons, and the capture of the Ark. Upon hearing this news, Eli falls from his seat, breaks his neck because he is an old man, and dies. His pregnant daughter in law, the wife of his son, Phineas, then gives birth to a son and dies. But before she dies, she names the baby Ichabod, which means, "No glory," or "the glory is gone," to symbolize the absence of the divine presence from Israel to symbolize the magnitude of the defeat.

Two major features of this narrative are important for characterizing Eli. First, his blindness is a key element insofar as the narrative portrays him as a high priest who remains unaware of the religious controversies around him. This in itself makes Eli and incompetent priest because he is unaware of what YHWH does in the world. The second major issue is Eli's inability to maintain oversight over the people, the Ark of G-d, and his sons and family. As a priest and a father, Eli would be expected to reserve final authority and responsibility for all of them. Having seen in the narrative the condemnation of his house, a reader might expect him to object to Israel going into the battle in the first place; Deut. 20:1-4 indicates that the priest has the authority to supervise Israel in times of war, and Samuel later leads Israel in battle in 1 Samuel 7. But Eli also could have objected to bringing the Ark of G-d to the battle and thereby jeopardizing the safety of the Ark and the presence of YHWH. But Eli does none of this, and the result is an absolute catastrophe for Israel and for his family.

Once again, Eli is characterized as an incompetent father and as an incompetent priest. Overall, the reader of the book of Samuel would have to conclude that the house of Eli does need to be replaced because of the lack of responsibility and oversight on the part of the high priest, Eli, and the associated house of Eli.

VI

In the end, the narratives in 1 Samuel 1–3; 4 present Eli, the high priest of Israel and of the nation of Israel at large, as an incompetent high priest. He is frequently portrayed as blind, insensitive, and completely unaware of his responsibilities or even of his strengths. Such a characterization builds the case in the larger narrative of Samuel and Kings that the house of Eli had run its course, and so Solomon, on David's advice in 1 Kings 1–2, replaces Eli's descendant, Abiathar, who had rendered loyal service to the King, with Zadok, the founder of the priestly house of Zadok, who would exercise authority and responsibility to maintain the sanctity of YHWH's

Temple at Jerusalem. It is striking that the critique of Eli also foreshadows the critique of David, especially in 2 Samuel 9–24, and raises questions concerning the role played by David's inadequacies as father and monarch in the ultimate demise of the house of David at the conclusion of the book of Kings.[24]

---

24. See my comments on the significance of Jehiachin's eating at the table of the Babylonian monarch, Evil Merodach (Amel Marduk), for the future of the house of David (Marvin A. Sweeney, *1 and 2 Kings: A Commentary*, OTL [Louisville: Westminster John Knox, 2007]), 464–5, 469–70.

Chapter 6

ORTHODOX THEOLOGY, ULTERIOR MOTIVES
IN SAMUEL'S FAREWELL SPEECH?:
THE CHARACTERIZATION OF THE PROPHET
IN 1 SAMUEL 12[*]

J. Richard Middleton

Until the rise of critical biblical scholarship, pious readings of the figure of David dominated Judaism and Christianity, aided and abetted, no doubt, by his image in Chronicles and in Psalms superscriptions. In more recent times, however, it has become common for contemporary interpreters to question David's motives and strategies in his rise to power in 1 Samuel in such a way as to anticipate the character defects that led to David's crashing fall in 2 Samuel 11–12.[1]

With few exceptions, however, the prophet Samuel has been read as a faithful (if strident), representative of YHWH's will—especially in contrast

---

[*] This chapter is based on material originally presented at the 2013 annual meeting of the Canadian Society of Biblical Studies, at the University of Victoria, Victoria, BC.

1. For my own analysis of David's character, see J. Richard Middleton, "The Battle Belongs to the Word: The Role of Theological Discourse in David's Victory over Saul and Goliath in 1 Samuel 17," in *The Hermeneutics of Charity: Interpretation, Selfhood, and Postmodern Faith*, ed. James K. A. Smith and Henry Isaac Venema (Grand Rapids: Brazos, 2004), 109–31; and Middleton, "A Psalm against David? A Canonical Reading of Psalm 51 as a Critique of David's Inadequate Repentance in 2 Samuel 12," in *Explorations in Interdisciplinary Reading: Theological, Exegetical, and Reception-Historical Perspectives*, ed. Robbie Castleman, Darian Lockett, and Stephen Presley (Eugene: Pickwick, 2017), 26–45.

to Saul, who is typically viewed negatively.[2] In contrast to this approach, I have been developing a reading of the character of Samuel that is suspicious of the prophet, by attending to his narrated abuse of power vis-à-vis Saul; and I have been teaching 1 Samuel 1–15 from this point of view.[3]

My Approach to 1 Samuel 12

This essay engages in a close reading of Samuel's so-called farewell speech at Gilgal in 1 Samuel 12, though its character as a farewell speech is disputed, since Samuel doesn't retire afterwards.[4] Indeed, he continues to have a determinative influence on Saul, the newly installed king (though he has not a whit of influence on David). And while some scholars dispute the intended location of the speech at Gilgal, since the link between chs. 11 and 12 is unclear, it makes perfect sense to view the speech as a continuation of the narrative of Saul's installation as king at the end of ch. 11.[5]

The characterization of Samuel has been developing from the opening narratives of his birth and childhood in 1 Samuel 1–3. At his birth his

---

2. Significant exceptions to this typical reading include Keith Bodner, *1 Samuel: A Narrative Commentary*, HBM 19 (Sheffield: Sheffield Phoenix, 2008); Marti J. Steussy, *Samuel and His God*, Studies on Personalities of the Old Testament (Columbia: University of South Carolina Press, 2010); and Tamás Czövek, *Three Seasons of Charismatic Leadership: A Literary-Critical and Theological Interpretation of the Narrative of Saul, David and Solomon*, Regnum Studies in Mission (Milton Keynes: Paternoster, 2006), esp. Chapter 2.

3. This approach is being developed into a monograph, tentatively entitled: *Portrait of a Disgruntled Prophet: Samuel's Resistance to God and the Undoing of Saul* (in preparation). For a summary, see Middleton, "Samuel Agonistes: A Conflicted Prophet's Resistance to God and Contribution to the Failure of Israel's First King," in *Prophets, Prophecy, and Ancient Israelite Historiography*, ed. Mark J. Boda and Lissa M. Wray Beal (Winona Lake: Eisenbrauns, 2013), 69–91.

4. Whereas Robert D. Bergen claims that here "Samuel closed the books on his own lengthy tenure of service as a leader for all Israel" (Bergen, *1, 2 Samuel*, New American Commentary 7 [Nashville: Broadman & Holman, 1996], 140), Keith Bodner's comment about Samuel's continuing role is more on target: "the reader may be tempted to think that…Samuel is going out to pasture. But, like the odd *professor emeritus*, Samuel has no immediate plans to retire" (Bodner, *1 Samuel*, 149). Although Bodner's comment has to do with Samuel's role after his criticism of Saul in 1 Sam. 13, it is *apropos* also of his continuing role after the speech of ch. 12.

5. Given that the chapter divisions are a late phenomenon, a number of scholars follow Josephus, who has Samuel assemble the Hebrews for his speech (*Ant.* 6.86), right after the confirmation of Saul's kingship at Gilgal (6.83).

mother, Hannah, explains Samuel's name in relation to the verb "to ask" or "lend" (1:20), which is more clearly linked to Saul's name, thus putting the reader on notice of the coming rivalry between them. Indeed, at one point (1:28) Hannah says that as long as Samuel lives he is "lent" (šā'ûl) to YHWH (where the Hebrew for "lent" is identical to the name *Saul*). After Samuel's introduction to YHWH by the priest Eli in 1 Samuel 3, his "character zone" develops especially throughout 1 Samuel 7–16, from the first account of his public leadership to his anointing of David as a replacement king after Saul's rejection.[6] It even continues post-mortem in 1 Samuel 28, where the dead prophet, still in character, speaks to Saul from the grave. Yet there is warrant for focusing on 1 Samuel 12, since it contains Samuel's longest discourse in the entire book.[7] This chapter is thus particularly revelatory of the character of the prophet.

In my reading of 1 Samuel 12, I will juxtapose the "orthodox," so-called Deuteronomistic, theology to which Samuel appeals in his speech with the complex rhetorical strategy of his words, examining his possible motivations and the effect of Samuel's rhetoric on his audience. I do not intend to try to get behind the text to putative sources, with their varying ideological points of view.[8] My focus will be on the "Samuel" presented in the world of the text.

Samuel's speech in 1 Samuel 12 has a relatively clear structure. Samuel first looks back to his impeccable career as judge (vv. 1-5), then

---

6. The notion of a "character zone" is derived from Mikhail M. Bakhtin, "Discourse in the Novel," in *The Dialogical Imagination: Four Essays by M. M. Bakhtin*, ed. Michael Holquist, trans. Caryl Emerson and Michael Holquist (Austin: University of Texas Press, 1981), 259–422; see esp. 316. This notion is used to great effect in the writings of Keith Bodner (for his definition, see *1 Samuel*, 7).

7. I am not particularly interested in parsing whether (on source critical or other grounds) the chapter represents two or three separate speeches or simply one continuous discourse in three parts (my divisions are vv. 1-5, 6-13, 14-25, though others divide the chapter differently). For the claim that vv. 6-15 (along with vv. 20b-22, 24-25, and possibly 19b) are later Deuteronomistic insertions into an earlier speech, see P. Kyle McCarter, Jr., *1 Samuel: A New Translation with Introduction, Notes and Commentary*, AB 8 (New Haven: Yale University Press, 1980), 214, 219.

8. We should note that there is considerable disagreement about the extent that this chapter represents the work of a Deuteronomistic editor (who may or may not be anti-monarchic in outlook). For a nuanced analysis of the supposedly pro- or anti-monarchial sources in 1 Samuel, see Lyle Eslinger, "Viewpoints and Point of View in 1 Samuel 8–12," *JSOT* 26 (1983): 61–76. My use of "Deuteronomistic" is not meant to come to a decision about sources or tradents, but simply to recognize ways in which the theology articulated by Samuel in this chapter reflects language and ideas usually attributed to the Deuteronomistic history.

reviews the history of God with Israel, from the exodus to the monarchy (vv. 6-13), with a focus on the people's sin in asking for a king and on his own indispensable role as prophet (vv. 14-25). All of these foci—Samuel's impeccable career, his recounting of Israel's history, the people's sin, and the prophet's indispensable role—are the clear emphases of Samuel's rhetoric. The question is: What is Samuel (the character in the text) trying to accomplish by this rhetoric?

At this point an interpreter of the Bible may be expected to say something about their methodology or theoretical orientation, as a prolegomenon to the actual interpretation. However, my experience of biblical studies as a discipline over the years has led me to be less impressed by textual analyses that are over-determined by methodological issues, since the interpretation of Scripture (or any literature) is much more a matter of practiced art than extrapolation from theory.

Nevertheless, perhaps something of my assumptions about the Samuel narrative might be helpful at the outset—though these assumptions are not formulated in advance, but have been developed via my engagement with the text itself (indeed, the best theory is a reflection on praxis).[9]

To begin with, I treat the text of Samuel as opening up a narrative world that readers are invited to enter.[10] This world is both continuous with, and discontinuous from, the world of the reader (or of the succession of readers, over time). While discontinuities have to do with the temporal,

---

9. This coheres with Greger Andersson's suggestion that theory is often based on the memory of prior readings; see Andersson, *Untamable Texts: Literary Studies and Narrative Theory in the Books of Samuel*, LHBOTS 514 (New York: T&T Clark, 2009), 69–70, 260 (thanks to Benjamin J. M. Johnson for this reference). Special thanks are due my former student T. L. Birge for suggestions about relevant literature (below) that intersects with my methodological comments (from her doctoral proposal on reading biblical narrative).

10. For a long time, formalist approaches to biblical narrative, derived from the literary discipline of "narratology" (a term coined by Tzvetan Todorov in *Grammaire du Décaméron*, 1969) have dominated the field. These approaches laudably attempt to understand the internal reality created by the narrative, based on various semantic cues; however, such approaches have tended to minimize the role of the reader. In recent times alternative approaches have been developing (so-called post-classical narratology), which attempt to understand how narrative and reader interact and affect each other. See David Herman, "Cognitive Narratology" (online article revised September 22, 2013) in *The Living Handbook of Narratology*, ed. Peter Hühn et al. (Hamburg: Interdisciplinary Center for Narratology, Hamburg University Press), http://www.lhn.uni-hamburg.de/article/cognitive-narratology-revised-version-uploaded-22-september-2013 (this is an ongoing revision of *Handbook of Narratology* [Berlin: de Gruyter, 2009]).

linguistic, cultural, and conceptual distance of the reader(s) from the context of the author(s), the continuity is rooted in the shared human experiences of both, since contemporary readers are acquainted with transitions of power, the role of speeches in such transitions, and ways in which rhetoric may be used to manipulate a situation.[11]

Admittedly, there are many gaps or lacunae in the account in 1 Samuel 12, as there are in any biblical narrative. And readers (whether scholarly/technical or ordinary/naïve readers) will always fill in the gaps, either from either own expertise or from some common realm of human experience. Narratives invite us in to inhabit their world for a while, which allows that world to impact our own world—and vice versa.[12]

Is there subjectivity in my reading of 1 Samuel 12? Undoubtedly. But subjectivity is not a vice to be avoided. Rather, subjectivity is a pervasive feature of being human, and thus intrinsic to all interpretation. The question is never *whether* a reading is subjective; all readings are subjective. The question is whether a particular reading is helpful in opening up the meaning of a text. This means that not all interpretations (including attempts to fill in narrative lacunae) are equally successful and thus legitimate.[13]

I take it as axiomatic that no interpreter worth their salt would settle for the first, seemingly obvious, way they understand the meaning of a given text. Rather, the interpreter needs to live with the text, inhabiting its narrative world—in multiple ways, on many occasions, open to learning new meanings and correcting initial impressions (even if those initial impressions are shaped by scholarly training).[14]

---

11. Post-classical narratologists have begun using the term "storyworld" to describe the space that opens up between the world of the text and the world of the reader. It is a function neither of the literary text alone nor of the reader's imagination, but is dialectically related to both. This concept is central to David Herman, *Storytelling and the Sciences of the Mind* (Cambridge, MA: MIT, 2013). For a short definition, see Marie-Laure Ryan, "Space" (online article revised April 22, 2014) in Hühn et al., eds, *The Living Handbook of Narratology*, http://www.lhn.uni-hamburg.de/article/space), para. 9.

12. Gap-filling is discussed by Catherine Emmott and Marc Alexander, in "Schemata" (online article revised September 22, 2014), in Hühn et al., eds, *The Living Handbook of Narratology*, http://www.lhn.uni-hamburg.de/article/schemata.

13. For more in-depth exploration of the constitutive nature of subjectivity for interpretation, see J. Richard Middleton, *The Liberating Image: The* Imago Dei *in Genesis 1* (Grand Rapids: Brazos, 2005), 34–42.

14. Indeed, Ehud Ben Zvi is famous for suggesting that no text is meant to be read just once; rather, texts are meant to be reread repeatedly. See Ben Zvi, *The Signs of Jonah: Reading and Rereading in Ancient Yehud*, JSOTSup 367 (Sheffield: Sheffield Academic, 2003), 1–14.

This developing sense of the text's meaning will be strengthened by challenges from other interpretations—including both alternative perspectives and previously unexamined data. Such challenges may come through reading secondary literature (both contemporaneous and historical) or through interacting with an embodied community of learners (whether in academic or faith settings), who are invested in grappling with the meaning of a common text.

In my own case, my reading of the character of Samuel has been developing through twenty years of teaching 1 Samuel, while attending to a wide variety of scholarly perspectives on this material, as well as to the insights of my students (which have proved to be just as helpful as scholarly perspectives).[15]

The Prophet Doth Protest Too Much, Methinks (1 Samuel 12:1-5)

From the start, Samuel's rhetoric is highly confrontational. He frames his speech as a series of quasi-legal disputations, first concerning his own innocence (in the first five verses), then concerning the people's guilt (in the rest of the chapter). Throughout, we find an abundance of attention-getting language—*wĕ'attâ* ("and now") with one *gam-'attâ* ("even now"), and lots of *hinnê* ("behold"), with *hinnām* ("behold them") and *hinĕni* ("behold me").[16]

In his opening salvo, in 12:1-5, out of the blue and in the absence of explicit accusation by anyone, Samuel jumps to defend his past career as judge. Here we find an accumulation of "behold" (four times), with the first "and now" (*wĕ'attâ*) at the start of 12:2. After this *wĕ'attâ*, Samuel contrasts the king's present leadership (12:2a) with his own past leadership (12:3a), using the metaphor of "walking before" in each case. This contrast leads the reader to think that he is handing over the reins of power; he must diminish, the king is taking over (hence the idea that this is Samuel's farewell speech).

---

15. For post-classical perspectives on narrative characterization, see Herman, *Storytelling and the Sciences of the Mind*, Chapter 5: "Characters, Categorization, and the Concept of Person"; and Keith Oatley, "On Truth and Fiction," in *Cognitive Literary Science: Dialogues Between Literature and Cognition*, ed. Michael Burke and Emily T. Troscianko, Cognition and Poetics (New York: Oxford University Press, 2016), 259–78. Oatley's essay is helpful in reflecting on how readers run simulations of reality through their minds as they read, testing the narrative world and the characters therein by their own experience of extra-narrative reality.

16. All biblical translations in this essay are my own, unless otherwise stated.

Yet sandwiched in the middle of this contrast between Samuel and the king is the distinction between his old age and his sons' current presence among the people (12:2).[17] This muddies the waters somewhat; is it the king who is replacing Samuel or is it his sons? Indeed, given the unethical behavior of his sons, it is unlikely that he is suggesting that they would replace him (even though he had appointed them as judges; 8:1-2). So the question arises as to why Samuel mentions his sons here. Whereas some suggest that this is Samuel's last nostalgic look back at the possibility of his sons' dynastic succession as judges, others more plausibly suggest that Samuel intends a contrast between his own practice of judgeship and that of his sons.[18]

Then Samuel calls the people to testify against him "before YHWH and before his anointed" concerning his tenure as judge, with a series of questions about his honesty and lack of profit from his position (12:3). These questions implicitly contrast Samuel's impeccable leadership with that of his sons; "from whose hand have I taken a bribe?" distinguishes Samuel's behavior from the bribery of his sons, which was mentioned in 1 Sam. 8:3.

But his use of the verb "take" both in the question about the bribe and in two other questions ("Whose ox have I taken? Or whose donkey have I taken?") suggests, instead, a contrast with the way Samuel had previously portrayed the typical behavior of kings, who, according to ch. 8, would *take* (*lāqaḥ*) the people's sons, daughters, fields, vineyards, slaves, cattle, donkeys, and sheep, until finally they became slaves to the reigning

---

17. This could be thought of as a chiasm. While the two outer lines (1 and 4) contrast the king with Samuel (using the language of walking before), the two inner lines (2 and 3) contrast Samuel with his sons (as for me, as for my sons):

1. And now, behold [*hinnê*] the king who is walking before you.
2. As for me, I am old and gray.
3. As for my sons, behold they [*hinnām*] are with you.
4. As for me, I have walked before you from my youth until this day—behold me [*hinĕni*].

However, it is possible that these verses are not chiastic, but should be read as two sets of sequential contrasts—between lines 1 and 2 (Samuel and the king) and between lines 3 and 4 (Samuel and his sons).

18. For the former suggestion, see Robert Alter, *The David Story: A Translation with Commentary of 1 and 2 Samuel* (New York: Norton, 2000), 65. For the latter suggestion, see Barbara Green, *How Are the Mighty Fallen? A Dialogical Study of King Saul in 1 Samuel*, LHBOTS 365 (Sheffield: Sheffield Academic, 2003), 188.

monarch (8:11-17).[19] So Samuel may be contrasting his leadership with both his sons and the king—at least in his description of what a king would do.[20]

It is clear what answer Samuel expects to all of his questions—namely, "No-one." That is essentially what he gets in 12:4, when the people reply: "You have not defrauded us or abused us and you have not taken anything from the hand of anyone." I would interject, however, that the narrative of 1 Samuel 9–15 suggests that Samuel has indeed defrauded and abused *Saul* so that his leadership ability becomes compromised (and he becomes mentally unstable), though this, admittedly, takes us beyond the narrative of ch. 12. And while Samuel may not have taken anything from the hand of anyone, the narrator tells us in 9:22 that "Samuel *took* Saul and his servant and brought them into the hall" (where the addition of the verb *lāqaḥ* is technically unnecessary; "brought" works just fine by itself).[21]

But my main point here is that instead of Samuel's questions functioning to clear his name from any evildoing as he prepares to pass the torch of leadership, they seem intended to portray his past leadership as superior to either that of his sons or of the newly installed king, with the implication that there was no need for his replacement. Especially in the absence of any accusation of wrongdoing by anyone, the prophet "doth protest too much, methinks."[22]

---

19. Samuel's speech also echoes language from Moses's prayer to YHWH in response to the accusations of Dathan and Abiram, when he says: "I have not taken (even) one donkey from them" (Num. 16:15).

20. This point is widely noted in the commentaries. Here I would emphasize that this contrast is between Samuel and *his prediction* of what a king will do (fulfilled in the case of Solomon and Rehoboam, for example); it is not an accurate contrast between Samuel and Saul specifically, since the latter is not portrayed by the narrator as fulfilling this prediction. Indeed, while Saul does (later) "gather" men into his military service (1 Sam. 14:52), the verb "take" is not used there.

21. Many commentaries note that Samuel, in contrast to his description of the king in ch. 8, is clearly innocent of "taking." I suggest that this is not so clear to the reader who attends to the phrasing of 1 Sam. 9:22 as a clue to Samuel's treatment of Saul (especially in 1 Sam. 9–10). But Samuel is not the only one who "takes" Saul; the people "took" Saul from hiding among the baggage (1 Sam. 10:23). Thus Saul is more typically on the receiving end of taking than being the one who takes (at least, early in his reign). For further analysis of chs. 9–10, see Middleton, "Samuel Agonistes," 73–4.

22. Here I refer to the words of Queen Gertrude in Shakespeare's *Hamlet*, Act 3, scene 2: "The lady doth protest too much, methinks."

And if one might be inclined to a charitable reading of the protesting prophet, I would point to two items in the text that corroborate my reading. The first is Samuel's rhetorical shift from defense to accusation in 12:5. Whereas he had challenged the people (in the absence of any accusation) to "testify against" him "before YHWH and before his anointed" (12:3), when the people admit that he is guiltless (12:4) Samuel turns the tables from defending himself to accusing them, by stating: "YHWH is witness against you, and his anointed is witness that you have not found anything in my hand [i.e. you have found me guiltless]" (12:5).[23]

How does an accusation against the people follow from Samuel's proven innocence? Are guilt and innocence a zero-sum game such that Samuel's impeccable leadership implies the people are guilty? Of what would they be guilty? Certainly not of accusing him directly of impropriety. They do no such thing.[24]

As we shall shortly see, the missing part of Samuel's argument is that the people are guilty for seeking to replace Samuel's impeccable leadership as judge with a king. That is, their asking for a king implied—from Samuel's point of view—that he had been lacking as Israel's leader. Methinks the prophet definitely doth protest too much.

The second corroborating item that something strange is going on here is Samuel's opening sentence in 12:1, which begins with *hinnê* and continues with two falsehoods—or at least two cases where he has massaged the truth.

First, Samuel states that he has listened to the people's voice in all that they said to him—whereas he had clearly resisted the people's voice. This resistance began in ch. 8, when the people asked for a king. God had to twice tell him to "listen to the people's voice" (1 Sam. 8:7, 22) and he still ignored their request for a king at the end of ch. 8, even after God added the explicit command "and install a king for them" (8:22).

---

23. Note that Samuel avoids calling Saul by name anywhere in his speech. In the first five verses he refers only to "a king" (12:1) or to YHWH's "anointed" (12:3, 5), while in the rest of the speech he speaks only of "a king" (12:12, 13, 17, 19), "the king" (12:13), or "your king" (12:14, 24; also 12:15 LXX). Samuel's use of the verb "asked" (*šā'al*) in 12:13 (referring to the people's request for a king) is the only allusion to the name Saul in the entire chapter.

24. Given the absence of any accusation from the people, it is difficult to understand Robert Bergen's claim that "the people were prosecutors" (Bergen, *1, 2 Samuel*, 140). This might be a case of taking Samuel's point of view over that of the narrator, who is mum on that point.

And if anyone would defend the prophet by noting that in the end he did give them a king, I would point out that it was only reluctantly, with many obfuscating moves and feints (throughout ch. 10) to delay the process as long as possible—a secret anointing, followed by convoluted instructions to the new king, and then the casting of lots to discover who the king would be (as if God had not revealed his choice of king to Samuel in ch. 9 and as if the king had not already been anointed).

The second case of massaging the truth, if not outright falsehood, is Samuel's statement in 12:1 that he has installed a king for them (the Hiphil of *mālak* followed by *melek*; he has kinged a king). This identical verb was used only one verse earlier (in the last verse of ch. 11) to describe *the people* installing Saul as king (11:15).[25] And while technically Samuel might be able to take credit for what turned out to be inevitable, despite his objections, the fact that two adjacent sentences (separated by an artificial chapter division) make contradictory *prima facie* claims about who it was that installed Saul as king should arouse our suspicions about Samuel's motives here. By taking credit for a situation that he had long resisted, but now realizes is inevitable, Samuel is here attempting to take control of the fledgling monarchy as it gets underway.[26]

Samuel's Confusing Retelling of Israel's Story
(1 Samuel 12:6-13)

Our suspicions about Samuel's motivations are put on high alert when we turn to Samuel's creative (and initially confusing) retelling of Israel's story in 12:6-13. Near the start (in 12:7), Samuel utilizes the language of legal challenge: "take your stand and I will enter into judgment with you before YHWH" (12:7). Whereas in 12:1-5 YHWH and "his anointed"

---

25. This is the same Hebrew phrasing used in God's original instruction to Samuel to install a king (1 Sam. 8:22).

26. Evidence for Samuel's sense that the monarchy is now inevitable (despite his aversion to it) is that although he affirms in no uncertain terms that asking for a king was a great evil (which the people admit), nowhere in 1 Sam. 12 does he call the people to repent of this sin (there is simply no going back at this point). This is astutely observed by Robert Polzin, who contrasts this with Samuel's earlier speech against idolatry in ch. 7, where Samuel explicitly calls the people to repent (*šûb*; 7:3) and they respond by putting away their idols (7:4). See Polzin, *Samuel and the Deuteronomist: A Literary Study of the Deuteronomistic History*, Part 2: *1 Samuel*, Indiana Studies in Biblical Literature (Bloomington: Indiana University Press, 1989), 122–3.

have been witnesses, the single witness to the proceedings from here on is YHWH. This is rhetorically significant, in that the king will be taken to be part of the problem (so he cannot function as witness here).[27] In other words, the purpose of the retelling of Israel's story is to provide the basis for an accusation against the people precisely for wanting a king. This accusation leads some scholars to view the chapter as a covenant lawsuit (and there is, indeed, language here that might be taken from the covenant lawsuit of Mic. 6:1-5, along with similar texts).[28] However, this is much more a lawsuit between *Samuel* and the people than between God and the people.[29]

Samuel tells Israel's story in three stages. Beginning with the exodus (12:6-8), he then moves to the time of the judges (12:9-11), and ends with a reference to contemporaneous events (12:12-13). In all three stages of the story we find contradictions between his retelling and what we know from elsewhere in the Bible.

---

27. This rhetorical shift is noticed by A. Graeme Auld, who correctly attributes it to the fact that from here on the king and people are together treated as defendants. Auld, *I and II Samuel: A Commentary*, OTL (Louisville: Westminster John Knox, 2011), 131. In contrast to this shift, Josephus's version of Samuel's speech (*Ant.* 6.86-94) consistently has God and the king as witnesses to Samuel's challenge and warning to the people (which may suggest his more sanguine view of the monarchy), while the version in Pseudo-Philo (*LAB* 57) pits God and Samuel (and Moses) consistently against the people and king (and Korah) throughout the entire speech (the king is never a witness, only a defendant). See Joachim Vette, "Samuel's 'Farewell Speech': Theme and Variation in 1 Samuel 12, Josephus, and Pseudo-Philo," in *Literary Construction of Identity in the Ancient World*, ed. Hanna Liss and Manfred Oeming (Winona Lake: Eisenbrauns, 2010), 325–39.

28. Samuel's speech shares with Mic. 6 mention of Gilgal (Mic. 6:5; 1 Sam. 11:14), Moses and Aaron (Mic. 6:4; 1 Sam. 12:6), the call to "testify against [lit. "answer"] me" (Mic. 6:3; 1 Sam. 12:3), and the "righteous deeds of YHWH" (Mic. 6:5; 1 Sam. 12:7). Other parallels can be found in other prophetic or covenantal contexts, such as Amos 5:12 ("take a bribe"; 1 Sam. 12:3), Deut. 28:33; Amos 4:1; Hos. 5:11 (the verbs "crush" [or "defraud"] and "oppress"; 1 Sam. 12:3), and Isa. 1:15 ("hide my eyes"; 1 Sam. 12:2). On these, see Auld, *I and II Samuel*, 128–9.

29. Some scholars think that Samuel's speech in ch. 12 represents a covenant-renewal ceremony, parallel to the one in Josh. 24, as a means of providing continuity in a transitional time. A prime example is J. Robert Vannoy, *Covenant Renewal at Gilgal: A Study of 1 Samuel 11:14–12:25* (1978; repr. Eugene: Wipf & Stock, 2008), 178. Although David G. Firth disputes that the chapter represents a covenant-making ceremony, he admits that it uses terminology typical of covenant speeches by Moses (Deuteronomy as a whole) and Joshua (ch. 24). Firth, *1 & 2 Samuel*, ApOTC 8 (Nottingham: Apollos; Downers Grove: InterVarsity, 2009), 144.

The Exodus (1 Samuel 12:6-8)

In his summary of the exodus, Samuel focuses on the role of Moses and Aaron. His focus on these two leaders is usually thought to emphasize that they were personally chosen by YHWH, in contrast to the king whom *the people* asked for (thus Samuel will later mention "the king whom you have chosen, for whom you asked"; 12:13). If this is the point, like all of Samuel's points it is tendentious, since we might note that in response to the people's asking for a king, YHWH specifically selects Saul (1 Sam. 9:15-17). And in the following chapter, Samuel admits that YHWH has "chosen" Saul (1 Sam. 10:24).[30]

Samuel makes two narrative claims about Moses and Aaron, namely that they brought the ancestors up from Egypt (12:6 and 8) and that they settled the ancestors in the land (12:8). Whereas the former claim is uncontroversial, the latter claim does not fit any known account of Israel's founding narrative. Not only was it Joshua who settled them in the land, but Moses died on the other side of the Jordan (Deut. 34:1-5; Josh. 1:1-2). So Samuel seems a tad confused here. Or, more plausibly, Samuel is at pains to deny the passing of the torch from Moses to Joshua, since this might justify the transition from judge to king, thus granting legitimacy to Saul.[31]

The Judges (1 Samuel 12:9-11)

Samuel's retelling of the story of the Judges is even more confusing than his version of the exodus. Admittedly, Samuel follows the basic pattern of the cycles (or spirals) of sin, oppression, cry of distress, and deliverance or salvation found in the book of Judges. Samuel even utilizes stereotypical language found in Judges, such as Israel *forgetting* or *abandoning* YHWH their God (1 Sam. 12:10; Judg. 3:7; 10:10; also Deut. 6:12; 8:11, 14, 19; 32:18), YHWH *selling them into the hand* of various enemies (1 Sam. 12:9; Judg. 2:4; 3:8; 4:2; 10:7), and their *crying out* to YHWH (1 Sam. 12:10; Judg. 3:9; 10:10).

---

30. Bergen claims that Samuel's point is that YHWH specifically "appointed" and "sent" these human agents, in contrast to Saul (Bergen, *1, 2 Samuel*, 142). Firth has a somewhat more nuanced position, claiming that "this king is one he [God] has permitted, not one he desires" (Firth, *1 & 2 Samuel*, 144). While these explanations may reflect Samuel's perspective on the matter, neither one fits the facts of the case.

31. Thus even the nuances of Samuel's version of salvation history illumine his motivations, which contribute to his characterization throughout ch. 12.

What is strange, however, is that whereas the narrative of Judges 3–16 lists five cycles of oppression and deliverance, Samuel lists only three sets of oppression in 12:9 and four deliverers or judges in 12:11. Further, the three examples of oppression he lists are out of chronological order. To top it off, the second judge in Samuel's list (Bedan) is unknown from the book of Judges;[32] hence the replacement of Bedan with Barak in the LXX and with Deborah and Barak in the Peshitta (since Deborah is technically the judge and Barak is her lieutenant). The Peshitta also puts Gideon (a.k.a. Jerubbaal) after Deborah and Barak, presumably to correct Samuel's confused narrative order.[33] A further confusion is that Samuel gives his own name as the fourth judge, which seems so self-serving that this is replaced with Samson in the Lucianic text of the LXX and in the Peshitta.

32. Some Rabbinic traditions interpreted Bedan as meaning "from Dan" (*b. Roš Haš.* 25a) or "son of Dan" (Kimchi), taking this as a reference to Samson, the Danite. Serge Frolov attempts to explain the presence of Bedan as a judge in Samuel's version of the narrative by postulating a rhetorical situation (internal to the narrative) in which Samuel wants to avoid upsetting the Philistines, who had been active in 1 Sam. 4–7 and would plausibly have been dominant in the region at the time of his speech. To accomplish this, Samuel focuses on Transjordan events (in the east), where the Philistines (on the western coast) had no stake. Thus, he cites two deliverers (Gideon/Jerbbaal and Jephthah) of Transjordan origin, who fight against Transjordan enemies (Midianites and Ammonites). And he will soon introduce the Ammonite threat to Jabesh-Gilead (in Transjordan) as the basis of the people's request for a king (replacing the Philistine threat, which had been the real reason)—all in an effort to convey to any Philistine agents who might overhear his speech that he was concerned only with Israel's liberation from oppression in the east (far from Philistine interests). In this context, Frolov speculates that Bedan is introduced into Samuel's narrative based on his lineage from Manasseh, a Transjordan tribe (1 Chron. 7:17). See Frolov, "Bedan: A Riddle in Context," *JBL* 126 (2007): 164–7. Whether or not we buy Frolov's explanation of the occurrence of the name Bedan (and his thesis about the Philistines seems contraindicated by their occurrence in 12:9), he is surely correct that "the mention of Bedan as a deliverer is but a relatively minor component of the massive twisting of biblical traditions that takes place in Samuel's overview of the Israelite history" (ibid., 165).

33. The replacement of Bedan with Barak is found in three versions of the LXX: Codex Vaticanus (LXX^B), Codex Alexandrinus (LXX^A), and the Lucianic recension (LXX^L).

MT (Hebrew)	LXX^BA (Greek)	LXX^L (Greek)	Targum (Aramaic)	Peshitta (Syriac)
Jerubbaal	Jerubbaal	Jerubbaal	Gideon	Deborah, Barak
Bedan	Barak	Barak	Samson	Gideon
Jephthah	Jephthah	Jephthah	Jephthah	Jephthah
Samuel	Samuel	Samson	Samuel	Samson

Figure 1. Textual Traditions for 1 Samuel 12:11

If we were to correlate the examples of oppression and deliverance in Samuel's retelling (from the MT), we have oppression by Sisera of Hazor, with rescue by Jerubbaal (Gideon); then oppression by the Philistines, with rescue by Bedan; then oppression by the king of Moab, with rescue by Jephthah; and finally rescue by Samuel himself, with no oppression listed.

Judges 3–16 (5 sets of oppression and deliverance by judges)	1 Sam. 12:9-11 (3 oppressors, 4 judges)
Eglon, King of Moab → Ehud (ch. 3)	Sisera of Hazor → Jerubbaal
Sisera of Hazor → Deborah (and Barak) (chs. 4–5)	Philistines → Bedan
Midianites → Gideon (= Jerubbaal) (chs. 6–9)	King of Moab → Jephthah
Ammonites → Jephthah (chs. 10–11)	? → Samuel
Philistines → Samson (chs. 13–16)	

Figure 2. Samuel's Implicit Narrative of Oppression and Deliverance

Instead of trying to get behind the text to putative alternative traditions of Israel's history that Samuel may be drawing on (as some scholars are wont to do), I am interested in the rhetorical effect of portraying the prophet as either confused about Israel's past or as outright rewriting history for his own purposes (or some combination of the two).[34] I will soon address the missing oppression in Samuel's recounting of Israel's history and how it serves his agenda.

---

34. Tony W. Cartledge notes that the difference between Samuel's version of the story and that found in the book of Judges suggests "the presence of an older variant tradition." Cartledge, *1 & 2 Samuel*, Smyth & Helwys Bible Commentary (Macon: Smyth & Helwys, 2001), 162. Likewise Ralph W. Klein affirms the antiquity of this material in this chapter because it "seems to represent a different history than that recounted in Dtr." Klein, *1 Samuel*, WBC 10 (Waco: Word, 1983), 112. Neither considers these variants as part of the narrative characterization of the prophet.

But for now we can see one way that Samuel selectively uses history for his purposes by attending to the confession of sin that he quotes from the time of the Judges. After listing the three sets of oppression by enemies, Samuel claims: "Then they cried out to YHWH, and said, 'We have sinned, for we have forsaken YHWH, and we have served the Baals and the Astartes. And now deliver us from the hand of our enemies, and we will serve you'" (1 Sam. 12:10). Whereas this confession is supposed to serve as a typical example of Israel's cry for help in the time of the Judges, we should note that of all the times when Israel cries out to YHWH for help in Judges, only *once* do they ever confess their sin. According to Judg. 10:10, "The Israelites cried out to YHWH, saying, 'We have sinned against you, because we have abandoned our God and have worshiped the Baalim.'" In every other case in Judges when Israel cries out to God for help, there is no specific acknowledgment of sin. So Samuel is being very selective in his recounting of the time of the Judges, since he wants a precedent for the people acknowledging their sin.[35]

The Origin of Israel's Monarchy (1 Samuel 12:12-13)

Samuel's confusion (or his bending of the facts) is evident in his account of the recent events that led to the people's request for a king. According to Samuel, it was in response to the Ammonite threat that the people demanded a king (12:12). However, Samuel here juxtaposes language from 1 Sam. 8:19 (where the people say, "No! but a king shall reign over us") with the narrative of Nahash and the Ammonite threat recounted at 11:1-5, which comes *after* Saul's anointing (and certainly after the people's request for a king). Some commentators try to harmonize Samuel's statement with a passage from Qumran (4QSam^a) that suggests that Nahash had been terrorizing Israel for at least a month before the incident at Jabesh-Gilead; so they postulate that this threat could have been part of the motivation for the people's request for a

---

35. The particular confession of sin that Samuel cites comes in the context of the Ammonite threat in the book of Judges; and Samuel will soon connect a more recent Ammonite threat with the people's request for a king, thus implying that they might have followed their ancestors in confessing their sin, instead of asking for a king (which in his view simply compounded their sin). Bergen comments: "Israel's oft-repeated pattern of repentance and return to the Lord in the face of a foreign threat was broken...in their demand for an earthly king" (Bergen, *1, 2 Samuel*, 143). Here I simply note that Bergen has accepted Samuel's reconstruction of this "oft-repeated pattern" over the pattern actually found in Judges.

king (depending on how much time is supposed to have passed between 1 Sam. 8 and 11).³⁶

Some justification for this postulate could be found in the fact that when God brings Saul to Samuel's attention in ch. 9 as the one to be anointed *nagid* over Israel, the reason given is that YHWH has heard the cries of his people under Philistine oppression and will deliver them by the hand of Saul (1 Sam. 9:16-17). Yet note that YHWH lists Philistine oppression and not the (later) Ammonite threat. Plus, when the people reaffirm their request for a king in 1 Sam. 8:19 (the line quoted by Samuel) they make no mention of Nahash or the Ammonites, though they do say they want the king to go before them and fight their battles.

Perhaps more importantly, Samuel seems to ignore the original reason for the people's request for a king at the start of ch. 8, namely Samuel's old age and his sons' corruption (8:4); new leadership is therefore necessary. Samuel's reframing of the reason for the people's request for a king to omit mention of the need for new leadership further supports my claim that the prophet protests too much at the start of ch. 12; his defense of his previous leadership seems like an anxious act of self-justification.

We should also note here the significant disjunction between the way that Samuel and YHWH frame the need for a king qua deliverer. Whereas YHWH (in 9:16) portrays Saul's deliverance of Israel as part of the pattern of the Judges as a *legitimate* response to the people's cry of distress, Samuel (in 12:12) portrays it as an *illegitimate* request to replace YHWH's kingship. God and prophet are not on the same page here.³⁷

---

36. The passage from 4QSamᵃ seems to have been known by Josephus (*Ant.* 6.68-71). It is placed in the NRSV prior to 1 Sam. 11:1, without verse numbering. This passage makes sense of the LXX of 1 Sam. 11:1, which begins with "And it came to pass about a month after" by supplying the missing information.

37. This is not the place for a detailed analysis of how Samuel and God differ about the validity of the monarchy. But a summary may suffice. God explained to Samuel (1 Sam. 8) that the people were not rejecting him (Samuel); rather, the request for a king was simply a new form of rejecting YHWH's rule, which they had already been doing even during the time of the judges (so this was nothing new for God). However, Samuel delayed in carrying out God's explicit command, "listen to the voice of the people" (8:7), even after God repeated the command, along with the clarification "give them a king" (8:22), just in case he didn't understand. Not only did Samuel send the people home at the end of ch. 8, without giving them a king (or even letting them know that God has acceded to their request), but after God pointed Saul out as the king designate (9:15-17), Samuel anointed Saul in secret (9:26–10:1), so no-one knew he was king, gave him a series of convoluted instructions (10:2-6), including the following—"do what your hand finds to do" (10:7) and "I will tell you what to do" (10:8)—then publicly cast lots to decide who the king would be

The Self-Serving Result of Reframing Israel's Story: Samuel as Israel's Deliverer

It is now time to turn to the lacuna in Samuel's reframing of the cycle of oppression and deliverance in 12:11. Having mentioned the lack of reference to the oppression to which he is the answer, it is time to figure out why Samuel leaves the oppression unsaid at this point.

We could fill in the lacuna by looking to *the past*, specifically to ch. 7, where Samuel is clearly portrayed as a judging Israel, though primarily through the exercise of a juridical function (7:6, 15-17). Yet Samuel is also instrumental (in that chapter) in delivering Israel from the Philistine threat, though not by military action (as is typical of the judges), but by prayer and sacrifice (7:7-12), in response to the people putting away their idols (7:3-6). However, in ch. 12 Samuel does not mention the Philistines as the oppression from which he delivers Israel, which he easily could have done.

Instead of looking to the past, it makes sense to look to *the future*, to Samuel's expected rescue of Israel from oppression, at least as he envisions it. Samuel's rhetorical framing of Israel's past and current history leads the reader to expect that it is *the monarchy* that will fill the lacuna, since this is the new form of oppression that Israel will need deliverance from. In other words, Samuel's rhetorical lacuna is intentional, to be filled in by what the prophet says in the remainder of ch. 12. This will reveal Samuel as Israel's true deliverer.

Now, someone might object that back in ch. 8, Samuel ended his warning about the monarchy by stating that the people would cry out for deliverance from the king, but that YHWH would not answer them (8:18). So that constitutes a clear contradiction with Samuel portraying himself as the deliverer from the monarchy in ch. 12. But what's a little contradiction among friends? Or perhaps we should say enemies—since it is clear from 12:14 following that Samuel places himself (along with YHWH) in an adversarial stance vis-à-vis the people (and also the king). It also turns out that Samuel seems quite comfortable with contradictions (or, at least, tensions) in what he says in the remainder of ch. 12.[38]

(10:17-23), as if the king hadn't already been chosen by God and also anointed (with a tiny *vial* of oil as opposed to a horn, as is usual—which suggests how grudgingly Samuel performed his role as kingmaker). And then there is Samuel's condemnatory speech in ch. 12, *after* the king has been formally installed. God and prophet are clearly not on the same page about the monarchy.

38. Contradictions do not seem to faze Samuel, who, as we have seen, is willing to massage the facts in the service of his rhetorical ends. As Frolov notes, "to put it mildly, factual accuracy was not among his [Samuel's] primary concerns" (Frolov, "Bedan," 167).

These tensions can be read as a function of the adversarial stance that Samuel takes in the rest of ch. 12, through which he communicates both subliminally and openly his opposition to the monarchy.

First, the subliminal communication.

Samuel's Lopsided Statement of Covenant Sanctions (1 Samuel 12:14-15)

Having recounted Israel's history in 12:6-13, Samuel moves on to challenge the people, using traditional covenantal categories, with the alternatives of obedience and disobedience, which are articulated as (1) fearing YHWH and listening to his voice versus (2) not listening to YHWH's voice, but rebelling against his mouth (12:14-15). In one sense these alternatives constitute "orthodox" Deuteronomistic theology. The trouble is that Samuel's statement of the traditional covenant sanctions is lopsided. Whereas the consequence of rebellion (12:15) is that YHWH's hand will be against the people ("and their ancestors," MT; or "and their king," LXX), there is no positive consequence stated for obedience (12:14). Many translations therefore supply something like: "it will be well with you."[39]

This lopsidedness leads some commentators to take Samuel's words in 12:14 to include both the protasis and apodosis (the latter being, "*then both you and the king who reigns over you will follow YHWH your God*"); but this makes for a tautology, not a consequence.[40] Whereas in the case of many imprecations in the Hebrew Bible the actual curse is missing, perhaps because it is too terrible to be said, here the blessing is missing.[41] Could Samuel omit the positive apodosis because he can't force himself to countenance a positive outcome of the monarchy?[42]

---

39. Some variant of this positive outcome is found in the NRSV, ESV, NIV, NAB, GNB, NJB, and McCarter, who claims that without this we are accusing Samuel (or the Deuteronomistic editor) of "some rather bewildering speechmaking" (*1 Samuel*, 209).

40. That this makes for a tautology is noted by Firth, *1 & 2 Samuel*, 143. Some variant of this tautology is found in the NLT, NASB, HCSB, and Klein, *1 Samuel*, 110–11.

41. An example of a missing apodosis in an imprecation is found in Uriah's oath to David in 2 Sam. 11:11, which the NRSV renders as "As you live, and as your soul lives, I will not do such a thing." However, instead of "I will not do this thing," the Hebrew simply says, "if I do this thing…," without stating the consequence.

42. Peter D. Miscall wonders if the apodosis is missing because Samuel "simply will not connect the king with things going well" (though he also suggests other possibilities). Miscall, *1 Samuel: A Literary Reading*, Indiana Studies in Biblical Literature (Bloomington: Indiana University Press, 1986), 76.

Support for this possibility is found in the fact that Samuel continues to harp on the evil of the monarchy even *after* YHWH has given Israel permission for a king in ch. 8 and specifically chosen Saul in ch. 9; indeed, Samuel's affirmation of the evil of the monarchy comes even after he anointed Saul in ch. 10 and after Saul is installed as king in ch. 11. Clearly, Samuel cannot accept the fact that the monarchy (with Saul as the first king) could ever be legitimate.

The depth of Samuel's antipathy to the monarchy in ch. 12 is seen by his association of the monarchy with nothing less than idolatry; he makes this association in a series of subtle and not so subtle rhetorical moves.

Samuel Intimates That Monarchy Equals Idolatry (1 Samuel 12:10, 12)

First, the cry of distress that Samuel quotes from the book of Judges (in his retelling of the cycles of oppression and rescue) has the people identifying their forsaking of YHWH with serving the Baals and Astartes (12:10). This is not controversial for covenantal theology. But then Samuel goes on in 12:12 to identify asking for a human king with rejecting YHWH as king. If we put these two statements together, from vv. 10 and 12, we have an implied identification of forsaking or rejecting YHWH both with *following idols* and with *asking for a king*. So the monarchy is thus tantamount to idolatry in Samuel's eyes; both constitute rejection of YHWH.

Samuel Gets the People to Admit that the Monarchy is Evil (1 Samuel 12:16-19)

Perhaps this is too subtle.

So, having laid out the two ways, of obedience followed by… (whatever) and disobedience followed by YHWH's adamant opposition, Samuel goes on (in 12:16 and following) to predict and then perform a miraculous sign; this sign is meant as a show of power to convince the people of their *great evil* in asking for a king (12:17), and this right after the king has been installed. This sign is introduced with *gam- 'attâ* ("even now"), followed by a call for them to take their stand and see the "great thing" that YHWH will do.

The fact that the storm for which Samuel prays would in all likelihood have damaged (if not destroyed) the wheat that Samuel himself acknowledges is ready for harvest (12:17), simply demonstrates that the miracle is not for the people's benefit, but to exalt Samuel's prestige and authority in their eyes. And the miracle has the desired effect. The people "greatly feared" YHWH *and Samuel* (12:18); and they ask him to pray for them that they do not die.⁴³ Then they acknowledge that asking for a king was *an evil* that they have added to all their other sins (12:19). To their idolatry, in other words—of which they repented in ch. 7—they have now added monarchy.⁴⁴

Samuel Identifies Monarchy with Idolatry (1 Samuel 12:20-21)

The parity or equivalence between monarchy and idolatry is confirmed in Samuel's response to the people's confession of the evil of monarchy.

In his response, in 12:20-21, Samuel contrasts, on the one hand, serving YHWH with all your heart and, on the other, turning aside after *tohû*, which (he adds) cannot profit (*lo' yô'ilû*) and cannot deliver. Now, *tohû* has a variety of contextual uses in the Hebrew Bible, but in Isa. 41:29 it is used of idols and in Isa. 44:9 it is a description of those who make idols. Likewise *lo' yô'ilû* ("they do not profit") can be used in different contexts, but is used to describe the impotence of idols in Isaiah's famous diatribe

---

43. That God backs Samuel up with the miraculous storm does not mean that God either initiated Samuel's words of judgment about the monarchy or approved of the miraculous storm (given the damage it would do). A key to understanding the YHWH–Samuel relationship is found in the earlier announcement (1 Sam. 3:19-20) that God ensured that none of Samuel's words would fall to the ground (the text ambiguously says "his words," which is appropriate since Samuel's words will henceforth be treated as God's words). The implicit rationale for this verse is that in light of the coming monarchy (which God foresaw), God rescinded his promise of a faithful/trustworthy (*ně'eman*) priest, who was to replace the Elide line (2:35), and provided, instead, a faithful/trustworthy (*ně'eman*) prophet (3:19) in the person of Samuel, in order to balance the power of the king, since that was more needed. Here faithful/trustworthy (*ně'eman*) refers not to the personal character of the prophet, but to the reliability of the prophetic word. On 1 Sam. 3:19-20, see Middleton, "Samuel Agonistes," 87–8 (*Thesis 5: God has chosen to be constrained by the choice of Samuel as the authoritative representative of God's will*).

44. J. P. Fokkelman makes an astute comment about a possible thematic connection (as well as a disconnect) between Samuel's miracle in ch. 12 (where he calls on YHWH to send thunder; 12:17-18) and Hannah's song in ch. 2 (where she affirms that the Most High will thunder in heaven; 2:10a). While the theme of thunder (the lexemes are different) links the words of mother and son, the very next line of Hannah's song states: "May YHWH give strength to his king / and exalt the horn of his anointed" (2:10b)—something her son could never affirm (for Samuel, YHWH's thundering is a condemnation of the monarchy). See Fokkelman, *Narrative Art and Poetry in the Books of Samuel: A Full Interpretation Based on Stylistic and Structural Analyses, Vol. 4: Vow and Desire (1 Sam. 1–12)*, SSN 31 (Assen: Van Gorcum, 1993), 525.

(Isa. 44:10) and in the covenant lawsuit of Jer. 2:8, where it stands in parallel with Baal, a clear reference to idolatry.[45]

Samuel's use of these terms in 12:21, in his response to the people's admission that they sinned in asking for a king, clarifies the alternatives, at least in Samuel's mind: *either* serve YHWH wholeheartedly *or* turn aside to the monarchy, which (like idolatry) is described as *tohû* and that which cannot profit.[46] Interestingly, according to Samuel the monarchy cannot profit *and it cannot deliver*, even though YHWH intended the king to deliver Israel from the Philistines (1 Sam. 9:16-17), and the new king has in fact already delivered them from the Ammonites.

Samuel's Prima Facie Theological Contradictions

At this point I want to explore what look suspiciously like theological contradictions internal to Samuel's own words to the people, beginning in 12:14 and continuing through the end of the chapter.[47]

To Fear or Not to Fear (1 Samuel 12:14, 20, 24)

The first contradiction has to do with the motif of *fear*. Having listed *the fear of YHWH* as one of the covenantal alternatives (in 12:14), Samuel gives a miraculous sign, which results in the people *fearing YHWH and Samuel* (12:18). However, in 12:20 Samuel's identification of monarchy with *tohû* is prefaced by the exhortation *Fear not!* This is, paradoxically, followed in 12:24 by the warning "Only *fear YHWH*." Now I am fully aware that it is possible to argue for two meanings of "fear" here, one being the legitimate awe of God (12:24), the other unnatural terror (12:20); and, indeed, there need not be an intrinsic contradiction between these two

---

45. The phrase *loʾ yôʿilû* is a also linked to idolatry (though less directly) in Isa. 57:12 and Jer. 16:19.

46. Bill T. Arnold acknowledges that v. 21 represents Samuel's identification of the monarchy with a new form of idolatry, while arguing for a particular origin of the verse as a pre-Deuteronomistic adage that derives from the struggle against the Baals and Astartes in ninth-century Israel. Whether one agrees with Arnold's reconstruction of the origin of this verse (or with the more common view that it is a later post-Deuteronomistic addition to the text, or neither), Arnold is right to see this mention of idolatry as part of Samuel's critique of kingship as an institution. Arnold, "A Pre-Deuteronomistic Bicolon in 1 Samuel 12:21?" *JBL* 123 (2004): 137–42.

47. My terminology of theological contradictions is paralleled by Peter Miscall's reference to Samuel's "paradoxical assertion" and his combining themes "in oxymoronic fashion" (Miscall, *1 Samuel*, 77).

meanings of "fear" (as in Exod. 20:20). However, it seems clear that the very point of the miraculous sign was (to use a contemporary idiom) to put "the fear o' God" into the people, to scare them into acknowledging their guilt (which worked). So Samuel is being a bit disingenuous in his exhortation *not* to fear (12:20) after his (intentionally) fear-producing performance of the miraculous sign (12:18).[48]

Guilt Tripping and Love Bombing (1 Samuel 12:22 and 25)

But there is another contradiction in Samuel's concluding words (in 12:20-25) that parallels the two uses of *fear*.

On the one hand, Samuel affirms in 12:22 that "YHWH will not forsake his people, for the sake of his great name, for YHWH has resolved to make you a people for himself." These are words of assurance and comfort; they fit with *fear not* and suggest that no matter what the sin, YHWH's love is unconditional.

Yet in the last sentence of the chapter (just three verses later), we find the words, "But if you dare to do evil [*hārē'a tārē'û*; the infinitive absolute followed by the finite form of the verb], both you and your king will be swept away" (12:25).

So, which one is it? *Fear YHWH*? Or *Don't be afraid*?

Are we to believe *YHWH will not forsake you*? Or *You will be swept away*?

Having grown up in the era of new religious movements (also known as cults), I am struck by the parallel between Samuel's emotional manipulation of the people with his rhetoric and what was known in cult circles as "love bombing" and "guilt tripping." It is precisely the alternation between positive affirmation and negative condemnation that characterizes what has come to be known as the initial stages of cultic "brainwashing."[49] This immediate and irrational alternation between affirmation and condemnation served to keep new converts off balance and make them easily subject to manipulation by cult leaders. This is also practiced in terrorist

---

48. For a similar interpretation, see Czövek, *Three Seasons of Charismatic Leadership*, 65.

49. The term "love bombing" was coined by the Unification Church (with an initially positive meaning), but it has now become a central feature in psychological descriptions of sociopathic, narcissistic behavior. Although guilt tripping has not had the same attention in the psychological literature, ex-cult member Michael Bluejay describes the relationship between these two poles in "How Cults Recruit and Indoctrinate Their Members," June 2013, https://michaelbluejay.com/x/how-cults-recruit.html.

interrogation, vividly portrayed in the movie *Zero Dark Thirty*, which recounts the search for Osama bin Laden.⁵⁰

I submit that something analogous is going on throughout 12:20-25 (though more like cultic practice than what we find at Guantanamo). Witness Samuel's three opening affirmations in 12:20:

1. "Fear Not!"—comfort.
2. "As for you, you have done all this evil"—condemnation.
3. "Only, do not turn aside from following YHWH with all your heart"—warning.

And so it goes throughout the following verses, alternating comfort, condemnation, and warning. And in the midst of this rhetoric, Samuel makes an oath not to "sin against YHWH by ceasing to pray for you"; indeed, he promises to "instruct them in the good and straight way" (12:23), which is his way of guaranteeing continuing influence among the people after the monarchy has begun.

We are not told the people's immediate response to Samuel's concluding words in 12:20-25. But we can imagine with the help of an analogy.

An analogy for what Samuel is up to in the entire chapter would be to think of the installation of the king at Gilgal as a wedding, where the father of the bride (Samuel) is also the officiating minister and disapproves in no uncertain terms of the marriage of his daughter (the people). After the ceremony, which is meant to formalize and celebrate the relationship of bride and groom (read people and king), the disgruntled minister makes a speech at the wedding banquet in which he gets the bride to admit that he has always been an exemplary father to her, and he promises to be available at any time for marriage counseling, no matter what problems the ill-conceived marriage may bring. Having lectured the newly married bride on her sin in desiring this husband, he then gets her to admit publicly (on her wedding day) that the marriage was a bad idea from the beginning.

The question I have is: What possible chance would such a marriage have of succeeding? And what would be the effect of this speech on the groom?⁵¹

---

50. *Zero Dark Thirty* (Sony Pictures, 2012), screenplay by Mark Boal, directed by Kathryn Bigelow.

51. A possible effect of Samuel's speech on the fledgling monarchy is suggested by Joachim Vette, in his proposal that the fear the people have of Samuel (1 Sam. 12:18) continues into the next chapter. Thus, instead of coming out "as one man" (11:7) as they did in response to Saul's call to battle with Nahash, we find in ch. 13 that in preparation for the imminent Philistine attack "all the people trembled after him [Saul]" (13:7). This fear that Samuel has generated in ch. 12, Vette concludes,

Ulterior Motives, Deficient Theology: Samuel as Anti-Prophet

In the end, I need to answer the question in the title of this chapter: "Orthodox Theology, Ulterior Motives?" Clearly, Samuel's motives are mixed here, though he seems to appeal to standard covenantal (Deuteronomistic) categories.[52]

But that distinction is too simple; there is something else going on here. Samuel's rhetoric serves to position himself on the side of YHWH in opposition to king and people. That the people understand the force of this rhetoric is evident in their plea for Samuel to pray for them "to YHWH *your God*," which suggests that Samuel's seemingly indispensable connection to YHWH prevents the people from having their own independent relationship with Israel's God.[53]

However, as Abraham Heschel has shown, prophets are meant not just to identify with God, but also to identify with *God's people*. This is because they participate not in God's transcendent sovereignty, but in God's *pathos*.[54] This pathos is the wellspring of the biblical tradition of prophetic intercession, as numerous prophets not only bring YHWH's word of judgment to the people, but simultaneously stand "in the breach" (Ps. 106:23) in order to stave off God's judgment as long as possible.[55]

"has a major part in driving a wedge between the king and his people" (Vette, "Samuel's 'Farewell Speech,'" 338–90). More radically, Czövek notes that by his tendentious speech "the prophet destines Saul to inevitable failure" (Czövek, *Three Seasons of Charismatic Leadership*, 62).

52. My point here is similar to Keith Bodner's: "When the speech as a whole is evaluated, it is much like the characterization of Samuel himself: some personal crustiness mixed with some highly orthodox theology that Israel needs to hear in these first days of the monarchy" (Bodner, *1 Samuel*, 116). My characterization, however, has gone a bit beyond "personal crustiness," and will soon question the orthodoxy of Samuel's theology.

53. As Czövek puts it, "By now the audience has been convinced that rebelling against Samuel, Yahweh's mouthpiece, amounts to rebelling against Yahweh" (Czövek, *Three Seasons of Charismatic Leadership*, 63). Saul's threefold use of this same expression ("YHWH your God") in ch. 15 confirms that this conviction comes to be shared by the king (15:15, 21, 30).

54. For the classic analysis of God's pathos, in which the prophet participates, see Abraham Heschel, *The Prophets*, Perennial Classics (New York: Harper & Row, 1962, 2001), esp. vol. 1, Chapter 6: "Jeremiah," and vol. 2, Chapter 1: "The Theology of Pathos."

55. On the theme of prophetic intercession, stemming from Moses, see Michael Widmer, *Standing in the Breach: An Old Testament Theology and Spirituality of Intercessory Prayer*, Siphrut 13 (Winona Lake: Eisenbrauns, 2015).

Thus Moses (the paradigmatic prophet) intercedes on behalf of the people after the Golden Calf episode.[56] But Samuel, having promised not to cease praying for both people and king (1 Sam. 12:23) reneges on his oath when he outright refuses to intercede for Saul in ch. 15.[57]

When I began working on this chapter I expected to be able to affirm the terms of my title: "Orthodox Theology, Ulterior Motives." However, I am now of the opinion that Samuel's speech in ch. 12 not only reflects *ulterior motives*, but represents a *deficient theology of prophecy* as well.

---

56. True, not all prophets intercede on behalf of the people; but I am focusing here on Moses as the paradigmatic prophet. For my own exploration of the motif of prophetic intercession, see J. Richard Middleton, "God's Loyal Opposition: Psalmic and Prophetic Protest as a Paradigm for Faithfulness in the Hebrew Bible," *Canadian-American Theological Review* 5, no. 1 (2016): 51–65.

57. For an exploration of the contrast between Moses in the Golden Calf episode and Samuel in the narrative of 1 Sam. 15, see Middleton, "Samuel Agonistes," 89–91. Widmer discusses Samuel as intercessor in Chapter 4: "Samuel: Israel's Second Legendary Intercessor (1 Samuel 7, 12, 15)," focusing on similarities between Samuel and Moses, without addressing the differences. Yet Widmer is forced to note that "in contrast to Moses, none of Samuel's actual prayers are recorded in the canon" (Widmer, *Standing in the Breach*, 174).

Chapter 7

From a Head above the Rest to No Head at All: Transformations in the Life of Saul

Paul S. Evans

The best stories feature characters who change in significant ways and the book of Samuel is no exception. In modern fiction, some of the most popular stories are about characters who experience positive changes and improve as people, or experience long sought for success. However, there are many stories about characters who do not improve but change for the worse, or are in a sense tragic characters. While not as uplifting or inspirational as stories of a character who overcomes obstacles to succeed and improve as a person, characters who end up making bad choices and even become the villain are also compelling.[1] In fact, their story may be like watching a train wreck—you just can't look away. Part of you wants them to stop, but another part doesn't. Perhaps the most captivating character of all is a character who struggles against their dark side, and "flirts for awhile with the idea of being good, then decides that his true self is on the dark side of the street."[2] A famous example would be Gollum in *The Lord of the Rings*, who reverted to Sméagol for a while, and looked like he might be redeemed, only to turn in the end towards the dark—to his own doom. Using insights about negative character arcs and negative traits in modern fiction writing, the present essay examines the transformation of

---

1. E.g. Roger in *Lord of the Flies*, Allie Fox in *The Mosquito Coast*. Cf. Jeff Gerke, *Plot Versus Character* (Cincinnati: Writer's Digest Books, 2010), 78.
2. Ibid.

the character of Saul in the book of Samuel as an example of a negative character arc who flirts with greatness, but eventually turns to the darkness and to his own doom.³

In some recent scholarship Saul's characterization has been viewed as somewhat ambiguous or ambivalent, with clearly positive aspects highlighted as well as very negative.⁴ This is usually explained by an appeal to putative distinct sources, some of which were thought to be originally positive about Saul,⁵ to which were added sources negative about him.⁶ Many find in the final redaction by the Deuteronomistic Historian an almost wholly negative portrayal of Israel's first king. For example, Mobley suggests that in DtrH, Saul "is debased just short of caricature" and McKenzie finds him "a one-dimensional character who provides a contrast to David."⁷

Against the view that Saul's characterization is ambivalent, owing to its redactional history, or that he is a one-dimensional character, this essay will argue that Saul is a remarkably multi-layered character who is characterized consistently in the Samuel narrative. The seeds of his downfall are present from the beginning, and what accounts for the positive and negative aspects of his characterization is not the vestiges of diverse

---

3. My use of the terms "character arc" and "negative traits" is heuristic, providing new ways of looking at Saul's characterization that foregrounds overlooked facets of his character that drive his actions.

4. E.g. Ralph K. Hawkins, "The First Glimpse of Saul and His Subsequent Transformation," *JSOT* 22 (2012): 353–62. Some view him as tragic. E.g. Diana V. Edelman, *King Saul in the Historiography of Judah*, JSOTSup 121 (Sheffield: Sheffield Academic, 1991); J. Cheryl Exum, *Tragedy and Biblical Narrative: Arrows of the Almighty* (Cambridge: Cambridge University Press, 1992); W. Lee Humphreys, "The Tragedy of King Saul: A Study of the Structure of 1 Samuel 9-31," *JSOT* 6 (1978): 18–27. Others have suggested he was a victim of a capricious deity. E.g. D. M. Gunn, *The Fate of King Saul: An Interpretation of a Biblical Story*, JSOTSup 14 (Sheffield: JSOT Press, 1980), 40.

5. E.g. 1 Sam. 9:1–10:6; 11:1-15; 13:3-14.

6. E.g. 1 Sam. 8:1-22; 10:17-27; 12:1-25.

7. Gregory Mobley, "Glimpses of the Heroic Saul," in *Saul in Story and Tradition*, ed. C. S. Ehrlich and M. C. White, FAT 47 (Tübingen: Mohr, 2006), 80; and in the same volume Steven L. McKenzie, "Saul in the Deuteronomistic History," 68, though McKenzie holds that in the "original story" of Saul, before redactional additions, he may have been a "more complex and intriguing character." Similarly, Van Seters finds the original story sympathetic to Saul, but that the addition of the "Story of David's Rise" made him only a foil for David. Van Seters, *In Search of History: Historiography in the Ancient World and the Origins of Biblical History* (New Haven: Yale University Press, 1983), 263.

sources but his transformation throughout the story. A key text for Saul's characterization is 1 Samuel 15 with Samuel's direct characterization of Saul as "small in his own eyes" (15:17) and his prediction that Yahweh had chosen a successor who is "better" than him (15:28). Saul's character deficiencies displayed throughout contribute to the reader's understanding of David as "better" than Saul.

Saul's Fatal Flaw

In fiction, characters with a negative character arc usually experience a downfall due to their tragic flaw; a lacking in their lives, or a "besetting sin" of sorts. This fatal flaw is something internal. They are somehow incomplete within. This lack becomes the problem that creates the necessary conflict to drive the plot. Such flaws can at first even seem to be a positive aspect of their character, but in the end prove to be their undoing.[8] In this essay I will argue that Saul's fatal flaw is his low self-esteem which, despite initially making him a sympathetic character, underlies his insecurity, weak will, jealousy, paranoia, instability, and addictions, which lead to his self-destruction. Saul's flaw leads him to make bad choices, to rebel against the divine word, and disastrously prevents him from repenting.

Saul's Appearance

When we first meet Saul in 1 Samuel 9 the narrator tells us he is more handsome and taller than anyone else in all of Israel (1 Sam. 9:22).[9] Descriptions of physical attributes are rare in Hebrew narrative, as many studies have noted, and the function of these references has been debated by scholars. Eslinger suggested that Saul's height was an obstacle that God put before Israel.[10] That is, the people took to the tall Saul instinctively, but God intended him to be no more than a puppet. Against this view, Avioz suggested that the references to Saul's height were meant to

---

8. As K. M. Weiland has noted, "In some instances, it may start out seeming to be a strength, but as the story progresses, it will become his Achilles heel" (*Creating Character Arcs: The Masterful Author's Guide to Uniting Story Structure, Plot, and Character Development*, EBL ed. [PenForASword Publishing, 2016], Chapter 1).

9. Interestingly, Saul's stature is noted a second time later in the story (1 Sam. 10:23).

10. Lyle M. Eslinger, "A Change of Heart: 1 Samuel 16," in *Ascribe to the Lord: Biblical and Other Studies in Memory of Peter C. Craigie*, ed. Lyle Eslinger and Glen Taylor (Sheffield: JSOT Press, 1988), 341–61.

show Saul's great potential to lead Israel, absolving God of any fault in the king's later downfall.[11] I understand the narrator's grand description of Saul's appearance as inferring him to be a man of great physical attributes, who is set up for success.[12]

Saul's Heritage

Saul is also introduced as being from the tribe of Benjamin. Some have suggested that at the time the connotations of being a Benjaminite were negative due to Benjamin's role in the horrible events relayed in Judges 19–21, especially those that occurred in the Benjaminite town of Gibeah, which is actually likened to Sodom (compare Gen. 19 and Judg. 19).[13] Since Saul is actually from Gibeah (1 Sam. 10:26) his association with this notorious village is thought to be somewhat of a stigma on his otherwise impressive pedigree.

Against this negative-Benjaminite view is the prominence of Benjaminite cities in the story. The Benjaminite city of Mizpah clearly has an honored reputation in the book of Samuel, being the place where Samuel assembled Israel before Yahweh's deliverance of Israel from the Philistines (1 Sam. 7), and where he gathered them together to choose their king (1 Sam. 10:17). The Benjaminite city of Gilgal was an important cultic center at this time (1 Sam. 10:8),[14] and where Samuel officially coronates Saul as king (1 Sam. 11:14-15). As well, later in the story when David returns from exile, Judahites meet at Gilgal to greet him (2 Sam. 19:15). Furthermore, Samuel's home was Benjaminite Ramah (1 Sam. 7:17; cf. Josh. 18:25) and his regular judicial cycle (1 Sam. 7:16) took

---

11. Michael Avioz, "The Motif of Beauty in the Books of Samuel and Kings," *VT* 59 (2009): 346.

12. Cf. Humphreys ("Tragedy of King Saul," 20) understands this description to indicate that "Saul is a man of heroic potential." Alternatively, taking his lead from Rashi, Hawkins ("First Glimpse of Saul," 357–8) suggests the use of the word "good" (טוב) to describe Saul in 9:2 indicates he was righteous, not good looking, even speculating it meant he kept God's covenant. This suggestion seems quite unlikely, though I agree with Hawkins that this is "intended to be a positive depiction of Saul."

13. E.g. Robert Polzin, *Samuel and the Deuteronomist: A Literary Study of the Deuteronomistic History: Part Two: 1 Samuel* (San Francisco: Harper & Row, 1989); Moshe Garsiel, *The First Book of Samuel: A Literary Study of Comparative Structures, Analogies and Parallels* (Ramat-Gan, Israel: Revivim, 1985), 78–84; Keith Bodner, *1 Samuel: A Narrative Commentary*, HBM 19 (Sheffield: Sheffield Phoenix, 2008), 79.

14. Wade R. Kotter, "Gilgal," *ABD* 2:1022.

place in the Benjaminite cities of Bethel (cf. Josh. 18:21-22), Mizpah, and Gilgal, indicating the centrality and prominence of Benjamin. In fact, in the book of Samuel the putatively notorious Gibeah is *not* presented negatively but as the site of a prophetic band to whom Samuel sends Saul (1 Sam. 10:10). In sum, Saul's being a Benjaminite does not characterize him negatively.[15]

Saul's First Challenge

Immediately after Saul's introduction, the character's first challenge is set before him—he must recover his father's lost donkeys (1 Sam. 9:3). Saul immediately obeys, which is a positive part of his characterization, as it contrasts the disobedience of other sons in the story thus far (e.g. Eli's sons and Samuel's sons).[16] When the initial challenge proves difficult, Saul despondently suggests abandoning the quest (9:5). Alter has argued that "the first reported speech of a character is a defining moment of characterization" and Saul's first words "let's go back" suggest to Alter Saul's "uncertainty."[17] Instead of uncertainty, I understand Saul's initial words, a suggestion to go back, to show a lack of confidence in successfully completing the assigned task.

Saul's characterization here is in contrast to the attitude of the lad who accompanied him who comes up with a possible solution—ask a seer (9:6). Despite what will prove to be an astute suggestion, Saul disparages the plan on grounds that they did not have sufficient means to fund the proposed course of action (9:7). Saul's words here suggest a lack of self-confidence and somewhat pessimistic stance.[18] On the other hand, when the young lad informs Saul that he happens to have sufficient money on his person for the prophetic inquiry, Saul is quick to follow the lad's lead (9:10). This lack of self-confidence coupled with a willingness to let others take the lead is an enduring aspect of his characterization.

---

15. This is not to say that the shadow of the events in Judg. 19–21 do not hang over the story and anticipate the inter-tribal conflict to come.

16. Bodner, *1 Samuel*, 80.

17. Robert Alter, *The David Story: A Translation with Commentary of 1 and 2 Samuel* (New York: Norton, 1999), 47. Bodner (*1 Samuel*, 81) has further suggested the words are ironic and may be an "intentional literary strategy," alluding to the fact that "there is no returning from…kingship."

18. This lack of confidence and hesitance is further underscored when contrasted with David's first words, which are clearly imbued with confidence and intent to act (1 Sam. 17:26).

The Hero Blows the "Sure Thing"

Not long after his Hollywood good looks are described Saul comes upon some young women at a well (1 Sam. 9:11). Of course, meeting a young marriageable woman at a well is not a unique occurrence in biblical literature, as scholars have pointed out. Such an encounter is understood to be a betrothal "type-scene" and a literary sign of a forthcoming "romantic" encounter.[19] Saul's good looks and impressive size may be in view here, as the women who speak to him at the well appear flustered by his presence and perhaps flirtatious (as evidenced by their "confused" speech).[20] In this instance, however, contrary to the reader's expectations, the type-scene does *not* end with Saul's betrothal as it comes to a halt before its happy conclusion.

Some have suggested that the significance of the so-called "aborted type-scene" is to foreshadow the "aborted" nature of Saul's kingship.[21] Alter, for example, opines "the deflection of the anticipated type-scene somehow isolates Saul, [and] sounds a faintly ominous note that begins to prepare us for the story of the king who loses his kingship."[22] While this may explain the significance of the failure, it does not account for the failure at the story level. Saul's failed "first date" with a water-drawing maiden contributes to his characterization. The reader might wonder if the tall, dark, and handsome Saul "struck-out" with these eligible maidens at the well due to a self-confidence problem. After all, in Jacob's betrothal type-scene (Gen. 29:1-12), Israel's eponymous ancestor displayed great confidence in order to "get the girl." Upon seeing the young maiden (Rachel) Jacob proceeded to "roll away the stone from the mouth of the well" (Gen. 29:10) which the narrator had informed us was "large" (גדלה; Gen. 29:2), suggesting his action was a purposeful show of strength to impress the girl. Furthermore, Jacob proceeded to show his kindness by "watering the flock" (Gen. 29:10). If that show of strength and kindness wasn't enough, Jacob proves himself *extremely confident* as he next "kissed Rachel" (Gen. 29:11)—a bold move to say the least. In another betrothal type-scene in Exodus 2 Moses himself makes a show of strength in defending the maidens from some hostile shepherds who had driven

---

19. Robert Alter, *The Art of Biblical Narrative* (London: G. Allen & Unwin, 1981), 51–62.

20. Shimon Bar-Efrat, *Narrative Art in the Bible*, JSOTSup 70 (Sheffield: JSOT Press, 1997), 97; Gary A. Rendsburg, "Confused Language as a Deliberate Literary Device in Biblical Hebrew Narrative," *JHS* 2 (1999): 197–213; Avioz, "Motif of Beauty," 346; Bodner, *1 Samuel*, 85.

21. Bodner, *1 Samuel*, 78.

22. Alter, *Art of Biblical Narrative*, 60.

them from the well (Exod. 2:17). Similar to Jacob, Moses also shows his kindness in proceeding to water the girls' animals. Saul, on the other hand, despite the apparent flirtatious ways of the maidens at the well, does not pursue them. He makes no move to impress them either with strength or kindness. His inaction here might belie a lack of confidence in Saul.

Meeting the Seer

When Saul first meets Samuel he apparently does not recognize his prophetic status, instead asking him for directions (1 Sam. 9:18). Did Samuel not "look the part" of a prophet? Later in the story Saul can identify Samuel with only a loose description given by the medium of Endor to go by (1 Sam. 28:14). Does Saul suspect this is the seer, but lack the confidence to ask directly? After all, the maidens at the well appear to have already told Saul exactly where to find the seer, saying "As *soon as you enter the town*, you will find him... Go up at once, for you will find him right away" (1 Sam. 9:13). The narrator tells us as Saul entered the gate והנה שמואל "behold Samuel" (1 Sam. 9:14). The expression והנה suggests Saul recognized the prophet.[23] As Alter explains, "The presentative 'look' (*hineh*)" functions "as an indicator of transition from the narrator's overview to the character's point of view."[24] Saul *recognized* Samuel when he entered the gate, finding him exactly where the girls from the well said they would find him. What is more, Samuel is going up to the high place, just as the maidens had predicted. It was pretty clear this is the seer he was looking for. Yet Saul seems too lacking in confidence to address the seer directly so as to confirm his identity.

After Samuel identifies himself and tells him that his donkeys have been found, Samuel informs Saul of his status as Israel's most desirable bachelor—the one "on whom is all Israel's *desire* fixed" (1 Sam. 9:20).[25] Given his great wealth, unmatched height, and good looks, such a description of Saul might have seemed fitting. Saul's response to this remark, however, further bolsters his characterization of low self-esteem. He says "I am only a Benjaminite, from the smallest (מקטני) of Israel's tribes, and my family is the littlest (הצערה) of all the families of the tribe of Benjamin" (1 Sam. 9:21). Clearly this self-description is out of

---

23. As BDB (243) notes "in historical style, esp. (but not exclusively) after verbs of seeing or discovering, making the narrative graphic and vivid, and enabling the reader to enter into the surprise or satisfaction of the speaker or actor concerned."

24. Alter, *The David Story*, 186.

25. One commentator translated Samuel's words to Saul here as "to whom is all the base desire of Israel directed" (Bodner, *1 Samuel*, 88).

touch with reality. At the beginning of the chapter in his genealogy (9:1) the narrator already told us that Saul's father was a "powerful man" (גבור חיל).[26] As Klein comments, "the intent of the genealogy is surely to emphasize the high status of Kish and therefore of Saul."[27] Again, Saul's oddly low self-esteem comes to the fore, as he refuses Samuel's compliment and denigrates his own pedigree.

The Reticent Anointed One

Answering Saul's hyper-humble assessment of himself, Samuel anointed Saul, gave him several miraculous signs of confirmation, and even arranged for Saul to join a prophetic band (10:1-6). Despite these affirming and potentially ego-boosting events, when Saul returned home we see a somewhat strange reticence to share the news with his family even under direct questioning by his uncle (10:15-16). Saul's keeping secrets here suggests a timid characteristic of the new king.

After Saul is chosen by lot out of all the tribes and families of Israel, Saul is nowhere to be found (10:9-21). Shunning the spotlight, it takes a direct word from Yahweh to locate him. Yahweh says "Look! He has hidden himself among the equipment" (10:22).[28] This contributes to his characterization as lacking a healthy perspective on himself. Seemingly to snap Saul out of his self-loathing, Samuel introduces him to the nation in extremely flattering terms. "Do you see the one Yahweh has chosen? There is no one like him among all the people" (10:24). If that wasn't enough, the people then all chime in, "Long live the king!" (10:24). Normally, one would think acclamation from all the people would help to bolster one's ego. However, it seems this did not awaken a healthier self-esteem in the newly minted king. Immediately after this, some from the crowd shouted insulting remarks (10:27). Saul's reaction is quite revealing here. Though most translations read something like "but he held his peace" (NRSV) or "but Saul kept silent" (NIV), the Hebrew literally translated (ויהי כמחריש) means "but he was as a deaf one," suggesting that Saul did not just keep quiet (i.e. choosing to not retaliate) but that he *pretended* not to hear them.[29] Instead of responding directly, either graciously or vindictively, Saul acts as if he did not hear the insulting comments. Rather than viewing Saul's inaction as gracious, it more easily reads as timidity (if not cowardice).

26. P. Kyle McCarter, *I Samuel*, AB 8 (Garden City: Doubleday, 1980).
27. Ralph W. Klein, *1 Samuel*, WBC 10 (Waco: Word, 1983), 86.
28. Klein understands this to mean that Saul was "shy or modest." Ibid., 99.
29. JPS translates as "He pretended not to mind."

The Ammonite Challenge

They say action is the implementation of character, and Saul's delivering Jabesh-Gilead from the Ammonites (11:1-11) is definitely the high moment in his characterization. When news of the Ammonite conquest of Jabesh-Gilead reaches him, Saul was "returning from the fields, behind his oxen" (11:5). Curiously, after being anointed as king, then chosen as king through lot ceremony, then acclaimed as king by the people, now Saul is back to farming. Is this due to an admirable reticence to take power, or to an unfortunate lack of confidence to lead?

Saul's reaction to the people's tears at the messengers' report shows Saul's sensitivity to the feelings of others (11:5). This could be attributed to his low self-esteem (always concerned with what others think or what they are feeling) but more likely functions to show a compassionate aspect of his character. Regardless, at this point Saul is changed and transformed from a follower into a true leader. The key moment that transforms Saul from the timid soul who would rather pretend not to hear (10:27) than to face a challenge is the coming of Yahweh's spirit on him (11:6). The one who followed the lead of his servant lad (9:6-10) now leads all of Israel to victory. The changed character of Saul can also be seen in his reaction to those who called for capital punishment for those who previously opposed Saul's kingship (11:12). Instead of feigning deafness, Saul asserts his authority and shows mercy; granting amnesty to the guilty and choosing to focus on God's granting of victory to Israel that day (11:13).

Put in his Place by the Prophet

In ch. 12 Samuel gives something like a farewell speech, boasting of his achievements (i.e. *not* stealing from them), ignoring his failures (12:2; his sinful sons), and warning his audience to trust in God and not in "useless things that cannot profit or save" (12:21). While "useless things" likely means "idols," as the story proceeds it foreshadows Saul's reliance upon superstitious rituals. This connection is clear when Samuel later equates Saul's disobedience to idolatry (15:23). What is more, in ch. 12 it is clear that Samuel's words are directed not only to the people but the king whose presence is explicitly mentioned throughout the speech (12:1, 13, 25). The diatribe concludes, "but if you surely do evil, both you *and your king* will be swept away" (12:25). In response, Saul says nothing. This could reflect well on the king, deferring to Yahweh's prophet appropriately. On the other hand, it could reflect Saul's reluctance to assert himself.

The Philistine Challenge

When Saul faced a new challenge with Philistia (13:5), and Samuel did not come at the appointed time, the new king acts decisively and offers the sacrifice himself, rather than wait any longer for the dilatory prophet. Saul's actions may strike the reader as reasonable in this context, given Samuel's tardiness and the life-and-death situation with which Saul was faced. After all, Samuel had told Saul to wait "seven days" until he arrives (1 Sam. 10:8), and Saul did, in fact, properly wait until the appointed time (13:8).[30] Furthermore, Saul's initiative here may have been emboldened by Samuel's earlier advice of doing "whatever you see fit to do, for God is with you" (1 Sam. 10:7). Further, it is open to question whether Samuel set Saul up for failure in this instance, given his impeccable timing of showing up immediately after Saul offered the sacrifice.[31]

While this potentially confusing advice may elicit sympathy for Saul from the reader, the prophet clearly did not view it this way. Saul had been given the freedom and license to do whatever "his hand finds to do" (1 Sam. 10:7), but at the same time he was given strict parameters as regards to what he must do at Gilgal (1 Sam. 10:8). The situation is not dissimilar to the situation in the garden of Eden, where the first human couple are given freedom but are restrained as well. The Lord God first says, "You are free to eat from any tree in the garden" (Gen. 2:16) but immediately afterwards states, "but you must not eat from the tree of the knowledge of good and evil" (Gen. 2:17). Similarly, Saul was given freedom to act, but was also called to obey the prophet.

While the reader may question whether Saul was guilty of anything in this matter, Saul's own consciousness of his guilt is revealed in his lengthy response (27 words) to Samuel's terse inquiry (2 words).[32] Regardless of the ambiguous nature of Saul's "sin" here, or whether the prophet was complicit in the monarch's failure, of most interest for our purposes here is Saul's explanation of his motivation to Samuel (13:12) wherein two aspects of Saul's character come to the fore: his susceptibility to peer pressure and his penchant for superstitious ritual.[33] The first is seen in

---

30. Cf. Polzin, *Samuel and the Deuteronomist*, 129; Gunn, *The Fate of King Saul*, 33–40; Exum, *Tragedy and Biblical Narrative*, 27.

31. As Exum (*Tragedy and Biblical Narrative*, 27) writes, "Samuel's failure to keep the appointment on time, followed by his arrival just as Saul finished offering the sacrifice, suggests something beyond mere chance."

32. As Bodner writes, "Human speech is often difficult to gauge, but still, the 'numbers' can be helpful." Bodner, *1 Samuel*, 121.

33. Long ago John Henry Newman understood Saul similarly, writing: "Saul in his way was a religious man; I say, in *his* way, but not in God's way; yet His very

Saul's concern that the people were "scattering" (נפץ) away from him (13:11). While it is human to be flustered by this state of affairs, one might expect more from the commander-in-chief. Saul appears overly dependent upon public opinion. Furthermore, Saul's reliance on superstition is evident in Saul's feeling compelled to offer the sacrifice in order to gain Yahweh's favor. Here Saul shows his deep concern for the "good luck" that offering sacrifices might bring. This need for superstitious confirmation rears its head again and again throughout the rest of the Saul story.

Again, these weaknesses seem related to his fatal flaw. Saul's low self-worth meant he inordinately relied upon others' opinions. His lack of confidence created a need for constant affirmation. Most significantly from here on out is Saul's reliance upon—if not addiction to—superstitious ritual for affirmation and assurance of success. Persons with self-esteem issues often show addictive character traits. The *Negative Trait Thesaurus* defines the "addictive" character flaw as "a predisposition to becoming unhealthily dependent upon a substance, practice, person, habit, or other intangible."[34] Causes for this addictive flaw are listed as "low self-esteem and insecurity."[35] Addicts often end up "blowing off important commitments" in order to feed their addiction, and Saul is no different.[36] Here Saul forgets his commitment to wait for Samuel, and undertakes a ritual on his own.

Saul's lack of confidence underlies his reliance on superstitious ritual and his susceptibility to peer pressure, both of which are evinced in the next chapter with the persistence of the Philistine threat.[37] As Saul waits with his army at the outskirts of Gibeah (1 Sam. 14:2) he ensures he has ready access to ritualistic guidance as he is accompanied by a priest who is explicitly said to have with him an ephod (1 Sam. 14:3). Saul's

disobedience *he* might consider an act of religion. He offered sacrifice *rather* than go to battle without a sacrifice. An openly irreligious man would have drawn up his army and fallen upon the Philistines without any religious service at all." John Henry Newman, "The Trial of Saul," in *Parochial and Plain Sermons* (San Francisco: Ignatius, 1997), 1593. More recently, Steven Chapman has highlighted Saul's superstitious piety, noting that "Saul approaches God's presence in a manner more superstitious than devout." Steven B. Chapman, *1 Samuel as Christian Scripture: A Theological Commentary* (Grand Rapids: Eerdmans, 2016), 132.

34. Angela Ackerman and Becca Puglisi, "Addictive," in *The Negative Trait Thesaurus: A Writer's Guide to Character Flaws*, EBL ed. (JADD Publishing, 2013).

35. Ibid.

36. Ibid.

37. See my fuller treatment of chs. 13–14 in my commentary, *1–2 Samuel*, SOG (Grand Rapids: Zondervan, 2018), 148–55.

reticence to act without ritualistic guidance is evident in what follows. Jonathan spearheads a successful assault against the enemy (14:14) and Yahweh sends panic through the Philistine camp (14:15), yet Saul will not participate in Yahweh's deliverance until he gets ritualistic guidance. Instead Saul first says, "Bring the ark of God!" (v. 18)—which, at the very least, can be seen as a good luck charm.[38] Then he attempts to obtain an oracle from the ephod-bearing priest (v. 19), until the tumult in the Philistine camp increases to the point that it can no longer be ignored (14:19) and Saul interrupts the oracular process and sends Israel to battle.[39]

The superstitious characterization of Saul is further developed in a narratorial aside (14:24) of delayed exposition, which informs the reader that in an effort to obtain ritualistic insurance of success, Saul had bound the Israelites by an oath saying, "Cursed be anyone who eats food before evening comes, before I have avenged myself on my enemies!" (14:24). Here Saul takes the foolhardy action of making his army fast during a battle, risking his entire army for the sake of superstition. This behavior is typical of addicts, who frequently exhibit "obsessive tendencies" and take "foolhardy risks."[40]

The self-centered nature of Saul's vow is also informative ("avenged *myself* on *my* enemies") and contributes to his characterization. Twice later Saul mentions that he should be the subject of pity, berating his officers and servants saying "none of you is sorry for me (ואין־חלה מכם עלי)" (22:8) and later thanking the Ziphites who reported David's location to him saying "Yahweh bless you for your pity for me (חמלתם עלי)" (23:21). Why the tallest, best looking and most powerful man in Israel should be the subject of pity may not be obvious to others, but it seemed self-evident to the self-centered king.

Saul's superstition is again seen in his response to the Israelites eating meat with blood in it (14:32-33). After arranging a place for the people to slaughter their cattle, Saul proceeds to build an altar to Yahweh (1 Sam. 14:35). In keeping with the superstitious aspect of his character, Saul attempts to deal with his problems through the use of ritual. When this superstitious attempt fails, as Yahweh does not answer Saul's inquiry

---

38. Of course, instead of "bring the Ark" (הגישה ארון) the LXX reads "bring the ephod" (προσαγαγε το εφουδ), which may preserve the original reading (similar to David's request to the priest to "bring the ephod" [הגישה האפוד] before inquiring of the Lord in 1 Sam. 23:9).

39. Saul orders the priest to "withdraw your hand" (1 Sam. 14:19), likely meaning for the priest to withdraw his hand from the ephod. So David Toshio Tsumura, *The First Book of Samuel*, NICOT (Grand Rapids: Eerdmans, 2007), 366.

40. Ackerman and Puglisi, "Addictive."

(14:37) at the newly minted altar, Saul decides that it must be due to somebody's unknown sin. Therefore, he draws lots[41] to discover the culprit (14:41), invoking Yahweh's name in swearing that the guilty party must die—even if it is his own son (14:39). When the lot falls on Jonathan, Saul's superstitious characterization is again underscored as he utters another oath of self-imprecation, swearing that Jonathan be put to death (14:44).

Ironically, after committing publicly to his son's execution, the people reject Saul's leadership on this matter and "ransom" (14:45) Jonathan. (The reader might question whether the curse Saul uttered was then going to fall on Saul since he failed to execute Jonathan.) Initially, the people were following Saul loyally twice, saying, "Do whatever seems best to you" (14:36, 40). But now that the people have refused to execute Jonathan (14:45), Saul scraps his plan to pursue the Philistines (14:46)— who he had previously intended to chase all night long (14:36). Again, the king is surprisingly swayed by the dispositions of his subjects.

The Amalekite Affair

The subsequent scene (1 Sam. 15) provides a key text for Saul's characterization of low self-esteem and addiction to ritual. Saul is under divine orders to utterly destroy the Amalekites, including all people and animals (15:3). First, a sympathetic side of his characterization is underscored as Saul approaches the "city of the Amalek" and warns the Kenites who live there to leave before he attacks (15:6). This act shows a compassionate side to Saul's character once again, as seen earlier in his concern for the tears of the people who heard of the conquest of Jabesh-Gilead (11:5). After the Kenites evacuated, Saul led the attack and proceeded to "seize" the king of Amalek, Agag, but devoted the rest of the Amalekites to destruction (15:8).

Within this context of Saul's showing concern for the Kenites, it is interesting that Saul is said to "pity/spare" (ויחמל) Agag (15:9). There may be some purposeful ambiguity here. If we are to translate it as "pity," Saul's compassion comes to the fore again, though it is clearly misplaced. Did Saul pity Agag because he could relate to him *king to king* and felt sorry for the "burden" of kingship that Agag bore?[42] If we translate the word as "spared" we might understand this act as more about keeping the

---

41. Or uses the mysterious Urim and Thumin.
42. "With regard to the sparing of Agag", Exum doubts "we can second-guess Saul's intention" (*Tragedy and Biblical Narrative*, 160 n. 37).

enemy king alive as a prize—something to bolster the glory and honor of the victory (consistent with Saul's erecting a monument to himself in 15:12).[43] Regardless of what motivated Saul (or our choice of translation here) his actions are clearly in direct violation of God's command at the beginning of the chapter (15:3), where he is told not to "pity/spare" (לא תחמל) anyone. Thus, Saul is being negatively characterized here either way.

Saul also spared the best of the animals to use as sacrifices, again underscoring his obsession with superstitious ritual. Significantly, we are told that it was "Saul and the people" (15:9) who spared the Amalekite king and the animals. Saul later excuses his actions to Samuel because he was pressured by the people (15:24). Thus, Saul's disobedience here spawns from not only his superstitious penchant for ritual but also his susceptibility to peer pressure. In terms of a negative character trait one would call Saul "weak willed," as he is more comfortable following others than thinking for "himself."

When the prophet is sent to confront him, Samuel is told that Saul "has erected a monument for himself" (15:12). Given Saul's low self-esteem, his erecting a monument to honor himself might seem a bit out of character. However, lack of self-esteem can manifest in counterintuitive ways. Sometimes such a person displays overconfidence and boasting as a way of compensating for their lack of self-confidence—a defense mechanism of sorts. The person's insecurity leads to attempts to convince others of their worth (in this instance by erecting a monument to himself). His inordinate concern for being honored is underscored later in ch. 15, where instead of repenting of his sin, Saul requests that Saul "honor" him "before the elders of my people and before Israel" (15:30).[44]

In fact, it is in this context that the most explicit reference to Saul's low self-esteem is found as the prophet states: "You are small (קטן) in your own eyes" (15:17). Saul thought himself not worthy in the eyes of others, yet he desperately wanted their approval. This low view of himself meant a refusal to repent, lest Saul look bad in front of the people. In response to Saul's disobedience, the prophet equates Saul's rebellion to divination and idolatry (15:22-23). Remembering the warning to the king

---

43. Contra Exum, who does not "think this act helps us decide the issue of Saul's intentions" (ibid., 37).

44. As V. Philips Long comments, "The shift from 'forgive me' to honour me/ along with the other, more subtle alterations, captures the spirit of Saul's machinations in a way that could hardly have been achieved through straight exposition" (*The Reign and Rejection of King Saul: A Case for Literary and Theological Coherence* [Atlanta: Scholars Press, 1989], 38).

(and the people) about idolatry back in ch. 12:21, we can explicitly see its relevance for the king. The reader suspects that the prophet knew Saul's superstitious flaw beforehand.

When Samuel informs Saul that Yahweh has "torn" the kingship from him, he declares that God has given it to one of his "neighbors" (לרעך) who is "better than" him (הטוב ממך) (15:28). Given his self-esteem issues, this statement would have proved devastating but also rang true to Saul, and readers might suspect his irrational hatred of David owes to this comparison. Furthermore, Samuel's assertion of Saul's successor as "better" leads the reader to pay attention to Saul's character deficiencies.

The Evil Spirit

As the story proceeds, Saul's progression from low self-esteem to jealousy begins with Saul's envy of David's success, leading to resentment and irrational paranoia. Just as the coming of God's spirit (11:6) resulted in a transformation in Saul's character, now with the coming of the evil spirit (16:14) we see a dramatic change. From this point on we see an acceleration of Saul's negative characterization as he moves from weak-willed and superstitious, to defiant, cruel, and murderous. This evil spirit "terrifies" or "torments" (בעת) the king. Some have called this reference to an evil spirit as a "theological diagnosis" for Saul's presumably psychological "malady."[45] In the storyworld it would appear this tormenting exacerbated Saul's anxieties. Furthermore, being abandoned by both God's prophet (15:35) and God's spirit (16:14) lead to Saul's further reliance upon superstition for his much-needed affirmation.

A New Addiction

After David comes into the picture, first to exorcize Saul's demons (16:23), then to defeat the giant whom Saul refused to fight (ch. 17), Saul's self-esteem does not improve. His need for approval manifests in his jealousy when the Israelite women praise David alongside Saul for their military victories (18:7). Irrationally, he equates such praise as indicating that David is a step away from dethroning him (18:8). Saul attempts to murder David both by his own hand (18:11) and by sending him into harm's way in battle (18:13). Saul's obsession with David's demise becomes a new addiction for the king. The addictive nature of his obsession with David negatively affects Saul's interactions with his family. When having David fight with the army fails to result in his demise, Saul leads David to risk his

---

45. Klein, *1 Samuel*, 165.

life further in battles in order to acquire a bride price for Saul's daughters (18:17, 25). In this stratagem Saul shows himself willing to disregard the feelings and desires of his children (son and daughters) in order to achieve his goals. Addicts frequently end up "resenting family and friends who try to intervene,"[46] and Saul is no different. His son, Jonathan, attempted to convince Saul that David was innocent (19:4-5), but Saul resented him for it, and turned on him, vulgarly insulting his mother (1 Sam. 20:30) and impulsively throwing a spear at his own son (20:33).[47]

Addicts frequently become paranoid and feel alienated.[48] Saul displays classic paranoia with David, who is suspected of treason, despite his faithful service. Saul's paranoia was not limited only to David. Saul accused his children, loyal servants, and even priests of conspiring to kill him (22:8). Saul's paranoia led him to have all the priests of Nob slaughtered. With this act, the qualities that earlier made Saul a sympathetic character have disappeared. In contrast to Saul's earlier actions of granting amnesty to those who had opposed him (11:12-13), Saul now retaliates. In his paranoia Saul thought the priests were conspiring to help David kill the king (1 Sam. 22:13). Saul's paranoia is so strong that we see another change in his character at this point. While in the past Saul often followed the lead of his subjects when they refused an order (e.g. 14:45), now, when his servants refused to kill the priests, Saul orders Doeg the Edomite to do so (22:18). Shockingly, while Saul earlier failed to implement the ban on Amalek (15:3), he now does so against the priests and their town, killing "its men and women, its children and infants, and its cattle, donkeys and sheep" (22:19). Any attempt to absolve Saul of

---

46. Ackerman and Puglisi, "Addictive."

47. Of course, some think Saul's outburst regarding his wife, Ahinoam, may be explained by David's having taken her as his wife, since one of David's wives later has the same name (2 Sam. 2:2). E.g. J. D. Levenson, "1 Samuel 25 as Literature and as History," *CBQ* 40 (1978): 11–28; Levenson and Halpern, "Political Import of David's Marriages," *JBL* 99 (1980): 507–18. While identifying David's wife Ahinoam as Saul's wife is suggestive and might suggest a literal interpretation of Nathan's remarks to David about God giving him his "master's wives" into his hands (2 Sam. 12:7-8), the fact David's wife is consistently referred to as Ahinoam of Jezreel (1 Sam. 25:43; 27:3; 30:5; 2 Sam. 2:2; 3:2) and Saul's wife is referred to as "daughter of Ahimaaz" (1 Sam. 14:50) seems to indicate they are distinct characters in the story. I have dealt with Levenson and Halpern's arguments regarding the identity of David's wives more fully in a forthcoming essay "All in the Family of David: The Chronicler's Change from the Ammonite (2 Sam. 17:25) to the Davidic Zeruiah (1 Chr 2:16)," in *Community: Biblical and Theological Reflections in Honour of August H. Konkel*, ed. Rick Wadholm, Jr. (McMaster Divinity College Press, forthcoming).

48. Ackerman and Puglisi, "Addictive."

blame in his downfall must account for this murderous undertaking.⁴⁹ After this deplorable act it is no wonder Samuel later declares to Saul that "Yahweh has become your enemy" (28:16).

Denial is a hallmark of addiction. Despite Saul hearing repeatedly from Samuel that God was against him, Saul lived in denial. This can be clearly seen in the scene where Saul is told of David's location and he says, "God has given him into my hand..." (1 Sam. 23:7). Despite all evidence to the contrary, Saul was in denial about God's disposition toward him. In Saul's skewed view, God was on his side.⁵⁰

Addicts fail to live up to their responsibilities. As time goes on, Saul goes all-out in his pursuit of David, taking 3,000 men (1 Sam. 24:2; 26:2) to pursue David's 600 (an obvious misappropriation of resources) and disregarding his royal responsibility to secure Israel. This disregard comes to the fore when the Philistines attack (23:27) while Saul is closing in on David, forcing Saul to abandon his obsession temporarily (23:28).

Saul's addiction leads to mental instability as seen in his obsessive pursuit of David. When David spares his life in the cave (ch. 24), Saul is remorseful and weeps aloud (24:16), praising and blessing David. Yet Saul continues the pursuit shortly after (ch. 26). As Alter writes, this "underlines the compulsive character of his obsession with David. Whatever his avowed good intentions, Saul cannot restrain his impulse to destroy his rival."⁵¹ His instability is underscored again when David spares his life a second time, as Saul is repentant (26:21), and he blesses David (26:25), inviting David to return home with him (26:21) and promising not to harm him. Despite Saul's claims to no longer pursue David, the narrator says that Saul only stopped pursuing David when he heard David had fled to Philistia (27:4).⁵²

---

49. As noted, Gunn (*The Fate of King Saul*, 87) accentuates Yahweh's culpability in Saul's demise, but he glosses over this incident, merely noting that "it is hard to retain any sympathy for Saul in this scene, there is yet a certain pathos about it."

50. Another hint at denial may be present in 15:13 when Saul claims "I have carried out Yahweh's command" to Samuel after sparing Agag and the Amalekite animals. Did Saul's addiction to ritual (sacrificing the animals instead of destroying them) so deceive him that he was in denial about his disobedience to God's command? John Mauchline speculated that Saul's assertion to Samuel "reveals a lack of awareness that he had done wrong" (*1 and 2 Samuel* [London: Oliphants, 1971], 124).

51. Alter, *The David Story*, 163.

52. The reader might suspect that Saul's actions in both stories reveal a guilty conscience. Yet it is unclear whether this is the case. After all, following his disobedience with the Amalekite affair the narrator notes that Samuel is grieved over Saul's disobedience, and that Yahweh feels regret (15:35), but Saul is never said to be sorrowful, neither does he display any obvious regret.

Fatally Addicted

Saul's addiction and life of denial continues in the final pericope of his story. With imminent battle with the Philistines looming, Saul wanted to ensure his success through obtaining a divine oracle or sign, but Yahweh did not answer him (28:6). Despite a consistent word from Samuel that he was rejected, Saul risks everything (crossing enemy lines as Endor was north of Shunem, on the other side of the Philistine army) to get a post-mortem audience with the prophet by consulting a medium.

Ironically, Saul himself had expelled the mediums from the land (28:3). Given his quick turn to employ the services of those he expelled, one suspects Saul only deported said diviners under pressure from others—in keeping with his character thus far (giving in to peer pressure). The fact that his servants so quickly can point to a nearby medium also reflects poorly on the king, since it suggests Saul did a poor job of ridding the land of diviners.[53]

In his visit with the medium, it is revealed he had not eaten "all day and all night" (28:20). Another common symptom of addiction is "poor appetite or poor nutrition,"[54] but the reader suspects that Saul was fasting in hopes to gain supernatural insights or favor. After receiving a predictably negative word from Samuel's ghost, the medium urges Saul to eat (28:22), but he refuses (28:23a). In keeping with his original characterization that was so quick to follow the lead of others, Saul is quickly persuaded by the medium and his servants to eat (28:23b).

Saul's last moments come during battle with Philistia, and again his flaws come to the fore. First, his paranoia rises again in that Saul thinks the Philistines are about to capture him (31:4). While this fear seems quite legitimate, Saul is actually *not* found by the Philistines *until the next day* (31:8). Saul's concern with his reputation and his need to be honored also comes to the fore in his final moments. Despite the sympathy with which one might view Saul's suicide, its presentation here does not reflect well on the fallen king. Though some have viewed it as brave or noble,[55] there is little evidence to suggest it was viewed this way in ancient Israel.

---

53. As Hildebrandt observes, Saul's request "leads to a re-evaluation of the efficacy of his cleansing—after all, it implies that there are still mediums in the country and that people know where they are to be found." Samuel Hildebrandt, "The Servants of Saul: 'Minor' Characters and Royal Commentary in 1 Samuel 9–31," *JSOT* 40 (2015): 194.

54. Ackerman and Puglisi, "Addictive."

55. E.g. Humphreys writes, "In death Saul attains a stature that escaped him in life. He assumes some control over his fate by knowingly confronting it" ("Tragedy of King Saul," 24).

After all, when Job suffered so intensely, suicide is never brought up as an option either by Job or his friends.[56] Therefore, from an Israelite perspective, Saul's suicide continues his negative character arc to the end. In fact, the suicide again shows Saul's "concern for his 'image.'"[57] The stated reason that Saul wants to die before the Philistines get to him is his fear they would "make sport of me" (31:4). Saul was so concerned about his image that he could not bear to be humiliated and made the object of scorn. Saul's concern with his honor is in keeping with ancient Mesopotamian thought on suicide, which was primarily viewed "as a means of retrieving honor."[58] Ironically, Saul's suicide did not prevent the Philistines from making "sport" of him, as his head, body, and armor were all used to this end (31:9-10).

The conclusion to the Saul story is sympathetic to the now-dead king, with the people of Jabesh Gilead retrieving the bodies of Saul and his sons. Reference here to Jabesh Gilead leads the reader to recall the high point of Saul's kingship (1 Sam. 11), thus creating a sympathetic conclusion to the narrative, as "Saul is dignified in death by the remembrance of his moment of glory."[59] Conversely, remembering his glory puts into relief the dark depths to which Saul had sunk.

Conclusion

This analysis of Saul's characterization has shown that the seeds of Saul's self-destruction were present from the beginning of his narrative. The king's low self-esteem led to his insecurity, weak will, jealousy, paranoia, instability, and addictions, which resulted in his defiance of the prophetic word, refusal to repent, and outright rebellion against Yahweh. Saul's negative character arc provides a foil[60] for viewing David as "better" than him—a theme of the larger narrative. From the heights of the deliverance of Jabesh Gilead to his death on Gilboa, Saul's story is tragic as we watch the son of Kish flirt with greatness only to crash and burn. The one who

---

56. Polzin, *Samuel and the Deuteronomist*, 271 n. 16.

57. Edwin M. Good, *Irony in the Old Testament* (Philadelphia: Westminster, 1965), 78.

58. Jo Ann Scurlock, "Death and the Afterlife in Ancient Mesopotamian Thought," in *Civilizations of the Ancient Near East* (New York: Charles Scribner's Sons, 1995), 1890.

59. Francesca Aran Murphy, *1 Samuel*, BTCB (Grand Rapids: Brazos, 2010), 284.

60. John Van Seters, *In Search of History: Historiography in the Ancient World and the Origins of Biblical History* (New Haven: Yale University Press, 1983), 259–60.

was a head taller than anyone in Israel (10:23) is eventually relieved of his head by the Philistines (31:9). As tragic as Saul's story is, it is also captivating. As Gerke has commented: "There's something fascinating about watching people make choices and live with the fallout. Perhaps that is why we read fiction."[61] Perhaps this is what makes Saul's story enduringly compelling.

---

61. Gerke, *Plot Versus Fiction*, 152.

Chapter 8

DAVID: KALEIDOSCOPE OF A KING[*]

Keith Bodner and Benjamin J. M. Johnson

Introduction

In his aptly titled, *David's Secret Demons*, Baruch Halpern writes, "David, in a word, is human, fully, four-dimensionally, recognizably human. He grows, he learns, he travails, he triumphs, and he suffers immeasurable tragedy and loss. He is the first human being in world literature."[1] Similarly, Robert Alter claims, "The story of David is probably the greatest single narrative representation in antiquity of a human life evolving by slow stages through time, shaped and altered by the pressures of political life, public institutions, family, the impulses of body and spirit, the eventual sad decay of the flesh."[2] Superlatives abound when it comes to talking about the character of David. However, the range of interpretations of this character are immense. Put another way, "As certain modern writers have observed, he is a symbol of the complexity and ambiguity of human experience itself."[3] Some of this complexity and ambiguity is certainly due to the character of David himself, some of it is also likely due to us as readers.

[*] Our thanks to David Firth, David Shepherd, James Patrick, and Rachelle Gilmour for their helpful comments and suggestions on this essay.

1. Baruch Halpern, *David's Secret Demons: Messiah, Murderer, Traitor, King* (Grand Rapids: Eerdmans, 2001), 6.

2. Robert Alter, *The David Story: A Translation with Commentary of 1 and 2 Samuel* (New York: W. W. Norton & Co., 1999), ix.

3. Raymond-Jean Frontain and Jan Wojcik, "Introduction: Transformations of the Myth of David," in *The David Myth in Western Literature*, ed. Raymond-Jean Frontain and Jan Wojcik (West Lafayette: Purdue University Press, 1980), 5.

In their work on biblical interpretation, Robert Morgan and John Barton write that "Texts, like dead men and women, have no rights, no aims, no interests. They can be used in whatever way readers or interpreters choose."[4] Of course, readers often choose to attempt to come to grips with the "so-called" authorial intent of a text. The point Morgan and Barton make is that it is the reader's decision to do so. It is commonplace now to recognize the importance of readers' perspectives in biblical interpretation, and though there may be disagreements about how much freedom and authority a reader has to create meaning, most recognize that readers play an active role in the interpretive process.[5] That reality is no less true when it comes to the character of David. As we will argue in this essay, the biblical portrayal of David can perhaps best be perceived as something of a kaleidoscope in that it changes shape depending on how one holds the textual lens. The David the reader sees will depend on the decisions about what one is willing to look at and what questions one is willing to entertain. Are we interested in the David of Samuel or Chronicles or Psalms? Are we interested in the David of history or of the text? Are we interested in the text as it stands or the possibility of layers within the text? Do we trust the text or do we not? And while it seems certain that the text constrains our interpretation of David so that he may not mean just *anything*, it also seems clear that to many and various different readers he does in fact mean *many things*.

David and History

One of the possible twists of the kaleidoscope is to focus the lens on the David of history. The range of views on the David history span from general trust in the historical reliability of the biblical story, to trust of the historical reliability of the biblical story when read as propaganda, to distrust that we can even say there was a David of history.[6] For those

---

4. Robert Morgan with John Barton, *Biblical Interpretation*, Oxford Bible Series (Oxford: Oxford University Press, 1988), 7.

5. See, for example, David M. Gunn and Danna Nolan Fewell, *Narrative in the Hebrew Bible*, Oxford Bible Series (Oxford: Oxford University Press, 1993), Chapter 9, for a relatively active role for readers in approaching Hebrew narrative. One of the best detailed discussions of the role of the reader in biblical interpretation is Kevin J. Vanhoozer, *Is There a Meaning in This Text? The Bible, the Reader, and the Morality of Literary Knowledge* (Grand Rapids: Zondervan, 1998). His suggested model for the reader is as an active yet subservient disciple of the text.

6. For a survey of some historical issues and various opinions on the historicity of the story of David see Benjamin J. M. Johnson, "Israel At the Time of the United

that are interested in seeking the David of history, a common reading strategy is to view the story of David in the book of Samuel as an ancient apology.[7] The assumption in this reading strategy is that, as an example of an ancient apology, the biblical story of David in the book of Samuel is offering the best possible spin on the character of David. Thus, for example, in 1 Samuel 25, the text is clear to point out that Abigail kept David from incurring blood-guilt by slaughtering Nabal and all his men and instead God himself struck down Nabal. Those who understand the book of Samuel as a piece of ancient apology read this passage and suggest that the one thing we know for sure is that David assassinated Nabal and took his wealth and his wife.[8]

The portrait of David that is painted utilizing this reading strategy is not a positive one. As Joel Baden has so aptly put it in his recent attempt at sketching a historical David, "David was a successful monarch, but he was a vile human being."[9] Those that utilize this twist of the kaleidoscope find a historically plausible David as Steven McKenzie concludes his portrait: "The fact is we can never know for certain what actually happened in David's lifetime. We can only make an educated guess… Our biography of David, therefore, is not an exact recounting of history but is rather, to borrow another scholar's title, a plausible tale."[10] While attempts at reconstructing the historical David certainly look through the David of

---

Monarchy: David and Solomon," in *The Biblical World*, ed. Katharine Dell (Oxford: Routledge, forthcoming). A good sampling of various perspectives would include, Philip R. Davies, *In Search of "Ancient Israel": A Study in Biblical Origins* (Sheffield: Sheffield Academic, 1992); Steven L. McKenzie, *King David: A Biography* (New York: Oxford University Press, 2000); and Iain Provan, V. Philips Long, and Tremper Longman III, *A Biblical History of Israel* (Louisville: Westminster John Knox, 2015).

7. See the earlier work of Lemche and McCarter: Niels Peter Lemche "David's Rise," *JSOT* 10 (1979): 2–25; P. Kyle McCarter, Jr., "The Apology of David," *JBL* 99, no. 4 (1980): 489–504; idem, "The Historical David," *Int* 40, no. 2 (1986): 117–29. The most recent work along this line is Andrew Knapp, *Royal Apologetic in the Ancient Near East*, Writings from the Ancient World (Atlanta: SBL, 2015). For a critique of the "apology" view see J. Randall Short, *The Surprising Election and Confirmation of King David*, HTS 63 (Cambridge, MA: Harvard University Press, 2010).

8. For examples of this reading see Steven L. McKenzie, *King David: A Biography* (New York: Oxford University Press, 2000); Halpern, *David's Secret Demons*; and more recently Joel S. Baden, *The Historical David: The Real Life of an Invented Hero* (New York: HarperOne, 2013). For a critical assessment of this reading strategy see Steven Weitzman, "King David's Spin Doctors," *Prooftexts* 23, no. 3 (2003): 365–76.

9. Baden, *The Historical David*, 259.

10. McKenzie, *King David*, 186.

the text to try to ascertain the David of history, nevertheless, they do not ignore the text. As McKenzie notes, "In a sense, this biography is truer to the Bible than the more traditional images of David… The Bible never denies or downplays David's humanity."[11]

David: Narrative Critical Readings

While we might be interested in looking through the biblical narrative to try to see back to the David of history, another possible twist of the lens would be to try to interpret the literary portrayal that we find in the text of the book of Samuel itself. Attending to the text as it stands is in many ways not novel; however, there has been a distinct move toward literary readings in the last half century.[12] Interestingly, those whose primary interest is the text as it stands find in the text nearly diametrically opposed readings of the character of David.

David, a Man after His Own Heart: Critical Readings

Most traditional religious readings of David, both Jewish and Christian, have seen David as a character worthy of praise and emulation (for the most part). He is said to be a man after God's own heart after all (1 Sam. 13:14).[13] However, the turn toward literary readings of the final form of the text coincided with a growing number of readings that were less-than-glowing of David.

One of the earlier and ground-breaking examples of this tactic was the work of David M. Gunn.[14] This reading strategy does not see apology or propaganda in the text of Samuel but rather a sophisticated literary presentation that is far from overly positive about the character of David. In this view the book of Samuel "is the work of no propagandist pamphleteer nor moralizing teacher: the vision is artistic, the author, above all, a

---

11. Ibid., 189.

12. For a survey see Stephen D. Moore, "Biblical Narrative Analysis from the New Criticism to the New Narratology," in *The Oxford Handbook of Biblical Narrative*, ed. Danna Nolan Fewell (Oxford: Oxford University Press, 2016), 27–50.

13. On the complexity of that verse see the discussion in Benjamin J. M. Johnson, "The Heart of Yhwh's Chosen One in 1 Samuel," *JBL* 131, no. 3 (2012): 455–66; George Athas, "'A Man After God's Own Heart': David and the Rhetoric of Election to Kingship," *JESOT* 2, no. 2 (2013): 191–8; and Jason S. DeRouchie, "The Heart of Yhwh and His Chosen One in 1 Samuel 13:14," *BBR* 24, no. 4 (2014): 467–89.

14. David M. Gunn, *The Story of King David: Genre and Interpretation*, JSOTSup 6 (Sheffield: JSOT Press, 1978); idem, *The Fate of King Saul: An Interpretation of a Biblical Story*, JSOTSup 14 (Sheffield: JSOT Press, 1980).

fine teller of tales."[15] An example of this reading strategy can be seen in David's lament for Abner in 2 Samuel 3. On one level, the text narrates David's innocence in the death of Abner and his lament for a "great man" in Israel (2 Sam. 3:31-39) so that we know that David "had no part in the killing of Abner son of Ner" (2 Sam. 3:37).[16] So surely David is innocent, right? Well, a close reading of this text may suggest that the answer to that question might not be as straightforward as it seems on the surface. First, it is sometimes noted that David's lament for Abner and his claim that a "great man" has fallen in Israel seems suspiciously to be "only for public consumption."[17] Second, the seemingly confirming statement that all Israel knew of David's innocence (2 Sam. 3:37) may not fully confirm David's innocence, for it is entirely possible to read this as a confirmation that the people have been convinced (or possibly duped!) without confirming that the narrator assumes David's innocence. The narrator may in fact even being drawing some distance between his view and the view of "all the people."[18]

Another example that might highlight this reading strategy is David's first spoken words in 1 Sam. 17:26.[19] After hearing Goliath's challenge, David inquires: "What shall be done for the man who kills this Philistine, and takes away the reproach from Israel? For who is this uncircumcised Philistine that he should defy the armies of the living God?" (1 Sam. 17:26). According to Robert Alter, in biblical narrative, a character's first words are often "a defining moment of characterization."[20] A number of scholars have noted the potentially negative way that David is characterized by his opening speech. Marti Steussy argues, for example, that David "has one eye on God, but the other watches greedily for reward (17:26)."[21] Alter, in commenting on David's opening words, suggests that "The inquiry about personal profit is then immediately balanced (or

---

15. Gunn, *Story of King David*, 111.
16. Unless otherwise noted, all translations are NRSV.
17. Gunn, *Story of King David*, 96.
18. See Robert Polzin, *David and the Deuteronomist: A Literary Study of the Deuteronomic History: Part 3: 2 Samuel* (Bloomington: Indiana University Press, 1993), 40–1. Keith Bodner, *David Observed: A King in the Eyes of His Court*, HBM 5 (Sheffield: Sheffield Phoenix, 2005), 38–66, has argued that this looks like a case of what Russian literary theorist Mikhail Bakhtin called "pseudo-objective motivation."
19. Of course, David's first words in the shorter LXX^B text would be in 1 Sam. 17:32, which would make for an interestingly nuanced characterization.
20. Alter, *The David Story*, 105.
21. Marti J. Steussy, *David: Biblical Portraits of Power* (Columbia: University of South Carolina Press, 1999), 4.

covered up) by the patriotic pronouncement."[22] In this reading, David, in other words, may have a veneer or at least modicum of piety and patriotism, but what likely motivates him is his ambition. What readings that utilize this strategy show is that the text allows for and may even suggest a predominantly negative portrayal of David.

A Man after God's Own Heart: Affirmative Readings

Not every narrative critical reading of David's story sees him in a predominantly negative light. A number of readings of David suggest that with the right twist of the lens a more positive characterization of this biblical hero is possible. Paul Borgman, a professor of English literature, turned his literary eye on the David story and suggested that attentiveness to patterns of repetition in the David story unlocks the "defining clues of what makes David a mystery, but also what unfolds as a resolution to that mystery."[23] David, for Borgman, is a complex character. He is flawed, but, unlike Saul, not tragically so.[24] Another way to twist the lens along these lines would be to follow the lead of Stephen Chapman, whose work is attentive to the literary *and theological* nature of the book of Samuel, in offering a distinctly Christian reading of 1 Samuel. In Chapman's reading with the grain of the text he suggests that while David is certainly complex and far from perfect, he nevertheless possesses an "innately spiritual orientation…[which] leads him consistently to seek God's guidance and forgiveness, even when he succumbs to the worldly temptations that surround him."[25] By giving space to the specifically theological issues present in the text, Chapman allows for some level of positive characterization for David. In a forthcoming work, Benjamin Johnson has argued that if the reader takes seriously the text's claim that there is something positive about David's heart (1 Sam. 13:14; 16:7), then there is a possibility to see him in at least a partially positive light.[26] If we read through the lens of the handful of references to David's heart we can see him positively compared to Saul who is disobedient (1 Sam. 13:14) and fearful (1 Sam. 17:32). We can see that he has a heart that is able to be convicted of wrongdoing (1 Sam. 24:5; 25:31; 2 Sam. 24:10)

22. Alter, *The David Story*, 105.
23. Paul Borgman, *David, Saul, & God: Rediscovering an Ancient Story* (New York: Oxford University Press, 2008), 6.
24. Ibid., 7.
25. Stephen B. Chapman, *1 Samuel as Christian Scripture: A Theological Commentary* (Grand Rapids: Eerdmans, 2016), 237.
26. Benjamin J. M. Johnson, *David: A Man after God's Own Heart*, Cascade Companions (Eugene: Cascade, forthcoming).

and that he has a heart that is willing to be aligned or realigned with God's (2 Sam. 7:3, 27).

It needs to be said that the division between what we have termed "critical readings" and "affirmative readings" is largely artificial. Such is the beautifully complicated character of David that few readings find him either entirely praiseworthy or utterly irredeemable. Instead, our binary division is just a helpful heuristic to see various emphases in different literary analyses of David's character. A good example of the non-binary nature of literary studies on David is the recent work of Barbara Green.[27] Her study, which is subtitled a literary-hermeneutical study, recognizes the importance of the range of lenses that a reader may utilize when accessing the David story. On the one hand, she fits our "critical reading" category. This can be seen by her suspicion of the narrator's comment concerning David's innocence in the death of Abner. She writes: "Is it at odds with the portraiture of the implied author for us to credit that *everyone* is pleased with *everything* that David did? I find it a suspicious statement."[28] On the other hand, the basis of her study is a wager, as she terms it, "that David can be shown as a flawed human being with deep moments of turning toward God and as demonstrating compassion while often falling short of that capacity,"[29] suggesting she perhaps fits with our "affirmative reading" category. Perhaps it is not surprising that readings of David's character resist easy categorization. After all, what all this variability in the analysis of David shows is that he is a character that resists easy categorization.

Which David? What Text?

What the previous section showed was that the presentation of David in the text has led interpreters to argue for a range of characterizations for this enigmatic character. What was consistent about the scholars and approaches surveyed above was the decision to interpret the text as a whole. That tendency has not been the predominant strategy of biblical interpretation historically. Furthermore, the character of David is such that it has led scholars to see in the text various traditions that had various perspectives on him.[30] Two interesting attempts along these lines are

---

27. Barbara Green, *David's Capacity for Compassion: A Literary-Hermeneutical Study of 1–2 Samuel*, LHBOTS 641 (London: Bloomsbury T&T Clark, 2017).

28. Ibid., 144.

29. Ibid., 32.

30. See Timo Veijola, *Die ewige Dynastie: David und die Entstehung seiner Dynastie nach der deuteronomistischen Darstellunmg*, AASF Series B 193 (Helsinki: Suomalainen Tiedeakatemia, 1975); and idem, *Das Königtum in der Beurteilung der*

the work of K. L. Noll and John Van Seters.[31] Noll's contribution to the study of David is in his attempt to read the narrative as a whole and to come up with a literary reason for the disparate presentation of David in 1–2 Samuel. His working hypothesis begins with the literary insight that differentiates the implied author from the narrator. He suggests that "The degree of complexity in David's character is partially the result of the dual presentation of him; the narrator presents David one way, the implied author, while not completely undermining that characterization, deepens it, rounds it, presents David as more human, more opaque."[32]

For Noll the varying perspectives on David are due to different voices within a unified text. For John Van Seters the seemingly contradictory presentation of David is due to two traditions within the David story. Van Seters's solution to the complexity of the portrayal of David is to suggest that there are

> two extensive and competing presentations of David that extend from the beginning of David's career under Saul to the succession to David's throne by Solomon. These two narratives are obviously contradictory in the sense that one idealizes David as the model king for all future monarchs, as embodied in the ideology of the messiah, Yahweh's anointed and chosen king, and the other regards both David's rise to the throne and the manner of his reign as typical of oriental despots and hardly a fitting model for a just society.[33]

While Van Seters's proposal of multiple textual traditions within the book of Samuel is far from unique,[34] his contribution is unique in the dialogue that he sees as occurring between the two. In Van Seters's view, the more critical *David Saga* is meant to undermine the more positive presentation of David in the Deuteronomist's work. What these reading strategies suggest is that the complex portraiture of David need not be held artificially together, but instead the various presentations of him need

---

deuteronomistischen Historiographie: Eine redaktionsgeschichtliche Untersuchung, AASF B198 (Helsinki: Suomalainen Tiedeakatemia, 1977) for earlier analysis of the pro- and anti-monarchic and in turn Davidic tendencies in the book of Samuel.

31. K. L. Noll, *The Faces of David*, JSOTSup 242 (Sheffield: Sheffield Academic, 1997); John Van Seters, *The Biblical Saga of King David* (Winona Lake: Eisenbrauns, 2009).

32. Noll, *Faces of David*, 39.

33. Van Seters, *Biblical Saga*, 1.

34. For a detailed discussion of redactional theories, see Jeremy M. Hutton, *The Transjordanian Palimpsest: The Overwritten Texts of Personal Exile and Transformation in the Deuteronomistic History*, BZAW 396 (Berlin: de Gruyter, 2009). Van Seters himself includes a lengthy discussion of precursors to his own study (*Biblical Saga*, 3–34).

to be allowed to have their own voice. Our job is to understand how they work together or communicate to each other.[35] Whether or not one agrees with these two strategies, they highlight the complexity of the character of David and offer two ways of dealing with that complexity.

Characters around David

What if we twist the lens such that instead of focusing on David, it brings other characters into focus? A number of scholars have highlighted what we can learn about the characterization of David by paying attention to the characters that swirl around him.[36] One interesting recent contribution along these lines is the work of April Westbrook who has argued that the stories of women surrounding David offer significant characterization of him. After surveying the stories of Abigail, Michal, Bathsheba, Tamar, the wise woman of Tekoa, the ten women left behind when David flees Jerusalem, and Rizpah, Westbrook concludes that "Again, and again, the woman stories in the David narrative call into doubt the ability of the monarchy to do justice by highlighting David's questionable acts. Though David may have bright moments in the narrative overall, no woman story presents him in a singularly positive light."[37] What this study and others like it show is the risk that tunnel-visioned focus on David may have. Ironically, by letting David fade into the background he may come into greater focus.

A Type of Repentance: David in Chronicles[38]

So far in our survey of diverse twists of the lens of the kaleidoscope of David, we have focused on the varying presentations of him in the book

---

35. In this sense we are reminded of Walter Brueggemann's earlier work on David, *David's Truth in Israel's Imagination and Memory* (Minneapolis: Fortress, 1985).

36. See Bodner, *David Observed*; and Cephas T. A. Tushima, *The Fate of Saul's Progeny in the Reign of David* (Cambridge: James Clarke & Co., 2011). See also the contribution of David Firth in the present volume.

37. April D. Westbrook, *"And He Will Take Your Daughters..." Woman Story and the Ethical Evaluation of Monarchy in the David Narrative*, LHBOTS 610 (London: Bloomsbury T&T Clark, 2015), 227. Westbrook uses the term "woman story" as a technical term for a pattern that develops in each episode that features David's dealings with prominent women.

38. This and the following section are adapted and developed from Keith Bodner, "David: The Anointed Israelite," in *Sources of the Christian Self: A Cultural History of Christian Identity*, ed. James M. Houston and Jens Zimmerman (Grand Rapids: Eerdmans, 2018), 36–53.

of Samuel, a fitting choice for a book on characterization in Samuel. However, the character of David in Samuel exists always within the canonical work of the Hebrew Bible, in conversation with the character of David in the book of Chronicles.[39] The character of David in Samuel has always garnered more interest than the character of David in Chronicles. Why this is so was hinted at already by Julius Wellhausen in his influential *Prolegomena*: "See what Chronicles has made out of David! The founder of the kingdom has become the founder of the temple and the public worship, the king and hero at the head of his companions in arms has become the singer and master of ceremonies at the head of a swarm of priests and Levites; his clear cut figure has become a feeble holy picture, seen through a cloud of incense."[40] Despite the dismissive posture of Wellhausen and those who followed in his wake, in recent times Chronicles has been reevaluated much more positively for its literary, historical, and theological richness. Thus, if we allow a twist of the lens that includes Samuel and Chronicles an additionally complex picture of David can be offered.

David is uniquely profiled in 1 Chronicles, and despite the more positive characterization, the king is configured as the archetypal repentant sinner. Readers have long noticed some startling omissions in the story when compared with the Former Prophets: there is no protracted civil war with the house of Saul, the debacle with Bathsheba and Uriah's murder is essentially elided, and instead of the deadly succession struggle between Adonijah and Solomon there is a smooth and bloodless transition set in motion as early as 1 Chron. 22:5. If David is essentially an absent father in 2 Samuel, he is a sage guide and mentor in Chronicles. Rather than the

---

39. The dominant scholarly view remains that the book of Chronicles utilized a version of Samuel-Kings in its composition. However, some recent scholars have argued that Chronicles, rather than being based on Samuel-Kings, is actually a contemporary competing history that is based on the same source(s) as Samuel-Kings. For an articulation of the dominant view see Sara Japhet, *I & II Chronicles: A Commentary*, OTL (Louisville: Westminster John Knox, 1993). For recent arguments for Chronicles as a contemporary of Samuel-Kings see A. Graeme Auld, *Kings without Privilege: David and Moses in the Story of the Bible's Kings* (Edinburgh: T. & T. Clark, 1994); and Raymond F. Person, Jr., *The Deuteronomistic History and the Book of Chronicles: Scribal Works in an Oral World*, AIL 6 (Atlanta: SBL, 2010).

40. Julius Wellhausen, *Prolegomena to the History of Israel*, trans. J. S. Black and A. Menzies (Edinburgh: Black, 1885), 182, cited in Mark J. Boda, "Gazing through the Cloud of Incense: Davidic Dynasty and Temple Community in the Chronicler's Perspective," in *Chronicling the Chronicler: The Book of Chronicles and Early Second Temple Historiography*, ed. Tyler F. Williams and Paul S. Evans (Winona Lake: Eisenbrauns, 2013), 215.

sphere of human machination receiving extensive attention, other aspects of David's reign and legacy are highlighted, and there is a concentrated focus on matters relating to the temple or Israel's worship, in keeping with the theme of Chronicles as essentially a biography of the temple: the spatial center of Israel's worship. David emerges from the text as the leader of the nation's chorus of praise and founding father of the temple's schematics.

As one comparative example, consider the Chronicler's treatment of the conquest of Jerusalem. The parallel text in 2 Sam. 5:6 reads, "The king and his men marched to Jerusalem against the Jebusites, the inhabitants of the land," whereas in 1 Chron. 11:4 we read, "David and all Israel marched to Jerusalem, that is Jebus, where the Jebusites were, the inhabitants of the land." The reader straightaway observes that the capturing of Jerusalem—the urban center of the story for the rest of the Chronicler's narrative—is a corporate undertaking of considerable proportion. In 2 Sam. 5:6 it is the king *and his men* who march against the city, meaning David and his personal militia (a group of figures presumably from Judah who are distressed and in debt, according to 2 Sam. 22:2). By contrast, in Chronicles it is a unified and national effort involving all the tribes, and not only Judah. Moreover, this collective takeover of Jerusalem is David's first action as king in Chronicles, and it is much less the acquisition of a personal throne and more the procurement of a national capital.[41] The value of this kind of comparison is that the major and differing emphases of the Chronicler and author of Samuel can be discerned, not least the compelling vision of the identity of God's people in Chronicles versus the more personal portrayal of David and his achievements in Samuel.

While it is true that David's catastrophic failings of 2 Samuel 11 are not detailed in Chronicles, the "census narrative" certainly appears to be afforded a prominent position in 1 Chronicles 21, which departs in various ways from its parallel in 2 Samuel 24.[42] Indeed, in the context of

---

41. Steven L. McKenzie, *1–2 Chronicles*, AOTC (Nashville: Abingdon, 2004), 124. There may also be a further contrast with Saul's aborted kingship in this episode: in 1 Chron. 10:7 the Philistines (first mentioned in 1 Chron. 1:12 as a potentially dangerous group) occupy Israelite cities vacated in the wake of Saul's death, but now David occupies the city of the dislodged Jebusites, also mentioned among the nations of 1 Chron. 1:14 (see John Jarick, *1 Chronicles*, Readings [London: Sheffield Academic, 2002], 86). Consequently, David's kingship is presented as the paradigm in the Chronicler's narrative.

42. For a helpful survey of the differences in these two accounts see Ralph W. Klein, "David: Sinner and Saint in Samuel and Chronicles," *CTM* 31, no. 4 (2004): 274–81.

David's career in Samuel-Kings the census narrative is attached as part of a concluding and dischronologized appendix to David's reign,[43] whereas the Chronicler includes it as a central episode in the story.

As one leading scholar summarizes in relation to Chronicles, "The stress on Davidic responsibility may be understood in the context of a larger movement characterized by wrongdoing, confession, intercession, renewed obedience, and divine blessing. The story of the census, plague, and establishment of a permanent altar underscores the highly positive consequences of David's ability to confront and manage his own failure."[44] David's career in Chronicles, it could be argued, is typologically configured to provide a portrait of the king as exemplar of a repentant sinner, because in "the context of a national disaster of his own making, David is able to turn that catastrophe into the occasion for a permanent divine blessing upon Israel."[45]

Overall, the Chronicler's subtle and sophisticated portrait of David as *the representative of God's people and a figure of their identity* draws attention to the reality of continuing divine faithfulness in accordance with the great ancestral promises. The Chronicler's extended portrait of David's repentance and the legacy of atonement for God's people accords with the larger profile of the king in the book of Psalms and offers an alternative to the portrait of David in the book of Samuel. In the Chronicler's portrait, David becomes more of a type than a person. In the Samuel presentation of the Davidic census, David's repentance is clearly seen. However, rather than conforming to a set pattern, it more closely emphasizes David's turning of his heart as seen by the phrase "David was stricken to the heart" (2 Sam. 24:10). This phrase, not present in Chronicles, highlights the personal conviction of David before any divine consequences are narrated. The Chronicler is often accused of whitewashing David so that he becomes more palatable. Perhaps we might

---

43. Of course the idea of an "appendix" is something of a misnomer as it is entirely possible that this is the intentional conclusion of the narrative of Samuel. On the importance of 2 Sam. 21–24 see Herbert H. Klement, *II Samuel 21–24: Context, Structure and Meaning in the Samuel Conclusion*, European University Studies Series (New York: Lang, 2000).

44. Gary N. Knoppers, "Images of David in Early Judaism: David as Repentant Sinner in Chronicles," *Bib* 76 (1995): 454. Knoppers further notes: "David's unequivocal admission of guilt, his mediation on behalf of Israel, his diligent observance of divine instructions, and his securing a site for the future temple contribute positively to his legacy."

45. Ibid., 469.

suggest that the Chronicler takes aspects of the character of David that are present in Samuel, like his repentance, and repackages them or cleans them up to better suit his purposes and audience. Either way, when we read Samuel and Chronicles together we are given another possible twist in the kaleidoscope that gives us a nuanced picture of David.

The Poet: David in the Psalms

Most scholarly readings of the character of David take it as axiomatic that the book of Psalms is out of bounds when considering David. The association between David and the Psalms is looser than popularly recognized by most lay readers. There was a tendency for the scribal tradition to add headings that attributed psalms to David and those that do connect a psalm to a particular part of his life often do not always fit clearly the context they are connected to.[46] However, even apart from the Psalms, David is by far the most prominent poet amongst Israel's royal personages, as his sonorous eulogy for Saul and Jonathan (2 Sam. 1:17-27) and purported last words in 2 Sam. 23:1-7 variously testify. Moreover, his prayer in 2 Sam. 7:18-29 is one of the longest by a reigning king, and David is prominently associated with the Jerusalem temple from its inception. So, there are a host of compelling reasons why David should be closely identified with the Psalms. Furthermore, as Brevard Childs has argued, whether or not we can ascertain any historical association between David and the Psalms, it is entirely legitimate in hermeneutical terms to explore the relationship between David and the Psalms because of the superscriptions.[47] So what happens when we widen our lens to include the psalms as providing some possible characterization of David?[48]

---

46. For an overview of these issues see John Day, *Psalms*, Old Testament Guides (Sheffield: JSOT Press, 1992).

47. Brevard S. Childs, "Psalm Titles and Midrashic Exegesis," *JSS* 16 (1971): 137–50. See also Rolf Rendtorff, "The Psalms of David: David in the Psalms," in *The Book of Psalms: Composition and Reception*, ed. Peter W. Flint and Patrick D. Miller, Jr., with the assistance of Aaron Brunell and Ryan Roberts (Leiden: Brill, 2005), 53–64.

48. While the issue of David's characterization in the Psalms in general is an interesting subject, our focus in this chapter is on David in the book of Samuel so we are concerned primarily with how including the Psalms in our analysis may color our reading of the Samuel text. For that reason, it is interesting to note that when Psalm superscriptions mention an episode in the life of David it is always to an episode in Samuel not in Chronicles (thanks to David Firth for this insight).

In the history of the religious reception of David, it is probable that the book of Psalms is just as influential as the book of Samuel. As James Luther Mays suggests:

> The David of the Psalms has always been an important feature of the church's traditional understanding of Scripture, liturgy, and prayer. Prompted by the way in which David and the Psalms are connected in the Old Testament canon, Christians have understood David in terms of the Psalms and have viewed the Psalms as belonging to David. Because Christians have continuously used the Psalms as the core of their praise and prayer, and in doing so have believed that David was both type and prophet of the Christ, the David of the Psalms has had an immense influence on Christian belief and practice. The psalmic David remains more real for most Christians than the David of history, and probably even than the David of the Samuel story.[49]

A good example of reading David between psalm and narrative can be seen in the relationship between Psalm 142 and 1 Samuel 24. The superscription of Psalm 142 reads "A Maskil of David. When he was in the cave. A Prayer." While there are a number of possible contexts when David is in a cave, a good case can be made for seeing the superscription as connecting this Psalm with the cave at En-gedi in 1 Samuel 24.[50] What happens when we widen our literary lens on 1 Samuel 24 to include Psalm 142? The results are interesting.

The context of 1 Samuel 24 is David on the run from Saul. On the one hand it is clear that Saul has the upper hand, is more powerful with his three thousand men to David's few hundred. On the other hand, in the span of narrative from ch. 18 onward, Saul's violent intentions toward David are thwarted time and time again. The reader gets the clear sense that God is truly with David and God has clearly abandoned Saul, because David can do no wrong and Saul can do no right.

In that context we find David hiding in a cave when Saul comes in "to relieve himself" (1 Sam. 24:3 [v. 4 MT]). David's men think that this is an opportunity given by God who, according to them, promised David to "give your enemy into your hand, and you shall do to him as it seems good to you" (1 Sam. 24:4 [v. 5 MT]). Apparently, what seemed good to

---

49. James Luther Mays, "The David of the Psalms," *Int* 40 (1986): 144.

50. This was argued by Elieser Slomonovic, "Toward an Understanding of the Formation of the Historical Titles in the Book of Psalms," *ZAW* 91 (1979): 377, based on the threefold lexical word link of צדיק, סגר, and גמל respectively. This is picked up by Vivian L. Johnson, *David in Distress: His Portrait through the Historical Psalms*, LHBOTS 505 (New York: T&T Clark, 2009), 103–4.

David was to cut off a corner of Saul's robe, presumably as a warning. Immediately after David cuts off a corner of Saul's cloak, he is "stricken to the heart" (ויך לב, 1 Sam. 24:5 [v. 6 MT]) because of it.

When we look at Psalm 142 in light of this context, the results are a bit complex. On the one hand, Psalm 142 is a personal psalm but a little generic. The voice of the Psalm reflects that "they have hidden a trap for me" (Ps. 142:3 [v. 4 MT]), "no refuge remains to me; no one cares for me" (Ps. 142:4 [v. 5 MT], "they [my persecutors] are too strong" (Ps. 142:6 [v. 7 MT]. On the other hand, there are aspects of the psalm that seem not to fit the context of David hiding in the cave in 1 Samuel 24. The psalmist speaks of a plurality of enemies laying a trap for him ("they have hidden a trap," v. 3 [v. 4 MT]), whereas David is on the run from Saul alone. The psalmist claims that "no one is concerned for me" (v. 4 [v. 5 MT]), whereas David has several hundred men with him.[51] The psalmist laments to the Lord "no one cares for my life" (v. 4 [v. 5 MT]), whereas the narrative has been clear to point out that Jonathan and Michal both clearly care for his life (chs. 19–20) and his men seem to care for his life by trying to convince him to dispatch his enemy. In many ways the content of the psalm seems to sit light to the context of the narrative. However, if, as creative interpreters, we read the scene of David in the cave of En-gedi with Psalm 142 offering some characterization of David, the results are fruitful and interesting.

Others have pointed out the theological connection between the psalm and the narrative. In her discussion of Psalm 142, Vivian Johnson notes that if we read Psalm 142 as a prayer of David prior to Saul's arrival, then "when Saul enters the cave and David gains the upper hand, it is not a coincidence. Rather, it is a divine act that comes about as an answer to David's prayer (Ps. 142:4)."[52] This is a very interesting aspect of characterization because throughout the narrative of ch. 24 David's men have attributed this act to God (1 Sam. 24:4 [v. 5 MT]) and Saul has attributed this act to God (1 Sam. 24:19 [v. 20 MT]), but David does not explicitly attribute this to God. If we allow the psalm to characterize David, we are invited to see it as a response to David's prayer.

---

51. The number of David's fighting force is a complex issue with variants throughout the MT and LXX of 1 Samuel. See 1 Sam. 22:2; 23:13; 25:13; 27:2; 30:9, 10, 21.

52. Johnson, *David in Distress*, 104. She is drawing this from previous study by Yair Zakovitch, *From Shepherd to Messiah* (Jerusalem: Yad Ben-Tsvi, 1995), 159 (Hebrew).

We can press this reading further, however, as this is not the only significant aspect of characterization that happens when we read this psalm next to this narrative. As we have noted, the whole narrative progression up to 1 Samuel 24 has made it clear that God is with David and God has abandoned Saul. One of the key ways that this has manifested narratively is that in some ways David can do no wrong and Saul can do no right. Every attempt that Saul makes on David's life gets immediately foiled. It is thus possible to read this portion of David's story and not have any actual fear for David's life. Just as some movies and books put their heroes in danger but no one is actually concerned for them because we all know that they will be fine in the end, David's story can be read that way. David has no real reason to be afraid because we all know God is on his side. However, if we allow Psalm 142 to offer some of the character portrait for David, the picture becomes a little more nuanced.

Thus, while the David of the narrative may have no real reason to fear because we know God is with him, the David of the psalm can write of his spirit growing faint (Ps. 142:3 [v. 4 MT]), of persecutors who are too strong for him (Ps. 142:6 [v. 7 MT]). The David of the narrative has several hundred men surrounding him. And if Hushai is at all depicting the reality, we know that David's fighting men are a seriously formidable force, probably especially in rocky terrain where guerrilla warfare might be effective (2 Sam. 17:7-10). The David of the psalm, however, can say that there is no one at his right hand, there is no one concerned for him, and that no one cares for his life (Ps. 142:4 [v. 5 MT]). As far as David is concerned, he is in that cave alone. As a piece of dramatic characterization, it depicts David as someone who is surrounded by people and yet feels utterly alone. This is an interestingly relevant piece of characterization for our contemporary culture, which is more connected to others than ever before and yet reports of depression and loneliness are extremely high. Thus, when 1 Samuel 24 is read in light of Psalm 142, not only is the theological aspect of God's delivery of David heightened but the dramatic and personal characterization of David is given much greater emphasis.

Of course, the most famous characterization of David in the book of Psalms occurs in Psalm 51.[53] In the famous narrative of David's evil and murderous interactions with Bathsheba and Uriah, his simple confession "I have sinned" in 2 Sam 12:13 after Nathan exposes his crime(s) can be

---

53. For a useful bibliography and review of scholarship, see R. Christopher Heard, "Penitent to a Fault: The Characterization of David in Psalm 51," in *The Fate of King David: The Past and Present of a Biblical Icon*, ed. Tod Linafelt, Claudia V. Camp, and Timothy Beal, LHBOTS 500 (London: T&T Clark, 2010), 163–74.

seen as terse and underwhelming after the extended account of David's horrible actions.[54] If we include Psalm 51 into the narrative, David's brief confession of "I have sinned" becomes an extended meditation on the nature of sin's infiltration, the theology of sacrifice and atonement, and the journey toward restoration, with three different Hebrew words for *sin* balanced by three different Hebrew words for *grace*.[55] Thus, the resolution to the famous episode of David, Bathsheba, and Uriah takes on a very different flavor when the characterization of David in the Psalms is taken into account. What we see when we include the David that is reflected in the Psalms is another possible twist of the kaleidoscope.

Time Would Fail Me to Tell

To steal a line from the writer of the Hebrews (11:32), time would fail me to tell of the many and various other ways that we could twist the kaleidoscope to see David. We could discuss the significance of seeing the end of his story in 2 Samuel 21–24 versus seeing the end of his story in 1 Kings 2.[56] We could discuss David's afterlife in the book of Kings.[57] We could discuss David's afterlife in the history of the reception of his story.[58] What we have offered here is but a limited, representative example of the ways that one may twist the lens to view David. Is it possible to put this picture together? Works like those by Walter Brueggemann and Marti Steussy attempt to do so,[59] but David may always be something of a Rorschach test.

---

54. See, for example, Westbrook's questions about the sufficiency of David's confession in *"And He Will Take Your Daughters,"* 139.

55. Goldingay, *Psalms*. Vol. 2, *Psalms 42–89*, BCOTWP (Grand Rapids: Baker, 2007), 87.

56. For the significance of 2 Sam. 21–24 see Klement, *II Samuel 21–24*. For some hermeneutical reflections on deciding on an ending see Green, *David's Capacity for Compassion*, 36–8.

57. See, e.g., Alison L. Joseph, *Portrait of the Kings: The Davidic Prototype in Deuteronomistic Poetics* (Minneapolis: Fortress, 2015).

58. See, e.g., Sara Kipfer, *Der bedrohte David: Eine exegetische und rezeptionsgeschichtliche Studie zu 1Sam 16—1 Kön 2*, SBR (Berlin: de Gruyter, 2015); Linafelt, Beal, and Camp, eds, *The Fate of King David*; or Raymond-Jean Frontain and Jan Wojcik, eds, *The David Myth in Western Literature* (West Lafayette: Purdue University Press, 1980).

59. Brueggemann, *The David Story*; Marti J. Steussy, *David: Biblical Portraits of Power* (Columbia: University of South Carolina Press, 1999).

However, the biblical presentation of the character of David has great staying power. This character will long outlast our attempts to come to grips with him. Some years ago, Greger Andersson wrote a book on literary theory and the books of Samuel, entitling it *Untamable Texts*.[60] His thesis was that the books of Samuel resist our theory-laden readings. Our attempts to grapple with the poetics of the book will always run aground against the text itself which is, to use Andersson's term, untamable. By way of conclusion, we suggest that David is much the same. David resists easy categorization; he resists our literary theory and our aims of interpretation. In as much as David may mean many things to many people, he cannot just mean anything, because the David of the text has his own obduracy. That is why the character of David has so much to offer. However much we may think we have some control of the ways that we twist the kaleidoscope that is David, the image that we see will often be different and surprising, but always we will see something that is uniquely and recognizably David.

---

60. Greger Andersson, *Untamable Texts: Literary Studies and Narrative Theory in the Books of Samuel*, LHBOTS 514 (London: T&T Clark, 2009).

Chapter 9

THE HEIR OF SAUL:
JONATHAN'S LIFE AND DEATH
IN THEOLOGICAL PERSPECTIVE

Diana Abernethy

As 1 Samuel traces the transition from Saul's reign to David's, two extended episodes (1 Sam. 14; 20) focus on Jonathan, Saul's son who does not succeed him as king. Though Jonathan's death robs him of an ongoing role in David's kingship, significant narration time develops Jonathan as a character with independent motivations and goals. Jonathan's characterization contributes to 1 Samuel's theological portrayal of the transition from Saul to David. While some accounts of the historical David behind 1–2 Samuel posit that David participated in the deaths of Saul and his sons, the narrative locates David far from the battle of Gilboa (1 Sam. 29–31) and focuses on theological reasons for their deaths.[1] Jonathan's character highlights the theological reasons why David succeeds Saul as king. By characterizing Jonathan as theologically astute and as a capable potential heir to Saul, the narrative directs the reader to the Lord's choice of David as the primary reason why he, not Jonathan, succeeds Saul as king. By extensively developing Jonathan's loyalty to David over Saul before Jonathan's death, the narrative presents Jonathan as unable to use his choices and actions to separate himself from the fate of Saul's

---

1. For such historical arguments, see Baruch Halpern, *David's Secret Demons: Messiah, Murderer, Traitor, King* (Grand Rapids: Eerdmans, 2001), 78–81 and Steven L. McKenzie, *King David: A Biography* (Oxford: Oxford University Press, 2000), 108–10.

house. Jonathan dies alongside Saul and his brothers on Mount Gilboa for theological reasons—because the Lord has rejected Saul as king.

The Man According to the Lord's Heart

After Samuel asserts that a "man according to his [the Lord's] heart" (איש כלבבו) (1 Sam. 13:14) will succeed Saul as king, the narrative invites the reader to consider Jonathan in relation to this man.[2] It focuses on Jonathan in 1 Samuel 14, where it initially presents him positively as a faithful and capable military strategist by depicting his confidence in the Lord's power to deliver, his cooperation with the Lord in battle, and his victory over the Philistines (1 Sam. 14:1-23). However, 1 Sam. 14:24-46 raises questions about Jonathan's future as it foreshadows his death as a consequence of Saul's actions. Thus, the narrative follows an arc in which it first encourages the reader to see Jonathan as a capable successor before redirecting the reader to David's rise.

1 Samuel intertwines Jonathan's introduction with that of the man according to the Lord's heart. After Saul offers sacrifices before Samuel's arrival—and thus contrary to Samuel's instructions (10:8; 13:8-9)—in 13:13-14, Samuel declares:

> You have been foolish. You did not keep the commandment of the Lord your God that he commanded you so that now (כי עתה) the Lord would have established your kingdom (ממלכתך) to Israel forever. And, now your kingdom will not rise. The Lord sought (בקש) for himself a man according to his heart (איש כלבבו), and he commanded him to be prince over his people because you did not keep what the Lord commanded you.[3]

Though the implication of the perfect verb בקש is debated, Samuel's words prompt the reader to look for Saul's replacement.[4] Most commentators

---

2. When I refer to "the reader," I draw on Seymour Chatman's notion of an "implied reader": the implied reader exists immanent in the narrative, and "real readers"—the actual individuals reading a narrative—can embrace or challenge the position of the implied reader as they place the narrative in conversation with their experiences and other texts. I use "the reader" as a trope to describe how syntax and literary features affect meaning for an ideal reader implied in the narrative (*Story and Discourse: Narrative Structure in Fiction and Film* [Ithaca: Cornell University Press, 1978], 146–51).

3. All translations are mine unless otherwise indicated, and I use the Masoretic text as the basis for this reading.

4. Robert Alter and David Firth interpret בקש as having a past sense here and implying that the Lord has already chosen a new king (*The David Story: A Translation*

interpret Samuel as indicating that the Lord is ending Saul's dynasty (ממלכתך), which as a result excludes Saul's son Jonathan from acceding to the throne.[5] However, Diana Vikander Edelman intriguingly contends that Samuel's pronouncement does not necessarily preclude Jonathan from succeeding Saul on the throne at this point, even as the narrative later obscures whether the Lord ever chose Jonathan as Saul's successor.[6]

The narrative leaves space for the reader to consider Jonathan a potential successor because Samuel does not name one in 1 Samuel 13; Samuel only indicates that he will be a man according to the Lord's heart. The meaning of this designation has been debated. P. Kyle McCarter interprets "a man according to his heart" as "a man of his own choosing," arguing that it describes the Lord's choice of the king itself rather than particular qualities of the candidate or the Lord's affection for the selected one.[7] However, Benjamin J. M. Johnson contends that the phrase describes the character of the Lord's chosen king and that qualities of the heart function as a significant "narrative thread."[8] In light of Johnson's reading, Samuel's pronouncement cues the reader to look for a man whose heart resembles the Lord's in some way.

---

with Commentary of 1 and 2 Samuel [New York: Norton, 1999], 73 and *1 & 2 Samuel*, ApOTC 8 [Nottingham: Apollos, 2009], 155–6). Alternatively, Stephen B. Chapman contends that Samuel indicates the Lord is looking for another king with a specific kind of heart, though the Lord may have not yet selected the individual (*1 Samuel as Christian Scripture: A Theological Commentary* [Grand Rapids: Eerdmans, 2016], 128). Diana Vikander Edelman explores whether to interpret בקש with a past sense or as "the 'prophetic perfect' or the 'perfect of confidence,'" and she contends that the timing and extent of Samuel's predicted rejection remain unclear (*King Saul in the Historiography of Judah*, JSOTSup 121 [Sheffield: Sheffield Academic, 1991], 80–1). Robert Polzin interprets Samuel's phrase כי עתה as marking a "contrary-to-fact" description; the Lord would have established Saul's kingdom but did not do so (*Samuel and the Deuteronomist: 1 Samuel*, Vol. 2 of *A Literary Study of the Deuteronomic History* [Bloomington: Indiana University Press, 1989], 136).

5. While Keith Bodner sees Jonathan as a "son with no future," David Jobling and David Firth explore how the narrative both presents and excludes Jonathan as Saul's successor (Keith Bodner, *1 Samuel: A Narrative Commentary*, HBM 19 [Sheffield: Sheffield Phoenix, 2008], 130 and 135; David Jobling, *1 Samuel*, Berit Olam [Collegeville: Liturgical Press, 1998], 94; and Firth, *1 & 2 Samuel*, 156).

6. Edelman, *King Saul*, 80–1, 83, 87, and 96.

7. P. Kyle McCarter, *I Samuel*, AB 8 (Garden City: Doubleday, 1980), 229.

8. Benjamin J. M. Johnson, "The Heart of YHWH's Chosen One in 1 Samuel," *JBL* 131, no. 3 (2012): 455–66.

The narrative juxtaposes Jonathan and the "man according to his [the Lord's] heart" by revealing Jonathan's filial connection to Saul shortly after Samuel's announcement and by drawing attention to Jonathan's heart through his armor bearer's words in 1 Sam. 14:7. While the narrative introduces Jonathan in 13:2 as a commander in Saul's army, it does not identify him as Saul's son—and thus possible heir—until 13:16, two verses after Samuel's declaration. With Samuel's pronouncement, the narrative invites the reader to think about Saul's successor, and with Jonathan's identification as Saul's son, it encourages the reader to consider how Jonathan is related to this successor.[9]

The possibility that Jonathan could be a man according to the Lord's heart gains momentum with his positive portrayal in 1 Sam. 14:1-23. In 14:6, Jonathan discloses his confidence in the Lord's capacity to overcome the Philistines: "Perhaps the Lord will do for us because there is not to the Lord any restraint to deliver (להושיע), with many or with few." By introducing his observation with "perhaps" (אולי), Jonathan does not make a definitive statement about whether the Lord will choose to intervene at this juncture, but he clearly expresses confidence in the Lord's power to achieve victory, regardless of the number of troops.[10]

Right after Jonathan expresses his assurance of the Lord's ability to fight, his armor bearer affirms the content of Jonathan's heart. In 1 Sam. 14:7, his armor bearer says, "Do all that is in your heart—reach out for yourself. Here I am with you as your heart" (עשה כל־אשר בלבבך נטה לך הנני עמך כלבבך). Though the translation of this phrase is debated, Jonathan's armor bearer encourages him to act according to the content of his heart.[11]

---

9. Edelman emphasizes the significance of Jonathan emerging as Saul's son in 1 Sam. 13:16 and draws on this sequence in her exploration of the possibility that Jonathan is the Lord's chosen successor (*King Saul*, 80–1).

10. David J. Reimer argues that Jonathan's use of "perhaps" portrays his recognition of the Lord's freedom and the place of the Lord's freedom in Israel's covenant theology ("An Overlooked Term in Old Testament Theology—Perhaps," in *Covenant in Context: Essays in Honour of E. W. Nicholson*, ed. A. D. H. Mayes and R. B. Salters [Oxford: Oxford University Press, 2003], 339). Fokkelman, Polzin, and Chapman similarly contend that Jonathan's approach acknowledges the Lord's freedom, a theological perspective endorsed by the narrative (Jan P. Fokkelman, *Narrative Art and Poetry in the Books of Samuel: A Full Interpretation Based on Stylistic and Structural Analyses: Vol. 2, The Crossing Fates [I Sam. 13–31 & II Sam. 1]*, SSN 23 [Assen: Van Gorcum, 1986], 54; Polzin, *Samuel and the Deuteronomist*, 137; and Chapman, *1 Samuel as Christian Scripture*, 130–1).

11. The Masoretes pointed נטה as an imperative, and the following prepositional phrase has a second-person pronominal suffix serving as an object. The *atnach*

Johnson connects the armor bearer's statement in 1 Sam. 14:7 with Samuel's phrase in 13:14, using this link to argue that this heart language describes the qualities of one's heart and character. He challenges McCarter's use of 14:7 as evidence for the heart language referring to "an individual's will or purpose."[12] Particularly in light of Johnson's reading, the narrative highlights Jonathan's faithful heart while the reader searches for the man according to the Lord's heart, thereby encouraging the possibility that Jonathan could be the one to succeed Saul in the kingship.

The narrative reinforces Jonathan's confidence in the Lord when he uses cledonomancy to determine whether to proceed with the offensive against the Philistines (1 Sam. 14:8-12).[13] Jonathan describes two possible Philistine spoken responses, and in 1 Sam. 14:10, he asserts that the second scenario will reveal the Lord's assurance of success: "for the Lord will have given them into our hand, and this will be for us the sign." Jonathan reasserts the Lord's agency in the battle in 1 Sam. 14:12, when the second scenario comes to pass: "for the Lord has given them into the hand of Israel." Through his cledonomancy, the narrative underscores Jonathan's ability to perceive the Lord's work and boldness in participating in it.

Not only does Jonathan accurately recognize the Lord's guidance of his military initiative, but the narrative also confirms his cooperation with the Lord in the victory. After describing Jonathan's elaborate secret attack that catalyzes Israel's victory, the narrator reports in 1 Sam. 14:23, "the Lord

---

appears under בלבבך just prior to this phrase, which suggests that נטה begins a new phrase that may or may not have heart as the subject. Firth translates it as "reach out," implying Jonathan is the subject (*1 & 2 Samuel*, 158). Alternatively, Alter follows the LXX and translates the phrase, "Do whatever your heart inclines" (*The David Story*, 77). Chapman renders it as "Do whatever is in your heart" (*1 Samuel as Christian Scripture*, 131). *HALOT* suggests a textual emendation and presents נטה with a ל preposition as "devote oneself to" ("נטה," *HALOT* 1:692–3).

12. Johnson, "The Heart of YHWH's Chosen One," 457–8 and McCarter, *I Samuel*, 229 and 236. V. Philips Long follows McCarter in seeing the Lord's choosing as an important resonance in the phrase, but he argues that McCarter "perhaps overstates his case" in completely excluding the "unity of purpose" implied in linked hearts in 1 Sam. 13:14 as well as 1 Sam. 14:7 (*The Reign and Rejection of King Saul: A Case for Literary and Theological Coherence*, SBLDS 118 [Atlanta: Scholars Press, 1989], 92–3).

13. Solomon Nigosian describes cledonomancy as "divination by the acceptance of a fatal word, or of a spoken omen" (*Magic and Divination in the Old Testament* [Brighton: Sussex Academic, 2008], 47–9).

delivered (וַיּוֹשַׁע) Israel on that day."[14] The narrator uses the same verb (ישׁע) as Jonathan does in his initial statement of confidence, which reinforces the Lord's work through his attack.

In addition to the narrator's explicit statement regarding the Lord's involvement in 1 Sam. 14:23, the narrative also more subtly implies the Lord's role in the course of the battle. In 14:14-15, after Jonathan and his armor bearer's initial attack, the narrative describes its effects, including terror among the Philistines. In 14:15, "the land quaked, and it became the terror of God (וַתְּהִי לְחֶרְדַּת אֱלֹהִים)." Nouns in construct with a name of God have a superlative sense while also connecting an action to God.[15] By describing a new form of fear in relation to God, the narrator implies that God caused the earthquake in order to enhance the effects of Jonathan and the armor bearer's assault. Furthermore, this phrase reminds the reader of God shortly after Jonathan declares that the Lord has given the Philistines into Israel's hand in 14:12. Thus, the narrative invites the reader to see the Lord's involvement in this battle and view Jonathan's plan favorably.[16]

Not only does the narrative portray Jonathan positively through his cooperation with the Lord, but his success against the Philistines also augments his favorable depiction. In 1 Sam. 9:16, the Lord tells Samuel to anoint Saul, who "will deliver (ישׁע) my people from the hand of the Philistines." This goal functions as a measure by which the reader can track Saul's success as king through 1 Samuel. Though Saul leads a successful defeat of the Ammonites in 1 Samuel 11, Jonathan—not Saul—works with the Lord to deliver Israel from the Philistines in 1 Sam. 14:1-23.[17] As Jonathan fulfills this hope for Israel's king, the narrative continues to present him as a capable successor to Saul.

---

14. Fokkelman aptly describes Jonathan's collaboration with the Lord: "Jonathan's raid and God's help are completely and inseparably interwoven. The victory is entirely the work of the heroic Jonathan and at the same time entirely an act of his God" (*The Crossing Fates*, 52–3).

15. Bruce K. Waltke and M. O'Connor, *An Introduction to Biblical Hebrew Syntax* (Winona Lake: Eisenbrauns, 1990), 268.

16. For further discussion of the theological portrayal of the earthquake, see Firth, *1 & 2 Samuel*, 164; Fokkelman, *The Crossing Fates*, 57–8; Long, *The Reign and Rejection of King Saul*, 111; Edelman, *King Saul*, 86; Chapman, *1 Samuel as Christian Scripture*, 131–2; Gerhard von Rad, *Holy War in Ancient Israel*, trans. and ed. Marva J. Dawn (Grand Rapids: Eerdmans, 1991), 42–3, 48–9; and Millard C. Lind, *Yahweh Is a Warrior: The Theology of Warfare in Ancient Israel* (Scottdale: Herald, 1980), 104.

17. In 1 Sam. 14:47-48, the narrative reports Saul's success against the Philistines and other groups. By listing the Philistines last, the narrative invites questions about whether the Philistines are Saul's primary focus. In 1 Sam. 14:52, the narrative indicates that conflict with the Philistines continues during Saul's reign, so Saul does

However, after the reader sees Jonathan's confidence in the Lord's deliverance and his cooperation with the Lord in Israel's victory over the Philistines in 1 Sam. 14:1-23, the narrative redirects the reader's expectation that Jonathan could be a man according to the Lord's heart. In 14:24-46, Saul declares that Jonathan will die for breaking Saul's vow—a death sentence that overshadows Jonathan in the rest of 1 Samuel.

As Jonathan continues to fight against the Philistines, he eats some honey, unaware that Saul made the troops swear that anyone who ate before he avenged his enemies would be cursed (14:24, 27).[18] As another soldier informs Jonathan of the oath, the narrative creates an expectation that this oath will affect Jonathan.

After Saul receives no answer from the Lord about whether to attack the Philistines, he casts lots to determine the cause of the Lord's silence. At the outset of his investigation, Saul introduces the possibility of Jonathan's death (14:39): "Indeed, as the Lord who delivers Israel lives, for if it [the offense] is in Jonathan, then he will surely die (מות ימות)." In the second round of lots, the lot falls on Jonathan; after explaining that he ate some honey, Jonathan accepts the consequences (14:43): "Here I am: I will die" (הנני אמות).[19] In 14:44, Saul reaffirms that Jonathan will "surely die" (מות תמות), but the troops intervene and spare Jonathan on account of his cooperation with the Lord in the victory (14:45).

Though the troops protect Jonathan's life, this scene encourages the reader to imagine his death, specifically as a consequence of Saul's actions, and it signals that Jonathan's life hangs in the balance as 1 Samuel proceeds.[20] This image of Jonathan's death directs the reader away from

---

not have lasting success against them. Nowhere does 1 Samuel devote significant narration time to Saul leading a victory over the Philistines, as it does for Jonathan (14:1-23) and David (chs. 17–18), and Saul kills himself during a battle with the Philistines (ch. 31). Thus, Jonathan's and David's successes against the Philistines contrast markedly with Saul's failure to end the Philistines' threat to Israel, and they contribute to their positive portrayal in 1 Samuel.

18. For readings that Saul intentionally tries to target Jonathan, see Bodner, *1 Samuel*, 144, and Edelman, *King Saul*, 90–1.

19. Fokkelman interprets Jonathan's willingness to die positively, since he is not striving to be Saul's successor (*The Crossing Fates*, 74). When Jonathan facilitates David's rise, the reader remembers this detachment that Jonathan shows toward the throne, and Jonathan's commitment to David appears all the more sincere in light of Jonathan's willingness to die at this point.

20. See Barbara Green for further exploration of how "Jonathan lives the rest of his life under this proleptic death sentence" (*How Are the Mighty Fallen? A Dialogical Study of King Saul in 1 Samuel*, JSOTSup 365 [Sheffield: Sheffield Academic, 2003], 247).

the possibility that Jonathan is the man according to the Lord's heart who will succeed Saul as king, thereby renewing questions about the succession shortly before the narrative returns to Saul's rejection in 1 Samuel 15. Thus, 1 Samuel 14 presents Jonathan as a faithful and capable successor before leading the reader away from him as a viable candidate.

However, the presentation of Jonathan's positive qualities lingers with the reader as the narrative introduces David in 1 Samuel 16–17.[21] Several similarities emerge as the reader juxtaposes Jonathan in 1 Samuel 14 with David in 1 Samuel 17, including their successes against the Philistines when the rest of Israel fears them, their confidence in the Lord, and their unconventional use of weapons. Because Jonathan and David share these positive qualities, they do not provide sufficient reason for why Jonathan is passed over and David is anointed as Saul's successor. Instead, these similarities direct the reader to seek another explanation for David's anointing. In this search, the theological dimensions of the narrative rise to the fore: David, not Jonathan, succeeds Saul because the Lord has rejected Saul (13:13-14; 15:28) and chosen David (16:12).

Jonathan and David each strike the Philistines when fear incapacitates their fellow soldiers. In 1 Sam. 13:6, Saul's troops "saw that distress was to them" (ראו כי צר לו) and "hid" (ויתחבאו). While the army hides, Jonathan leads his secret attack. Similarly, Goliath threatens a fearful Israelite army for forty days before David offers to face him. In 17:11, Israel's troops "were dismayed and feared greatly" (ויחתו ויראו מאד), and the narrator returns to the Israelites' response to Goliath in 17:24: they "fled from before him and feared greatly" (וינסו מפניו ויראו מאד).[22] Thus, both Jonathan and David intervene while the rest of the army struggles to find a way forward, and they each enact brave and independent initiatives.

---

21. In the sequence of 1 Samuel, David enters the narrative in Jonathan's shadow, but if actual readers of 1 Samuel already know that David will succeed Saul, 1 Samuel presents Jonathan in 1 Sam. 13–14 for these readers to compare with David in 1 Samuel and in the impressions of David they bring to 1 Samuel.

22. Jonathan is absent in 1 Sam. 15–17 in the sense that the narrative does not mention his name. However, when Jonathan reemerges in 1 Sam. 18:1 and knows of David's victory over the Philistines (19:5), the reader wonders whether Jonathan was present in Saul's army in 1 Sam. 17 and whether he was among all Israel who feared the Philistines (17:11, 24). By omitting Jonathan's name, the narrative leaves Jonathan's location conspicuously ambiguous, and it focuses the reader on other dynamics, including Saul's failure to end the Philistine threat and David's success. For example, Saul's name begins the description of Israel's fear (17:11). Additionally, the narrative does not explain how Jonathan's trial (14:38–46) affects his place in Saul's army and court. Since Jonathan's presence in 1 Sam. 17 is not narrated, it remains only a downplayed possibility for the reader filling in the narrative's gaps.

Jonathan's and David's successes against the Philistines contrast with Saul's secondary role in chs. 14 and 17, especially in light of the Lord's hope that Saul would deliver Israel from the Philistines (9:16).

In 1 Samuel 14 and 17, Jonathan and David exhibit confidence in the Lord's power to deliver them in battle.[23] While Jonathan asserts the Lord's power to deliver in any circumstance in 14:6, David makes more specific predictions about the Lord's protection of him in the imminent conflict with Goliath. In 17:37, David assures Saul that "the Lord who delivered me (הצלני) from the hand of the lion and from the hand of the bear—he will deliver me (יצילני) from the hand of this Philistine." David echoes this conviction when he addresses Goliath. In 17:46, David declares, "this day the Lord will shut you (יסגרך) in my hand," and he concludes in 1 Sam. 17:47, "because to the Lord is the battle, and he will give (ונתן) you into our hand." Jonathan and David use different verbs but both look to the Lord for deliverance, and David makes stronger claims about the Lord's actions in this situation.

When Jonathan and David collaborate with the Lord, they achieve victory without superior weapons. Jonathan initiates his assault when the Philistines have limited the Israelites' access to weapons; only he and Saul have sword and spear (1 Sam. 13:19-22). Jonathan's surprise attack and the Lord's intervention precipitate victory as the Philistines use their swords against each other (14:14-20). In contrast to Goliath's extensive armor, David declines Saul's offer of his armor and sword (17:5-7, 38-39). When Goliath is insulted that David faces him with shepherd rods (במקלות), David claims a more powerful weapon: the Lord, who does not need sword and spear to achieve victory (17:43-47). Before David uses Goliath's own sword to behead him, the narrator reminds the reader that "a sword there was not in the hand of David," which highlights David's reliance on the Lord at the climax of his victory (17:50-51). Since David does not carry a sword into battle, his success against Goliath is even more significant than that of Jonathan, who has his own sword.[24]

---

23. For further discussion of the connection between Jonathan's and David's expressions of confidence in the Lord, see Fokkelman, *The Crossing Fates*, 80–1; Long, *The Reign and Rejection of King Saul*, 108; and Chapman, *1 Samuel as Christian Scripture*, 130.

24. Jonathan's possession of a sword and spear is narrated in 1 Sam. 13:22 but not in 1 Sam. 14. The narrative implies that Jonathan and his armor bearer have weapons in 1 Sam. 14:13–14 when they kill the first twenty Philistines, but the narrative does not narrate their possession of a sword or spear at this point. In 1 Sam. 14, the word חרב only appears in 1 Sam. 14:20 when the Philistines turn their swords to their neighbors, and the word חנית does not appear in 1 Sam. 14.

Both Jonathan and David lead Israel to victory over the Philistines with inferior conventional weapons and confidence in the Lord's power to deliver. Though David exhibits a greater degree of confidence in the Lord and slays Goliath more impressively, these similarities encourage the reader to conclude that these shared positive qualities do not constitute the reason David is anointed instead of Jonathan.[25] The narrative presents the Lord's choice of David as the primary reason for his ascension, not the faithfulness and military skill that Jonathan also possesses.[26]

Bonds of Covenant and Blood

The Lord's choice of David explains why he is anointed instead of Jonathan, but David's anointing and success against the Philistines raise questions about his relationship with Jonathan. Though the images of Jonathan's positive portrayal in 1 Samuel 14 linger with the reader as 1 Samuel progresses, Jonathan disappears from the narrative in 1 Samuel 15–17, causing the reader to wonder how he will figure in David's coming reign. When Jonathan reenters the narrative in 1 Sam. 18:1-4, he initiates a relationship with David that reflects a solid commitment to him.

Jonathan's actions in 1 Sam. 18:1-4 show the kind of relationship he seeks with David. The narrator first describes Jonathan's attachment to David: "and the life of Jonathan was bound with the life of David, and Jonathan loved him as his life" (ונפש יהונתן נקשרה בנפש דוד ויאהבו יהונתן כנפשו). As Jonathan's life ties (קשר) to David's, the narrative signals that Jonathan's and David's lives will intertwine as the plot progresses.[27] In the context of two potential political rivals making a covenant, the verb

---

25. Fokkelman similarly recognizes that in 1 Sam. 17, David emerges as "more than Jonathan's equal" (*The Crossing Fates*, 83).

26. Jonathan Y. Rowe also highlights the theological significance of Jonathan and David's shared qualities: "We have seen that Jonathan and David are portrayed in very similar terms: both men are independent, valiant, militarily successful and, most importantly, YHWH is with them. The similarity of characterization is highly significant for as 'another self' Jonathan is a 'proto-David' who enables the author to make three related assertions: (1) David is a worthy king regardless of the slurs of other characters; (2) Jonathan *would have been* a worthy king of Israel had he not died on Mount Gilboa; and (3) Jonathan, as the rightful heir, recognized David as YHWH's chosen leader of Israel" (*Sons or Lovers: An Interpretation of David and Jonathan's Friendship*, LHBOTS 533 [New York: Bloomsbury T&T Clark, 2012], 132).

27. "קשר," *HALOT* 2:1153–4. *HALOT* renders the Niphal of קשר in 1 Sam. 18:1 as "commit oneself," thereby interpreting it with a reflexive sense. This reflexive sense highlights Jonathan's response to David without implying David's reciprocity.

אהב includes political nuances.²⁸ Since the verb אהב has a wide semantic range, its emotional resonances also contribute to the reader's understanding of Jonathan and David's relationship, but the narrative does not clarify to what extent Jonathan's attachment to David is motivated by political or emotional loyalty. As a result of these narrative gaps, interpretations of Jonathan and David's relationship range from a political alliance to the bond between comrades in arms and homosexual love.²⁹ Rather than clarify the precise nature of Jonathan's inner feelings about David, the narrative focuses on the effects of his relationship with David, particularly how he protects David from Saul and facilitates David's rise.

In 1 Sam. 18:3, the narrative foregrounds Jonathan's agency when he and David first make a covenant: "and Jonathan and David cut a covenant" (ויכרת יהונתן ודוד ברית). Though the narrative includes Jonathan and David as subjects for this action, the singular verb (ויכרת) highlights the action of the first stated subject—Jonathan. In their initial covenant, Jonathan is the primary actor while David participates in a secondary way.³⁰ In explaining

---

28. J. A. Thompson argues that in the context of Jonathan giving David weapons and David's military successes in 1 Sam. 18:1-5, the political resonances of the verb אהב dominate. Thompson builds on William L. Moran's connections between the political uses of the verb אהב in Assyrian vassal treaties and covenants in the Old Testament, especially Deuteronomy (J. A. Thompson, "The Significance of the Verb *Love* in the David-Jonathan Narratives in 1 Samuel," *VT* 24 [1974]: 334 and 336, and William L. Moran, "The Ancient Near Eastern Background of the Love of God in Deuteronomy," *CBQ* 25 [1963]: 81–2).

29. For additional bibliography on Jonathan and David's relationship, see Erin E. Fleming, "Political Favoritism in Saul's Court: חפץ, נעם, and the Relationship between David and Jonathan," *JBL* 135, no. 1 (2016): 20–1 nn. 1–3. James E. Harding and Mark S. Smith describe the openness of the David and Jonathan texts to more or less erotic readings. Harding charts this openness as a preface to his study of the reception history in which homoerotic readings of David and Jonathan emerged (*The Love of David and Jonathan: Ideology, Text, and Reception* [Sheffield: Equinox, 2013], 122–273). Smith argues that ancient Near Eastern warriors were frequently portrayed in poetry as attractive to both women and men. This poetry often uses language for love between men and women as analogies for the relationships between men, and in these analogies, the poems create space for emotional intimacy between men without specifying whether or not it is sexual (*Poetic Heroes: Literary Commemorations of Warriors and Warrior Culture in the Early Biblical World* [Grand Rapids: Eerdmans, 2014], 91–4).

30. Alter contends, "This is one of the most significant instances of the expressive grammatical pattern in which there is a plural subject with a singular verb, making the first member of the plural subject the principal agent: the initiative for the pact of friendship is Jonathan's, and David goes along with it" (*The David Story*, 112).

why Jonathan initiates the covenant, the narrative echoes his love for David as the motivation for his actions (1 Sam. 18:1, 3). Jonathan's love for David "as his life" (כנפשו) signals that this love parallels his concern for his own well-being (1 Sam. 18:1, 3).

In 1 Sam. 18:1-4, Jonathan pledges loyalty to David by making a covenant. He symbolizes his endorsement of David as Saul's successor by removing his cloak, robe, sword, bow, and belt, and offering these to David.[31] Jonathan initiates the relationship with David, but it becomes more mutual as Jonathan repeatedly demonstrates his loyalty to David in 1 Samuel 19; 20; 23.

In 1 Sam. 19:1-7, Jonathan informs David of Saul's plan to kill David, and skillfully orchestrates a reunion of the two. In 19:1, the narrator reports that Jonathan's "delight" (חפץ) for David motivates him to warn David.[32] Though 1 Samuel 19 does not mention Jonathan and David's covenant per se, the verb חפץ reminds the reader of Jonathan's commitment to David that motivates him to make the covenant in 18:1-4. Jonathan enacts his loyalty in 19:1-7 as he alerts David to Saul's murderous intentions, devises a plan, and independently executes his scheme. The narrative underscores Jonathan's initiative in this scene with his speeches and actions. While David is silent, Jonathan utters two long speeches, one to David and one to Saul, and the narrative only mentions David as the object of Jonathan's actions and the subject of his instructions.[33] Not only does Jonathan seek out David, but he also tells him what to do—hide in the field—while Jonathan speaks to Saul (19:2-3). Jonathan successfully convinces his father not to kill David by highlighting the contrast between David's good actions for Israel and Saul's hope for David's death (1 Sam.

---

31. Ora Horn Prouser explores how clothing functions to enhance narrative effects, and she uses the theme of Saul's fall and David's rise in 1 Samuel as a case study. For Prouser, David receives clothing that symbolizes his growing relative power ("Suited to the Throne: The Symbolic Use of Clothing in the David and Saul Narratives," *JSOT* 71 [1996]: 31–2 and 34). See also Fokkelman, *The Crossing Fates*, 198–9, and David Gunn, *The Fate of King Saul: An Interpretation of a Biblical Story*, JSOTSup 14 (Sheffield: JSOT Press, 1980), 80.

32. Fleming argues that like the verb אהב, the verb חפץ "should be understood primarily as political support" in David and Jonathan's relationship. For Fleming, the verb חפץ signifies consciously chosen favor within a political alliance, either from the superior or inferior party ("Political Favoritism," 28).

33. In 1 Sam. 19:1-7, Jonathan speaks sixty-six words while Saul replies with four. For more on the narrative focus on Jonathan and on David's passivity in 1 Sam. 19, see Bodner, *1 Samuel*, 202, and Fokkelman, *The Crossing Fates*, 250.

19:4-5).³⁴ Though Saul soon tries to break his pledge not to kill David, Jonathan's actions in 19:1-7 demonstrate his allegiance to David over Saul (19:6, 10).

Jonathan's loyalty in 1 Sam. 19:1-7 impresses David enough to return to him for assistance, and Jonathan agrees to do whatever David specifies (20:1-4). As David requests, Jonathan lies to his father to gain information about Saul's current plans, further solidifying his loyalty to David over Saul (20:5-8, 28-29). When Saul responds to Jonathan by throwing his spear, Jonathan's loyalty brings him alongside David as the object of Saul's attempts at violence (18:11; 19:10; 20:33).³⁵ In response to Jonathan's demonstrations of loyalty in 1 Samuel 20, David's appreciation for their relationship increases.

As in 1 Sam. 18:1-4, David and Jonathan understand that Jonathan initiated their covenant at the beginning of 1 Samuel 20. However by the end of 1 Samuel 20, David demonstrates an increased interest in their relationship. When David appeals for Jonathan's help in 1 Sam. 20:8, he cites "the covenant of the Lord" (בברית יהוה) into which Jonathan "brought" (הבאת) him as the reason Jonathan would help him. As David uses a Hiphil verb (הבאת), he underscores that Jonathan instigated the covenant. When Jonathan appeals for David's faithfulness to him and his house in 1 Sam. 20:14-16, he reiterates that he cut a covenant with David;

---

34. For further discussion of Jonathan's skilled rhetoric in 1 Sam. 19:4-5 see Firth, *1 & 2 Samuel*, 216; Bodner, *1 Samuel*, 204; and Fokkelman, *The Crossing Fates*, 254.

35. For further discussion of how Saul's attempt to strike Jonathan places him with David, see Fokkelman, *The Crossing Fates*, 325, and Jobling, *1 Samuel*, 98. Furthermore, when Saul addresses Jonathan as "son of an unchaste woman" (1 Sam. 20:30), he likens Jonathan to one who disregards family obligations, which accords with Jonathan's loyalty to David over his father. I am following Paul Haupt in translating בן־נעות המרדות as "son of an unchaste woman." Haupt argues that the phrase refers to a "woman who who been led astray with regard to discipline or moral training, chastity" ("Heb. *mardût*, Chastisement and Chastity," *JBL* 39 [1920]: 156). Bodner also discusses the possibility that David marries Saul's wife Ahinoam (1 Sam. 25:43-44). Such a connection would help explain Saul's anger with Jonathan as well as David (*1 Samuel*, 272). Rowe argues that Jonathan negotiates different moral goods, and that the narrative portrays Jonathan favorably for prioritizing his commitment to David, his friend and the Lord's chosen successor: "Just as Jonathan in preferring David stood against not only Saul but also the dominant moral schema of family loyalty and filial obedience, so readers should recall that loyalty to YHWH's anointed—and his successors—is paramount." For Rowe, Jonathan is "honourably disloyal" in cooperating with the Lord's choice of David at the expense of socially expected obligations to his own family (*Sons or Lovers*, 131–2).

Jonathan's singular verb (ויכרת) echoes the beginning of their covenant in 1 Sam. 18:3 and acknowledges his agency in making the covenant.[36]

After Jonathan demonstrates his loyalty by lying to Saul, Jonathan and David express mutual affection for the first time, and David shows more involvement than Jonathan (1 Sam. 20:28-42). The narrator makes explicit that the two kiss and weep with each other; the narrator attaches the phrase "each man…his friend" to both verbs: "and each man kissed his friend and each man wept for his friend" (וישקו איש את־רעהו ויבכו איש את־רעהו). While the repeated phrase emphasizes the mutual nature of their actions, the narrator also indicates that David engages in these actions to a greater extent: "until David increased" (עד־דוד הגדיל).[37] David's greater participation in these gestures signals that Jonathan's fidelity in 1 Samuel 18–20 prompts growth in the mutuality of their relationship.[38]

Jonathan recognizes this change, and the narrator's last description of their covenant reflects this growth. When Jonathan responds to David and declares that they have sworn in the name of the Lord in 1 Sam. 20:42, he uses two phrases to emphasize their joint action: an independent personal pronoun (אנחנו) as a stated subject and the phrase "the two of us" (שנינו). During Jonathan and David's last meeting, the narrator describes their covenant-making with unprecedented mutuality: "And the two of them cut a covenant before the Lord" (1 Sam. 23:18). While singular verbs express previous iterations of their covenant (18:3; 20:8, 16), a plural verb (ויכרתו) here describes their joint participation. Furthermore, with "the two of them" (שניהם), the narrator echoes Jonathan's recognition of David's increasing investment in their relationship after Jonathan's repeated demonstrations of loyalty.

Jonathan's covenant and enacted allegiance to David reveal the future for which Jonathan longs—attachment to David and detachment from Saul—and Jonathan's final words exemplify this hope. In 1 Sam. 23:17, Jonathan not only recognizes that David will replace Saul as king, but

---

36. Though Jonathan does not include the noun ברית in 1 Sam. 20:16, the verb ויכרת implies the covenant as its object (Alter, *The David Story*, 126, and Firth, *1 & 2 Samuel*, 221 and 225–6).

37. Alter renders this as a temporal phrase in which David weeps longer than Jonathan (*The David Story*, 130). Chapman notes that the phrase could connote the duration or degree of David's weeping (*1 Samuel as Christian Scripture*, 170). Regardless of the precise nuance of the phrase, David's weeping marks him as participating in his relationship with Jonathan to a greater degree than he has previously.

38. On the development of David and Jonathan's relationship in 1 Sam. 20, see also Firth, *1 & 2 Samuel*, 225–6; Fokkelman, *The Crossing Fates*, 293 and 440; and Smith, *Poetic Heroes*, 66.

he also states his place in these developments: he will remain faithful to David as his second-in-command (למשנה). Jonathan's repeated demonstrations of loyalty have given David no reason to doubt his intentions, which the narrative reinforces with David's first mutual participation in their covenant in 1 Sam. 23:18.

In David's lament for Jonathan in 2 Sam. 1:22-27, he expresses appreciation for both Jonathan's military prowess and personal commitment.[39] Thus, David's lament reveals that Jonathan has convinced David of his loyalty and benefit.[40] With this culmination of Jonathan and David's relationship, the narrative presents Jonathan as a steadfast asset for David's coming reign rather than a threat to be eliminated.[41]

Since the narrative has traced Jonathan's repeated acts and expressions of allegiance to David, Jonathan's death does not remove a dangerous rival. Instead, it serves a different function, one tied to his relationship to Saul. As Jonathan repeatedly proves his loyalty to David, he attempts to distance himself from his father.

Jonathan helps David at Saul's expense to the point of lying to his father (1 Sam. 19–20), and he has sought independence from Saul since 1 Samuel 14. When Jonathan attacks the Philistines, he conceals his plan from Saul, and the narrative uses the *Leitwort* עבר to highlight Jonathan crossing over toward the Philistines and away from Saul. The root עבר occurs seven times in 1 Sam. 14:1-8 to describe Jonathan's movement,

---

39. Smith argues that David expresses a "great attachment" to Jonathan in 2 Sam. 1:26-27 (*Poetic Heroes*, 275–83). Fleming highlights the political nuances of נעם in 2 Sam. 1:23, 26: it refers to the expected, rather than voluntary, benevolence of the superior party in a political alliance ("Political Favoritism," 33).

40. Though Orly Keren helpfully explores the "complex" emotional and political relationship between Jonathan and David, Keren argues that Jonathan invests in a consistently one-sided relationship with David. This reading depends on seeing David's lament as not "supported by the previous narrative" rather than as a development anticipated by David's greater weeping in 1 Sam. 20:41 and David's participation in the covenant making in 1 Sam. 23:18. While Keren contends that David's "public eulogy" focuses on Jonathan's commitment to him and how Jonathan's loyalty benefits him, Smith identifies David's "private voice" in 2 Sam. 1:26-27, analogous to that of Gilgamesh for Enkidu: "This is a first person singular voice locked in lament over a second person singular intimate. Such singular devotion to Jonathan is what an audience might expect from David" (Keren, "David and Jonathan: A Case of Unconditional Love?," *JSOT* 37 [2012]: 22–3, and Smith, *Poetic Heroes*, 277–8).

41. Steven Weitzman argues that part of the narrative function of David's lament is to clear David of charges that he participated in the deaths of Saul and his sons ("David's Lament and the Poetics of Grief in 2 Samuel," *JQR* 85 [1995]: 354–5).

path, and destination.⁴² Jonathan's independence from his father continues to emerge in 1 Sam. 14:29-30, when he criticizes Saul's vow.

As Jonathan attempts to separate from Saul and attach to David, the narrative reminds the reader that Jonathan is Saul's son. For example, when Jonathan conceals David from Saul, the narrative frequently highlights Saul and Jonathan's connection. 1 Samuel 19:1-7 mentions their bond six times. The narrator twice refers to Jonathan as Saul's son in 19:1 and describes Saul as Jonathan's father in 19:4. When Jonathan speaks to David, he refers to Saul as "my father" three times in 19:2-3.⁴³ Similarly, as Jonathan and David conspire to protect David from Saul in 20:1-23, David refers to Saul as "your father" five times in 20:1, 3, 6, 8, 10, and Jonathan mentions "my father" six times in 20:2 (twice), 9, 12, 13 (twice).⁴⁴ Thus, the narrative intertwines Jonathan's increasing loyalty to David with reminders of his familial connection to Saul—the relationship that will precipitate Jonathan's death.

Jonathan succeeds in attaching to David but fails to detach from Saul. In 2 Sam. 1:23, David laments Jonathan and Saul: "in their death they were not separated" (ובמותם לא נפרדו). Despite Jonathan's initiatives to make a covenant with David and repeated displays of his allegiance to David, he remains Saul's son. None of Jonathan's choices separate him from the fate of Saul's house, and the death sentence Saul pronounces in 14:24-46 comes to fruition. In 28:16-19, Samuel announces that Saul and his sons will join him in death because Saul failed to heed the Lord's instructions. Here, Samuel does not mention Saul's sons by name, which

---

42. Eleven of the thirty-five occurrences of the root עבר in 1 Samuel appear in 1 Sam. 14: 1 Sam. 2:24; 9:4 (four occurrences), 27 (two occurrences); 13:7; 14:1 (two occurrences), 4 (three occurrences), 6, 8, 23, 40 (two occurrences); 15:12, 24; 16:8, 9, 10; 20:36; 25:19; 26:13 (two occurrences), 22; 27:2; 29:2 (two occurrences); 30:10; 31:7 (two occurrences). For further discussion of this *Leitwort*, see Bodner, *1 Samuel*, 131 and 137; Polzin, *Samuel and the Deuteronomist*, 132–3; and Edelman, *King Saul*, 84.

43. Alter (*The David Story*, 118) and Jobling (*1 Samuel*, 97) contend that the repetition of Jonathan and Saul's filial relationship in 1 Sam. 19:1-7 emphasizes their connection when Jonathan does not act like a loyal son. Alternatively, Edelman (*King Saul*, 143) interprets this repetition as marking Saul's concern for Jonathan's future in light of David's growing relationship with the Lord and support from the people.

44. In 1 Sam. 20, only the narrator refers to Saul by name (1 Sam. 20:25, 26, 27, 28, 30, 32, 33). During Jonathan and Saul's confrontation, the narrator also highlights their familial connection (1 Sam. 20:27, 32), and Jonathan responds to "his father" in 1 Sam. 20:33-34. For further discussion of the prominence of familial language in 1 Sam. 20 see Firth, *1 & 2 Samuel*, 223–4, 227–8, and Fokkelman, *The Crossing Fates*, 296, 302, 337, 441.

underscores that their filial connection accounts for their deaths alongside their father. However, in 1 Sam. 31:2, the narrator names them when they die. With Jonathan's name, the reader remembers all his attempts to assert his independence from Saul and become David's second-in-command, none of which effectively split him from his father.

As Jonathan's initiatives fail to secure him a permanent place at David's side, his own words and actions reveal the theological dimensions of 1 Samuel that illuminate his fate. In 1 Samuel 14, Jonathan confesses the Lord's power to deliver and collaborates with the Lord in Israel's victory. In 1 Sam. 20:12-16, 18-23, Jonathan identifies the Lord as being active in his covenant with David, punishing him if he fails to warn David, being present with David as with Saul in the past, cutting off David's enemies in the future, and sending David securely away from Saul.[45] The narrative does not explain how Jonathan perceives the Lord working on David's behalf. However, in light of the narrator's confirmation of Jonathan's collaboration with the Lord in 14:1-23 and the Lord's choice of David in 16:12, the narrative creates an expectation that Jonathan accurately intuits the Lord's role in David's rise.

Jonathan's theological insights direct the reader to the primary narrative explanation of why David becomes king instead of him: the Lord has rejected Saul's house and chosen David to reign in Saul's place. With

---

45. Keren concludes that Jonathan acts "contrary to his own best interests" when he supports David and abdicates his claim to the throne. When Keren contends that "Jonathan's anxiety about his future is unmistakable," Keren identifies Jonathan's self-interest in securing a place for himself in David's reign as a primary "hidden" motivation in Jonathan's actions. Though Keren considers Zehnder's insights about the role of Jonathan and David's friendship in "the divine plan," Keren does not consider Jonathan's perception of the Lord's choice of David as a contributing motivation for his actions ("David and Jonathan," 11, 13, 18, 21, and 23). However, Jonathan frequently describes the Lord's role in his relationship with David, which marks it as a prominent factor in Jonathan's understanding of his relationship with David. Since the Lord's choice of David and rejection of Saul drive 1 Samuel, Jonathan cooperates with the Lord when he assists David and places David's future above his own. Though Jonathan does seek protection for his family and a place for himself with David, Jonathan's words and actions expose his theological perception as the primary motivation for his commitment to David. In 1 Sam. 20, Jonathan recognizes the Lord's presence with David before he asks David to protect his family. Immediately after this first request for David's reciprocal faithfulness, the narrator reiterates Jonathan's love for David that continues to be his stated motivation in the narrative (1 Sam. 20:12-17). Likewise, before Jonathan asserts that he will be David's second-in-command, he encourages David to strengthen himself in the Lord (1 Sam. 23:16-17).

the similarities between Jonathan's and David's faithfulness and success as military strategists in 1 Samuel 14; 17, the narrative highlights that Saul's house falls for theological reasons, rather than for lack of a capable successor. Likewise, when Jonathan dies with Saul's family, he does not die as a threat to the rising king; Jonathan has convinced David of his allegiance and has clarified his intention to serve him. Since Jonathan's initiatives have failed to sever his filial bond with Saul, he inherits the consequences of the Lord's rejection of Saul and dies alongside Saul as his heir. Jonathan's connection to Saul thereby foils his hope to continue assisting David—the Lord's chosen heir for Saul.

Chapter 10

Analogies between Minor Characters: The Example of Michal

Jonathan Jacobs

Biblical stories generally feature a single main character, accompanied by several minor characters.[1] Professor Uriel Simon began his classic article on minor characters with the following statement: "The number of characters who appear in biblical narrative, of every period, is extremely small." Later he wrote:

> In general, then, the actions and feelings of secondary characters are described only when they are required to advance the plot or to shed light on another actor, and not out of a genuine interest in these characters themselves... A primary function of some minor characters is to move the plot forward; others endow the narrative with greater meaning and depth.[2]

---

1. It is not always easy to ascertain who is the main character, and which characters are minor. Some scholars claim that the main character is the one who is "onstage" during the entire narrative, while the minor characters enter and exit as necessary. Others claim that the main character is rounder, and develops while the minor characters are superficial and unidimensional. In many cases, these definitions indeed help us identify the major and minor characters. But there are always borderline cases. Therefore, it is better not to speak of clearly differentiated categories but rather of a scale with clear endpoints and range of intermediary possibilities. For more on this see, E. M. Forster, *Aspects of the Novel* (London: Edwin Arnold, 1949), 67–78; William K. Wimsatt, *The Verbal Icon: Studies in the Meaning of Poetry* (London: Noonday, 1970); Josef Even, *Character in Narrative* (Tel Aviv: Hapoalim, 1993), 33–44 (Hebrew), and regarding biblical narratives, Shimon Bar-Efrat, *Narrative Art in the Bible* (New York: T&T Clark, 2008), 86–92.

2. Uriel Simon, *Reading Prophetic Narratives*, trans. Lenn J. Schramm (Bloomington: Indiana University Press, 1997), 263, 266, 267.

From his statement, it emerges that the biblical narrative focuses on the main character and his or her development. Simon points out that the secondary characters have two significant roles: advancing (and stopping) the narrative, and furnishing it with meaning. To be more specific, we might say that the second role of minor characters is to cast light on the main character, to draw him or her out, and, at times, provide background for understanding a particular situation.

Since Simon's work was published, there has been more research on minor characters. For example, some scholars have pointed out that there are analogous characterizations that compare and contrast the main character and accompanying minor characters. A famous example of a contrasting characterization is the comparison the Bible draws between the character, actions and temperament of David, as the main character, and the character, actions and temperament of the minor character Uriah the Hittite in the story of David and Bathsheba. This analogy casts a negative light on the behavior of David in this incident.[3]

This essay presents a similar literary phenomenon that has not yet been adequately explored: stories designed to create an analogy between two *minor* characters within the narrative.

Just as analogies between minor characters and the main character can be used to cast light on the main character, so too can analogies between minor characters contribute to characterizing and illuminating the main character. However, it would also be interesting to consider whether there are any cases in which comparing two minor characters serves to define each of them, beyond casting light on the main character. If we find a case of this type, it will show that the minor characters are significant in and of themselves, not just as a means for casting light on the main character.

I will begin with three short examples of analogies between minor characters, which are based primarily on the plot. I will then present, at greater length, the analogy between Michal and Jonathan, the children of David. All of the examples are drawn from the books of Samuel.

1. It is agreed that Hannah is the main character in the books' opening stories (1 Sam. 1), accompanied by three minor characters: Elkanah, Peninnah, and Eli. Of these characters, two—Elkanah and Eli—are contrasted, an analogy being made between their responses to the main character's tears. Hannah cries twice in this chapter, and the two men respond in opposite manners. Elkanah responds to his wife's tears by attempting to placate her. Conversely, Eli in the

---

3. Bar-Efrat, *Narrative Art*, 87.

Tabernacle reprimands her severely. At this stage it appears that Elkanah's response is more sensitive and appropriate, but Hannah does not share her inner feelings with Elkanah; rather, she shares her distress and sorrow with the more aloof high priest. In the end, it is Eli who gives his blessing to Hannah, rather than Elkanah her husband.[4] In this case it seems that the analogy between two minor characters sheds light on the main character, Hannah, and teaches about the turmoil in her soul, her doubts, and inner feelings when facing infertility and isolation.

2. In 1 Samuel 26, an analogy of contrast is created between two military commanders, Abishai son of Zeruiah and Abner son of Ner. On the one hand, Abishai is loyal to his master, and is prepared to kill Saul on his behalf, while Abner is unable to protect his master. This instance is a minor chapter in the overall comparison that the Bible draws between David, whose path to the summit is paved, and Saul, who is progressively declining. The generals are miniature reflections of their masters: the successful Abishai reflects the image of the successful David; Abner, who cannot protect his master, reflects Saul's deteriorating fortunes.

3. 2 Samuel 9 deals with the meeting of David and Mephibosheth in the wake of the fulfillment of the covenant between the latter's father Jonathan and David, the main character in the story. In addition to Mephibosheth, another minor character is mentioned: Ziba, a servant in the house of Saul, who is in possession of his late master's property. These minor characters stand in opposition to each other: Mephibosheth suffers from a very poor self-image—three times in vv. 9-10 he refers to himself a "the son of your master." On the other hand, although the biblical narrator indeed refers to Ziba as a "servant" (vv. 2, 9, 12; trans. NSRV; the Hebrew words differ) three times, he actually has great self-confidence. Mephibosheth is indeed the grandson of King Saul, but he is handicapped and destitute. Conversely, although Ziba is a simple servant in Saul's house, he has great wealth. Mephibosheth has only one child, while Ziba has fifteen sons. These distinguishing details, which contrast the minor characters, seem to portray Ziba as superior to Mephibosheth. However, David faithfully keeps his promise to Jonathan and exalts Mephibosheth, granting him honor and property, at the expense of Ziba, who is humiliated by

---

4. For this analogy, see Robert Alter, *The Art of Biblical Narrative* (New York: Basic Books, 1981), 81–6.

David and forced to hand his possessions over to Mephibosheth.[5] The apparent aim of this comparison is to cast a positive light on David, who faithfully keeps his promises, does justice, and returns lost property to its rightful owners. However, the contrasting analogy between Mephibosheth and Ziba presented in this chapter also forms the foundation for their future clash in the story of David's escape from Absalom (2 Sam. 16:1-4). Indeed, David will eventually return half of the property to Ziba, so it is divided equally between them (2 Sam. 19:31).

In the brief examples presented above, the comparisons between the minor characters serve to illuminate the character of the protagonist.

I now proceed to 1 Samuel 18–20 where I believe a broader comparison is constructed between two minor figures, both children of Saul, Jonathan, and Michal. Michal has been the subject of extensive research.[6] Jonathan, too, has received more than a little attention,[7] yet it seems to me that the analogy between these minor characters can add new perspectives for understanding not only Michal and Jonathan, but also the main character in these chapters, David.[8]

---

5. For this analogy, see Shimon Bar-Efrat, *I Samuel*, Mikra Leyisra'el (Tel Aviv: Am Oved, 1996), 97 (Hebrew).

6. See, for example, Alter, *The Art*, 114–25; David J. A. Clines, "Michal Observed: An Introduction," in *Telling Queen Michal's Story: An Experiment in Comparative Interpretation*, ed. David J. A. Clines and Tamara C. Eskenazi (Sheffield: Sheffield Academic, 1991), 24–63; J. Cheryl Exum, "Michal: The Whole Story," in *Fragmented Women: Feminist (Sub)versions of Biblical Narratives* (Sheffield: JSOT Press, 1993), 42–60; Chaya Shraga Ben-Ayun, *David's Wives—Michal, Abigail, Batsheba* (Israel: Levinsky, 2005), 21–85 (Hebrew); Ellen White, "Michal the Misinterpreted," *JSOT* 31 (2007): 451–64. Other articles may be found in Clines and Eskenazi, eds, *Telling Queen Michal's Story*.

7. R. B. Lawton, "Saul, Jonathan and the Son of Jesse," *JSOT* 58 (1993): 35–46; Orly Keren, "Saul's Son Jonathan: Light and Dark in His Character," *Beit Mikra* 53 (2008): 124–44 (Hebrew); David Jobling "Jonathan: A Structural Study in 1 Samuel," *Society of Biblical Literature: Seminar Papers* 10 (1976): 15–32. Additional articles will be mentioned below.

8. From the comparison between the siblings, Berlin learns that Jonathan has feminine characteristics, while Michal has masculine traits; see Adele Berlin, "Characterization in Biblical Narrative: David's Wives," *JSOT* 23 (1982): 70–2, and compare with J. P. Fokkelman, *Narrative Art and Poetry in the Books of Samuel: Vol. 2, The Crossing Fates*, SSN 23 (Assen: Van Gorcum, 1986), 195. Exum, "Michal," 52, expresses doubts about Berlin's approach. Ben-Ayun also disagrees, and suggests that the comparison between the siblings teaches that Jonathan acts out of warmth and loyalty, while Michal uses sophistication and guile; see Ben-Ayun, *David's Wives*, 72–3.

It should be noted that the Midrash already proposed an elementary analogy between these characters: "Michal, the daughter of Saul, and Jonathan, both loved David; Michal helped escape inside the house, and Jonathan outdoors" (*Midr. Ps.* 32:1).

We shall begin with 1 Samuel 18, where the foundation for an analogy between Jonathan and Michal is laid: of Jonathan it says, "And the soul of Jonathan was bound to the soul of David, and Jonathan loved him as his own soul" (v. 1),[9] while of Michal it is written, "Now Saul's daughter Michal loved David" (v. 20). Jonathan makes a covenant with David, "Then Jonathan made a covenant with David, because he loved him as his own soul" (v. 3). Michal also enters into a covenant with David, a covenant of marriage, "Saul gave him his daughter Michal as a wife" (v. 27). In this chapter, the analogy between the siblings is direct, and sheds light on both the overall love David enjoyed from all segments of the population, and the fact that Saul is exceptional in his hatred and envy of David.[10]

In 1 Samuel 19, the narrator continues to augment the analogy between the two minor characters. Careful reading of the chapter reveals two efforts to rescue David from Saul: Jonathan attempts to save David by achieving a temporary reconciliation between him and Saul (vv. 1-7), but this attempt fails (vv. 8-10); Michal's effort to save David by smuggling him out of the house results in the final separation between David and Saul (vv. 11-17).

From a literary standpoint, the two rescue attempts have the same form, with four stages: Saul's intentions to kill David immediately, "in the morning" (vv. 1-2, 11); the child talks to David, and informs him about the father's intentions (vv. 2, 11),[11] and then acts to counter the father's intentions (Jonathan, by way of reconciliation; Michal, by separation); and Saul's reaction to his children's actions. It should be emphasized that in neither case does Saul mention David's name (vv. 6, 17).

---

9. In this context I will not discuss the nature of the relationship between David and Jonathan. For a survey of the various opinions found in the scholarly literature, see Avraham, "David and Jonathan," 215–16 and nn. 1–4.

10. Ralph W. Klein, *1 Samuel*, WBC 10 (Waco: Word, 1983), 191; Bruce C. Birch, *The First and Second Books of Samuel*, NIB (Nashville: Abingdon, 1998), 1118; P. Kyle McCarter, Jr., *1 Samuel*, AB 8 (Garden City: Doubleday, 1980), 317–18.

11. On the similarities in the second stage, the reports to David, see Fokkelman, *Crossing Fates*, 262–3; Robert Polzin, *Samuel and the Deuteronomist: A Literary Study of the Deuteronomistic History. Part 2: 1 Samuel* (Bloomington: Indiana University Press, 1993), 185; Diana V. Edelman, *King Saul in the Historiography of Judah*, JSOTSup 121 (Sheffield: Sheffield Academic, 1991), 149.

The following table shows the stylistic affinities between the portrayals describing the actions of each minor character:

	Jonathan and David *(1 Sam. 19:1-7)*	*Michal and David* *(1 Sam. 19:11-17)*
Saul's intention to kill David	[1] Saul spoke with his son Jonathan and with all his servants about *killing David*. But Saul's son Jonathan took great delight in David.	[11] Saul sent messengers to David's house to keep watch over him, planning *to kill him in the morning*.
The children inform David	[2] *Jonathan told David*, "My father Saul is trying to kill you; therefore be on guard *tomorrow morning*; stay in a secret place and hide yourself. [3] I will go out and stand beside my father in the field where you are, and I will speak to my father about you; if I learn anything I will tell you."	[11] *David's wife Michal told him*, "If you do not save your life tonight, tomorrow you will be killed."
The children act for David's welfare	[4] *Jonathan spoke well of David to his father Saul*, saying to him, "The king should not sin against his servant David, because he has not sinned against you, and because his deeds have been of good service to you; [5] for he took his life in his hand when he attacked the Philistine, and the Lord brought about a great victory for all Israel. You saw it, and rejoiced; why then will you sin against an innocent person by killing David without cause?"	[12] So *Michal let David down* through the window; he fled away and escaped. [13] Michal took an idol and laid it on the bed; she put a net of goats' hair on its head, and covered it with the clothes. [14] When Saul sent messengers to take David, she said, "He is sick." [15] Then Saul sent the messengers to see David for themselves. He said, "Bring him up to me in the bed, that I may kill him." [16] When the messengers came in, the idol was in the bed, with the covering of goats' hair on its head.
Saul's response to his children's actions	[6] *Saul heeded the voice of Jonathan*; Saul swore, "As the Lord lives, he shall not be put to death." [7] So Jonathan called David and related all these things to him. Jonathan then brought David to Saul, and he was in his presence as before.	[17] *Saul said to Michal*, "Why have you deceived me like this, and let my enemy go, so that he has escaped?" Michal answered Saul, "He said to me, 'Let me go; why should I kill you?'"

Figure 3. Jonathan and David/Michal and David

Jonathan works by persuasion and reconciliation. Michal, however, makes not attempt to appease; she takes the drastic steps of exclusion and separation. What drives them to act differently?

It should be noted that at the beginning of the narrative Jonathan is referred to as "the son of Saul" (v. 1). Conversely, Michal is called "David's wife" (v. 11).[12] This emphasis indicates a possible difference between the two children: Jonathan remained loyal to his father while still maintaining his love for David. Michal, however, transferred her full loyalty to David. In vv. 1-7, Saul presents his hatred of David explicitly, unlike the previous chapter where he tried to rid himself of David clandestinely. It seems that Saul intends to kill David immediately, so Jonathan tells David to hide in the morning until he is able to calm his father. The filial relationship is emphasized with two mentions in v. 1: "his son Jonathan"; "Saul's son Jonathan." Jonathan retains loyalty to his father, and therefore acts to reconcile them. Indeed, Jonathan says "my father" (vv. 2-3) three times, which indicates the great difficulty he faces when he is torn between loyalty to his father and his love for David.[13]

Michal is referred to as David's "wife" (v. 11), and she evinces no signs of struggle or hesitation. She helps David flee, and uses a trick, placing idols in David's bed, to buy time so David can gain some distance (vv. 13-14). Michal does not attempt to compromise or mediate. In v. 17, the last word is indeed given to Michal, thereby expressing her father's helplessness in the face of his daughter's actions.[14] The sevenfold use of the Leitwort "kill" (vv. 1, 2, 5, 11, 15-17) also helps to shape Michal's character as being willing to risk her life for her husband: six times, "kill" refers to David, but the seventh time it refers to Michal, symbolizing her

---

12. Clines has examined all references to Michal, and has shown that when she acts for David's good, she is called "David's wife," and whenever she criticizes David, she is "Saul's daughter." See David J. A. Clines, "X, X ben Y: Personal Names in Hebrew Narrative Style," *VT* 22 (1972): 269–72; see also D. Seeman, "The Wacher at the Window: Cultural Poetics of a Biblical Motif," *Prooftexts* 24 (2004): 22; Moshe Garsiel, "The Relationship between David and Michal, Daughter of King Saul," *Studies in Bible and Exegesis* 10 (2011): 119–20 (Hebrew).

13. For Jonathan's considerations, see also, Klein, *Samuel*, 210. I disagree with the scholars who claim that Jonathan conspired with David against Saul, see for example, David M. Gunn, *The Fate of King Saul: An Interpretation of a Biblical Story*, JSOTSup 14 (Sheffield: JSOT Press, 1980), 81; Joyce G. Baldwin, *1 and 2 Samuel*, TOTC (Downers Grove: IVP, 1988), 131; Walter Brueggemann, *First and Second Samuel*, Interpretation (Louisville: John Knox, 1990), 141.

14. See, for example, Fokkelman, *Crossing Fates*, 264–70.

devotion to her husband. The bottom line is that Jonathan's method for saving David failed, while Michal's method succeeded. 1 Samuel 18, presents the analogy between Jonathan and Michal: both of them love David, and both of them make a covenant with him (a covenant of love or a covenant of marriage); ch. 19 presents the siblings' actions to save David, each one in a unique way. It has been suggested that Jonathan acted as he did because of his dual loyalty, while Michal's loyalty was fully given to her husband David. Michal is not explicitly mentioned in ch. 20, but it seems to me that the Bible shapes the character of Jonathan in this chapter in a way that is analogous way to Michal's actions in ch. 19.[15]

David flees from Saul, then returns to Jonathan and asks him to ascertain Saul's intentions. In my opinion, David himself is well-aware of Saul's decision to cause him harm; his purpose is not to determine the king's plans, but rather to convince Jonathan that there is no chance of reconciliation between Saul and David. Jonathan agrees to cooperate, and in order to clarify matters David asks Jonathan to deceive his father—to tell him that David has gone to his family instead of dining at the king's table.

The Bible makes stylistic and substantive connections between the two stories in which Saul's children deceive him. In both cases, the word "escape" is used to describe David's departure but its use in ch. 20 is artificial; and I think this usage is intended to strengthen the analogy between the two figures.[16] In both cases, the children of Saul claim that David asked or demanded that they "send him"; in both cases, Saul is angry at the child who deceived him, and claims that his children are cooperating with his enemy David.

Michal's deception (1 Sam. 19)	Jonathan's deception (1 Sam. 20)
[11] David's wife Michal told him, "If you do not *save* [מְמַלֵּט] your life tonight, tomorrow you will be killed."	[29] My brother has commanded me to be there. So now, if I have found favor in your sight, *let me get away* [אִמָּלְטָה], and see my brothers.

---

15. Jonathan Grossman, *Text and Subtext: On Exploring Biblical Narrative Design* (Tel Aviv: Tvunot, 2015), 65 (Hebrew), briefly discusses some aspects of this analogy.

16. Other scholars think putting the word "escape" in Jonathan's mouth is intended to hint that David did not go to brothers for an ordinary visit, but rather to get away from Saul. See, for example, H. P. Smith, *A Critical and Exegetical Commentary on the Book of Samuel*, ICC (Edinburgh: T. & T. Clark, 1899), 193; Fokkelman, *Crossing Fates*, 332; Edelman, *King Saul*, 159.

¹⁷ Michal answered Saul, "He said to me, '*Let me go*; why should I kill you?'	^{28–29} Jonathan answered Saul, "David earnestly asked leave of me to go to Bethlehem; he said, '*Let me go* for our family is holding a sacrifice in the city.
¹⁷ Saul said to Michal, "Why have you deceived me like this, and *let my enemy go*, so that he has escaped?"	³⁰ Then Saul's anger was kindled against Jonathan. He said to him, "You son of a perverse, rebellious woman! Do I not know that *you have chosen the son of Jesse* to your own shame, and to the shame of your mother's nakedness

Figure 4. Michal's Deception/Jonathan's Deception

There is indeed a similarity between the actions of Jonathan and Michal, but the difference between them is also evident: Jonathan deceives his father with the thought of, and perhaps hope for, reconciliation between Saul and David. Michal, on the other hand, deceives her father with the understanding that there will be no reconciliation, and with the intention of separating her father from her husband.

In conclusion, it seems that Jonathan remains, to the best of his ability, loyal to both sides, to his father and to David, and tries his best to persuade Saul not to harm David.[17] Conversely, Michal is loyal only to David. Jonathan's action to save David fail, while Michal's action to save David succeed.

I have shown that the analogy between the minor characters, Michal and Jonathan, illuminates their characters by contrasting them. However, in the final analysis it seems that the purpose of the analogy is to teach us something about the main character, about David. Initially, we saw that Jonathan and Michal sought to save David in opposing ways. Yet in the second stage, Jonathan follows his sister's example, and uses deceitful tactics, similar to the tricks that Michal uses against Saul. If we compare the parting of David from each of the siblings, we find that David separated from Jonathan with great warmth (1 Sam. 20:41). As we know, there is no such separation from Michal (1 Sam. 19:12). How can David's behavior be understood?[18]

---

17. Here I disagree with the few scholars who believe that Jonathan had made his peace with the divine plan that chose David, and was entirely on David's side. See, for example, Edelman, *King Saul*, 144.

18. Exum claims that the difference in the siblings' fate is the result of gendered preference for the male; see Exum, "Michal," 51–9. Ben-Ayun contends that their fates differ because Jonathan is loyal and does not express any criticism while Michal gets and angry at David and provokes him; see Ben-Ayun, *David's Wives*, 74.

Much has been written about David's relationship to Jonathan and Michal.[19] I would like to add an additional layer to the subject, focusing on the analogy suggested above. As mentioned, Jonathan tries to remain loyal to both Saul and David. Michal, on the other hand, is extreme in her love for David, and therefore rebels against her father and abandons him for David's sake. But David himself is more like Jonathan than Michal: David maintains his allegiance to the kingdom, and as long as Saul is the legitimate king, David demands respect for him, from both himself and his men. In the parallel stories in 1 Samuel 24 and 2 Samuel 26, David prevents his men from hurting Saul, and defines Saul as the Lord's anointed: "The Lord forbid that I should do this thing to my lord, the Lord's anointed, to raise my hand against him; for he is the Lord's anointed" (1 Sam. 24:6); "But David said to Abishai, 'Do not destroy him; for who can raise his hand against the Lord's anointed, and be guiltless?'" (1 Sam. 26:9). On this basis, I would like to suggest that David's attitude toward Jonathan is more sympathetic than his attitude toward Michal. David respects Jonathan's dual loyalty while deeming Michal's blind loyalty to himself unacceptable. From a personal perspective, Michal is distanced from her father because of her love of David; but Michal is actually rebelling against the Lord's anointed, an approach to kingship which David is unwilling to accept.

It should be remembered that the Bible contains no explicit censure of David's behavior toward Michal (as opposed to the Bathsheba story, for example, where the Bible explicitly criticizes David's behavior). However, David's estrangement from Michal suits his overall image as someone who remains loyal to the monarchy and reigning king, as long as he remains on the throne.

We have thus learned that the analogy of contrast between Jonathan and Michal might shed further light on the behavior and character of the protagonist of the book of Samuel, David.

In conclusion, this essay presents an instance in which the biblical narrator creates an analogy between minor characters in the narrative. Biblical analogies between secondary characters usually contribute to a deeper understanding of the motives and character of its protagonist, but sometimes also contribute to understanding the character of the minor characters themselves.

---

19. See nn. 6–7 above.

Chapter 11

ABIGAIL:
A WOMAN OF WISDOM AND DECISIVE ACTION

Philip F. Esler

The world in which 1 Samuel 25 was written and which it assumes was contoured with cultural forms and practices very different from those with which people reading this text in a modern Western context are familiar. One way—but surely not the only way—of exploring Abigail and how she functions in the narrative is to situate her character, understanding and actions within the framework of the distinctive social setting that was ancient Israel. The main benefit of this approach, which is adopted here, is that it highlights the degree to which Abigail's exercise of agency in relation both to her husband and David cuts across and subverts the male roles and male power that customarily held such ample sway in that culture. In other words, unless we do our best to understand the usual state of affairs in Abigail's world, we will not appreciate how she upends convention and reveals her character in doing so. In this way, Abigail plays a crucial role in the events described in 1 Samuel 25. This chapter in 1 Samuel rehearses one of many incidents in the larger narrative that recounts David's attempts to survive Saul's animosity towards him. Nevertheless, what we find in it is a short but exciting and vividly rendered story where the character of Abigail proves decisive in propelling the plot towards a resolution that is a happy one for her and David, although not for her husband. Nothing written below assumes the historicity of the events of this narrative, which remains an open question; rather, the issue is how the details of the narrative would have been understood by an ancient Israelite audience, whether they had actually happened or not.

The Social Context

To set the scene, it is necessary to summarize certain aspects of this context that will prove relevant in how Abigail is presented and the story unfolds.[1] Speaking at a fairly high level of generality, this was a patrilineal society, where fathers bequeathed property, land especially, to their sons, while helping their daughters in other ways, by the provision of dowries for example.[2] It was also patrilocal, with wives leaving their natal families to go off and live in their father-in-law's house or their husband's if his father was dead. Women married at a very young age, often shortly after puberty (see Ezek. 16:4-8). Like most human cultures it was group-oriented, which meant that individuals tended to be more closely embedded in their relevant groups, families or villages for example, than in individualistic cultures. Honor was a pivotal value and one aspect of honor was that men had to protect their daughters, sisters and wives from the sexual attentions of other men. Another aspect was the need to be successful in the jostling with other men that is common in settings where men value their honor, a social pattern known as "challenge and response."[3] Although in this context men had great power over women in their family, the idea that women had little or no power has been comprehensively discredited by Carol Meyers. A better understanding of the situation is that women "in peasant households dominate in certain household activities and men in others, with significant contributions from both."[4] Women's household activities covered a whole range of complex and vital skills, especially rearing children, preparing food and spinning and clothes making. Their power in household decision-making was not a trivial matter.[5] Men were particularly active in activities outside

---

1. For more details, see Philip F. Esler, *Sex Wives, and Warriors: Reading Biblical Narrative with Its Ancient Audience* (Eugene: Cascade, 2011), 35–76.

2. For a discussion of the anthropology of dowries and bride-prices, and their application to some of the papyri in the Babatha archive from the late first and early second century CE, see Philip F. Esler, *Babatha's Orchard: The Yadin Papyri and An Ancient Jewish Family Tale Retold* (Oxford: Oxford University Press, 2017), 90–3.

3. Bruce J. Malina, *The New Testament World: Insights from Cultural Anthropology. Third Edition Revised and Expanded* (Louisville: Westminster John Knox, 2001), 33–6. Malina was reliant on the discovery by Pierre Bourdieu of this pattern among the Kabyle of North Africa ("The Sentiment of Honour in Kabyle Society," in *Honour and Shame: The Values of Mediterranean Society*, ed. J. G. Peristiany [London: Weidenfeld & Nicolson, 1965], 191–241, at 197).

4. Carol Meyers, *Rediscovering Eve: Ancient Israelite Women in Context* (Oxford: Oxford University Press), 186.

5. Ibid., 185.

the household, for example, growing crops and raising livestock, and in building and maintenance activities. In most cases, men probably took the visible lead in relations with outsiders (even if women were offering advice behind the scenes).

David, Nabal, and Abigail

The story is predicated on the circumstance that David is in the wilderness of Paran on the run from Saul (1 Sam. 25:1). Unstated but implied is that he is accompanied by a band of young men who need to be fed, 600 of them according to 25:13! At this point the narrator introduces us to the possible solution to David's problem: a very rich man, who lived in Maon and kept his flocks of sheep and goats in Carmel. Carmel was about one mile north of Maon.[6] With 3,000 sheep and 1,000 goats he was extremely wealthy. By way of comparison, Job owned 7,000 sheep, 3,000 camels, 500 yoke of oxen and 500 she-asses, but then he was "the greatest of all the people of the east" (Job 1:3). At this time the man was sheering his sheep, always in Israel an occasion of celebration and plenty.

The narrator next supplies the man's name, Nabal, and also that of his wife, Abigail, before launching into brief descriptions of them. In those descriptions, it is interesting to note, Abigail is mentioned first, presumably because the story to come will pivot around her. She is of good understanding (טובת־שכל) and beautiful in appearance (יפת תאר). Only a small number of women are described as "beautiful" in the Hebrew Bible apart from Abigail.[7] The combination of beauty and intelligence (with the word discretion [טעם] also used of Abigail at 1 Sam. 25:33) in a woman is not unknown to the Hebrew Bible, since it is implied in Prov. 11:22 by the problem of someone who has the former but not the latter. Nevertheless, Abigail is the only woman expressly described as possessing both qualities. Accordingly, the combination of the two features here is highly significant for the story. Nabal, on the other name, is very different; he is "harsh," "severe" (קשה) and "evil," "unpleasant" (רע). His very name means "fool," as Abigail will later point out (1 Sam. 25:25).

---

6. Hans Wilhelm Hertzberg, *I & II Samuel: A Commentary* (London: SCM, 1983), 247.

7. They are: Sarah (Gen. 12:11); Rachel (Gen. 29:17); Bathsheba (2 Sam. 11:2); Tamar, Absalom's sister (2 Sam. 13:1); Tamar, Absalom's daughter (2 Sam. 14:27); Abishag the Shunammite (1 Kgs 1:3); Vashti, Queen of Persia (Est. 1:10-11); Esther (Est. 2:7); Job's daughters (Job 42:15); the royal princess (Ps. 45:11); and the beloved (Song 1:5).

We are, however, able to say rather more about Abigail by exploring details of the narrative within this particular social context. To begin with, we must ask how Nabal has come to marry Abigail. This would certainly have been a marriage arranged between him (there is no mention of his father, who was probably dead at the time of the marriage) and Abigail's family. It would not have been a marriage for love. Nabal was certainly able to pay a significant bride-price to her father, if that was the dominant custom of the time (and Saul demands a bride-price from David in 1 Sam. 18:25). On the other hand, if Abigail came from a family of some wealth, we would expect her father to have settled some form of dowry upon her in the event of her husband dying or divorcing her. For in a patrilineal society such as this, if Nabal died, Abigail would not inherit his property, since it would pass instead to the nearest heir on his patriline. This point is regularly misunderstood by interpreters who automatically and erroneously assume that after Nabal's death David acquired his property when he married Abigail.[8] In fact, it does appear that Abigail's dowry was a very limited one, consisting of the one ass and her five maidens who accompanied her when she went off to become David's wife (v. 42). No gold or silver, jewelry or fine clothes are mentioned. All this suggests that she came from a family that was not particularly wealthy and which could not provide her with an ample dowry. By way of comparison, in Genesis 24 the arrangements for Rebekah's betrothal to Isaac involve Abraham, through his servant, giving rich presents to her brother and mother (these being akin to a bride-price), as well as silver and gold jewelry and rich clothes to Rebekah, while her family sends her off with camels and servants, these constituting a dowry (Gen. 24:53, 61).

Abigail has no children. This is not stated expressly, but the omission of any reference to her being a mother is socially significant. In a patrilineal and patrilocal society, the position of a new bride among her affinal kin can be very difficult until she has produced a child, ideally a son.[9]

---

8. For this assumption, see Joyce G. Baldwin, who believes David had a right to Nabal's estates (*1 and 2 Samuel: An Introduction and Commentary* [Leicester: Inter-Varsity, 1988], 153). Similarly, Hertzberg (*I & II Samuel*, 205) claims the text assumes the widow of a rich sheep-owner represented material support for David. Mary J. Evans (*1 and 2 Samuel*, NIC [Peabody: Hendrickson, 2000], 115) assumes that marrying Abigail provided David with extra funding because "she almost certainly brought more than just five maids with her." Steven L. McKenzie (*King David: A Biography* [Oxford: Oxford University Press, 2000], 146) states that David acquired Calebite property on his marriage to Abigail.

9. J. K. Campbell, *Honour, Family and Patronage: A Study of Institutions and Moral Values in a Greek Mountain Community* (New York: Oxford University Press, 1964), 59–69.

Since Abigail's having given birth to a son would have greatly enhanced her status in the eyes of Nabal and of other people in their setting, one would expect it to be mentioned if it had happened. Clinching the view that she has no children is the fact that towards the end of the narrative, when Abigail marries David, although she goes to him with five maids, no children are mentioned (v. 42). Later she will bear a son to David (called Chileab in 2 Sam. 3:3 and Daniel in 1 Chron. 3:1). These considerations suggest that an ancient audience would have understood her as quite young (since women married very young) and probably not married to Nabal for very long.

Accordingly, the picture that emerges of Abigail is not only of a woman who is beautiful and intelligent, but also of one who is young, childless and not from a particularly wealthy family. The fact that Abigail is intelligent and yet young assumes added significance in a social context where wisdom was generally regarded as something a person acquired with age. Thus we find in Job 12:12: "Wisdom is with the aged, and understanding in length of days" (RSV). Yet this general picture still allowed for exceptions: "But it is the spirit in a man, the breath of the Almighty, that makes him understand; It is not the old that are wise nor the aged that understand what is right" (Job 32:8-9; RSV). A statement in Ps. 119:100—"I understand more than the aged, for I keep thy precepts" (RSV)—both implies the general rule but also allows for deviations from it for those who do God's will. Abigail's intelligence, therefore, was not in the usual run of things, but nor was it utterly unlikely. Here it aligns with her closeness to the Lord God as seen in how she addresses David in 1 Sam. 25:24-31.

That Abigail does not have a son is particularly problematic for her position in the family. If she and Nabal had had a son, in the event of her husband's death, her son would have inherited his property and, in most cases, could be expected to have looked after his mother. With no son, Nabal's property would pass to a more distant member of his patriline, someone who might have been quite happy to show Abigail the door upon his coming into the estate, leaving her only recourse the shameful return to her birth family. In short, therefore, Abigail's position is extremely vulnerable in the event that her husband dies or divorces her.

David's Messengers and Nabal

After the mini portraits of Abigail and Nabal, which we have now complemented from the wider narrative in its social context, the narrator turns back to David: "David heard in the wilderness that Nabal was shearing his sheep" (v. 4). David's mention of Nabal's name and the fact that he was shearing his sheep render it likely that the narrator wants his audience to assume that the information expressly supplied in vv. 2-3 about Nabal and Abigail was known to David. The severity of Nabal's character helps explain why, when David sends ten men to request supplies from Nabal, he instructs them to extend great respect and elaborate courtesy to the man (vv. 5-8). Lest it pass unnoticed, however, it must be stressed that, in line with the nature of the social context outlined above, it is to Nabal, at the shearing at Carmel, that David sends his men, not to Abigail. We must imagine a scene at Carmel where Nabal has laid on large amounts of food (bread and meat) for his men. Although Abigail was probably in their house a mile away in Maon, there must have been food there too (even if not as much as at the shearing). Yet, although he probably knows of Nabal's wife, David automatically assumes that a request like this must be made to the senior man in the family, not to his wife. It falls within the husband's prerogative, not the wife's. It is "men's business." The choice of Nabal rests partly on his being the property owner (vv. 6-8), but also on his honor as the senior male of the family. The latter factor explains why David diminishes the status of himself and his men in relation to Nabal by telling his men to say to him, "Pray give whatever you have at hand to your servants and to your son David" (v. 8).

Daniel Bodi has suggested that David and Nabal's interaction should be understood within the culture of hospitality in the ancient Near East. Such a comparison would bring out how seriously Nabal has breached hospitality customs, thus implying a reading more sympathetic to David than many modern readings suggest.[10] Yet it is not obvious that it is hospitality, with the guest typically resident with the host for a period (one night at least), which David is seeking. Rather, a more likely social dynamic is at hand.

Within the social dynamic of challenge and response mentioned above, David's request for help was a challenge. Since the dynamic of challenge-and-response can proceed through many stages,[11] it is probably best to regard David's challenge as the latest gambit in a continuing process that had already begun with interactions between his men and Nabal's shepherds mentioned in the text (1 Sam. 25:7-8, 15-16). A positive answer from Nabal would have represented a satisfactory response for both parties, since his honor would have been enhanced at the expense of David's, and the exchange would have come to a peaceful end. David is ready to accept a diminution of his honor in relation to Nabal's in this

---

10. Daniel Bodi, "David as an 'Apiru in 1 Samuel 25 and the Pattern of Seizing Power in the Ancient Near East," in *Abigail, Wife of David, and Other Ancient Oriental Women*, ed. Daniel Bodi, HBM (Sheffield: Sheffield Phoenix, 2013), 24–59.

11. Malina, *New Testament World*, 33–6.

exchange because it is the price he needs to pay to get his men fed. But Nabal's scornful rejection of David's request represents a very different response, and one that will keep the exchange open and thus invite David to provide his own response to Nabal's, a very dangerous one as it will turn out.

It is worth examining the basis for Nabal's refusal to help David. Although David's request is really akin to seeking food for protection, that is not why Nabal says no. Instead, Nabal's response is tied to the group-oriented nature of this culture. He will not assist since he does not know David, nor where his people have come from, and is troubled by the trend for servants to break away from their masters. He will keep his bread, water and meat for his own people, the shearers. So David's men depart. The irony is that in looking after his people in relation to a small amount of food, Nabal is exposing them to real peril. In fact, he is endangering their lives by ignoring the likelihood that David will not accept Nabal's rebuff but will continue the exchange in his own deadly way. Although Nabal does not understand this, a servant of his (possibly) and his wife (certainly) will. For when David's envoys report back to him, he orders 400 of his men to arm themselves and follow him (v. 13). Later we learn he intended to kill every male in Nabal's house, literally "every one of them who urinates against a wall" (vv. 22, 34).[12]

Abigail

Meanwhile, the focus shifts to Abigail. One of the young men tells her what has happened. Presumably, Abigail was a mile away at Maon when the messengers visited Nabal at Carmel and thus she needed someone to tell her what had transpired there. The young man notes that David had sent messengers "to bless (ברך) our master" and, adding a new detail, says that he "screamed (עיט) at them." He also confirms the messengers' assertion that David's band had done Nabal's men no harm and that they and their flocks were safe when David's men were nearby (vv. 14-16). The young man finishes his report with the following statement:

> Now therefore know this and consider what you should do; for evil is determined against our master and against all his house, and he is so ill-natured (literally, "a son of Belial") that one cannot speak to him. (1 Sam. 25:17; RSV)

---

12. The other instances of this idiom all have this meaning: 1 Kgs 14:10; 16:11; 21:21 and 2 Kgs 9:8.

This concluding remark is noteworthy for three reasons.

Firstly, although Abigail was young and childless and probably not from a wealthy family, the young man credits her with the capacity to do something to retrieve the situation. He is assuming that she has agency to take action in some way that might save the family from the (unspecified) evil that David now intends against them. This is quite remarkable, especially in a social context where David's initial approach to Nabal reveals that this sort of issue would normally be sorted out by the senior men involved.

Secondly, by having the young man urge Abigail into action (of some unspecified sort) for the reason that an (unspecified) evil is impending on Nabal and all his house, the narrator has, nevertheless, somewhat circumscribed the intelligence to be imputed to Abigail. For the narrator could have had the young man come to Abigail and merely relate what had transpired between Nabal and David's messengers, leaving everything else to her. But he has him go further, by emphasizing the magnitude of the threat and by encouraging her to think about taking action. Abigail's intelligence at this point emerges in her having the wit to take the young man's advice on the threat seriously and to devise and implement a speedy and appropriate way to meet it. In addition, however, it will turn out that her understanding of the potential situation is more astute than that of the young man. For he does not go so far as to suggest precisely what David will do and does not specify that David is intending to kill people. He is also wrong in thinking that David has evil in mind for all Nabal's household (כל־ביתו), when David will only have the males in view. Abigail will prove she has understood David's intentions with more perspicacity.

Thirdly, in saying that Nabal is impossible to talk to, the young man assumes that other men in his position were open to taking advice from their servants. This affords us a rarely seen glimpse into the dynamics of master–servant relations in ancient Israel. In approaching Abigail, however, the young man is confident, rightly as it turns out, that she is a mistress to whom one can talk and offer advice.[13] This is in spite of the fact that she is likely to be quite young and has still not solidified her place in the house by the production of a son. He clearly understands that she is intelligent.

So Abigail, well appreciating the imminence of the threat—that David was not someone who would regard revenge as a dish best served cold—makes haste (תמהר) to gather provisions for David and his men: 200

---

13. Mary J. Evans aptly notes that the fact that Abigail had managed to build up a good relationship with the farm workers was a tribute to her character (*1 and 2 Samuel*, 114).

loaves, two skins of wine, five dressed sheep, five measures of parched grain, 100 clusters of raisins and 200 fig-cakes laid on donkeys (25:18). The narrator then informs us that Abigail told her young men to go on ahead of her, while she followed after them, and that she did not tell her husband (25:19). Her directions to her servants are best explained as a stratagem to avoid arousing her husband's suspicions were she to be seen leading burdened donkeys and attended by her young men. Having thought it necessary to hide her purpose from Nabal in this fashion, it is natural that she does not tell him. Both of these precautions imply that if Nabal had discovered what she was intending, he would have stopped her. After all, she was defying the will of her husband, by treating him as the fool his very name implied he was, and in such a situation he would certainly have put a stop to her mission. Indeed, had he known he would have been beside himself with anger at the attack on his honor his wife's actions necessarily entailed. For she had boldly usurped his role as manager of the household's relations with outsiders. He may very well have divorced her in consequence or subjected her to physical violence. If he did divorce her, a shameful return to her own home most probably awaited her. While commentators at times comment on Abigail's courage in going out to face David,[14] they rarely mention this quality in relation to her so emphatically flouting the will of her own husband. She was young (perhaps no more than fifteen), childless and probably not from a wealthy family and yet here she was boldly standing up to a man of great wealth, and hence great power.

Abigail and David

The next verse describes the initial meeting between Abigail (riding on her ass) and David and his men (v. 20). But it is apparent from what is said later in the text that by this time Abigail had joined up with her men and the asses with the provisions: the reference to "this present" in v. 27 and the statement that "David received from her hand what she had brought with her" in v. 35.[15] Her initial caution is no longer necessary because she (and, by implication, her servants) are descending under cover of the mountain (בסתר ההר). This must mean that they can no longer be seen from Maon. Here we have further evidence for her insight into practical

---

14. For example, Alice Bach, "The Pleasure of Her Text," in *A Feminist Companion to Samuel–Kings*, ed. Athalya Brenner (Sheffield: Sheffield Academic, 1994), 110–28, at 110.

15. This must be a reference to the provisions mentioned in v. 18: so Ralph W. Klein, *1 Samuel*, WBC 10 (Waco: Word, 1983), 250.

situations: a precaution necessary on departure from the farm at Maon, her separation from the asses and men, is no longer necessary when they are out of sight of the house. David and his men were in the same place, presumably to take Nabal and his men by surprise. It is unlikely that David and Abigail had a "private conversation."[16] More plausible are the numerous paintings of the meeting of David and Abigail in the Western pictorial tradition that regularly depict them in the presence both of David's men and her laden asses and servants. Did Abigail know where David and his band were camped and head in that direction? Or did she cleverly anticipate the route he would follow to preserve the element of surprise and go there? The logic of the narrative bends us towards the latter option.

On his journey David has been mulling over Nabal's insult and swearing to kill all males for whom he is responsible (vv. 21-22). This is a classic vignette of a man whose honor has been sullied and who is thirsting for revenge. Abigail senses accurately what he is feeling, homicidal and bloody violence, no doubt on the basis of her total familiarity with the structures of honor and shame in this culture (and possibly what she already knows of David). Her reaction to David, in her actions and in her words, involves both of the features attributed to her earlier: that she is a woman of good understanding (טובת־שכל) and beautiful in appearance (יפת תאר). Abigail stage-manages her arrival to considerable effect. Having alighted from her ass, she bows and falls on her face before David, at his feet (25:23). She also lowers her status in comparison with him by referring to him as "my lord" (אדני) and herself as "your handmaid" (אמתך), thus creating, in effect, a master and servant relationship. These actions and words of submission and supplication on the part of a beautiful and probably well-dressed woman arriving with asses bearing gifts must surely have had a major impact on him. Most importantly, by diminishing her own honor in this fashion, she restores, indeed magnifies, his. What Abigail says to David is notable for its sheer length (eight verses [vv. 24-31] and 332 words in the RSV translation) and the cunning construction of her argument.

Abigail begins with a rather surprising gambit, which boils down to: "Blame me, not the oafish Nabal" (vv. 24-25). Precisely what Abigail says is let the "punishment-for-the-offence (עון) be upon me alone, your handmaid" (v. 24). Then she adds "let my lord pay no regard to (literally: 'set not his heart on') this son of Belial, upon Nabal, for as his name is, so too is he; churlish folly is his name and churlish folly is with him. But

---

16. As suggested by Klein, *1 Samuel*, 250.

I, your handmaid, did not see the young men of my lord whom you sent" (v. 25). In terms of challenge and response, Abigail is saying that the wrong response was made to David's request for help and she asks him to disregard the refusal to help by the oafish Nabal and now accept her acceptance of David's request instead. This would bring the interaction to a successful, that is, peaceful conclusion. She knows exactly how the game of challenge and response is played. Abigail can so boldly offer to take on her husband's guilt because she shrewdly appreciates that David will not slake his anger on a woman, at least not on a woman like her. She must have assumed that he would go after the men in her husband's house. This is coupled with a bid to portray her husband as too churlish to be worth bothering about.

Abigail's confidence that David will not harm her tends to knock away arguments for her exhibiting courage in going out to confront him.[17] While she is indeed a courageous woman, her courage emerges, as already noted, in defying her husband, with the very real risk of Nabal's divorcing her, in spite of the fragility of her social situation in his household.

Her implication that the result would have been different if she had been present when David's messengers arrived forms part of this argument: she is the one with responsibility for such matters, not Nabal. We should not overlook the social significance of this idea. Abigail is asking David to take seriously the claim that in the household of Nabal it is his wife who makes the decisions in matters of this sort, not him. The claim presupposes that such an arrangement was socially possible in this ancient Israelite setting and amply corroborates Carol Meyers' arguments that we should be far more open to the power of ancient Israelite women in domestic settings. Nevertheless, while Abigail's claim confirms such an arrangement was imaginable in Israelite families, Nabal's family was not one of them and to this extent she is spinning a tale to David. A Nabal whom Abigail feared would prevent her sending supplies to David if he knew that was her intention was a not a person who would have yielded to her view when David's messengers arrived. In short, what she must do covertly she could not have achieved overtly. Nevertheless, Abigail's agency emerges very clearly in the audacity of the proposition, even if the facts do not support it. David must have been impressed even if he was not convinced.

Abigail's agency also surfaces in her confidence that merely by this opening statement she has succeeded in deflecting David from what he was intending. For next she says:

---

17. Such as that made by Bach, "The Pleasure of Her Text," 110.

> Now then, my lord, as the Lord lives, and as your soul lives, seeing the Lord has restrained you from shedding blood, and from taking vengeance with your own hand, now then let your enemies and those who seek to do evil to my lord be as Nabal. (v. 26)

Since Abigail here assumes she has convinced David (and thus anticipates the conclusion of the story), some commentators believe that v. 26 has been misplaced (perhaps from between vv. 41 and 42).[18] Others suggest it is due to the redaction history of the text.[19] But such interpretations disregard the literary and dramatic qualities of the narrative. Presumably, if we were to dramatize this encounter, we would need to allow time between Abigail completing what she has just said, so that David is able to make plain—perhaps by facial expressions or gestures—that he has accepted her argument. Surely we should assume an ancient reader taking the view that her beauty aided her persuasive power, otherwise why would the narrator mention it at the outset of the story? Without David's acceptance, her statement that the Lord has restrained him from shedding blood and taking vengeance would represent a very bold assumption indeed. At this point, moreover, Abigail reveals another dimension to her character: her devotion to Yahweh, her belief in his involvement in human affairs and her confidence in her ability to interpret the divine will. This will become a prominent theme as her address to David continues.

The initial statement in v. 26 is expressed as the basis for Abigail's wish that David's enemies may be as Nabal (although it could also be construed as a statement of fact and not a wish: "and they will be as Nabal"). Rather opaque here is the common element desired (or in view) between Nabal and David's enemies. Is Abigail praying for, or at least anticipating, the demise of, or at least serious harm for, both Nabal and the enemies? Or just that they be affected by his churlish (in her view) fecklessness? If the former is case, namely, a prayer for Nabal's demise, which seems highly likely,[20] we see an Israelite wife with zero regard for her husband, which is an unsurprising attitude for a wife in an arranged marriage to a most unpleasant man. Here again the curtain is suddenly drawn back on the social realities of this world, here those of a young bride in an arranged marriage. Perhaps more surprising, however, is the assertion of this view to a stranger, since it seems to go beyond what is necessary, given that

---

18. P. Kyle McCarter Jr., *1 Samuel: A New Translation, with Introduction and Commentary*, AB 8 (New York: Doubleday, 1980), 394.

19. Klein, *1 Samuel*, 250.

20. Robert Gordon rightly notes that v. 26 "anticipates David's relenting, and also the death of Nabal" (*1 & 2 Samuel: A Commentary* [Exeter: Paternoster, 1986], 184).

David already seems to have relented of what he was intending for Nabal and the males of his household. Certainly her negativity towards her husband reinforces the sense of personal autonomy in Abigail's character. Moreover, toward the end of the story we learn that God kills Nabal, thus responding positively to Abigail's prayer!

Some scholars have suggested a much darker reading of the relationship between David and Abigail than that just proposed. In 1978 Jon Levenson surmised that David may have picked a fight with Nabal precisely with marriage to Abigail in mind.[21] Taking a more extreme position, scholars like Steven McKenzie and Yitzhak Berger have interpreted David's venture against Nabal as an attempt to steal Nabal's property and his wife, in which attempt, Berger suggested, Abigail acted as his "scheming accomplice."[22] Similarly, McKenzie, who despite having noted (correctly) that as far as Nabal and Abigail were concerned, "the writer goes to great lengths to explain how David was innocent of any wrongdoing," nevertheless suggested that Abigail proposed a plan for Nabal's death, in which plan David acquiesced.[23] McKenzie also argued that the David–Bathsheba story was essentially the same as the Nabal–Abigail episode "only without the cover-up."[24] These interpretations, however, have very little to recommend them. Firstly, they anachronistically assume that David obtained Nabal's property by marrying Abigail, property which, as noted above, in the patrilineal society of ancient Israel would have passed to Nabal's male relatives; all that Abigail brought with her on her marriage to David were five maids (1 Sam. 25:42). Secondly, they misunderstand the comparison to be drawn between this episode and the story of David and Bathsheba. The latter can hardly be "like a straightforward version of the Abigail and Nabal story,"[25] when Uriah is not described as owning property and, if he did, it is entirely irrelevant to the narrative. The real point of comparison between the two stories is to reveal the progressive deterioration in David's character over time. Whereas he formed an intention to kill Nabal (and all the males in his house) but was persuaded by Abigail (on the basis of high principle) not to, in relation to Uriah he both formed that intention and then acted on it. His behavior

---

21. Jon D. Levenson, "1 Samuel as Literature and History," *CBQ* 40 (1978): 11–28, at 26.

22. Yitzhak Berger, "Ruth and Inner-Biblical Allusion: The Case of 1 Samuel 25," *JBL* 128 (2009): 253–72, at 269. Also see Steven L. McKenzie, *King David: A Biography* (Oxford: Oxford University Press, 2000), 100.

23. McKenzie, *King David*, 33 and 100.

24. Ibid., 156 (also at 173). For a similar view, see Berger, "Ruth," 263.

25. McKenzie, *King David*, 173.

was bad in the first instance, but far worse in the second. A latent potential in the first case becomes actualized as homicide in the second. Thirdly, these interpretations wrongly (and lamentably) characterize Abigail and Bathsheba as complicit with David in their husbands' death, for which there is no evidence in the text. While it is unnecessary to repeat what I have said above concerning Abigail's motivation, it is worth emphasizing that the author describes Bathsheba as a passive victim of the royal will: "So David sent messengers, and (he) took[26] her; and she came to him, and he lay with her" (2 Sam. 11:4).[27] David, moreover, compelled Bathsheba to have sex with him without any intention of killing Uriah and taking her as his wife. It was only Uriah's refusal to go home to his wife, as a demonstration of solidarity with his fellow soldiers still in the field, which induced David to take the ultimately ruinous path of having him killed. At this juncture, Abigail points to the supplies (literally "blessing") she has brought and invites David to give them to his men (1 Sam. 25:27). She then asks that he forgive her trespass (פשׁע), thus continuing her earlier request that he blame her for what has happened. Next she flatters him with the suggestions that the Lord will support his house because he is fighting the Lord's battles and that evil will never be found in him (v. 28). Here the relevant aspects of her character are knowledge concerning the current position of David (including his role in the divine plan), her rhetorical skill, and (in spite of her being unaware of the evil that David will later commit) a measure of prophetic power that will become more prominent as the narrative advances.

Abigail's final remarks are heavily theological, aimed at reassuring David that he will be protected by the Lord and is his agent. Firstly, the Lord will protect him from his enemies (v. 29). She speaks with eloquence and conviction:

> If people rise up to pursue you and to seek your life, the life of my lord shall be bound in the bundle of the living with the Lord your God; and he shall sling out the lives of your enemies as from the hollow of a sling. (25:29)

Secondly, Abigail reveals the basis for connecting David with the Lord's will, namely, that she knows that the Lord has already favored him. She envisages a time when the Lord will have done to David all the good that he has spoken concerning him and will have appointed him prince (נגיד)

---

26. The third person singular of the Hebrew word for "took" at this point is meant to underline that the messengers were agents of his will.

27. For my views on this passage, see Esler, *Sex, Wives, and Warriors*, 314 and 330.

over Israel (v. 30). Abigail is thus aware of, believes and looks forward to prophecies that have been made concerning David, including his future leadership role. As Klein comments, "Abigail joined the chorus of those prophesying David's kingship (Samuel, Jonathan, Saul)."[28] These sentiments would have been well received by David, particularly since his closeness to the Lord had been a central feature in his life to this point, with the Lord having looked into his heart and liked what he saw (1 Sam. 16:7), and with David reciprocating, by being the only Israelite who saw Goliath's insult to Israel as an insult to Israel's God (1 Sam. 17:26). In her ultimate words, Abigail makes clear that when all this transpires in David's favor, he will have no cause for grief or perturbation of the heart for having shed blood and taken vengeance, and in that time she hopes he will remember her (25:3).

David's initial response to Abigail valorizes that part of her character that comprises her devotion to the Lord. Indeed, he views her as an agent of the Lord, the God of Israel, sent to meet him (v. 32). Next he blesses her discretion (טעם) and Abigail herself for having hurried to him to restrain him from violence that would have extended to his killing all the males in Nabal's care (vv. 33-34). So David takes the supplies and grants her petition (v. 35).

Abigail and Nabal

Back home Abigail, acting courageously once again, means to tell Nabal what has happened. For all she knows, he is likely to beat or divorce her in consequence of her action. But she will be honest with him. He is drunk that evening, so she waits until morning. Many translations render the Hebrew near the start of v. 37 (בצאת היין מנבל) as "when the wine had gone out of Nabal." Peter Leithart, however, has creatively argued that this should be given a present meaning: "while the wine was going out of Nabal," meaning when he was emptying his bladder after his heavy drinking the night before. On this basis, Abigail's encounter with him occurs in the midst of this process! Leithart further surmises that the reader is meant to understand that Nabal was the pre-eminent urinator against the wall in his household threatened by David (1 Sam. 25:22, 34) and that in rejecting David's request for supplies he had, metaphorically speaking, urinated against the "wall" that David's men had erected for the protection

---

28. Klein, *1 Samuel*, 251. Hertzberg comments that Abigail "represents the prophetic voice" (*I & II Samuel*, 203).

of his sheep (25:16).[29] When she tells him the next day, the shock of the message causes his heart to die within him, so that he becomes as a stone. This reaction is probably to be interpreted as caused by the fatal attack on his honor caused by his wife so entirely subverting his authority and besmirching his honor in his household. Perhaps, also, he is shocked by how close he had come to causing all the males in it, himself included, to be killed by David and his men (vv. 36-37). Ten days later the Lord kills him (v. 38). This action provides divine legitimation for the negative view of Nabal and the prayer for his demise previously expressed by Abigail, while also being interpreted by David as turning Nabal's evil-doing on his own head (v. 39). But Nabal's death also conveniently opens the way for David himself to marry Abigail (vv. 39-42).

Conclusion

While there is truth in Hertzberg's claim that Abigail "is an instrument of the Lord to keep the future king's escutcheon clean for David,"[30] that view nevertheless seriously underestimates the extent to which Abigail is her own agent. The narrative portrays Abigail—in spite of her occupying the fragile social position of a young and childless wife in the house of a very rich husband—as not only intelligent and beautiful, but also very confident in her own views, courageous, quick and decisive in action, incapable of suffering a fool gladly and yet closely understanding of, and aligned to, the divine will. Moving out of the domestic realm, she ably shoulders the responsibility for the household's protection that her husband has so dangerously prejudiced, subverting male dominance even in the arena of relationships with important outsiders. The outer reaches of her push to agency extend to her ridiculing her husband to David and even to uttering a prayer for her husband's demise, an outcome Yahweh soon grants her. Abigail acts successfully not only to push her life-story to a happier outcome, but also David's. Hers is a rich and nuanced character and one could only wish that the subsequent story of the Israelite monarch had more to tell of her doings than the bald facts of her marriage to David and the production of a son.

---

29. Peter J. Leithart, "Nabal and His Wine," *JBL* 120 (2001): 525–7.
30. Hertzberg, *I & II Samuel*, 203.

Chapter 12

Joab's Coherence and Incoherence:
Character and Characterization

Barbara Green

Introduction

Joab is the most prominent character in the David stories, excepting possibly the figure of Saul. Indeed, just when Saul vanishes from David's narrative life, Joab appears to contend, over the rest of their lives and across 2 Samuel into 1 Kings. When recently I completed a substantial book on the figure of David in these materials, I acknowledged I had not settled for myself the nature of the David–Joab relationship, a project to which I now turn. I rely upon a broader and deeper conversation in that earlier work for both methodology and many narrative issues.[1] Though work with David is always controversial, much is gained from studying his biblical footprint. But Joab? Why explore Joab? First, the literary challenge is steep, given Joab's prominence, the subtlety of his presentation, and the wide range of interpretation of him. Second, though Joab appears to be rather a gangster,[2] that view may not be inevitable or adequate.

I propose to explore the question of whether Joab "is" coherent or incoherent: whether he acts consistently or inconsistently as a character, whether he is skillfully drawn to show him coherent at a level deeper

---

1. Barbara Green, *David's Capacity for Compassion: A Literary-Hermeneutical Study of 1–2 Samuel*, LHBOTS 641 (London/New York: Bloomsbury, 2017).
2. So Keith Bodner, *The Rebellion of Absalom* (New York: Routledge, 2014), 47.

than some of his surface twists and turns. The question takes us to some historical issues, to literary artistry, to reader responsibility. Though those realms can seem disparate and even hostile, my hope is to correlate them, so the rationale for my particular interpretation is clear, whether inviting assent or not. In place of an extensive presentation of methodology, let me name my three basic moves. First, I will work a set of distinctions for managing Joab: discrepancies between non-verbal experience and its literary presentation; between actual and implied authors and readers; between extradiegetic and intradiegetic narration; between story and discourse; between character and characterization.[33] My reading exploits these interlocking but distinguishable concepts. Second, I have drawn my initial wager—now developed into a thesis—by identifying an underlying artistic supposition, a matter that—if we discern and name it—brings coherence to Joab's character and characterization. And third, I rely on a more detailed draft of this essay to expose the reasoning in greater detail than is possible here, where seven complex scenes need attention.[4]

Of the many aspects of character begging attention, I limit my focus to the spectrum called character/ization: the transaction between authors and readers, mediated through a narrative "score." Terminology: *character* comprises authorial detailing of actant information, conscious and otherwise, while the *characterization* challenge asks readers to establish the traits composing character and distilling more widely across its presentation, to weigh them as to adequacy, to engage, interpret them. If we consider the analogy of one person extending an object to another, we imagine the actual moment of exchange, where both participants are guiding the object. How is a character *drawn* such that the portrait is meaningfully coherent (or not), and how is the character *received* with those same issues in view?[5] A character might be inconsistent, or the characterization might be inadequate and inconsistent. Is Joab offered to us as a character who is not quite sure what he wants to accomplish, who cannot muster the capacity to do so? Or is his characterization flawed, so that he does not quite "hang together"? Since my argument will be that the *character* Joab is largely consistent though with short-term divergences from

---

3. These issues are laid out at length in Green, *Capacity for Compassion*, Chapter 1.

4. Barbara Green, "As David and Joab Dance, Who Leads?" (paper presented at the SBL Annual Meeting, Book of Samuel Session, Boston, MA, 2017).

5. For discussion of these matters, see David Herman, "Character," in David Herman et al., *Narrative Theory: Core Concepts and Critical Debates* (Columbus: Ohio State University Press, 2012), 127.

a general path, and that his *characterization* can be generally coherent, though subtly so, I will not waste space here on the alternatives.

In a study generated earlier almost as a "cartoon" to this character/ization investigation, I worked with the simpler narrative tool of plot/plotting.[6] Posed as the question "When David and Joab dance, who leads?," I investigated the seven instances of their "dance" across 2 Samuel and into 1 Kings.[7] My conclusion from that work is that the *discourse-level plotting* consistently presents the issue of *who will rule besides David, who will not, how will that be determined*, and *how not*.[8] Seven times Joab is implicated in a major crisis of David's capacity to maintain his rule, with opposition rising from royal kin, not from outsiders. At the *story-level, plot* conflict between the David/Joab pair also seems construable around a pattern sustained generally across the material. Joab mostly works *with* David; but when *his own short-term good* is at issue, Joab acts for *that* good, jeopardizing—even abandoning—his obligations to David. As time goes on and episodes compound, Joab becomes ever-bolder and David seems ever-weaker, though David's backing off or failing to set limits is misleading. But in the end it is David's strong words, uttered in the first and last episodes (2 Sam. 2–3 and 1 Kgs 1–2) that are decisive. Joab, finally, defers and accepts their impact, ceases to avoid them.

In that plot/ting study, I sought a motivational key, a quirk to be construed as motivating Joab's behavior, an "if presumed, it makes sense," matter. This "navel" will be a submerged but proffered situation that makes sense of the disparate pieces we have.[9] How *does* Joab—how

---

6. Green, "As David and Joab Dance."

7. The episodes are the same ones treated here. Other brief mentions of Joab occur in 1 Sam. 26:6 and 2 Sam. 8:16; 9:23; 16:10; 23:18, 24, 37; 1 Kgs 11.

8. One might suppose that there is little else happening in these narratives, but much of what is related is not concerned directly with succession.

9. We are accustomed to such a phenomenon in modern literature, when we learn eventually of some factor that plausibly motivates characters' actions. In ancient literature, the factor is rarely made explicit. To inquire for such a literary element is a reader's choice to construe more actively than passively. Even if not able to be resolved definitively, the move exercises muscles of the imagination, useful in narratives so long-familiar and oft-interpreted. S. Min Chun, *Ethics and Biblical Narrative: A Literary and Discourse-Analytical Approach to the Story of Josiah*, Oxford Theology and Religion Monographs (Oxford: Oxford University Press, 2014), 224–5, poses a Josiah question, asking: What can we suppose about the assumptions of the character Josiah in 2 Kgs 22–23 that renders his moves sensible, given the information he has learned from Huldah? This is not a "happened" question but an artistic one, opening up subtle questions of characeral motivation and reader capacity to construe it in a given narrative.

is he shown to—work generally for the advancement of David's rule while also veering off with the effect of undermining it? If he acts so, do we know why so? *Does* Joab—or *can he be shown* to—have an eye toward moving himself nearer the throne, despite the fact that David has sons—as Saul had sons though his throne went to another? If we are solving for "x," is Joab's ambition to succeed David the "x"? Though *we* know that Joab will not succeed David, Joab might be drawn to think it possible, likely, worth a gamble as he manages his choices.[10] The particular feature I am positing relies on intended readers hypothesizing the possibility that Joab's desire to succeed David prompts him. This issue of kin usurpation must be understood as significant and engaging at the times of the narrative's production and its reception by intended readers, though such detail is beyond recovery.

Finally, prior to the careful consideration of seven passages where Joab and David engage, I offer several points as Joab's foundational default, to be held as the more finely detailed points are teased out. He is Zeruiah's son, David's nephew, brother of Asahel and Abishai, cousin to David's children. Narratively, Joab lacks wife and children. Joab acts most consistently as a skilled fighter and a bold talker. He seems strategic, though his strategies are often flawed. He is drawn as short-sighted, acting for near goals rather than farther ones, for his own limited good if it clashes with David's royal "corporate" goals. Joab is obeyed by his fighting men, save on one occasion, where he is bluntly countered. Though David's chief commander, Joab is conspicuously omitted from the list of mighty men (23:18, 24, 37), his name used to identify his "mighty" brothers, with no reason given for Joab's own exclusion. Typically a powerful, blunt talker, Joab has two places of careful, courtly talk amid most of his language to the king, direct to the point of disrespect. The primary character to oppose Joab verbally is David. The narrator does not sum Joab up, though at least once he will explain a particular action of Joab, though without endorsing it. Joab is shown missing from David's cultic actions—securing Jerusalem, bringing the ark there, planning to build the temple—though he does feature briefly in the odd event that secures the temple's eventual site.

---

10. To recall that, when the community of returning exiles made their decision about leadership, they selected from neither Judah nor Benjamin reminds us that "succession" may have been a central issue, the choice for something other than the obvious and past practice.

A Closer Look at Seven Episodes

With this summary of stable and non-controversial lineaments, we now examine seven narrated scenes where Joab and David contend, to argue with more detail Joab's character and characterization and to deepen his construction: co-operative except when he acts for his own limited good, though without, long-term, advancing his cause. Insofar as Joab anticipates himself on the throne, he is myopic, while David sees better and acts more skillfully.

Our first consideration is 2 Samuel 2–3, detailing *Joab's contributions to the general effort to establish David's rule* over the former adherents of Saul. Though David has initiatives that do not involve Joab, Joab is generally prominent. Key is Joab's tangling with Abner, who is shown struggling to establish Saul's son Ishbosheth as king. After a stylized event, where twelve of each side face off and then kill each other, a wider contest follows (2:17), with the advantage going to David's side. For a reason unspecified, Abner peels away from that fighting, pursued by the three sons of Zeruiah, most nearly by Asahel. Though Abner tries to avoid it, he eventually kills Asahel, who has pressed him too closely.[11] Abner first warns him that should he, Abner, kill Asahel, it would not go well with Joab: "Stop pursuing me, or I'll have to strike you down. How will I look your brother Joab in the face?" (2:23). Abner implies, and I infer, that the killing would be problematic in some way between the two kings' helpers, as turns out to be the case. We note Abner's evident regard for Joab's power.

While the two groups confront each other again, the leaders exchange recriminations (vv. 26-27): "Abner then called out to Joab, 'Must the sword devour forever? You know how bitterly it's going to end! How long *will you delay* ordering your troops to stop the pursuit of their kinsmen?' And Joab replied, 'As God lives, *if you hadn't spoken up*, the troops would have given up the pursuit of their kinsmen only the next morning'" (emphasis added). Abner names the cost of civil strife, perhaps the risk of men killing each others' near kin, as has just happened, twice, charging

---

11. The particular site of the stabbing is the fifth rib, the same anatomical place where Joab will stab Amasa, implies that Joab, the narrator, the authoring eye, and readers may see this as a justice-deed, performed by Joab when David does not do it, notes Keith Bodner in "Demise of Abner," 38–76 (56) in his *David Observed: A King in the Eyes of his Court*, HBM 5 (Sheffield: Sheffield Phoenix, 2005). Though Asahel's killing takes place generally in war time, after a battle, it is not unambiguously part of the battle, since Abner runs from the scene. We see the narrator refusing clarity so that we watch the conflict without being able to resolve it cleanly.

Joab as slow to call off his men, perhaps referring to the Zeruiad pursuit of himself. Joab's words seem to sling the accusation back to Abner, hinting that some speech of Abner had inflamed pursuit that might have stopped sooner. But the narrator indicates that the exchange, if opaque to us, effects a break in the hostilities. Joab's battle skill is attested here by narrator and characters.

The next phases of the struggle involve the abandonment of Ishbosheth by his own people, Abner in particular (ch. 3). Joab is absent from the phases leading to the final David–Abner negotiations. Returning with booty to David at Hebron after Abner has left, Joab learns of Abner's intervention and David's acceptance of it and confronts the king: "What have you done? Here Abner came to you; why did you let him go? Now he has gotten away! Don't you know that Abner son of Ner came only to deceive you, to learn your comings and goings and to find out all that you are planning?" (3:24-25).

There are several things to note in this direct discourse of Joab. First, it is blunt, shorn of courtesy and honorific language typically used to address kings. Second, Joab accuses Abner of double-dealing and says that David knows it as well. That Joab accuses it need not make it true, though it does suggest that either Joab believes it or wants David to think he does. Does Joab know it truly? We can see that Abner has betrayed his ancestral faction and that the move will succeed, even when Abner is dead, as is imminent.[12] Joab expresses outrage that David has not treated Abner as a traitor but trusted him. Some commentators think Joab is concerned lest Abner be given Joab's position—possible though not directly indicated. The third point to see is that David makes no reply to Joab's words, with the impact of his silence unclear.

Joab moves on to manage Abner himself, summoning him back to Hebron. Abner comes, apparently suspecting nothing until Joab takes him aside as if to speak but stabs him (v. 27). We do not hear Joab's words to Abner, but the narrator provides a motive for Joab, without necessarily endorsing it: "Now Joab and his brother Abishai had killed Abner because he had killed their brother Asahel during the battle at Gibeon." That is, though Joab has just accused Abner of treachery to the David side and implied that Abner was not a man of honor, the killing of Abner was not for those reasons but for the death of Asahel.

---

12. In a much earlier scene in 1 Sam. 26, when David and Abishai remove Saul's spear and water jug while his whole encampment has fallen into a deep sleep, David charges Abner with poor care for Saul, which Abner does not deny. Joab's charge is not perhaps so arbitrary as it may seem in the present scene.

Missing is Joab's claiming this motivation, and we may think he has delayed to act on the death of his brother, perhaps using it as pretext when his truer motive is Abner's initiative with David. As David *now* speaks at length about the death of Abner, assisted by narrator comment (3:28-39), the king's urgency seems to be to distance himself from it.[13] This time Joab is the silent partner, not responding to the words and gestures of the king, approved as they are by the people, the narrator says. Joab's silence is intensified by the verbosity of David's speech. David wants the allegiance of the Saul group, which he is on the verge of gaining when Joab kills Abner. David reasonably wants to limit the wider damage Joab may have inflicted. Joab neither rebuts nor denies what David says. In a sense, each benefits: David gains the allegiance of Saul's people without additional bloodshed.

By way of summary of this key framing episode: Joab is shown generally loyal to David's project of consolidating his reign, competent in his fighting against opponents led by Abner, doing well in the battle, losing fewer than he kills, gathering booty. I construe Abner's killing Asahel as a sort of ominous fluke amid various other scenes of strife. Joab's anger at both Abner and David follows from the killing, with words from the characters and the narrator offering diverse motivation. Joab charges David as both betrayed and betraying. The time lag between Abner's killing Asahel and Joab's killing Abner muddies the motive, as does David's non-response to the death of Asahel. That David can negotiate with the man who killed Joab's brother prompts Joab to kill Abner, a move not made until David collaborated with Abner. We hear Joab's outrage at David, not at Abner, without any firm sense that Joab's charges against Abner to David are true. David does not heed them—or has not by the time Joab takes the matter into his own hands. Joab then withholds response to David's barrage of criticism: because he owns the truth of the charges? Because he has already said too much? Because he feels justified in what he did, though for what specific reason? We can see an imbalance between the quality of David's outrage over the death of Abner and his silence in regard to his nephew Asahel. This first deviation of Joab from David's projects—which will end the set of episodes as well—leaves uncertain, even contested, the whole snarl of

---

13. Various commentators remark the odd blend of this fierce language and the ongoing dependence of David on Joab, suggesting that David's words may be understood as a strong statement designed to distance himself from reprisals. See Caleb Henry, "Joab: A Biblical Critique of Machiavellian Tactics," *Westminster Theological Journal* 69 (2007): 327–43.

factors composing the killing of Abner, rooting it in the set of actions bringing David to his position as king of Israel as well as Judah. And yet this episode underwrites Joab's death warrant.

Our second episode involves *Joab with Uriah and David* (chs. 10–12): Joab re-enters the narrative in a substantial way, first in material accumulating around the Ammonite war and then consequent upon David's stroll on his palace roof. The Ammonite war arises from a slight to David's honor, with Joab and a fighting contingent sent to respond. Joab and Abishai act strategically and successfully against Ammon and its coalition of fighters (10:11-12). The Ammonites withdraw to their capital and the Syrians regroup, only to be defeated by David and those with him. A truce is agreed, and by the end of ch. 10, the narrative summarizes Syrians subdued, Joab besieging Ammon, David in Jerusalem.

Though many criticize David for being in Jerusalem when spring weather makes war practical again, I see, rather, David crediting Joab as competent to manage the war, and in that appraisal, he is largely correct. But before hostilities resolve, another episode intervenes. David's unjust indiscretion with Bathsheba and Uriah panics the king into a cover-up. He enlists Joab to assist him, constructs Joab as reliable to eliminate Uriah while not exposing David's role, as capable of illicitly killing a man that David wants dead. In order to read Joab, Joab reading David, and David reading Joab reading David, we must study carefully the material in 11:14-25.

First, directions: "Place Uriah in the front line where the fighting is fiercest; then fall back so that he may be killed" (11:15). We see next Joab's implementation of that general order, provided by the narrator: "So when Joab was besieging the city, he stationed Uriah at the point where he knew that there were able warriors. The men of the city sallied out and attacked Joab, and some of David's officers among the troops fell; Uriah the Hittite was among those who died" (11:16-17). Though some think Joab changes the order, I am not so sure that is the case. The outcome remains consistent: Uriah dies. Whether David's directions specified that Uriah alone be assigned a place of extreme vulnerability or whether he goes accompanied—making the move less obviously aimed at Uriah—is not crucial. In either case, David trusts Joab to manage Uriah's death, and both are shown willing to subvert the war in order to do so. The narrator does not fulminate at this massive injustice, but the misuse of power stands exposed—collateral damage, as survivors are wont to say.

The next step is the report back to David, introduced first by way of summary—"Joab sent a full report of the battle to David" (v. 18)—then backing up to provide greater precision and more characteral exposure:

"When you finish reporting to the king all about the battle, the king may get angry and say to you, 'Why did you come so close to the city to attack it?... Was it not a woman who dropped an upper millstone on him from the wall at Thebez, from which he died? Why did you come so close to the wall?'" (vv. 19-21). The narrator does not repeat the summary, already provided for readers. Joab is shown, rather, to anticipate a spurt of outrage from David, who is just learning that a foolish tactic led to the death of several and presumably endangered the war. Joab even anticipates David's reference to a similar episode, known to us from Judges 9. Key is not the closeness of the fit but Joab's manipulating both messenger and king to indicate publicly what happened, the messenger clueless and the king feigning indignation. Joab continues the instruction that suits his strategy: "*Then* say: 'Your servant Uriah the Hittite was among those killed.'"

Both Joab's competence and knowledge are on display, also his plan to compromise David in public. Joab's final piece of information, to be dispensed at the strategic moment when the king—anticipated as exuding indignation—is a "game-changer," a reminder over the heads of other characters that Joab knows what David asked him to do and has done it. But our narrator thwarts Joab's game by having the messenger miss his cue, whether by stumble or skill. The messenger arrives to tell David all that Joab had sent him to say, in fact providing detail that we have not known previously (11:22-24): "The messenger said to David, 'First the men prevailed against us and sallied out against us into the open; then we drove them back up to the entrance to the gate. But the archers shot at your men from the wall and some of Your Majesty's men fell; your servant Uriah the Hittite also fell.'"

David has no chance to act as Joab has anticipated, since before he can grow indignant, the messenger blurts the punch-line. David now outfoxes the one who would "fox" him, seizing the initiative to send Joab advice to absorb in his context, again likely with witnesses to be presumed. "Give Joab this message: 'Do not be distressed about the matter. The sword always takes its toll. Press your attack on the city and destroy it!' Encourage him!" (v. 25). That is, David advises Joab: "Don't worry about your tactical blunder! These things happen in war!" David deftly constructs Joab as downcast over a failure rather than as triumphantly manipulative, urging that the messenger cheer him up. Insofar as Joab had appeared to have the upper hand, had seemed to feel and proceed as though he were managing the information, David sees through his strategy, subverts it, redirects it to draw Joab as at fault and in need of consolation.

We do not witness the messenger return with this word from the uncle-king, a narrative choice implying that David has foreclosed the transaction successfully. But there is actually one more round to be played here, coming after the confrontation between David and Nathan and the death of the child of David and Bathsheba. Joab is again a successful general and a bold speaker (12:26-31): "Joab attacked Rabbah of Ammon and captured the royal city. Joab sent messengers to David and said, '*I* have attacked Rabbah and *I* have already captured the water city. Now [*you*] muster the rest of the troops and [*you*] besiege the city and capture it; otherwise *I* will capture the city *myself*, and *my* name will be connected with it.'" Joab, successful again at his commission, threatens David to come himself and finish up what Joab has all but completed. The narrator spends no more direct discourse but tells us in emphatic detail the outcome of Joab's veiled threat to David. To highlight pronouns and adjectives is to show Joab's point, and the quantity of David's response provided by the narrator answers Joab's boldness.

To summarize: the two players are shown well-matched in both military skill and venality, working on a common project. Eventually they are shown as battling each other verbally to manage the "publicity." Joab designs to put David on the spot, and for a reason not explained, the messenger thwarts that plan. I construct David as understanding what Joab had intended and skillfully utilizing the same tactic on him, urging Joab not to feel bad about where he had failed his men, notably Uriah. A similar round is played at the end of the war, when Joab, competent and successful, threatens the king with what he, the commander might do if the king does not act. The bold speech of Joab to the king over Abner repeats here, as does the barrage of David's military response. Joab, again thwarted, falls silent, while seeming largely unscathed by consequences.

A third major scene involves *Joab with David and the Wise Woman* (ch. 14): the death of David and Bathsheba's infant initiates a chain involving David's sons and daughters, and in one of these early scenes Joab re-appears.[14] David's firstborn son, Amnon, longing to sleep with his half-sister Tamar, accomplishes it with the willful connivance of their cousin and the unwitting if heedless participation of David. Though angry, David does not act decisively in the justice-related matter of his son and daughter. But Tamar's brother, Absalom, biding his time for two years, assembles his brothers at a sheep-shearing, kills Amnon, then flees to his maternal kin at Geshur. David, though grieving, does nothing direct. As we get to the reappearance of Joab, the narrator provides us with the

---

14. For an argued demonstration of these links between David's crimes in ch. 11 and the deeds of his children in chs. 13–19, consult Bodner, *Absalom*, 26.

following information, in 13:39 and 14:1: "And King David was pining away for Absalom, for the king had gotten over Amnon's death. Joab son of Zeruiah could see that the king's mind was on Absalom." Any translation (this is TNK) makes the information clearer than the Hebrew allows for, with its predilection for ambiguity.[15]

We thus have an episode beginning with information both clear and unclear: we see David deferring response to the rape, the fratricide, and the flight, though he has strong feelings of some sort about Absalom and something related to him. Joab perceives something about David's feelings—whether correctly or not we cannot pronounce, and how motivated we cannot know.[16] These gaps risk making the characterization incoherent, though they also challenge us to construct it. What is clear is that while David delays, Joab acts. As before, when Abner slew Asahel and David did not react, now Joab makes moves, more intemperately than strategically. David earlier resisted taking a stance on whether a killing was licit or not, while Joab acted and interpreted (or so the narrator tells us) twice. Joab's tendency to act precipitously linked with David's slower instincts again stir up trouble.

But Joab is also more discreet on this occasion than before, avoiding apparent intervention for the exile in Geshur, acting instead by means of a proxy.[17] Gaps abound, though not all of them pertain to Joab's characterization.[18] Joab's proxy raises with the king, by degrees and with increasing directness, the matter of how justice pertains regarding a fratricidal son. The point seems not so much the exactness of the fit between her case and David's but the urgency of the topic. Her case is not tightly relevant to David's situation beyond the general scenario, but it jars him into making

---

15. Commentators explain their choices here, e.g., Bodner, *Absalom*, 47. The ambiguity of a common preposition like *'l*, which can signify "to" or "against," makes certainty elusive. Inevitably, an interpreter will have to name explicitly what assumptions are operative for the construction of how David feels and how Joab cues from it. Bodner supposes that Absalom nearer home is better controlled—plausible but not inevitable, not least since he turns out poorly controlled in Jerusalem!

16. Assumptions, explicit or not, control the pathways here. George Nichol, "The Wisdom of Joab and the Wise Woman of Tekoa," *Studia Theologica* 36 (1982): 97–104, supposes a whole set of alternatives to mine that have Joab helping David here. He argues plausibly but without foreclosing alternatives.

17. The fullest study of the many places of ambiguity and undecidability in this portion of ch. 14 is taken up in detail by Larry L. Lyke, *King David with the Wise Woman of Tekoa: The Resonance of Tradition in Parabolic Narrative* (Sheffield: JSOT Press, 1997).

18. The uncertainties facing Joab and the woman are more crucial when plot is under discussion than when the literary interest is in characterization.

the connection between "her son" and his own, to bring to attention the several reasonable options about handling the situation of justice and Absalom. How much of her language repeats Joab's and how much is her own improvisation is moot here. Joab has acted, verbally but somewhat discreetly, though by the end of the woman's presentation, David has both discerned the strategic presence of his nephew and made a decision about his son (14:21): "Then the king said to Joab, 'I will do this thing. Go and bring back my boy Absalom.'" David sounds decisive, clearer than before, though deceptively so.

Joab's reaction (v. 22) is puzzling: "Joab flung himself face down on the ground and prostrated himself. Joab blessed the king and said, 'Today your servant knows that he has found favor with you, my lord king, for Your Majesty has granted his servant's request.'" Joab expresses profound gratitude to the king, respect for him, speaking and acting in ways that are more suited for dialogue with royalty than anything we have heard from him. His relief and appreciation seem excessive. Perhaps Joab is drawn fearful of David's learning that he had acted. Expecting anger, he gushes relief when it does not come. We again wonder that Joab feels the need for a proxy, avoiding disclosure of his action. The woman claims that Joab's intent was to deceive the king, and perhaps Joab's excessive response to David's reaction is that his subterfuge has not turned out worse than it did—or seemed about to do, since this maneuver of Joab's cannot be said to turn out well in the long run. Joab seems short-sighted, compared to David, acting for the return of Absalom as though it were a clear *desideratum*. As the episode winds on, we see that David defers full reconciliation with his son and that Joab rests content with that, narratively speaking. So, in character/ization terms, David is shown cautious, Absalom impatient, Joab content—until Absalom's assault on Joab's property sends him to intervene for a fuller connection between Absalom and his father, the king.

So again David's throne is being undermined by Absalom's return, if not yet explicitly. Joab complexifies his characterization as a bold communicator, hiring someone to do his talking for him while scripting her at least partially. His motives remain opaque, perhaps even from his narrated character-self. Joab may want his cousin in Jerusalem for a variety of reasons, or he may want him back to please David—or to displease him. Earlier, Joab has not hesitated to jeopardize David's good when some urgent objective of his own intervenes, and arguably he does not hesitate now. His avoidance of speaking directly shows Joab as devious—differing from his way with David over the matter of Abner, more similar to Abner at the moment of assassination. But here Joab tries to conceal from David that he is the architect of the deed of Absalom's return from Geshur. The woman is the one whose language discloses Joab to David; there is no indication that Joab was about to claim his proper role. Is Joab too grateful, obsequious, even excessively fake? If so, it is a fresh condition, and perhaps he is shown insecure in it. We see neither Joab's reaction when David and Absalom finally are together nor Joab's responses to the early stirring of Absalom's revolt. Insofar as it is my plan to construct consistency, Joab once again puts some good of his own ahead of what is—as the story moves on—good for David in the return of Absalom to the palace. David sees the deed and Joab's hand but does not resist effectively.

Before moving on to the revolt of Absalom, sprawling within five chapters, we pass through episode four with its single verse where *Joab advises David* "too courteously." The moment comes in 2 Samuel 24, which many consider to be an appendix to the main narrative under discussion here.[19] The narrator, avoiding transparency, tells us that God's anger has initiated the census, and that David—not knowing what we know—orders Joab to get counting. Joab's response (24:3): "May the LORD your God increase the number of the people a hundredfold, while your own eyes see it! But why should my lord king want this?" The language is courtly and correct, even obsequious, formulaic. Joab's question seems a deterrent, an effort to slow the implementation: "Are you sure this a good idea?" But David runs right past that feeble restraint, and Joab without further cavil obeys, then drops out of the story. If Joab is generally consistent as a bold speaker, he does not manage it here; if he is learning to be a skilled and strategic speaker, this is a low point. If Joab is seen as acting for David's good without a thought to his own position, we are in fresh territory. If Joab's intervention is meant to provoke David to the opposite, there is a skill discernible. In the short run, Joab seems shrewder than David; in the longer run, David does well to have a hand in the temple project largely reserved to his son Solomon.

A fifth episode: *Joab with David and Absalom.* These chapters, 15–19, manage many things besides Joab's deeds, though we remain focused on those. The actual outbreak of the rebellion, gathering at Hebron, is reported to David, who acts with boldness and without Joab, all detailed

---

19. For a discussion of what comprises these two units, how each is grouped or structured, and why this is the least problematic pairing, see Fokkelman, *Throne and City*, 1–22. He argues that the material of chs. 21–24 needs not to interrupt the question of succession which trails into 1 Kings. An extensive study of the chapters is also provided by H. H. Klement, *II Samuel 21–24: Context, Structure and Meaning in the Samuel Conclusion*, Europäische Hochschulschriften 23 Theologie, 682 (Frankfurt: Lang, 2000).

in 15:13–17:29, where we witness the span of people with whom the king interacts, variously and not in primarily military ways. Joab first appears when sent out with the fighting men, split among three contingents to Absalom's one (18:2). David makes a move to join the fighters, but when countered by his men, agrees to remain apart from battle. That context of deploying his men to pursue the rebels occasions David's direction regarding Absalom (18:5): "The king gave orders to Joab, Abishai, and Ittai: 'Deal gently with my boy Absalom, for my sake.' All the troops heard the king give the order about Absalom to all the officers." This is firm characterization. Whether we feel as clear as is desirable about the word *l't*, we are sufficiently cued, as are characters in the story.[20] Whether the request is reasonable is also debatable, given Absalom's boldness. But that David wants him treated with care is clear. Strangely, there is little narrative interest in the culminating battle (18:6-8). The rebel leader, defeated, flees, pursued by at least one of the David contingents, led by Joab. Joab is informed that Absalom hangs, alone and vulnerable, trapped by his head, if not his famous hair. Joab's actions fall into three main parts, each needing scrutiny.

First, in 18:10-17, Joab shows not the slightest care for Absalom, despite David's plea. He first upbraids the soldier who saw and left Absalom alive for not having killed him, giving that character opportunity to draw a wide space between Joab and others alert to the king's words (18:11-13).

> Joab said to the man who told him, "You saw it! Why didn't you kill him then and there? I would have owed you ten shekels of silver and a belt." But the man answered Joab, "Even if I had a thousand shekels of silver in my hands, I would not raise a hand against the king's son. For the king charged you and Abishai and Ittai in our hearing, 'Watch over my boy Absalom, for my sake.' If I betrayed myself—and nothing is hidden from the king—you would have stood aloof."[21]

---

20. Robert Alter, *The David Story: A Translation with Commentary of 1 and 2 Samuel* (New York: W. W. Norton, 1999), 304, suggests its root (*lamed-aleph-tet*) is most likely to mean "to cover, protect." It is not utterly clear what David is asking, but generally he wants care for his son. It may be a foolish hope, given that Absalom is a rebel and involved in a civil war (so Bodner, *Absalom*, 92; Fokkelman, *Narrative Art and Poetry in the Books of Samuel, Vol. 1: King David [2 Sam. 9–20 and 1 Kgs 1–2]* [Assen: Van Gorcum, 1981], 262), but I am hesitant to think that the death of the rebel was the only option, a point that the non-killing soldier seems to hold as well.

21. Bodner, *Absalom*, 96, reminds us that in colloquial speech, the soldier indicates that he is sure had he killed Absalom, Joab would have "thrown him under the bus." The idiom captures exactly what the soldier boldly says to Joab.

The soldier is blunt in his assessment of Joab, leader of David's army. He disdains his opportunity and the reward Joab claims he would have gladly given, saying boldly that he would not trust Joab to have acted as he implies he would have done. This is intense characterization from one of Joab's fighters.

Joab dismisses—rather than disputes—the soldier's words: "'Then I will not wait for you.' He took three darts in his hand and drove them into Absalom's chest. [Absalom] was still alive in the thick growth of the terebinth, when ten of Joab's young arms-bearers closed in and struck at Absalom until he died" (vv. 14-15). Joab's is not the only hand involved, but involved he is in the death of Absalom.

The second section of Joab material, also echoing what we have seen before, involves his managing the messenger bringing news of the battle and its outcomes to David. His action is to inform the king of the results—the king who is also the father of the dead rebel. The news and its impact will thus be mixed: welcomed and dreaded. Joab has opportunities to play, and we are shown his concern in certain aspects, though little care for David, about to hear of the death of his son. Joab begins by refusing the initiative of Ahimaaz, son of David's priest Zadok, to run the report. That Ahimaaz sees only good news and wants to deliver it is made clear, and that Joab sees dual aspects is also manifest (18:19-20): "Ahimaaz son of Zadok said, 'Let me run and report to the king that the LORD has vindicated him against his enemies.' But Joab said to him, 'You shall not be the one to bring tidings today. You may bring tidings some other day, but you'll not bring any today; for the king's son is dead!'" Though the boy does not understand his news, Joab does. Joab shows, briefly, a strange concern for this young man, if not for the father of the dead son—as he expresses none for the defeated, fleeing, and trapped Absalom.

Joab next assigns the messenger task to a foreigner, a Cushite, telling *him* to tell the king what he saw. There is no effort to design the message. Joab seems unconcerned that David learn exactly what transpired: presumably the victory, the rebel's death, the manner of it (v. 21). But Ahimaaz, still not understanding, begs again that *he* might tell the news. Again, Joab tries to dissuade him, speaking almost tenderly to him (vv. 22-23). Joab does not explain to the priest's son how it is that victory can be other than well-received, and his allowing Ahimaaz to go registers with me as a sign of pitilessness for both David and Ahimaaz.

The king-and-father is anxiously awaiting news, anticipating by the identities of the messengers what it might be. The news is delivered twice, first by the priest's son, who suddenly understands what Joab has hinted, when David responds to his words (vv. 28-30): "The king asked,

'Is my boy Absalom safe?'" (v. 29a). Ahimaaz finds he cannot answer the question, and so the Cushite, also carefully, tells David what has transpired (vv. 31-33), occasioning the outcry of the father for his son. The contrast between David's grief and Joab's coldness is stressed, efficiently. It may be that Joab's practicality and David's lack of realism are also counterpointed, but the absence of any concern exhibited by Joab for David shrinks that point. Had we seen care earlier, it might be possible to see Joab here as simply trying to nudge David nearer to reality.

Though the passage pauses to stress David's grief, we move to Joab's third moment, his managing David's response to all that has happened. Joab is informed of David's "weeping and mourning for Absalom," and the narrator also tells us that the people respond to David's sorrow, their utterance framed as "the king is grieving for his son" (19:2). That is, focalized as their perception and utterance is the father's grief rather than something else that might have been said, for example, victory shared by leader, fighters, partisans. The implication, I think, is that the people sympathize with the father rather than feel Joab's irritation at a victorious king who cannot recognize his best interests.

Contrastively, then, Joab expresses anger and outrage at the king, nothing for the father. He upbraids David, publicly, disregarding all but one facet of the end of the rebellion (19:5-7):

> Joab came to the king in his quarters and said, "Today you have humiliated all your followers, who this day saved your life, and the lives of your sons and daughters, and the lives of your wives and concubines, by showing love for those who hate you and hate for those who love you. For you have made clear today that the officers and men mean nothing to you. I am sure that if Absalom were alive today and the rest of us dead, you would have preferred it. Now arise, come out and placate your followers! For I swear by the LORD that if you do not come out, not a single man will remain with you overnight; and that would be a greater disaster for you than any disaster that has befallen you from your youth until now."

His speech is tight if long, moving efficiently from point to point. Joab characterizes David as having insulted—dishonored—all his followers, who themselves acted to save David's life. Joab characterizes such treatment as perverse, loving and hating wrongly; he minimizes David's concern for any but the single son, pushes past the literal sense of David's words to suggest that—given the choice, David would exchange living and faithful allies for a dead and faithless son. Joab advises the king what to do and threatens that those who deserve to be greeted by the king would not fight for him again, should this gesture lack. The brutality of Joab's words does not occlude the fact that there is no evidence for anything

Joab says—in fact, the opposite, as David meets many loyal people as he re-enters Jerusalem. There is no indication that David's allies resent his grief, that they feel insulted, that David would choose their destruction to save his son—and be pleased to do so—or that their rebellion is simmering, to be stanched only by what Joab urges.

That David makes no demur but obeys Joab wordlessly may tempt us to think Joab correct in what he alleges, but I do not think so. Again, we have Joab acting in word and deed, generally advancing the purposes of David—until he opposes David's hope of a soft landing for Absalom. Military competence continues central and undisputed. Verbal cleverness, cruel boldness, again as well. The battle of wills and desires between David and Joab, in motion implicitly from the moment of David's seeing Bathsheba and explicitly from Amnon's lusting for Tamar is culminated here, as Joab eliminates the heir-apparent.[22] What each character has wanted is somewhat open to construction, and it seems best to suggest that the characters have not made evident what they most deeply desire as the drama has lurched from scene to scene. Joab's language has gone false. I see no sign that David's love is limited, even at the moment his language and demeanor are centered on the one son rather than more widely. This is argued in contrast to Joab's characterization of him, implying that David has chosen badly. From the moment the death-scene of Absalom begins, Joab's actions seem to rise from motives contrasting greatly with David's. The episode breaks off, with David resisting nothing that Joab has claimed, rather obeying Joab—except for the replacement of Joab with Amasa, words addressed to Amasa. We miss any moment where David excoriates Joab for these acerbic words, nor does anyone disagree with the content of the speech. Furthermore, no character is recorded as mentioning to the king that Joab is responsible for Absalom's death, no evidence that David knows how Absalom died.[23]

A sixth moment to examine is *Joab with David and Abishai* in ch. 20, set up at the end of the previous unit when David replaces Joab with Absalom's former commander, whether we infer simple contiguity or richer causality. The information comes as direct speech of David, spare and without explanation but intensified by an oath, uttered as David is returning to Jerusalem (19:14): "And to Amasa say this, 'You are my own flesh and blood. May God do thus and more to me if you do not become my army commander permanently in place of Joab!'" There is no immediate reaction from Joab, but his response is arguably the heart

---

22. Arguably, the pattern starts with Joab learning that David is negotiating with Abner, 3:23-25.
23. Bodner, *Absalom*, 106.

of what happens when revolt next erupts in the wake of David's quelling Absalom's attempt to unseat him. When David instructs Amasa with particulars he is unable to accomplish, David orders Abishai to pursue the rebel. But the narrator tells us that Abishai is accompanied by Joab, whom David has not charged. Joab reinstates himself at the head of the fighting men and then kills Amasa, moving past the corpse to lead the enterprise which the king charged Abishai (20:8–10).

The move seems reckless beyond what we have seen from Joab. Refusing to accept his replacement, first by Amasa and then by Abishai, he joins his brother and dispatches his cousin, who foolishly has not anticipated treachery. With Amasa removed, Joab leads pursuit of the rebels, tracking them north. He meets no opposition: not to his resuming leadership, nor to killing his cousin, not to pursuing the rebels, nor dealing with the people. Accumulating allies as he goes (20:11, 13, 15), Joab mounts a siege at a town called Abel, where again he connects with a wise woman who advises him that the revolt can be settled by the death of one man (20:16-21). Joab seems to want his usual two things: David's good—the crushing of the rebellion—and his own—command of David's fighters—and seems able to hear that she can offer him those. Joab once again does what needs doing for the good of David's rule, but also again without letting it take precedence over his own need of regaining his position at the head of David's fighting men. The narrator finishes the episode as follows (v. 23): "Joab was commander of the whole army of Israel." David's rule seems restored to stability. We hear no recriminations against Joab, no harsh words, no decisive gesture from David. Fallen silent, David virtually disappears. Joab is again drawn as a competent and shrewd commander, with his language serving primarily his own purposes, folding in David's objective incidentally. Joab shows himself superior to both his cousin Amasa and his brother Abishai, taking their king-assigned roles on himself. The wise woman of Abel reads him as practical, helps him win a victory with minimal loss of life. David constructs Joab by not—yet—resisting him effectively at any point in the scene. Joab's killing of Amasa echoes his slaying of Abner, as David will indicate when he gives Solomon the commission regarding Joab. We might classify Joab's deed as a personal killing in the midst of a war, his guilefully attacking a man on his own side who did not anticipate it. On the ever-bolder trajectory, it is a blunt move.

The seventh scene, *Joab with Adonijah and Solomon*, provides our last chance to scrutinize Joab making his final choices in 1 Kings 1–2. It is difficult to sequence these materials with what has preceded, as they conclude David's reign and introduce the time of Solomon. Insofar as modern literary studies have shown that what we are given in artistic literature is a series of brief scenes which we, reading, connect, we are "missing" a lot of scenes between when we last saw David ruling and when we find him now: old and cold, huddled and cuddled to preserve vitality. Consequently, we cannot know how Joab recovered from his crass disregard of his king's order in the previous scene. Actually, we have not seen much recovery between David and Joab. In narrative terms, Joab appears to have gotten away with his moves virtually unscathed. But not quite so, as we all are about to learn.

Another way to offer that point is to say that the David-plot has disintegrated, except for the matter of how kingship will be handed. From Joab's explicit narrative arrival, his plot-line has been consumed with such matters. Joab's presence marks the struggle of contenders for David's position, and so it concludes here. Joab, shown actively impatient and short-sighted in a number of ways, has nonetheless survived as part of David's kin group, entourage, and court from the early days of flight from Saul until now. The standard time for David's reign is forty years, and Joab has served David—for better or worse, well or poorly—for that length of time. So, though I will show how Joab "jumps ship" at the very end, his long "boat trip" needs to be remembered.

This final deed (1 Kgs 1:5-8) is set up by a narrator description of Adonijah, resembling Absalom in his aims and claims, also in his father's resistance to checking him. Insofar as David is feeble, as Adonijah is heir-apparent and never opposed by his father, and as he takes counsel before acting—if not before declaring his desire and acquiring royal accouterments—his move may not have been so rebellious as seems implied as the story unfolds.[24] Joab's choice here, provided by narrator summary, may have seemed like others he has made, acting for David's good when possible—until his own need interferes.

But, as the narrative moves along its stately way (1:9-53), the three main opponents of Adonijah show Joab on the wrong side, and the plan of Adonijah aborts, with Solomon established in his brother's stead. So thorough is the validation of Solomon's enthronement (and so familiar are most readers with its inevitability) that we may hardly notice that Adonijah's premature move dissipates without demur, let alone violence.

---

24. Some raise, even to dismiss, the matter that David can be seen as waiting for a move from God, such as the deity did when choosing Saul and David himself. Michael A. Eschelbach, *Has Joab Foiled David? A Literary Study of the Importance of Joab's Character in Relation to David*, Studies in Biblical Literature 76 (New York: Lang, 2007), 51–2, discusses this briefly, basically to dismiss it.

Joab moves aside (if not very far) without further mention as Solomon takes his rightful place. By comparison with other efforts to oppose David, this one is mellow.

But part of the transition from David to Solomon is David's charging Solomon how to clear certain injustices that David himself neglected. The pair that concerns us here involves Joab. After a general injunction about fidelity to God's *torah*, calling to mind not only the general Deuteronomic language and also that addressed specifically to David in 2 Samuel 7, David names the crimes (1 Kgs 2:5-6): Joab's killing of Abner and of Amasa: "He killed them, shedding blood of war in peacetime, staining the girdle of his loins and the sandals on his feet with blood of war. So act in accordance with your wisdom, and see that his white hair does not go down to Sheol in peace." Of the many ways we might anticipate David characterizing Joab, only these two are mentioned, and in fact as the scene develops, the matter to be cleared comes to one: unlawful bloodshed.[25]

The narrator joins Joab's last moves with Solomon's disposition of other rebellions:

> When the news reached Joab, he fled to the Tent of the Lord and grasped the horns of the altar—for Joab had sided with Adonijah, though he had not sided with Absalom. King Solomon was told that Joab had fled to the Tent of the Lord and that he was there by the altar; so Solomon sent Benaiah son of Jehoiada, saying, "Go and strike him down." Benaiah went to the Tent of the Lord and said to him, "Thus said the king: 'Come out!'" "No!" he replied; "I will die here." (1 Kgs 2:28-30)

Solomon is willing to order just that, reiterating David's charge against Joab. And so Joab dies.

Scholars query whether Joab had the right to seek sanctuary, but seek it he does.[26] Solomon's decision (and Benaiah's acquiescence to it) may hinge on the justice issues and the characters' presumed understandings of those, to which we have limited access. To lift out that matter more clearly: the story of David's rule has been filled with death, and for the most part,

---

25. Fokkelman, *King David*, 386–7, thinks the issue is about revenge.

26. Jonathan Burnside, "Flight of the Fugitive: Rethinking the Relationship between Biblical Law (Exodus 21:12-14) and the Davidic Succession Narrative (1 Kings 1–2)," *JBL* 129, no. 3 (2010): 430, suggests, that Joab may be shown to flee boldly to the horns of the altar, whether he deserves such sanctuary or not. His characterization is not inconsistent with such a view. On the other hand, Jerome T. Walsh, *1 Kings*, Berit Olam (Collegeville: Liturgical Press, 1996), 5–7, suggests that Joab is shamed by needing such a refuge.

it seems approved. Kingdoms are not run according to nonviolence. But from the first engagement of Joab with David to this last one, the issue is whether Joab's killing of Abner was a "licit" war death or not. Is Joab executed for—does he die as a result of—killing Abner (and Amasa) rather than for other things we might be able to name—though neither David nor the narrator brings them up. That Adonijah is not killed until he oversteps and that Abiathar is not executed for siding with the wrong throne-claimant suggests that the issue with Joab is, in fact, his early illicit shedding of blood, deeply offensive. David's deferring to settle is not a surprise, since David is characterized as dilatory, surely with Joab.

The explicit Joab issue in this scene, then, reduces to a single ethical one, perhaps not the one that bothers *us* the most or that *we* would think should bother David the most. Joab seems to me more cruel over the Absalom death than with Abner or Amasa. But Joab, refusing David's point of view as he did when Abner's death occurred, still refuses to abandon or acknowledge the wrongness of his position over against what David told Solomon. So in a sense, Joab is shown to die with some integrity as well as with courage—or perhaps with stubbornness. He is also consistent, I think, long-range faithfully serving David but short-range making a choice that suits his own good more closely: supporting Adonijah when he decides to usurp rather than waiting for David to declare an heir or to die, Joab does not back down when opposed. Twice we saw him grovel, at least verbally, but not here. His words are bold, and whereas David often took them without demur, Solomon refuses them.

Conclusions

Insofar as each of the seven Joab/David sections has been explored and then summarized, it remains to look across the episodes. At the level of authorial moves, explicit narrator comment, story-level assertions and character choices, Joab is largely coherent, consistent. He acts for David's benefit by default but diverges in each scene, when he has an alternative good to pursue—arguably for his own benefit—that his thwarting of David can plausibly advance. That we cannot quite name his goal does not occlude his *modus operandi*. His moves range from skilled and deft to naive and blunt, lacking subtlety and strategy, over time. Joab survives these moves and may plausibly feel emboldened as David resists him with diminishing immediate effect. But he dies, learning he has miscalculated.

Less clear, more reader-derived and inferrable, less comprehensible as characterization is a rationale for supposing that David might not be succeeded by a designated son. Given that Joab's narrative presence marks scenes where David's throne-position is under assault from his kin, my key to characterization has been to explore Joab *as if* aiming to succeed—granted, his hope is futile from our readers' angle. Why should such a contrary-to-fact situation seem available repeatedly? *Is* it proffered repeatedly? Joab opposes David's move with Abner and remains upbraided but unpunished. He slyly and then more boldly challenges David in war-linked moves; David bests him but leaves him in position, then fires him, ineffectually. Joab moves with more subtlety in bringing Absalom home but his tracks are spotted by David in any case, and the arrival of Absalom cannot be said to be a success. Joab can plausibly think he is gaining traction in his long-running effort to show the king's weakness. Always a skilled fighter, Joab is often but not always a skilled rhetorician: bold but not skilled.

But again, why should such a contrary-to-fact situation be proffered, repeatedly? No son of David until Solomon is shown more able than Joab, so his ambition is plausible, at the story level, though not obvious for readers, so long-familiar with the Davidic succession. For whom would such characterization be helpful, at the level of intended readers? We may think of Josiah's male progeny, or perhaps those surviving Jehoiachin. But power struggles among such characters as these are not rare. Joab's putative ambition is not wholly unfounded.

Chapter 13

KNOWING ABNER

David Shepherd

No one saw it, or knew it, nor did anyone awake; for they were all asleep.
—1 Sam. 26:12 (NRSV)

So long as I know it not, it hurteth mee not.[1]

Knowing Biblical Characters

The interpretive significance of what characters do and do not know is easily illustrated in literature of various sorts, so it should not surprise us if instances may also be gleaned from narratives of the Hebrew Bible.[2] Indeed, Meir Sternberg, in his important treatment of the poetics of the latter, offers just such an illustration from the books of Samuel when he poses the question: "Does Uriah Know about his Wife's Doings?"[3] In the

---

1. George Pettie, *A petite pallace of Pettie his pleasure contaynyng many pretie hystories by him set foorth in comely colours, and most delightfully discoursed* (R. Watkins, 1576), 168. In modern parlance, this proverb is often used to justify withholding information from someone so as to absolve them of responsibility or free them from worry. In George Pettie's sixteenth-century version of the classical story, *Cephalus and Procris*, the proverb is placed in the mouth of Procris, the jealous wife, who wishes to be spared the knowledge (and hurt) of her husband's infidelity.

2. For an exploration of "knowledge" in more modern literature see, for example, Donald Hardy, *Narrating Knowledge in Flannery O'Connor's Fiction* (Columbia: University of South Carolina Press, 2003).

3. Meir Sternberg, *The Poetics of Biblical Narrative: Ideological Literature and the Drama of Reading* (Bloomington: Indiana University Press, 1985), 201–9.

end, Sternberg's discussion plausibly suggests that the text permits two incompatible readings: the Uriah who does know, a complex figure "torn between his sense of betrayal and his sense of duty…[who] accepts his fate with an awe-inspiring dignity"[4] or the Uriah who doesn't know what has happened and who goes to his death as a heroic and idealistic innocent (though inevitably tinged with naivete?).[5]

In the course of his discussion, Sternberg observes that the interpretation of Uriah as unknowing is encouraged by the fact that Uriah doesn't explicitly admit that he knows.[6] While the possible reasons for Uriah refraining from admitting such knowledge (even if it was in his possession) caution us against seeing this as too great an encouragement, Sternberg's observation highlights the lack of explicit references to Uriah's knowledge within the narrative. Indeed, it is this very lack which allows Sternberg's two incompatible readings to be sustained by the reader's alternate interpretations of Uriah's actions and words as either knowing on one hand, or unknowing on the other.

Yet, it is worth noting that Hebrew Bible narratives are not always so reticent with regard to their characters' knowledge, and in some cases, as Shimon Bar-Efrat notes, more explicit indications of what a character does or doesn't know can be crucial for the development of the plot and characterization.[7] For example, Jonathan tells David that Saul knows that David will become king (1 Sam. 23:17), Nathan in turn suggests that Adonijah has been made king without David's knowledge in order to goad Bathsheba into action on behalf of her son (1 Kgs 1:11), and Solomon insists to Benaiah that Joab slew Abner (and Amasa) without David's knowledge (1 Kgs 2:32). As Bar-Efrat suggests, Solomon's accusation seeks to characterize Joab as murderous and David as innocent as a means of persuading Benaiah to kill Joab, which in turn advances the plot.[8] If this latter example well illustrates how what one character says about another contributes to the latter's characterization, we might also note that in doing so, Solomon contributes to his own characterization as a son bent on seeing that the wishes of his father, David, are fulfilled.

---

4. Ibid., 206.

5. Sternberg's discussion of incompatibility and ambiguity resonates with but does not reference that of Shlomit Rimmon-Kenan, *The Concept of Ambiguity—the Example of James* (Chicago: University of Chicago Press, 1977), 9–16. See further below.

6. Sternberg, *Poetics*, 205.

7. Shimon Bar-Efrat, *Narrative Art in the Bible*, JSOTSup 70 (Sheffield: Almond, 1989), 61.

8. Ibid.

In this case Solomon's own direct verbal insistence on David's lack of knowledge of (and thus, it is implied, responsibility for) Joab's intentions or actions, coincides with the view expressed by the narrator of 2 Sam. 3:26 that David knew nothing of Joab's retrieval and dispatching of Abner (a matter to which we will return below). While the historical David's ignorance and/or innocence of the deaths of various Saulides has of course been regularly interrogated,[9] there can be little doubt that the reliability of the biblical narrator may serve to encourage a particular appraisal of a character and what they may or may not know.[10]

While a character's own assertion of what they do or don't know may well be equally reliable, as when Jonah acknowledges that the storm sinking his ship is his fault (e.g. Jon. 1:12), Bar-Efrat rightly observes that it is not necessarily so. Thus, Cain's claim to not know the whereabouts of his dead brother (Gen. 4:9) is judged by the reader to be no more true than Ahimaaz's insistence to David that Ahimaaz doesn't know whether all is well with Absalom (2 Sam. 18:29).[11] If, as it seems, the above examples suggest that the books of Samuel display a considerable interest in what even minor characters such as Uriah do and do not know, it would not seem unreasonable to consider whether such an interest might also be evident in—and shed some light on—the characterization of Abner within these books.

Knowing Abner

As one might imagine, interpretations of the character of Abner in the books of Samuel begin with the Old Greek translation of these books and are to be found in subsequent rabbinica and in commentary literature right up to the present day. However, the only sustained and focused analysis of the character (and characterization) of Abner in his own right of which the present author is aware is the recent study of William Buracker, who

---

9. See, for instance, Steven L. McKenzie, *King David: A Biography* (Oxford: Oxford University Press, 2000), 113–26, who argues that the historical David not only sanctioned Abner's death, but must also be the prime suspect in Ishba'al's killing, and encouraged the Philistines into the conflict which claimed Saul's life. Cf. also Baruch Halpern, *David's Secret Demons: Messiah, Murderer, Traitor, King* (Grand Rapids: Eerdmans, 2003), 76–84.

10. By reliable we mean a narrator who does not relate things which they know not to be true. See Sternberg, *Poetics*, 51. Cf. the discussion in David Gunn and Danna Fewell, *Narrative in the Hebrew Bible* (Oxford: Oxford University Press, 1993), 53–6.

11. Bar-Efrat, *Narrative Art*, 62–3.

offers not only an analysis of the relevant passages in 1 and 2 Samuel in the MT but also the interpretation offered by the Old Greek.[12] For obvious reasons, the much more modest contribution offered here will not pretend to rival the comprehensiveness of Buracker's study, but will instead seek to discern the ways in which various passages in which Abner appears in the MT betray a particular interest in what he, and others to whom he relates, do and do not know. In addition to considering the knowingness of Abner, we will also attend to the question of how well the readers themselves are able to know Abner as a literary character.

1 Samuel 17:55-58

While Abner first appears in 1 Sam. 14:50-52, where his kinship to Saul and his position as commander of his army is noted, the passage offers little else by way of introduction.[13] However, Abner reappears in 1 Samuel following David's triumph over Goliath (17:55-58) in an episode whose initial curiosity lies in Saul's lack of knowledge:

> [55] When Saul saw David go out against the Philistine, he said to Abner, the commander of the army, "Abner, whose son is this young man?" Abner said, "As your soul lives, O king, I do not know." (חי־נפשך המלך אם־ידעתי) [56] The king said, "Inquire whose son the stripling is." [57] On David's return from killing the Philistine, Abner took him and brought him before Saul, with the head of the Philistine in his hand. [58] Saul said to him, "Whose son are you, young man?" And David answered, "I am the son of your servant Jesse the Bethlehemite."

That Saul does not appear to know whose son David is strikes the reader of 1 Samuel 17 as odd, given that in 1 Sam. 16:18-19, Saul is told that Jesse has a son, whom he proceeds to ask for by name ("David") from his father. While this curiosity may be best explained by supposing that the writer of one episode was not aware of the other,[14] the impression given

---

12. William Buracker, "Abner Son of Ner: Characterization and Contribution of Saul's Chief General" (PhD diss., Catholic University of America, 2017).

13. A conclusion drawn also by Buracker (ibid., 30).

14. So Gordon, *I and II Samuel*, 159; for the various ways commentators have sought to make sense of these chapters see John T. Willis, "Function of Comprehensive Anticipatory Redactional Joints in 1 Samuel 16–18," *ZAW* 85 (1973): 295–8, and subsequently Hugh Pyper, *David as Reader: 2 Samuel 12:1-15 and the Poetics of Fatherhood* (Leiden: Brill, 1996), 163–8. As Walter Dietrich ("Die Erzählung von David und Goliath in 1 Sam. 17," *ZAW* 108 [1996]: 183–4) notes, Saul's question is plausible (despite the observation by Benjamin Johnson, *Reading David and Goliath*

by the text as it stands is of Saul as oddly forgetful—a condition which is seen by some as symptomatic of his already troubled spirit (1 Sam. 16:14 et al.).[15] Of course, this will not be the last time that Saul seems not to know David.[16] Alternatively, it has been suggested that Saul's question should be read here as not so much ignorant as anxious—containing a coded-warning to Abner that someone as precocious as David needs to become a "son" of Saul to ensure that the young man's ambitions don't threaten both Saul and Abner.[17] While Saul's efforts to wed David to his daughters (1 Sam. 18) and references to David as "my son" (1 Sam. 24:17; 26:17) might point in this direction, it is difficult to be certain whether Saul's ignorance is best read here as genuine or calculated.

But Saul is not the only one who is presented as not knowing. So too Abner, whose first direct speech in the biblical tradition takes the form of not merely a confession of ignorance, but a seemingly emphatic one (17:55).[18] "As you(r soul) live(s)" (חי־נפשך) is also found in 1 Sam. 1:26 and in 2 Sam. 14:19, and in both the latter case and here, it is offered in response to a king's question presumably as a means of impressing upon him the respondent's earnestness and sincerity which may be perceived to

---

in Greek and Hebrew: A Literary Approach, FAT 2 [Tübingen: Mohr Siebeck, 2015], 201, that it is rather premature) given earlier reports (17:25) that the vanquisher of Goliath would be entitled to a daughter of the king and his own family's elevation.

15. Graeme Auld, *I & II Samuel*, OTL (Louisville: Westminster John Knox, 2011), 213, notes this possibility, having concluded that the text offers no sign that Saul's ignorance is feigned. Buracker, "Abner," 51, too is convinced that Saul's question is a genuine one, following Ralph W. Klein, *1 Samuel*, WBC 10 (Waco: Word, 1983), 181. The suggestion that Saul thought it was someone other than David going out against Goliath because David rejects Saul's armor (so Robert Polzin, *Samuel and the Deuteronomist: A Literary Study of the Deuteronomic History. Part Two: 1 Samuel* [Bloomington: University of Indiana Press, 1989], 173) seems rather implausible given that David's lack of armor should have rather facilitated Saul's recognition of him as he went out.

16. David Jobling, *The Sense of Biblical Narrative I: Structural Analyses in the Hebrew Bible*, JSOTSup 7 (Sheffield: JSOT Press, 1986), 28, suggests the possibility that this is part of Saul's characterization as one who is kept in the dark about things.

17. So suggests Keith Bodner, *1 Samuel: A Narrative Commentary* (Sheffield: Sheffield Phoenix, 2008), 189–90, apparently building on the very full discussion of J. P. Fokkelman, *Narrative Art and Poetry in the Books of Samuel: A Full Interpretation Based on Stylistic and Structural Analysis, Vol. 2: The Crossing Fates (1 Sam. 13–31 and II Sam. 1)*, SSN 23 (Assen: Van Gorcum, 1986), 190–1. See Buracker, "Abner," 48–50, for a fuller survey of scholarly opinions.

18. Fokkelman, *The Crossing Fates*, 191, seems to read Abner's ignorance as honest. So too Buracker, "Abner," 51.

be in doubt.[19] Indeed, the very fact that Abner feels the need to use such language may suggest that he perceives Saul's putting of the question to him to imply a suspicion that Abner does know more than the king does (and more than he should?) about this precocious young man.[20] Perhaps for that very reason, Abner's earnestness should not prevent us from considering whether we may be any more certain about Abner's ignorance than we are about Saul's. When read against the backdrop of 1 Samuel 17, Abner's claim to ignorance is at least as narratively plausible as Saul's.[21] Indeed, whereas Saul's claimed ignorance begins to ring false or at least odd when read in light of ch. 16, the absence of any mention of Abner in that chapter gives the reader little cause, on the face of it, to doubt the sincerity of Abner's claim that he doesn't know David's parentage (however implausible this might seem historically). Yet the reader, aware that the king has been well-furnished with information about David by his servants in 1 Sam. 16:18, might find it slightly dubious that Abner knows so little. While the reader cannot be certain at this point whether Abner does or doesn't know the answer to the king's question, a consideration of what Abner does (and doesn't) do next may offer a hint that Abner is more knowing than his reply to the king might seem to suggest.

Importantly, Abner's ignorance (whether genuine or feigned) leads to a continuation of the action and the conversation as Saul issues him orders to secure the information about David (v. 56) which both he and his general appear to lack. Given that the king's instructions are posed as David is

---

19. In 2 Sam. 14:19, the request for information is made by David of the woman of Tekoa, whom he rightly divines to be in cahoots with his general Joab. Fokkelman, *The Crossing Fates*, 192 sees the use of the vow formula as a hint that Saul's life is bound up with the crown, which is possible but doubtful. The suggestion of Yael Ziegler, *Promises to Keep: The Oath in Biblical Narrative*, VTSup 120 (Leiden: Brill, 2008), 109, that 1 Sam. 1:26, 17:55, and 2 Sam. 14:19 all offer contexts in which the recipient of this "vow" is threatened and needing to be reassured of their authority and their inferior's loyalty seems very strained in relation to 1 Sam. 1:26, but may have some relevance in the latter two texts (see also Johnson, *Reading David and Goliath*, 203). However, Ziegler's unwarranted assumption that Saul has no reason to suspect Abner of feigning ignorance stems from his failure to consider more fully what Abner might have to gain by doing so.

20. And if such a suspicion is plausible, it suggests that Abner's oath may be deployed here as a means of persuading his king of not only his deference but also his sincerity (contra Ziegler, *Promises to Keep*, 107, but in line with his comments on p. 109 and the relationship he observes elsewhere between oaths and sincerity (see 19, 60–2, 141).

21. This is perhaps what persuades Auld, *I & II Samuel*, 213, that Abner's ignorance here is as sincere as he judges Saul's to be.

going out to fight the Philistine (v. 55) the reader should presumably not make too much of the fact that Abner only acts on these orders after David has defeated Goliath. However, it is worth noting in what way and to what extent Abner does(n't) actually act on Saul's orders when he eventually does so. When the king orders Abner to inquire (v. 56), his use of the independent pronoun "you ask" (שאל אתה) makes it clear that he expects Abner to do so, rather than the king.[22] What Saul does not do, however, is suggest of whom Abner should inquire. If the reader recalls that Saul himself previously received quite detailed information about David from his servants (1 Sam. 16:18), one might imagine these same servants as a possible avenue of inquiry for Abner. At a minimum, it may be observed that Saul in no way specifies that Abner should inquire of David himself as he might have done if he so wished.[23] Moreover, even if Saul's order to Abner might allow for Abner to inquire of David himself, this does not obviously require Abner to bring David himself before the king to do so. It is thus noteworthy that Abner brings David before Saul (which he has not been asked to do), does not inquire about David (which he has explicitly been asked to do), but instead leaves it to the king to do so himself, at which point David himself furnishes the king with the solicited information.[24] While it is of course entirely conceivable for the reader to hypothesize that Saul might well have seen fit to summon David into his presence even if Abner simply told Saul that David was the son of Jesse, the narrative fact that Abner's claim to ignorance facilitates not only a personal audience for David with Saul, but also a conversation between them and David's eventual installation (again) in Saul's court, suggests the possibility that Abner may well have been more knowing than he let on—not least when one also considers the significant "liberties" Abner seems to take in fulfilling the king's command.[25] The text does not of

22. Fokkelman, *The Crossing Fates*, 192, suggests that Saul's emphatic insistence on Abner inquiring discloses Saul's discomfort with the growing realization that David will take his throne.

23. See, for example, Judg. 18:5, where the Danite spies ask the Levite to "inquire with/of God" (שאל־נא באלהים).

24. The contrast between Saul's orders and Abner's action is noted but without comment or analysis by Fokkelman, *The Crossing Fates*, 192, and by Buracker, "Abner," 52, who seems elsewhere (44) to see the text as implying that Abner's obedience was immediate, though neither immediacy nor obedience (as we have seen) are indicated by the text.

25. Abner is not the only general to take such liberties with their king's commands. Cf. for instance, Joab's "interpretation" of David's instructions in relation to Uriah (2 Sam. 11–12) and Absalom (2 Sam. 18).

course disclose Abner's motives in bringing together Saul and David, but it seems entirely possible that his "knowing ignorance" may play an important part in facilitating it.

1 Samuel 26

While Abner appears when David first goes missing from Saul's table in 1 Sam. 20:25, the brevity of his mention there means that one can say little about Abner here apart from observing that by appearing at Saul's side, Abner makes Jonathan's standing and David's absence all the more conspicuous.[26] If this mention underscores Saul's growing estrangement from David and Abner's close alignment to the king, Abner is more active in the account of the second of David's ambushes of Saul (1 Sam. 26; cf. also 1 Sam. 24). Indeed, one of the striking differences between these otherwise rather similar encounters is Abner's presence in the second episode, noted by the narrator through the eyes of David who sees Saul "with Abner, son of Ner, the commander of his army" (v. 5). This along with the noting of the men's encampment round about Saul is presumably meant to underline that there is no safer place for Saul to be than accompanied by his general and surrounded by his army (see also v. 7 where it is repeated). The falseness of this sense of security into which both Saul and the reader are lulled is, however, immediately and dramatically illustrated when David and Abishai manage to steal in and out of the camp taking with them from Saul's side evidence of the king's vulnerability in the shape of his spear and his water jar (vv. 6-12).

Having retreated a safe distance, David calls out perhaps surprisingly, not to Saul, but instead to the people and Abner (v. 14). Indeed, that David's interest is less in the army than its commander is confirmed by what he calls out: "Will you not answer, Abner?" (הלוא תענה אבנר, v. 14).[27] Unless we are meant to assume that David has called out something else in advance, querying the absence of an answer in an opening question does seem more than a little curious, even if David's intent to call Abner's capabilities into question is obvious. That Abner is capable of answering is proven in the same verse ("Abner answered"; ויען אבנר) by his own question of David which is, however, no less curious in its own way: מי אתה קראת אל־המלך, "who are you who calls out to the king?" Keith Bodner rightly points out the relevance of Abner's opening lines in the earlier episode (1 Sam. 17:55-58) for understanding this

---

26. See Buracker, "Abner," 54–5.
27. Perhaps Fokkelman, *The Crossing Fates*, 541, is right that David wishes to wake everyone up to hear his humiliation of Saul's commander.

one: whereas there Abner (and perhaps Saul too) professes his ignorance of David's parentage, here Abner seems ignorant of and thus queries David's identity.[28]

Yet, if we had cause to query whether Abner's claim to ignorance there was best understood as genuine or rather more "knowing," might we have reason to wonder whether here too Abner and his question should really be seen as genuinely ignorant, as has been assumed? Though it is hardly decisive, the fact that Saul will in short order manage to identify David by his voice (v. 17) might suggest that it would be odd if Abner could not.[29] More telling though is a less often queried aspect of Abner's question. Both the narrator's and David's own question have indicated to the reader that David's addressee has been Abner. It is thus rather striking that Abner asks "who are you that calls out to *the king*" (v. 14). While it has been suggested that David has initially addressed Abner here in this way to gain access to the king,[30] the fact that in the similar narrative (ch. 24) David has no qualms about speaking directly to Saul (24:9 [EVV 24:8]) and will do so again shortly here (26:17–20) would seem to make this rather unlikely. It is thus also unlikely that Abner's insistence that David is addressing the king rather than him is an attempt to contest David's right to do so.[31] Instead, it seems more probable that the reader should take their cue from Abner's previous appearance and his "knowing" ignorance there. In that passage, we may recall that Abner's claim to not know the identity of David serves to facilitate an actual exchange or dialogue between David and Saul. Here, we will see that Abner's claim to not know the addressee immediately sends the ball back into David's conversational court, while Abner's invoking of the king suggests his desire to ensure that David's conversation is, again, not with him, but with Saul.

While David will speak directly to Saul eventually, he does not do so before first seeking to impugn Abner and his efforts to protect Saul's life (vv. 15-16). In doing so, David ensures that his own preservation of Saul will seem all the more worthy, but the denigration of Abner's masculinity and competence as protector of Saul does rather rob David and Abishai's

---

28. D. Firth, *1 & 2 Samuel* (Nottingham: Apollos, 2009), 278 (followed at much greater length by Buracker, "Abner," 61–2) suggests that Abner's question may be entirely knowing and very much more contemptuous: "who are you to call out to the king?"; while this is not impossible (cf. 1 Sam. 24:16 and the possibility of legitimacy issues in 1 Sam. 17:55-58) the reading of "who are you?" (מי אתה) as a question of identity seems more natural and probable (see e.g. 2 Sam. 1:8; Gen. 27:18, 32).

29. So Buracker, "Abner," 62.

30. Firth, *1 & 2 Samuel*, 278.

31. Ibid.

own sortie of much of the daring it had seemed to require. Anyone at all, David seems to suggest, might threaten Saul with someone as incapable as Abner at his side. It is common amongst commentators to agree with David and happily add incompetence to ignorance on the list of Abner's demerits, perhaps because Abner's service to the house of Saul will be questioned later in 2 Samuel. But David goes still further in v. 16, by insisting that for not protecting the life of their "lord, the LORD's anointed" (24:6 [Heb. 7], 10 [Heb. 11]) as David has (26:11), Abner and his men are "sons of death" (בני־מות), a figure of speech used earlier in 1 Samuel by Saul to suggest to Jonathan that David himself should die (1 Sam. 20:31).[32] This underlines both David's perception of a duty of care for blood which is protected (in this case Saul's) and his conviction that one's failure to preserve blood which should not be shed might come at the price of one's own life. While this further conviction that Abner deserves to die garners fewer endorsements from commentators, might there be further reason to doubt David's judgment? With the preceding ch. 25 fresh in their mind, the reader will surely be inclined to note that even if David swears here that Abner and his men should die (as he has sworn that Nabal will die, 25:34), the difference is that here (unlike there) David shows no inclination to act as Abner's executioner.[33] But what finally and most tellingly puts paid to David's accusations against (and incriminations of) Abner in vv. 15 and 16 is a point which the narrator has made already three verses before David begins his diatribe (v. 12): "No one saw it, or knew it (ואין יודע), nor did anyone awake; for they were all asleep, because a deep sleep from the LORD had fallen upon them." If, as seems fair to assume, the thing no one (including Abner) knew about was David and Abishai's penetration of the camp and thieving of Saul's personal possessions, then the narrator's insistence that they didn't know it because they were deep in a divinely induced slumber must surely give the reader pause before acquiescing to David's indictment of Abner. Again, with reference to the previous chapter, whereas David's death sentence against Nabal is validated by the latter's divine execution, here David's similar verdict against Abner is surely invalidated by the narrator's report of divine sedation.

Unaware of his own exoneration by the narrator, Abner would seem to offer further evidence to the reader of his commitment to deflect David toward Saul by refusing to rise to the bait of David's mocking efforts

---

32. It is also possible, but less likely I think, that here David's accusation ("sons of death") implies that Abner has risked Saul's death (so Pyper, *Reading David*, 162).

33. Fokkelman, *The Crossing Fates*, 543, notes that neither in 25:34 nor here, does David's vow of death end in actual death.

to discredit him in front of his king and the troops under his command. Indeed, even when David concludes with a challenge to Abner in the form of a question which is as polemical as it is rhetorical ("where is the king's spear, or the water jar that was at his head?"), Abner's silence makes most sense not as "playing dumb" but simply "staying mum."[34] The shrewdness of doing so is suggested when Abner's silence is rewarded by Saul's belated entry into the conversation in v. 17 when he seeks to confirm his suspicion that this is David's voice calling out. Abner's cleverness in passing the ball back to David and suffering in silence might be seen to be further vindicated by the opportunity it allows for Saul to hear David's voice and identify him, even if his identification is less than entirely confident.[35] Here again, as in 1 Sam. 17:55-58, Abner's apparent, but arguably feigned "ignorance" and then reticence leads to an engagement between Saul and David.[36]

While Abner remains a relatively thinly drawn character in 1 Samuel, the departure of Saul from the stage at the end of the book paves the way for the much fuller portrait of Abner offered by the opening chapters of 2 Samuel. Accordingly, these chapters supply considerably more grist for the mill in assessing Abner's characterization, but also for tracing the contribution to this characterization made by the narrative's interest in what Abner knows and what he does not.

2 Samuel 2

With Saul and his son Jonathan dead, the narrator signals Abner's ascendancy by emphasizing his role in consolidating Saulide power and Ish-bosheth's kingship over Israel and the Jabesh Gileadites, despite David's overtures to the latter and reign over Judah from Hebron (2 Sam. 2:4-11). The remainder of ch. 2 is devoted to the violent conflict between forces loyal to Ishbosheth under Abner and those loyal to David under

---

34. Contra Buracker, "Abner," 63, who concludes (without arguing the case) that Abner's lack of response to David's insults shows that David has the upper hand.

35. Unlike the parallel episode, in which Saul's difficulty in identifying David's voice is belied slightly by David's bowing before Saul and the length of David's monologue, here the emphasis on the great distance which separates David from Abner and Saul gives the uncertainty a greater ring of narrative plausibility. H. J. Stoebe, *Das Erste Buch Samuelis* (Gütersloh: Gütersloher Verlagshaus Gerd Mohn, 1973), 468, seems to surmise that Saul sleeps more deeply and is only awakened by the exchange between David and Abner.

36. The theme of David's identity (and questions relating to it) thus recurs in 1 Samuel, even if in ch. 25, Nabal seems to question not primarily David's identity, so much as his legitimacy.

their commander Joab. The clash is precipitated by Abner's movement of troops across the Jordan from Mahanaim to Gibeon (El-Jib)—traditional Benjamite territory not far from Saul's Gibeah nor from Jerusalem—which may have been intended to bring matters to a head. Indeed, that Gibeon was of some strategic importance is suggested by the refusal of David to let this action go unchallenged by dispatching troops under Joab to meet the Benjamites.

Instead of a full military engagement, however, Abner suggests a kind of representative combat, akin to what the reader has already encountered in the case of David and Goliath (1 Sam. 17).[37] Some have suggested that Abner takes it upon himself to suggest this (here involving twelve men from each side instead of one) rather than a full engagement of the troops because he sought to gain an advantage or mitigate a weakness.[38] Indeed, it has also been suggested that the subsequent defeat of Abner's forces when full battle is finally joined might indicate as much.[39] However, if representative combat was advantageous to Abner in any obvious way, it is difficult to see why Joab would acquiesce so willingly to the suggestion, not least if Joab had any expectation of how thoroughly he might (and eventually did) rout his enemy. In light of these difficulties, it is worth considering the possibility that Abner suggests representative combat because he seeks to minimize the loss of life at least on his side, and perhaps on both sides.[40] While the representative combat here

---

37. For this suggestion and the reasons for preferring it to the idea that this was a game which got out of hand (so L. Batten, "Helkath Hazzurim, 2 Samuel 2,12-16." *ZAW* 26 [1906]: 90–4); see McCarter, *II Samuel*, 95–6 and the literature cited by him there. H. J. Stoebe, *Das Zweite Buch Samuelis* (Gütersloh: Gütersloher Verlagshaus Gerd Mohn, 1994), 115–17, offers a lengthy discussion which dismisses representative combat but fails to offer a more satisfying alternative. McCarter, *II Samuel*, 98, also follows F. C. Fensham, "Battle between the Men of Joab and Abner as a Possible Ordeal by Battle," *VT* 20 (1970): 356–7, in seeing the narrative here as implying that the result is a reflection of divine will (based on parallels with 1 Kgs 17 and comparable Hittite accounts)—a suggestion which is however rather weakened by the absence of both an explicit indication in this direction and—in the case of the representative combat—a result which might signal in whose favor the divine will has decided.

38. So seemingly Firth, *1 & 2 Samuel*, 338.

39. A possibility suggested by Firth (ibid.), who notes that it did not turn out this way.

40. So suggests Gordon, *I and II Samuel*, 214. J. P. Fokkelman, *Narrative Art and Poetry in the Books of Samuel: A Full Interpretation Based on Stylistic and Structural Analysis, Vol. 3: Throne and City (II Sam. 2–8 and 21–24)*, SSN 27 (Assen:

at Gibeon proves as unable to prevent full-scale battle as did David's monomachy with Goliath, this in itself does not make it impossible that Abner suggested it in the hope that it might. Moreover, what makes this reading of Abner's motivation here even more plausible is not only the absence of equally plausible alternatives but also the fact that it coheres well with the characterization of Abner when, later in the chapter, his forces are routed (v. 17) and he finds himself pursued by Asahel, the brother of Joab and Abishai, who evidently wishes to kill him and take his spoil.

With Asahel fleet of foot and in hot pursuit, the narrator reports that "Abner looked back and said 'Is it you, Asahel?' He answered, 'Yes, it is.'" Much like Saul's question of David in 1 Samuel 26, Abner's question does not seek to elicit truly new information, but rather to confirm a suspicion, which Asahel's response duly does.[41] There is no doubt then that Abner's question here is at least partly knowing, but what he goes on to say explains why he might be forgiven for wanting to know more, or to know more certainly.[42] After seeking to tempt Asahel to turn his attentions to one of Abner's underlings instead of him (v. 21), Abner makes clear his reasons for doing so: whereas Asahel's targeting of someone other than Abner might lead to only one death (presumably an anonymous member of Abner's army), Abner insists that Asahel's continuing pursuit of him risks not only Asahel's own death but an additional, and apparently serious complication, reflected in Abner's rhetorical question: "How then could I show (lit. 'lift up') my face to your brother Joab?" (ואיך אשא פני אל־יואב אחיך, 2:22)—a question on which commentators seldom linger.[43]

Van Gorcum, 1990), 44, notes that Abner's suggestion must "save face" by offering a battle of sorts, but "attempts to prevent mass bloodshed." This seems more likely than the possibility that Joab and Abner here take this encounter and the loss of life lightly, which Abner's suggestion that the men should "play/entertain" might suggest, if it were to be taken in its usual sense (cf. Judg. 16:25, 27)

41. Fokkelman, *Throne and City*, 51, notes the recognition and the need for confirmation and references Roman Jakobson's *phatic* communication. Cf. Buracker, "Abner," 93.

42. But the question is also a means of educating Asahel, who now knows that his identity is known.

43. Firth, *1 & 2 Samuel*, 339, suggests that the expression means that Abner will not "(be able to dialogue with him [i.e. Joab])," but it is not clear on what basis this suggestion is made. Buracker, "Abner," 132–3, mistakenly follows W. McKane, *I & II Samuel: The Way to the Throne* (London: SCM, 1963), 186, in assuming that Abner is expressing his fear that he will be shamed before Joab.

Rather than indicating that Abner's conscience will not be clear before Joab if he kills Asahel (so suggests BDB, but without parallel in the Hebrew Bible), Abner's worry about his inability to lift his face to/before Joab would seem to be more plausibly explained in light of David's lifting of Abigail's face in 1 Sam. 25:35. There, David explains to Abigail that he is permitting her to "go in peace to your house" (עלי לשלום לביתך), because "I have listened to your voice and I have lifted up your face" (ואשא פניך) (i.e. he has heard her request to be forgiven for failing to keep an eye on her foolish husband [1 Sam. 25:28] and granted her request to be forgiven).[44] Here Abner explains to Asahel that were Abner to kill him, Abner would *not* expect to be forgiven by Joab (his face would not be lifted up), a conclusion which the reader will discover to be well-founded when Abner is not allowed to "go in peace" by Joab in 2 Samuel 3 (v. 27), as we will see shortly. Whether Joab's predicted lack of forgiveness and intention to avenge Asahel ends up costing Abner his life at Joab's hands, or Joab's life at Abner's, this will be one more life lost than is necessary—and potentially more than one, if the cycle of vengeance is then permitted to spiral out of control.[45] While it will only be in retrospect that Abner's suspicion of Joab's vengefulness will be confirmed for the reader, and while Abner's tactic to dissuade Asahel from continuing his pursuit predictably fails, the suggestion that Abner's concern here is at least in part to minimize loss of life has the advantage of cohering with our reading of his suggestion of representative combat to avoid a full-on pitched battle.[46] Unfortunately for Asahel and indeed as we will see, unfortunately for Abner too, this latter attempt to minimize loss of life proves as fruitless as the first when Asahel refuses to give up his pursuit of Abner, which leaves Asahel dead and the reader to wonder whether Abner or Joab may be next.

That the reader may not need to wonder for long is suggested when the narrator notes that Asahel's brothers, Joab and Abishai, continue their pursuit (v. 24), and Abner, after rallying his troops for one last stand (v. 25), offers a final plea in the hope of pre-empting it:

---

44. For this reading of 1 Sam. 25 see D. Shepherd, "The Trespass of your Servant: Finding Forgiveness in 1 Samuel 25," paper presented at *Remember their Sins No More? Forgiveness and the Hebrew Bible/Old Testament*, a symposium held at the Trinity Centre for Biblical Studies, May 2018.

45. W. Brueggemann, *First and Second Samuel* (Louisville: Westminster John Knox, 1990), 222, agrees that Abner's purpose here is to forestall further violence.

46. Buracker, "Abner," 96–7, misreads Abner's flight and responses as indicating fear because he includes Abner in those who are afraid of Goliath (1 Sam. 17), but this is surely over-reaching.

²⁶ Then Abner called to Joab, "Is the sword to keep devouring forever? Do you not know that the end will be bitter? How long will it be before you order your people to turn from the pursuit of their kinsmen?"

The reader naturally assumes a concern for self-preservation to be foremost in Abner's mind here as he faces the prospect of his own death along with those not already perished. But Abner's appeal to Joab in a series of three questions certainly continues the theme—already implied by Abner's previous actions in this chapter—of someone concerned to avoid unnecessary loss of life. Leaving aside Abner's rhetorical appeal to the fraternal links between the combatants ("kinsmen"), the thrust of his appeal must be that with Joab's victory over the forces of Abner now decisively confirmed, the sword (a metonymy for armed conflict) should not be allowed to continue to consume both sets of troops.⁴⁷ Indeed, Abner's appeal to Joab to stand down his men is based on Abner's questioning of Joab's knowledge of how things will end. The most plausible way of making sense of Abner's question seems to be thus: if the reader and Joab assume from the tide of events thus far that the end will be bitter for Abner and his men alone, Abner's question is meant to communicate in no uncertain terms that the end will, in fact, be bitter for both. In other words, the cost of not merely defeating Abner and his men (which has been already accomplished) but killing them all (the "end") will be "bitter" because Joab should know (if he didn't already) that he will lose men of his own in the process. Thus, in questioning what Joab assumes to know (wrongly), Abner communicates what he wishes him to know (or assume). The advantage of such an understanding of Abner's rhetorical purpose is that it explains Joab's otherwise inexplicable standing down of his men.⁴⁸ In v. 27, Joab acknowledges that if Abner had not shared this "knowledge" (i.e. that the destruction of him and his men would be bitter for Joab and his men), Joab would have carried on.⁴⁹ Instead, Joab's

---

47. Firth, *1 & 2 Samuel*, 340, rightly divines that the point of Abner's questions is to cause Joab to consider whether further prosecution of the battle will be worth the price he and his troops may have to pay.

48. Stoebe, *Zweite Buch*, 118, finds both Abner's proposition and Joab's response curiously implausible.

49. Fokkelman, *Throne and City*, 59–60, follows C. J. Goslinga, *Het tweede boek Samuel*, Commentaar op het Oude Testament (Kampen: Kok, 1962), 54, and C. F. Keil and K. Delitzsch, *Biblical Commentary on the Books of Samuel* (Edinburgh: T. & T. Clark, 1876), 299, in reading לולא דברת כי אז מהבקר נעלה העם איש מאחרי אחיו (2:27) as Joab's accusation that if Abner hadn't suggested the representative combat (earlier that morning), there would have been no need to fight in the first

sounding of the trumpet and standing down of his troops (v. 28) signals his decision to content himself with a decisive victory over Abner and the servants of Ish-bosheth (as signaled by v. 30) rather than seeking a final annihilation of Abner and his troops, which Joab is persuaded by Abner's intimations (and his killing of Asahel) might result in a further loss of life on Joab's own side. Thus here again, for the third time in 2 Samuel 2, Abner seems to be characterized as one who is consistently interested in minimizing loss of life (including but not limited to his own), but also profoundly cunning and knowing in seeking to accomplish his purposes.[50]

2 Samuel 3

Following confirmation of the triumph of David's forces in the battle of Gibeon (2:30-31), the narrator's note of the waning strength of the house of Saul (3:1) but the waxing of Abner's power within it, prepares the reader for the events narrated in ch. 3. It is left unclear whether Ish-bosheth's accusation of Abner's presumption in relation to Rizpah (3:7-8) has any substance to it,[51] but it evidently offers Abner the pretense for ending the military conflict between the houses of Saul and David. Accordingly, following Abner's initial overture (v. 12) and David's recovery of Michal (vv. 13-16; on which he makes his covenant with Abner conditional), Abner communicates with the Israelites and the Benjamites and then goes to Hebron to parley with David and confirm his offer to rally Israel to him (vv. 20-21). David's agreement to this plan seems to be signaled by the narrator's report that David "sent Abner and he went in peace" (וילך בשלום). The otherwise redundant reappearance of "he went in peace" in the very next verse following the arrival of Joab (v. 22) ensures that the reader will not soon forget the manner of Abner's dismissal. Indeed, the *further* reiteration of it in the subsequent verse in

---

place. However, this fails to convince not only because the accusation is implausible (Joab's arrival and acceptance of Abner's suggestion indicates that a conflict of some sort was inevitable), but also because it is unnecessary, understanding the Hebrew as follows, in light of the loss of light at the end of the day (v. 24): "had you not spoken, then from the morning, the people would not have gone up from (i.e. given up) their pursuit, each one after his own brother."

    50. So also Buracker, "Abner," 123, 127.
    51. So rightly Firth, *1 & 2 Samuel*, 347, contra both W. Brueggemann, *First and Second Samuel*, 225–6, who sees Abner as guilty as charged, and A. A. Anderson, *2 Samuel*, WBC 11 (Waco: Word, 1989), 56, who finally suspects Abner's innocence. While the reader is not in a position to know whether Abner is guilty as charged by Ishbosheth, it seems safe to assume that Abner knows full well, but sees the fact as beside the point.

the report to Joab (David "sent him and he went in peace" (וישלחהו וילך בשלום, 2 Sam. 3:23) confirms that David's general too is in possession of this information.[52] The significance of this is clear: Joab now knows that so far as David is concerned, the state of war which has previously existed between David and Abner (המלחמה [2 Sam. 3:1, 6]) has now been replaced by peace. However, when Joab confronts David (3:25), it is precisely David's knowledge that Joab questions by insisting that David "knows" (ידעת) that Abner has deceived him and done so specifically to gain knowledge (ולדעת, 3:25[2×]), which Joab seems to imply Abner will use against David.[53] While Joab's assessment—that they are, in effect, still at war with Abner[54]—might well be intended to justify his subsequent killing of Abner, the reader is already prepared for both David and the narrator's objections to the contrary by the note that when Joab called Abner back, "David did not know" (ודוד לא ידע, 2 Sam. 3:26).[55] The narrator does not offer a similarly explicit judgment regarding Abner's knowledge, but given our and the narrative's interest thus far in what Abner does and does not know, it is worth attending to who knows what as we consider the account of Abner's killing by Joab.

The reader is of course not privy to how precisely Joab recalls Abner, but David's lament for Abner is often taken as an affirmation that it was what Abner didn't know, which hurt him:

[33] The king lamented for Abner, saying, "Should Abner die as נבל dies? [34] Your hands were not bound, your feet were not fettered; as one falls before the wicked you have fallen." And all the people wept over him again.

If David's question in v. 34 is a rhetorical one, as most assume, then David seems to imply that Abner should not have died the death he did, which was like that of a נבל. While most commentators (rightly) resist the

---

52. The repetition and its significance is noted by Gordon, *I and II Samuel*, 219, who also rightly finds suspect the LXX's inclusion of a fourth instance of "peace" at the end of v. 24.

53. The repetition of the verb ידע is noted at length by Fokkelman, *Throne and City*, 99–101, who does not however sense its connection to the wider theme in relation to Abner.

54. So Firth, *1 & 2 Samuel*, 350, notes that Joab "did not recognize David's peace under these circumstances…"

55. As Stoebe, *Zweite Buch*, 138, observes, the narrator notes twice over (3:27, 30) that it was to avenge his brother's death rather than for strategic purposes that Joab kills Abner; David's curse on Joab and his house (3:28-29) is clearly intended to disavow any responsibility for Abner's death.

temptation to follow the LXX in seeing this as an allusion to Nabal, who also dies an ignominious death in 1 Samuel 25,[56] the frequent reading of נבל as "fool"[57] here nevertheless reflects the well-enshrined misunderstanding of נבל as connoting mere "foolishness" in both narratives.[58] However, as careful analysis has shown, in both these instances and also in the narrative of Amnon's rape of Tamar in 1 Samuel 13, נבל refers to one who is guilty of a substantial transgression of acceptable boundaries or conventions.[59] That David is comparing Abner's death not to that of a "fool" but to that of a "transgressor" makes sense of his insistence that while Abner was executed in cold blood by Joab as if he was guilty of a crime, Abner was not bound hand and foot as a transgressor would be, for the very good reason that the wickedness was not to be found in Abner, but rather in the one who has executed him without warrant.[60] The other advantage of this understanding of נבל as connoting a transgressor is that because it clearly doesn't apply to Abner, it comports much better with the overall tenor of David's lament which is not merely an elegy but eulogistic.[61]

Perhaps what has encouraged the mistranslation of נבל as "fool," to whose death David likens Abner's, is the lingering suspicion in the minds of commentators that Abner's death arises because of his naivety in

---

56. For the LXX's reading of the proper name in vv. 33 and 34 see Auld, *I & II Samuel*, 382, 383.

57. So Firth, *1 & 2 Samuel*, 344, 351; Gordon, *I and II Samuel*, 221; Auld, *I & II Samuel*, 383: "Abner has fallen as a fool who has not looked out for himself against the wicked." Fokkelman, *Throne and City*, 103, sees Abner as dying because of a "somewhat naïve compliance after a deceitful approach." Stoebe, *Zweite Buch*, 138, 142 opts for "Narren." Buracker, "Abner," 172–3, 179, resists the translation of and comparison with "Nabal" but sees the presentation of Abner's death and David's words as confirming Abner's foolishness.

58. See Gordon, *I and II Samuel*, 221, for example.

59. See J. Marböck, "*nābāl*," *TDOT* 9:158–71 and literature cited there. McCarter, *2 Samuel*, 105, 119, is nearer the mark but not altogether on it, in translating "outcast" but rightly discerns David to be lamenting the execution of Abner like a criminal (in cold blood) despite him not being (shackled and imprisoned like) one.

60. While the binding of the hands and feet need not imply the treatment of a murderer, Firth, *1 & 2 Samuel*, 351, is right to emphasize the contrast between Abner's status and one who has been convicted (hence imprisoned) and will be justly punished.

61. If the reader sees Abner's earlier refusal to respond when charged with going in to Rizpah (3:7-8) as an admission of guilt, then David's question here might be read ironically, rather than rhetorically, as he clearly intends it.

approaching Joab in the gate.[62] On the face of it, the reader's sense that Abner should have "known better" is strengthened by their recollection of Abner's voicing of his own suspicion that if he was to kill Asahel, he would not be forgiven for doing so by Asahel's brother Joab (2:22). Before rushing to such a conclusion, it should be remembered that after Abner expresses his suspicions about Joab's vengefulness, Joab is persuaded by Abner to forego the killing of Abner and his men and to stand down his troops and return to Hebron. Moreover, whatever the reputation of the sons of Zeruiah, Abner knows that David's authority over them ensured that both Abner and Saul survived David and Abishai's nighttime sortie (1 Sam. 26) when Abishai might easily have dispatched Saul and Abner as they slept. Given both of these considerations, when David sends Abner away in peace, Abner should not too quickly be judged naïve for assuming that Joab's recalling of him might be on the authority and with the knowledge of David. Indeed, it is not impossible that Joab summons Abner to speak to him in the public space of the gate (v. 27), and thus not secretly but deceptively.[63] Yet, while these factors must surely mitigate to some extent Abner's fatal misstep, even those readers willing to forget Joab's subsequent bloody career (of which Abner knows nothing) might be forgiven for suspecting that Abner should indeed have "known better" and died because he didn't. If so, there is little doubt that such a fatal failure of wisdom/knowledge would seem to represent a tragic turn of events for a character who has appeared remarkably knowing and wise throughout the early chapters of 2 Samuel and, indeed, arguably also in his less frequent appearances in 1 Samuel.

It is, in fact, the quite unexpected nature of Abner's naivety here which requires us finally to consider another alternative. We have seen that Abner's cleverness and wisdom seem to have been deployed in 2 Samuel with the aim of mitigating the effects of the ongoing conflict (i.e. loss of life) between the houses of Saul and David, and then, when it became clear that there was only going to be one winner, with the purpose of seeking to bring peace by bringing Israel and Benjamin over to David. We have also argued that already in 1 Samuel, while serving Saul, Abner's apparent "ignorance" is more easily interpreted as a knowing one, calculated to facilitate direct engagement between Saul and David, even at the expense of Abner's own role or visibility in proceedings. Indeed, in 1 Samuel 26, Abner's willingness to sacrifice himself is most manifest

---

62. See, for example, McCarter, *2 Samuel*, 122, who notes that Abner is "easily to find himself embroiled in a quarrel, whether with friend or foe. He is a thoroughly unpredictable and controversial fellow, and he is fatally careless."

63. So Alter, *The David Story*, 213.

in his silent suffering of David's "public" humiliation of him to facilitate the necessary interaction between the one who was king and the one who would be.

In light of this characterization of Abner, might a reader not be entitled to wonder whether Abner's seeming "ignorance" in going to his death may have been as "knowing" as it was in his life? While the understandable tendency to impute to Abner the natural human instinct of self-preservation might make such a suggestion seem unlikely, a reader armed with an expectation of continuity or consistency of character might have plausible reasons to draw such a conclusion. Indeed, such a reader might find it eminently reasonable to assume that someone as wise as Abner had proven himself to be would understand that even if David did send Joab away in peace, the very personal vengeance which Abner fully expected might have been forgone by Joab at Gibeon, but not forgotten by him forever. This reader might also expect Abner to realize that someone as vengeful as he knew Joab to be was never going to allow a military commander of Abner's prowess and profile to rival his own position in David's court and that in a united Davidic kingdom, there was only room for one of them.[64] This reader might further assume Abner to calculate that for him to kill Joab in cold blood before Joab killed him would simply perpetuate the cycle of violence which Abner had already lamented and sought to avoid in 2 Samuel 3 (by motivating the remaining brother, Abishai, to avenge Joab). And that knowing only too well the weakness of Ish-bosheth, Abner's allowing himself to be removed from the equation would simply hasten David's uniting of the tribes under his rule—precisely the turn of events narrated in the aftermath of Abner's death (2 Sam. 4–5).[65] Indeed, it might be argued that the assumption of Abner's knowingly sacrificial "ignorance" in going to his death in the gate is the only way of making reasonable sense of so formidable and perceptive a fighter falling so "naively" to someone from whom he expects blood vengeance.[66]

---

64. Josephus, *Ant.* 7.31, 36-38, and various subsequent commentators including, for instance, J. A. Soggin, *Old Testament and Oriental Studies* (Rome: Pontifical Biblical Institute, 1975), 46.

65. While Firth, *1 & 2 Samuel*, 353, maintains that Abner's death delayed the unification of the kingdoms, it is hard to see how it does so (given that Ish-bosheth would presumably have needed to be eliminated or pacified whether Abner died or not), or especially to what extent it does so. Indeed, Ish-bosheth's failure of nerve and Israel's dismay are noted in the very first verse of chapter 4.

66. If so, one may be encouraged to ponder the violent end of Abner's killer and rival commander, Joab, whose death in the temple might be open to a similarly sacrificial interpretation (1 Kgs 2:28-34).

While the argument has been made here that a careful reading of Abner's portrayal in 1 and 2 Samuel (including the account of his death) supports the interpretation of his "ignorance" as much more "knowing" than previous commentators have suspected, the very fact that such an interpretation might have remained unsuspected for so long by so many offers a fine illustration of the challenges of studying characterization when narratorial judgments are comparatively rare. If the narrative evidence for Abner's "knowingness" strikes this reader as stronger, it would not be impossible to argue that Abner (at least in 1 Samuel and when he falls to Joab) is as unknowing as he appears to be. In this sense the challenge Abner poses for the reader is not entirely dissimilar to the one detected by Sternberg in Uriah. After all, only once, in 1 Samuel 26, does the narrator tell us what Abner really knows, and in that case, Abner is unknowing because God has put him to sleep. Otherwise we are dependent on reading between the lines of description and dialogue, which resist easy conclusions. All of which offers a salutary reminder not only of the challenges of determining how knowing Abner is at particular points, but also of the limited extent to which any reader may really lay claim to knowing Abner at all.

Chapter 14

"A MAN OF SHAME":
RIDICULING SAUL'S SON, ISHBOSHETH

Michael Avioz

Immediately after King Saul's death in the battle against the Philistines on Mount Gilboa (1 Sam. 31), we read of the son who succeeded him—Ishbosheth (2 Sam. 2–4).[1]

We are told of Ishbosheth's rise to the throne with Abner's help; the conflict between Ishbosheth's men and David's men; the confrontation between Abner and Ishbosheth; Abner's murder by Joab; and finally, Ishbosheth's brutal murder.

Most previous studies of Ishbosheth have focused on historical or chronological aspects,[2] while few studies have been devoted to his

---

1. According to 1 Sam. 14:49, Saul's sons are Jonathan, Ishvi, and Malchishua. 2 Sam. 2:8 adds Ishbosheth. However, the report of their death presents them as Jonathan, Abinadab, and Malchishua (1 Sam. 31:2), while 1 Chronicles lists them as Jonathan, Malchishua, Abinadab, and Ehba'al (8:33; 9:39). See Frederik E. Greenspahn, *When Brothers Dwell Together: The Preeminence of Younger Siblings in the Hebrew Bible* (Oxford: Oxford University Press, 1994), 76.

2. J. Alberto Soggin, "The Reign of 'Eshba'al, Son of Saul," in *Old Testament and Oriental Studies*, BibOr 29 (Rome: Biblical Institute, 1975), 31–49; Nadav Na'aman, "The Kingdom of Ishbaal," *BN* 54 (1990): 33–7; Alexander A. Fischer, *Von Hebron nach Jerusalem: Eine redaktionsgeschichtliche Studie zur Erzählung von König David in II Sam 1–5*, BZAW 335 (Berlin: de Gruyter, 2004), 85–93; Jeremy M. Hutton, *The Transjordanian Palimpsest: The Overwritten Texts of Personal Exile and Transformation in the Deuteronomistic History*, BZAW 396 (Berlin: de Gruyter, 2009), 69–73.

characterization.³ Moreover, scholarly focus on Ishbosheth tends to explore the integration of the episodes involving his character within the wider context of the so-called "History of David's Rise" or the "Succession Narrative,"⁴ with little scholarly attention paid to Ishbosheth's characterization.

This article attempts to fill this gap by providing a full literary analysis of the characterization of Ishbosheth.⁵

In his recent book on the characterization of Jesus in the book of Hebrews, Brian Small writes that characters have different traits and attributes, which include "name, age, gender, physical appearance, ethnicity, social location, or any other dimension of personhood that does not fall under the category of traits."⁶ I will use some of these categories in my essay. I will also present a comparison between Ishbosheth and other kings in the Hebrew Bible and the ancient Near East.

Characterization through Proper Names

Name is the "locus of qualities"⁷ or the "locus around which characterization actually takes place."⁸ Boris Uspensky⁹ demonstrates how names can be used to express different points of view within a given narrative. He brings several examples from world literature; one such example is his analysis of the various forms of Napoleon's name in Tolstoy's *War and Peace* and how they reflect different points of view and sentiments.

---

3. Keith Bodner, "Crime Scene Investigation: A Text Critical Mystery and the Strange Death of Ishbosheth," *JHS* 7 (2007), article 13, www.arts.ualberta.ca/JHS/Articles/article_74.pdf; repr. in idem, *The Artistic Dimension: Literary Explorations of the Hebrew Bible*, LHBOTS 590 (New York/London: Bloomsbury, 2013), 15–35.

4. See, e.g., Hutton, *The Transjordanian Palimpsest*; Sung-Hee Yoon, *The Question of the Beginning and the Ending of the So-Called History of David's Rise: A Methodological Reflection and Its Implications*, BZAW 642 (Berlin: de Gruyter, 2014), 23; Gillian Keys, *The Wages of Sin: A Reappraisal of the "Succession Narrative"*, JSOTSup 232 (Sheffield: Sheffield Academic, 1996), with earlier literature.

5. Unless otherwise stated, all biblical references are according to the NRSV.

6. Brian C. Small, *The Characterization of Jesus in the Book of Hebrews* (Leiden: Brill, 2014), 47.

7. Seymour Chatman, *Story and Discourse: Narrative Structure in Fiction and Film* (Ithaca: Cornell University Press, 1978), 131.

8. Thomas Docherty, *Reading (Absent) Character: Towards a Theory of Characterization in Fiction* (Oxford: Clarendon, 1983), 74.

9. Boris Uspensky, *A Poetics of Composition: The Structure of the Artistic Text and Typology of a Compositional Form*, trans. V. Zavarin and S. Wittig (Berkeley: University of California Press, 1973), 20–32.

In his book on biblical names, Moshe Garsiel[10] describes how the biblical literature operates with its own form of homiletics, which he calls "Midrashic name derivation." This sort of interpretation infuses the names with meaning based on sound or semantic potential. Only the context will indicate the exact meaning of the use of names in a given narrative.

The name Ishbosheth appears differently in Chronicles (1 Chron. 8.33; 9.39). There he appears as Eshba'al, which seems to be his original name. Scholars are divided in regard to whether the name "Ba'al" indicates the Israelite or the Canaanite deity. Without delving into this debate, I think that the focus should be on the intentions of the author/editor of Samuel.

The changes in the names of Saul's sons found in the book of Samuel should be attributed to an editorial stage in the book's composition and not to the hand of tradents. From a historical perspective, it is feasible that Saul did not perceive his sons' naming with the theophoric component of *ba'al* as incompatible with belief in the God of Israel, but evidently the author-editor of the book of Samuel did not share this viewpoint, since an anti-Saul orientation is apparent in his work. The change from *ba'al* to *boshet*, then, is seemingly calculated to protect Ishbosheth's character, yet this change is by no means complimentary towards the king, given that ancient readers would have immediately discerned its derogatory nature.

The fact that the lexeme *boshet* has negative connotations can be inferred from Saul's words to Jonathan in 1 Sam. 20:30: "Do I not know that you have chosen the son of Jesse to your own *shame* (לבשתך), and to the *shame* of your mother's nakedness?" Saul accuses Jonathan of shaming his parents and himself by his behavior. Ultimately, however, the shame is none but Saul's, and the irony is clear: Jonathan's name does not represent shame, but rather devotion to God, and it is undoubtedly a Yahwistic name. In his sermon, Samuel demands that the people "Serve Him (i.e., God) only" (1 Sam. 7:3), and as a result, "So Israel put away the Baals" (v. 4). Saul, it emerges, does not "put away the Baals," nor fulfill the injunction "and serve Him only"; rather, he perpetuates the Baals through the names of some of his sons.[11]

---

10. Moshe Garsiel, *Biblical Names: A Literary Study of Midrashic Derivations and Puns*, trans. P. Hackett (Ramat Gan: Bar-Ilan University Press, 1991).

11. See at length Michael Avioz, "The Names of Mephibosheth and Ishbosheth Reconsidered," *JANES* 32 (2011): 11–20, and the literature cited there. See further M. Golub, "The Distribution of Personal Names in the Land of Israel and Transjordan during the Iron II Period," *JAOS* 134 (2014): 621–42; Scott B. Noegel, "The Shame of Ba'al: The Mnemonics of Odium," *JNSL* 41 (2015): 69–94.

Ishbosheth's first mention in 2 Sam. 4:1 is significant: his nameless introduction as "the son of Saul" can be perceived as a sign of contempt.[12] This may, however, be a textual rather than a literary issue; in several places Ishbosheth appears with the appellation "Saul's son," so this may be a case of corruption.[13]

David Clines discusses Ishbosheth's appellations in 2 Sam. 3:14:

> Ishbosheth is here called "Ishbosheth son of Saul," while elsewhere in the chapter he is simply 'Ishbosheth' (vv. 7, 8, 11, 15). The reason is that David is saying to Ishbosheth: "[Michal] is my wife, not Paltiel's, and the responsibility for her being now with Paltiel is yours, since you are son and heir of your father who gave her to Paltiel (1 Sam. 25:44)."[14]

The names of Ishbosheth's murderers may have a comic effect: if Ba'ana refers to the Canaanite goddess Anat,[15] then this generates irony: a man with a Canaanite name kills a king with a Canaanite name—Eshba'al!

The name of the second killer, Rechab, may be an allusion to Deut. 24:6: "No one shall take a mill or an upper millstone (רכב) in pledge." The Hebrew word for the upper millstone is *rechev* and the lower *chechev*.[16] The murderers came to Ishbosheth when he was שכב ("sleeping") by disguising themselves as wheat buyers—generating wordplay with the same wheat mentioned in context of *recheb* in Deuteronomy.

Abner as a King-Maker

The narrative in 2 Sam. 2:8 reads: "But Abner son of Ner, commander of Saul's army, had taken Ishbaal (NJPS: Ish-bosheth) son of Saul, and brought him[17] over to Mahanaim." There is symmetry between the

---

12. S. Bar-Efrat, "Second Samuel", in *The Jewish Study Bible*, ed. A. Berlin and M. Zvi Brettler (Oxford: Oxford University Press, 2004), 626.

13. Cephas T. A. Tushima, *The Fate of Saul's Progeny in the Reign of David* (Cambridge: James Clarke, 2012), 144 n. 78.

14. David J. A. Clines, *On the Way to the Postmodern: Old Testament Essays 1967–1998, Vol. 1*, JSOTSup 292 (Sheffield: Sheffield Academic, 1998), 245–6.

15. See Samuel E. Lowenstamm, "Baana," *Encyclopaedia Biblica, Vol. 2* (Jerusalem: Bialik Institute, 1981), 301–2 (Hebrew).

16. Jeffrey E. Tigay, *Deuteronomy, with Introduction and Commentary*, 2 vols., Mikra Le-Yisrael (Tel Aviv: Am Oved; Jerusalem: Magnes, 2016), 1:600 (Hebrew).

17. MT: ויעבירהו. The LXX reflects a Hebrew variant: ויעלהו. Josephus (*Ant.* 7.9) has here ἐκαλεῖτο, reflecting a MT-like version.

first mention of Saul as Abner's commander and his latter mention as Ishbosheth's father. Ishbosheth is completely passive here: he is taken and transferred; Abner never asks him for his opinion; and he remains silent. This leads the reader to assume that this process is Abner's initiative.[18]

This passivity continues in v. 9, when Abner "made him king over Gilead, the Ashurites, Jezreel, Ephraim, Benjamin, and over all Israel." The reader may recall two anointment narratives: Saul's anointment in 1 Samuel 9 and David's anointment in 1 Samuel 16. In both narratives, the king was elected by God and anointed by a prophet. Neither God nor prophet is involved in Ishbosheth's case, and a third element—the people's consent (1 Sam. 10; 2 Sam. 5)—is also absent. In conclusion, God does not elect Ishbosheth, no prophet is involved in his anointment, and the people have no chance to express their attitude towards his election.[19]

Ishbosheth's Skills as a Judge

2 Samuel 3:7-11 describes the encounter between Abner and Ishbosheth. Ritzpah is identified in 2 Sam. 3:7 as Saul's concubine. Verse 7 reads:

וּלְשָׁאוּל פִּלֶגֶשׁ וּשְׁמָהּ רִצְפָּה בַת אַיָּה וַיֹּאמֶר אֶל אַבְנֵר מַדּוּעַ בָּאתָה אֶל פִּילֶגֶשׁ אָבִי

Now Saul had a concubine whose name was Rizpah daughter of Aiah. And Ishbaal said to Abner, "Why have you gone in to my father's concubine?"

Who is the subject of ויאמר? Many ancient translations have "Ishbosheth."[20] To complicate matters further, in 4QSam[a] the name appears as Mephibosheth.[21] If it is not a matter of a textual issue, it may be regarded as another case of an intentional ambiguity, caused as a means of the negative characterization of Ishboshesh, "what's his name."

---

18. Jan P. Fokkelman, *Narrative Art and Poetry in the Books of Samuel: A Full Interpretation Based on Stylistic and Structural Analyses: Vol. 3, Throne and City (II Sam. 2–8 & 21–24)* (Assen: Van Gorcum, 1990), 37.

19. Cf. David G. Firth, *1 & 2 Samuel*, AOTC 8 (Nottingham: Apollos, 2009), 332. See also William J. Buracker II, "Abner Son of Ner: Characterization and Contribution of Saul's Chief General" (PhD diss., The Catholic University of America, 2017), 80–1.

20. See Tushima, *The Fate of Saul's Progeny*, 127 n. 42.

21. Eugine Ulrich, *The Biblical Qumran Scrolls: Transcriptions and Textual Variants*, VTSup 134 (Leiden: Brill, 2010), 291.

Abner is accused of having sexual relations with Ritzpah. Abner responds angrily.[22] Note the word מדוע is not informative, but rather an indictment: "you have done so."[23] The reader does not know whether or not the accusation is justified.[24] This lack of information can be defined as a blank, not as a gap; a blank can be "disregarded without loss, indeed must be disregarded to keep the narrative in focus."[25]

However, we may mention in this regard that Iser's[26] use of "blank" is closer to what Sternberg characterizes as "gaps." It seems that the "boundary between gaps and blanks is admittedly hard to fix."[27]

Comparing this scene with other judicial scenes, the reader wonders whatever happened to the formal procedures of trial.[28] Given that this is not mere gossip,[29] but rather a king's accusation against his chief officer, the lack of formal trial is puzzling: no witnesses are summoned

---

22. Alice O. Bellis, *Helpmates, Harlots and Heroes: Women's Stories in the Hebrew Bible* (Louisville: Westminster John Knox, 1994), 144. Ken Stone, *Sex, Honor, and Power in the Deuteronomistic History*, JSOTSup 234 (Sheffield: Sheffield Academic, 1996), 85–93, reviews the opinion with regard to Ishboshet's argument. In his view, "The confrontation would instead be an entirely appropriate response from a man who, within a certain cluster of assumptions about gender, prestige, and sexual practice, wishes to assert that he can act appropriately with regard to the culturally defined protocols of gender performance" (91–2).

23. Pietro Bovati, *Re-Establishing Justice: Legal Terms, Concepts and Procedures in the Hebrew Bible*, JSOTSup 105 (Sheffield: JSOT Press, 1994), 76; George W. Ramsey, "Speech-Forms in Hebrew Law and Prophetic Oracles," *JBL* 96 (1977): 45–58.

24. See Soggin, "The Reign of Eshbaal," 45 n. 22; Craig E. Morrison, *2 Samuel*, Berit Olam (Collegeville: Liturgical Press, 2013), 48; April D. Westbrook, *"And He Will Take Your Daughters..." Woman Story and the Ethical Evaluation of Monarchy in the David Narrative* (London/New York: Bloomsbury, 2015), 91. LXX[L] adds "and Abner took her." It seems that the translator was trying to solve a gap in the text and it does not reflect an ancient reading/version. See Peter K. McCarter, *II Samuel*, AB 9 (New York: Doubleday, 1984), 105–6. Walter Brueggemann (*First and Second Samuel*, Interpretation (Louisville: Westminster John Knox, 1990]), 226, believes that Abner did have sex with Ritzpah.

25. Meir Sternberg, *The Poetics of Biblical Narrative* (Bloomington: Indiana University Press, 1985), 236.

26. Wolfgang Iser, *The Act of Reading: A Theory of Aesthetic Response* (Baltimore: Johns Hopkins University Press, 1978), 196.

27. C. Kavin Rowe, *Early Narrative Christology: The Lord in the Gospel of Luke* (Grand Rapids: Baker Academic, 2006), 38 n. 19.

28. See Bovati, *Re-Establishing Justice*, passim.

29. Buracker, "Abner," 155.

and no real process of investigation is initiated. Moreover, a comparison with Exod. 22:21-23 shows that such a crime is typically followed by anger and then punishment. In Samuel, however, the accused party is the one who becomes angry at the accuser: Abner becomes furious with Ishbosheth and reminds him of the political reality that Ishbosheth is a mere puppet in Abner's hands, and Abner could have easily handed him over to David. Abner becomes the accuser and even punishes Ishbosheth by swearing that he will transfer his support to David.

The king has no choice but to meekly accept Abner's version. What would have happened had the king in this scene been Saul rather than his weak son?[30]

The Non-speaking King

In her book "Characters Make Your Story,"[31] Maren Elwood writes that the four main purposes for dialogue are: (1) to reveal character; (2) to further the action of the plot; (3) to convey needed information; and (4) to show the emotional state of the speaker.

Kawashima notes that "dialogue functions as an important means of characterization in biblical narrative."[32] In the Ishbosheth narrative, the king barely speaks; his only words are a brief question: "Why have you gone in to my father's concubine?" (2 Sam. 3.7). This is unusual for any Israelite or Near Eastern king, for whom rhetorical skills were an important part of the royal position.[33] Kings ran their kingdoms with the power of words, so the silencing of Ishbosheth is a negative remark on his character.

---

30. This may remind us of the relationship between David and Joab, where David appears to be a weak character, next to Joab. See Michael A. Eschelbach, *Has Joab Foiled David? A Literary Study of the Importance of Joab's Character in Relation to David*, Studies in Biblical Literature 76 (New York: Lang, 2005).

31. Maren Elwood, *Characters Make Your Story* (Boston: The Writer, 1966).

32. Robert S. Kawashima, *Biblical Narrative and the Death of the Rhapsode* (Bloomington: Indiana University Press, 2004), 24; see also Robert Alter, *The Art of Biblical Narrative* (New York: Basic Books, 1981), 79–110; Sh. Bar-Efrat, *Narrative Art in the Bible*, JSOTSup 70 (Sheffield: Almond, 1989), 64–77, 88–9, 96–8, 147–9, 159–60, 242, 250–1; A. Berlin, *Poetics and Interpretation of Biblical Narrative* (Winona Lake: Eisenbrauns, 1994), 33–42.

33. Paul Y. Hoskisson and Grant M. Boswell, "Neo-Assyrian Rhetoric: The Example of the Third Campaign of Sennacherib (704–681 BC),'" *Rhetoric before and Beyond the Greeks*, ed. C. S. Lipson and R. A. Binkley (Albany: SUNY Press, 2004), 65–78.

Ishbosheth also remains silent when David demands Michal's return to him in 2 Sam. 3:14-15: "Then David sent messengers to Saul's son Ishbosheth saying, 'Give me my wife Michal, to whom I became engaged at the price of one hundred foreskins of the Philistines.' Ishbosheth sent and took her from her husband Paltiel the son of Laish." Once again, a more powerful character seizes a woman under Ishbosheth's dominion without any resistance on his part.

Michal's forced return to David also emphasizes Ishbosheth's passivity. Demands made from one king to another are typically characterized by negotiations, unless the inferior king is a vassal. However, even though Ishbosheth is not David's vassal, he immediately returns David's wife without demanding anything in exchange, or expressing any kind of resistance.

Alter[34] writes in this regard: "This silence with its explanation is politically portentous, for it demonstrates the unfitness of the pusillanimous Ish-Bosheth to reign."

The Non-warrior King

Another way of criticizing Ishbosheth is to leave the reader in the dark in regard to his participation in Saul's final battle against the Philistines.[35] The ancient king was also leader of his army.[36] Saul and three of his sons fell in battle, a death that some scholars view as heroic,[37] while Ishbosheth's absence from this scene is a foil to Saul and Jonathan's military valor. Whether Ishbosheth was entirely absent from the battle or whether he fled the scene, the reader will view his absence in a negative light.[38]

---

34. Alter, *Art of Biblical Narrative*, 106.

35. Exum, *Tragedy*, 97. The same question relates to Abner as well.

36. See Thorkild Jacobsen, *Toward the Image of Tammuz* (Cambridge, MA: Harvard University Press, 1970), 143–7; Roland de Vaux, *Ancient Israel: Its Life and Institutions*, trans. J. McHugh (London: Darton, Longman & Todd, 1961), 122; Alison K. Thomason, *Luxury and Legitimation: Royal Collecting in Ancient Mesopotamia* (Aldershot: Ashgate, 2005), 63.

37. See the discussion in Jacob L. Wright, "Making a Name for Oneself: Martial Valor, Heroic Death, and Procreation in the Hebrew Bible," *JSOT* 36 (2011): 131–62.

38. If it is true that Ishbosheth was not at the battle it offers another possible comparison with David. David also comes on the scene when his three older brothers are at war while he is at home. The difference is Ishbosheth is marked by timidity and inactivity, whereas David is, at least initially, marked by boldness and action (Benjamin Johnson, personal communication).

An intriguing hint in 2 Sam. 4:4 contributes to the impression that Ishbosheth did not participate in the battle: "Saul's son Jonathan had a son who was crippled in his feet. He was five years old when the news about Saul and Jonathan came from Jezreel." This verse could have been incorporated in 1 Samuel 31 and scholars view 2 Samuel 4 as a gloss. However, when this information is analyzed in its current position in the context of Ishbosheth's reign, it further implies that he was absent from the battle.

I do not accept Jeremy Hutton's[39] argument that "it would also be odd to conclude that Ishbosheth had not been at the battle, given that he is said to have been of sufficient age for battle." It is simply unclear whether or not Ishbosheth participated in the battle. This doubt itself casts a shadow of ineligibility and incompetence on Ishbosheth's character.

Buracker[40] adds another point: Abner leads Ishbosheth's subjects from Mahanaim across the Jordan to Gibeon, in Benjamin. It is worth noting that the text implies that this strategic decision was Abner's. In his words:

> The text never explicitly states that Ishbosheth gives any orders whatsoever here or elsewhere. In fact, Ishbosheth does not act in this section at all, and Abner, not Ishbosheth, is primary the subject [sic] of the masculine, singular verb יצא ("to go out") in v. 12.

Abner's character is utilized as a foil to Ishbosheth's character: Abner never takes orders from, advises, protects, or runs errands for Ishbosheth. This is extremely unusual for the army's chief commander.

In fact, besides the game between David's men and Ishbosheth's men, there is no depiction of any military involvement from the side of Ishbosheth. Ishbosheth stayed at Mahanayim. The fact that David fled to Mahanayim in the course of Absalom's rebellion (2 Sam. 17:24, 27) shows that it was a refuge in times of trouble. This can also show how irrelevant Ishbosheth was for his people.

The Murder of Ishbosheth

2 Samuel 4 narrates the murder of Ishbosheth. This scene raises many questions: How is it possible that two people could freely enter the king's house and murder him? Who are these "wheat buyers," and what is their connection with the killers? Was the king alone in the house—where

---

39. Hutton, *The Transjordanian Palimpsest*, 69 n. 74.
40. Buracker, "Abner," 89.

were the guards? The differences between the MT and the LXX further contribute to the mystery of this scene.

The story begins with the depiction of Ishbosheth's hands as feeble. Together with Mephibosheth's lameness, this conveys that none of Saul's heirs are capable of succeeding him.[41]

The Septuagint has another version of the murder scene: "the porter of the house was cleaning wheat, and he slumbered and slept."[42] This version is embraced by Josephus (*Ant.* 7.48), who describes how "She too had fallen asleep, due to fatigue and the labor she had performed as well as the noonday heat."[43]

Scholars are divided with regard to which version is preferable.

Segal[44] is skeptic of the authenticity of the LXX and suggests that it is a gloss, while many scholars such as Gordon,[45] McCarter,[46] and Fokkelman[47] prefer the LXX version. The fact that the MT's version is clearly corrupt is not sufficient proof that the LXX is correct—it too is somewhat problematic and seems secondary,[48] creating no fewer problems than the MT: is a doorkeeper supposed to be sufficient security for the life of a king?[49] Saul and David's bodyguards, mentioned in 1 Sam. 22:14 and in 2 Sam. 23:23, are a stark comparison. David himself is appointed as Achish's bodyguard in 1 Sam. 28:2. One may also recall the famous verse

---

41. Jeremy Schipper, *Disability Studies and the Hebrew Bible: Figuring Mephibosheth in the David Story*, LHBOTS 441 (New York: T&T Clark, 2006), 92.

42. See Bernard A. Taylor, "The Kaige Text of Reigns," in *New English Translation of the Septuagint*, ed. Albert Pietersma and Benjamin G. Wright (Oxford: Oxford University Press, 2007), 279. McCarter, *II Samuel*, 126, suggests that the retroverted Hebrew text was: והנה שוערת הבית לקטה חטים ותנום ותישן*.

43. A woman doorkeeper appears also in Jn 18:12-27. See Robert G. Maccini, *Her Testimony Is True: Women as Witnesses According to John*, JSNTSup 125 (Sheffield: Sheffield Academic, 1996), 237–8 n. 9.

44. M. Z. Segal, *The Books of Samuel* (Jerusalem: Qirayat Sepher, 1956), 256 (Hebrew).

45. R. P. Gordon, *1 & 2 Samuel: A Commentary* (Exeter: Paternoster, 1986), 222.

46. McCarter, *II Samuel*, 123, 126.

47. Fokkelman, *Throne and City*, 126. See also H. W. Hertzberg, *I and II Samuel: A Commentary*, trans. J. S. Bowden, OTL (Philadelphia: Westminster, 1964), 264; R. Alter, *The David Story* (New York: Norton & Co., 1999), 218.

48. M. Newkirk, *Just Deceivers: An Exploration of the Motif of Deception in the Books of Samuel* (Eugene: Pickwick, 2015).

49. Bodner, "Crime Scene Investigation." It is perhaps notable that Abner fails to protect Saul while he slept (1 Sam. 26), now with Abner's defection, Ishbosheth is not protected while he sleeps (Benjamin Johnson, personal communication).

from Song 3:7: "Look, it is the litter of Solomon! Around it are sixty mighty men of the mighty men of Israel."

From a literary point of view, this is another case of a Saulide king meeting his death in a brutal way, with his body dishonored. Like his father's, Ishbosheth's head is cut off. This shameful treatment of his body has a negative impact upon readers: "interment was accorded to all who served Yahweh; sinners were cursed with denial of burial or exhumation (Deut. 28:25-26; 1 Kgs 13:22; 14:10-11; Jer. 16:4)."[50] Nonetheless, there is a significant difference between father and son: Saul died for his own sins, while there is no clear evaluation of Ishbosheth's character. Rather, his death is necessary in order to clear the way for David's ascent to the throne as the successor of the Saulide dynasty.[51]

As for his burial, Gunn, Fokkelman, and Exum[52] have justly pointed out that it is ironic that Ishbosheth is buried "in the tomb of the very man who betrayed him." It is worth noting that the text does not relate what happened to the rest of Ishbosheth's body, in contrast with the bones of Saul and his sons, which are rescued by the people of Jabesh-Gilead.

Exum thinks that the character of Ishbosheth is "bound up" with that of Abner's: they both belong to the royal house of Saul; both are ruthlessly murdered; and both are buried in the same tomb.[53] Though there are clear similarities between Abner and Ishbosheth, their differences cannot be overlooked. The narrator employs Abner to highlight Ishbosheth's weakness. The text does not show any positive aspects of Ishbosheth's character at all, while the attitude toward Abner is more complex: both positive and negative aspects of his character emerge in different scenes. He is loyal and obedient to Saul, and he ultimately seeks peace. On the other hand, he is lustful[54] and manipulative.

---

50. Elizabeth Bloch-Smith, *Judahite Burial Practices and Beliefs about the Dead*, JSOTSup 123 (Sheffield: JSOT Press, 1992), 112.

51. Saul M. Olyan ("Some Neglected Aspects of Israelite Interment Ideology," *JBL* 124 [2005]: 603 n. 8) points out that even though Eshbaal's body was not reclaimed, burial in Saul's tomb was not possible: Eshbaal's head is buried in the Saulide branch tomb in Hebron.

52. David M. Gunn, *The Story of King David: Genre and Interpretation*, JSOTSup 6 (Sheffield: Sheffield University, 1978), 79; J. Cheryl Exum, *Tragedy and Biblical Narrative: Arrows of the Almighty* (Cambridge: Cambridge University Press, 1992), 96; Fokkelman, *Throne and City*, 136.

53. Exum, *Tragedy*, 95–7.

54. Buracker, "Abner," 73.

David's Reaction

After Ishbosheth's head is brought to David, the king is angry and he reproaches the killers for killing *ish zaddik*. Translating this phrase as "righteous" is not quite accurate; 'innocent" seems a more precise translation, due to the parallelism with אנשים רשעים. This is a trial scene, and one side will be convicted.

There is great irony in v. 8. We have no way of confirming Rechab and Ba'ana's claim that Ishbosheth hunted David, but it is unlikely that such a weak king would indeed pose a real threat to David.

David's description of Ishbosheth as *ish zaddik* may initially seem like a positive characterization and evidence that Ishbosheth was innocent. A more careful reading, however, reveals that this phrase, too, is somewhat derogatory—David himself calls Ishbosheth an איש, a mere "man," not a king!

Charles Mabee[55] learns from here that Ishbosheth was not actually anointed as king:

> The criminality of the defendants is clearly shown in their designation as רשעים, while the deceased is termed צדיק. Therefore, the crime is not regicide. It is Ishbosheth as "righteous man" that is the victim, rather than Ishbosheth as king. In other words, Ishbosheth's kingship is irrelevant insofar as the trial is concerned. Therefore the crime is not regicide—even though it is a king who is murdered.

McCarter[56] comments on David's referring to the murdered Ishbosheth as "an innocent man" (איש־צדיק, 2 Sam. 4:11): "In contrast to Saul, Ishbaal is not described as Yahweh's anointed or even as a king. His kingship is not recognized by David... Our narrator presents David as Saul's successor in Israel, not Ishbaal's." In my opinion, one cannot infer that David did not consider Ishbosheth a king. However, we may assign this evaluation to the author, not to David.[57]

Conclusion

The Saul-David narratives in Samuel contain both pro-Saulide and pro-Davidic ideologies.[58] In 2 Samuel 2–4, the author of Samuel continued

---

55. Charles Mabee, "David's Judicial Exoneration," *ZAW* 92 (1980): 104.
56. *II Samuel*, 128.
57. Arnold A. Anderson, *2 Samuel*, WBC 11 (Dallas: Word, 1989), 71.
58. See Marc Zvi Brettler, *The Creation of History in Ancient Israel* (London/New York: Routledge, 1995), 109.

to denigrate Saul through his unsuccessful heir—Ishbosheth. By changing his original name from Eshbaal into Ishbosheth, he ridiculed him. Saul gives his son a name that recalls the worship of Baal. This son is not portrayed as having achieved anything significant during his brief reign over Israel. His non-mention in the scene of the battle against the Philistines remains a mystery; he is virtually silenced (with the exception of one textually corrupt, unsubstantiated accusation against a stronger character); and his death is violent, just like his father's death. His death does not even occur during a battle; rather, it is the result of negligent security while he lies passive, fast asleep. This non-king is portrayed as the ridiculous opposite of David.

This portrayal is consistent with the motif of fathers and sons in Samuel: all the fathers in Samuel have unsuccessful sons, with ill-fated Jonathan the only exception. These fathers are Eli, Samuel, Saul, and David.[59]

The comparisons between Ishbosheth and his father, Ishbosheth and Abner, and Ishbosheth and David all lead to the conclusion that he is portrayed as a non-king or as a worthless, ridiculed king.

---

59. Lowell K. Handy, "The Characters of Heirs Apparent in the Book of Samuel," *BR* 38 (1993): 5–22.

Chapter 15

FOREIGNERS IN DAVID'S COURT

David G. Firth

Although David is clearly the central human character in the books of Samuel, he is surrounded by a host of others who interact with him in various ways. These characters are themselves developed to varying degrees, and they each contribute to the book's plot in different ways. More particularly, they also provide a mechanism for readers to evaluate David as the central human figure, though they can also be used to evaluate others. However, although some characters within the book have received considerable attention,[1] a feature of the book that has not received significant attention to this point is the large number of foreigners who are present in David's court as it is presented in 2 Samuel 5–24.[2] In this, David is contrasted with Saul for whom Doeg the Edomite is the only significant foreigner mentioned (1 Sam. 21:8, 22:6-23). In part, this is because Saul is not said to have developed his court to the same

---

1. E.g. Michal has been examined from a range of perspectives—see David J. A. Clines and Tamara C. Eskenazi, eds, *Telling Queen Michal's Story: An Experiment in Comparative Interpretation* (Sheffield: Sheffield Academic, 1991).

2. David, of course, becomes king of Judah from 2 Sam. 2:1-11, but there is little to indicate a well-established court while he was at Hebron, with the focus instead on the conflict between the house of Saul and the house of David, something which most likely prevented his court developing to any great extent. It is the "rest" from his enemies recorded in 2 Sam. 7:1 which enables David to develop a court. It is, however, notable that Ish-bosheth is reported as having foreigners working for him (2 Sam. 4:2-3), but they were also his murderers.

extent as David, though given the focus on David within the book it is not unexpected that aspects of Saul's court would remain underdeveloped in comparison. Nevertheless, there is an important function fulfilled by Doeg and the foreigners in David's court as they become figures through whom readers can evaluate the primary characters. That is, the presentation of these foreigners, especially in terms of their faithfulness to Yahweh (or not in Doeg's case relative to Saul) becomes a mechanism by which readers are enabled to evaluate the primary characters.

Each of these figures can justifiably be referred to as a minor character in that none of them are a protagonist whose decisions and actions drives the plot of the book. In this, they stand in clear contrast to Samuel, Saul, and David, each of whom is a protagonist, or even Yahweh who might also be thought of in literary terms as a protagonist within the book. But as Simon has helpfully argued, in a narrative world which values understatement, minor characters are a helpful means of pointing to the major theological themes which are developed, though often enough it is the ability of the narrator to say comparatively little about them which makes them so effective for this.[3] Simon highlights several ways in which minor characters can function within the Old Testament[4] which are helpful for our analysis:

- They can further the plot or provide greater depth to it.
- Expressively, they may:
  - Highlight the central focus through their presence, their subsequent absence showing their role is complete (e.g. Peninah, 1 Sam. 1).
  - By opposition to the protagonist they may highlight a dilemma they face (e.g. the confusion of David's servants following the death of Bathsheba's child, 2 Sam. 12:15b-23).
  - Through their ironic statements they can show the folly of other characters (e.g. Saul's servant better understands the man of God than Saul, 1 Sam. 9:1-14, or Jonadab can interpret events that David is unable to understand following Absalom's murder of Amnon, 2 Sam. 13:30-36).
- They can show the moral value of the protagonist (e.g. David's men were unwilling to rescue Keilah, unlike David, 1 Sam. 23:3-5).

---

3. Uriel Simon, "Minor Characters in Biblical Narrative," *JSOT* 46 (1990): 18.
4. Ibid., 14–18. Simon provides more than is covered here, but these are the elements which are deployed through the presentation of the foreigners.

Simon's elements are helpful, but his presentation of these elements is largely impressionistic. To take these observations further, we need to consider the process of characterization. As Walsh has noted, this involves attending to more than just the concept of "character," since characterization is concerned with the process by which a narrator endows a character with defining features.[5] That is, we can speak of characters in the classic sense defined by E. M. Forster as "flat" or "round," while acknowledging that most characters sit somewhere on a continuum between these points. This is because narrators tend to develop characters to the extent that is necessary for the plot, and as such their complexity is limited by this factor. Within Samuel, both Michal and David could reasonably be called "round" characters in that they demonstrate a degree of complexity. Consideration of their characterization involves more than noting this simple fact—it is a matter of attending to the mechanisms deployed by the narrator to provide this perspective on the characters.

Given that the common pattern across the Old Testament is that characterization is demonstrated through action rather than through direct comment, we obviously need to consider the particular element of what these foreigners do (including what they say).[6] However, a number of other techniques were deployed in antiquity to develop characterization and these can be drawn on to illuminate the elements of characterization in Samuel. Particularly helpful here is de Temmerman's analysis of characterization techniques discussed in Greek and Latin sources, notably the *progymnasmata*.[7] Since these works differ in significant respects to the material found in the Old Testament it is obvious that care must be used in drawing from them. Nevertheless, his careful treatment of the ways in which characterization is discussed in these contexts shows considerable overlap with the Old Testament's narrative traditions. Although the form by which characterization takes place in Samuel can differ from the Greek and Latin traditions, nevertheless the modes for expressing characterization discussed in these texts will be seen to be heuristically beneficial.

---

5. Jerome T. Walsh, *Old Testament Narrative: A Guide to Interpretation* (Louisville: Westminster John Knox, 2009), 33.

6. On the interface between presentation and action, see especially Meir Sternberg, *The Poetics of Biblical Narrative: Ideological Literature and the Drama of Reading* (Bloomington: Indiana University Press, 1985), 321–64.

7. Koen de Temmerman, "Ancient Rhetoric as a Hermeneutical Tool for the Analysis of Characterization in Narrative Literature," *Rhetorica* 28 (2010): 23–51.

De Temmeran notes that elements of characterization are discussed in several *loci* in these texts, and helpfully distinguishes between explicit and implicit characterization.[8] This is consistent with Sternberg's observations on the distinction between the description of the character and their presentation through their actions. Where de Temmeran's work is particularly helpful is in drawing together the options available for the description of a character and how this contributes to characterization. He notes the following as key points of discussion in the rhetorical texts, all of which have some relevance for the process of characterization in Samuel:[9]

- *Identification*—name giving was regarded as an important element in characterization. Some of the foreigners do not receive much more than a name, though in some instances the anonymity of a foreigner is itself an important element.
- *Direct Attribution of Characteristics*—a narrator may comment directly on an aspect of a character. For example, Mephibosheth is introduced as lame, although a brief explanation of this is also provided (2 Sam. 4:4).
- *Indirect Attribution of Characteristics* covers a range of techniques:
  - Comparison—a narrator can use a figure as a paradigm for others (as in the use of David as the paradigm king in Kings), or assess them relative to others (e.g. Absalom's beauty, 2 Sam. 14:25).
  - Metonymical techniques where one element stands for others, or perhaps better sheds light on them:
    - Emotions—for example, David's anger in response to Nathan's parable (2 Sam. 12:5).
    - Membership of a group—in particular, explicit identification with a people other than Israel is important here, but there is also a standard mode of identification in the Old Testament where characters are often introduced using the formula *X ben/bat Y*.
    - Action—this is an element that does not receive significant discussion in these texts, but (in light of Sternberg's observations) can be seen as significant for the Old Testament.
    - Speech—this covers a range of elements, including the extent to which someone speaks "in character." This element has been recognized in, for example, the speech of

8. Ibid., 28.
9. Ibid., 30–42.

the messenger to Eli (1 Sam. 4:16-17).[10] Speech can also be used by others to characterize someone, as for example when David is first mentioned to Saul (1 Sam. 16:18).
- ○ Appearance—comments on appearance are widely deployed in Samuel, mostly in explicit comments by the narrator (e.g. about David in 1 Sam. 16:12, or Goliath in 1 Sam. 17:4-7).
- ○ Setting—although only occasionally addressed in the rhetorical sources, this is arguably an important element in Samuel (e.g. the danger posed by the forest, 2 Sam. 18:8).[11]

As noted, care must be taken in transferring rhetorical discussions from another culture and applying them to the Old Testament. Nevertheless, the fact that so many of these can easily be mapped across to the books of Samuel indicates that they are useful markers of characterization which can be used in assessing the presentation of the foreigners in David's court.

Uriah the Hittite and David's Mighty Men

Although Obed-Edom the Gittite has been mentioned as the one with whom the ark was left after the disastrous first attempt to bring it to the City of David (2 Sam. 6:10-12), his exact relationship to David is unclear. As such, the first foreigner within the court to be noted is Uriah the Hittite (2 Sam. 11; 23:39). The story of his encounter with David is vitally important within the plot of 2 Samuel 11–20, and arguably for the subsequent story of Judah's monarchs since, for the writer of Kings, David's actions with regard to Uriah constitute his only obvious failure (1 Kgs 15:4-5).[12] The placement of references to Uriah are an important part of his contribution to the plot of Samuel since his introduction in 2 Samuel 11 obviously prepares for the events that follow, though arguably his mention at the end of the list of David's mighty men, where

---

10. David G. Firth, *1, 2 Samuel* (Nottingham: Apollos, 2009), 87.
11. De Temmerman, "Ancient Rhetoric," 40–1, also considers *ecphrasis*. Although important for the rhetorical texts, it is a more abstract element and more difficult to identify in Samuel.
12. This text might be unaware of the events of 2 Sam. 24, though since the observation is that David did not turn aside from all that Yahweh had commanded, and in Samuel at least the census goes back to Yahweh's command (2 Sam. 24:1), it could suggest that David had still been obedient in some way even there.

he is one of several foreigners, is also intended to encourage readers to re-evaluate their earlier interpretation of the events in 2 Samuel 11. That is, the process of characterization may well extend beyond the narrative section in which Uriah is active.[13]

Uriah is first introduced indirectly in a report about the identity of his wife (2 Sam. 11:3). Although brief, this statement immediately raises key issues about him that will be significant for interpretation and which can be related to many of the elements of characterization de Temmeran has noted. Although there are no direct attributions of characterization, or comments on his appearance or emotions, all of the other elements are utilized, and each contributes to Uriah's presentation.

From the outset, even before we meet him as a character within the narrative, we know Uriah's name, his ethnicity, and some details of his family, though the significance of his family only gradually comes to light. The combination of his name and ethnicity, however, raises an issue about how readers are to interpret him. As a Hittite he is immediately identified as belonging to a group outside Israel, though the name "Uriah" means either "Flame of Yah" or "Yah is my light" depending on which one of two possible roots we use to derive the first part of his name. There is no need here to resolve this issue, because the more important point to note is that his name is clearly Yahwistic. So, he is a Hittite, but he also clearly belongs to Israel in some sense. The exact sense of "Hittite" is also uncertain in that it could suggest he belonged to the people known by this name from Anatolia, though it is more probable that it means he is regarded as a descendant of Heth, who is listed as Canaan's second son in Gen. 10:15. If so, then he is reckoned as one of the Canaanites who had (according to Joshua) survived and integrated themselves in Israel. But whatever his precise ethnic background, his level of integration would be demonstrated by his name, which indicates that he was a Yahwist, though at the same time his ancestry continued to be noted. He is known as a foreigner.

As well as his ethnicity, which perhaps explains why his father remains unnamed since this rather than a patronym is decisive for his characterization, he is also immediately associated with a group. In this case, he is linked by marriage to Bathsheba, and through Bathsheba to her father Eliam. Since Eliam has not previously been mentioned readers may well conclude that mention of Bathsheba's patronym is more important for her characterization than for Uriah. Nevertheless, that Bathsheba can be

---

13. See David G. Firth, "David and Uriah with an Occasional Appearance by Uriah's Wife: Reading and Re-Reading 2 Samuel 11," *OTE* 21, no. 2 (2008): 210–28.

introduced by a standard Israelite technique has already made clear that Uriah has married into an Israelite family.[14] His introduction therefore has already characterized Uriah as a foreigner, a Yahwist, and someone who has married into an Israelite family. More troubling for him, his wife has attracted David's attention.

Uriah's next mention is in 2 Sam. 11:6, when David asks Joab to send him back to the palace. This continues to characterize him through his membership of a group, since v. 1 has already noted that David had sent Joab to lay siege to Rabbah. Without making the point explicit, readers discover that Uriah is a member of Israel's military. However, this mode of introducing the point means that readers do not know what Uriah's status might be. But they do know from v. 1 that David had sent "Joab, and his servants with him, and all Israel" to lay siege to the city. Joab's "servants" here would be his more immediate military associates, whereas "all Israel" would refer to the civil militia. That Uriah seemingly owns a house near the palace, or at least has access to one, might indicate that he is someone of some standing in the military, but the process of placing him in the army through metonymical techniques means the narrator can hold back from making this explicit.

This process also allows the narrator to characterize Uriah by means of his actions, setting, and speech. As these elements are closely integrated they can be treated together. The command to Joab to send him back to David has already used setting indirectly to characterize Uriah, but this method becomes more important once he returns to Jerusalem and then later goes back to Rabbah. On his return, Uriah came to David, but although speech is noted as happening, we do not actually hear anything from him. This element is held back as location is used at first. Having been encouraged by Uriah to go to his home and "wash his feet" (perhaps a euphemism),[15] Uriah left the palace with a gift from the king following him. But instead of going home to his wife, Uriah slept in the entrance to the palace along with various palace officials. This action is initially

---

14. It is surely significant that apart from her introduction in 2 Sam. 11:3, Bathsheba is "the wife of Uriah" until 2 Sam. 12:24. In Jesus' genealogy in Mt. 1:6, Bathsheba is again "the wife of Uriah."

15. Gale A. Yee, "'Fraught with Background': Literary Ambiguity in II Samuel 11," *Int* 42 (1988): 248, believes this phrase could be intentionally ambiguous since washing the feet of guests was a standard part of hospitality. This is plausible from David's perspective (in which case he speaks in character), but Uriah's response in v. 11 indicates that he understood it sexually. The chapter as a whole is certainly full of ambiguities, starting from the first verse—see Keith Bodner, *David Observed: A King in the Eyes of his Court* (Sheffield: Sheffield Phoenix, 2005), 77–88.

unexplained, continuing a pattern that is used throughout this chapter of characterizing Uriah in ways that leaves issues unresolved for readers. After all, why might he not have gone home? Both setting and action characterize Uriah, but in ways that need explanation, placing readers in the same position as David who also needs to know what these actions mean.

When David heard that Uriah had not gone home, he summoned him once again to see him, asking directly why he had not gone home. Uriah's response in v. 11 is the only time he speaks, but it is a vital element in his characterization. By holding back speech to this point, the narrator is able to focus the characterization of Uriah, whilst contrasting him with David. David speaks frequently in this chapter, with his every speech further convicting him of his wrongdoing. Uriah's speech is a masterpiece of condensed characterization and theology so that his claims as a Yahwist are made explicit. That is, he remains a Hittite, but his Yahwistic name is not the only evidence of his commitment. Rather, his speech shows a deep awareness of Israelite theology even as it challenges David. The opening of the speech is built around two participles (ישבים and חנים), both of which refer to the army's current place at Rabbah. This is a temporary condition, a life in booths while the soldiers camp, something happening even as Uriah speaks. But it is not just Joab and the army who are there— even before mentioning them, Uriah introduces the ark to the discussion. Readers have not previously been told of its relocation, so this introduces new information which characterizes the army camp as a holy place. Deuteronomy 23:10 [ET 23:11] would require soldiers to abstain from sex during warfare.[16] By noting that the army is still encamped as he speaks, and the particular holiness that would be expected because of the presence of the ark, Uriah presents himself as someone who is loyal to the king. But more than that, he is someone loyal to the rest of the army with whom he identifies and also someone committed to holiness as understood within Israel. David, of course, had not properly understood this in relation to the ark in his attempt to bring it to the city of David (2 Sam. 6:5-11). Uriah's commitment to holiness means he will not sleep with his wife.

David's response to this is to get Uriah drunk, but even so he would not return to his house and sleep with his wife.[17] Again, Uriah is characterized

---

16. This also seems to be the implication of David's response to Ahimelech in 1 Sam. 21:6 [ET 21:5].

17. Peter R. Ackroyd, *The Second Book of Samuel* (Cambridge: Cambridge University Press, 1977), 102, in a turn of phrase every Samuel commentator wishes they had come up with first, neatly observes that "Uriah drunk is more pious than David sober."

by his actions, all of which point to a loyalty which transcends even his marriage, and in so doing contrasts notably with David for whom sexual continence is not a notable characteristic. The final note of characterization for Uriah in 2 Samuel 11 occurs as he is sent back to the siege carrying the letter which contained David's order for Joab to arrange his death. That Uriah remained loyal to David is again demonstrated by what he does not do—the letter clearly remained unopened until received by Joab, even if the narrative restraint means we do not know how much Uriah had already pieced together. The narrator does not state this directly, but readers are left to infer it on the basis of the fact that Joab did indeed arrange his death (albeit not exactly as David ordered—Joab is far too canny to do that). Uriah is thus shown to be loyal—to his wife, his fellow soldiers, his commander, his king, and also to Yahweh. He is a foreigner who is treated as a dupe by his commander and his king as they conspire to arrange his murder, but the final note of 2 Samuel 11 indicates that Yahweh, at least, recognizes the wrong that has been done.

Uriah, however, shares an important characteristic with the prophet Samuel in that they are the two characters in the book who contribute to the narrative after their death.[18] Uriah's note in 2 Sam. 23:39 is not as noteworthy as Samuel's appearance at Endor, but it nevertheless plays an important role in his characterization while providing readers with a further mechanism for assessing David through him. Here, he is introduced as a member of the "Thirty." Questions about the nature of the "Three" and "Thirty" abound, but for our purposes it is sufficient to note that these most likely represent some form of military rank, and that all those listed in this section (2 Sam. 23:8-39) are elite soldiers who had a close relationship to David. Although likely quite ancient, the list shows signs of developing over time since the various soldiers are not listed by a standard pattern. However, Uriah's placement at the end of the list gives him a degree of prominence, whilst highlighting something important about him not made clear in 2 Samuel 11. Membership of this group shows not only that he was a soldier, but that he was a member of David's elite forces. Readers discovering this fact now may well be interested in returning to the previous narrative to see how this might change their view of events there. Moreover, in v. 34 we are told that another member of the

---

18. Samuel's death is reported in 1 Sam. 25:1, but he has an important narrative function in 1 Sam. 28:3-25. One could argue that they share this with Saul and Jonathan, but narratively (if not chronologically) David's lament over their death (2 Sam. 1:17-27) and commendation of the men of Jabesh-Gilead for the recovery of their bones (2 Sam. 2:4b-7) follow immediately on their death. By contrast, both Samuel and Uriah are introduced into key points of the narrative after their death.

Thirty was "Eliam ben Ahithophel the Gilonite." Only one other Eliam has been mentioned in Samuel—Bathsheba's father (2 Sam. 11:3). Likewise, the only Ahithophel previously mentioned was David's counsellor who had joined Absalom (2 Sam. 15:12), and he too is the called "the Gilonite" (since his home town was Giloh), making it likely that the one Ahithophel is meant both times. The ambiguity which was so evident in 2 Samuel 11 thus remains here in that it is possible to connect Uriah with Eliam, and hence reach conclusions about why Ahithophel joined Absalom, though without absolute certainty. Nevertheless, Uriah is here characterized by group membership as someone of particular importance to David. This group also contains foreigners—Eliphelet (v. 34) might be a non-Israelite depending on whether Maacah here is the Aramean state or the clan from southern Judah. Igal (v. 36) is from Zobah, a kingdom David had earlier defeated (2 Sam. 8:3-12), while Zelek (v. 37) is an Ammonite, the people who had triggered the war in which Uriah was killed (1 Sam. 10:1-14). The two Ithrites, Ira and Gareb (v. 38), might be descendants of the Canaanites left in the land, but this is not certain. Nevertheless, it is clear that Uriah is not the only foreigner among the Thirty, though he is the only one with a Yahwistic name. Even as he is placed in this group, he is distinguished from them.

This final element of Uriah's characterization functions to raise more questions about David's earlier actions, while remaining consistent with the pattern of the Samuel Conclusion (2 Sam. 21–24) of stressing the achievements of David's men more than David himself. A member of David's elite, he could reasonably have expected some access to the king, so his appearance before David earlier is now more explicable. But this merely shows even more the evil of David's actions there as readers now know that he knowingly entered into a sexual relationship with the wife of a close supporter. Each detail of Uriah's character is carefully drawn. Through him readers gain a greater understanding of David as he becomes the lens through which to evaluate David's actions and at least begin the process of working through the ambiguity in 2 Samuel 11.

Ittai the Gittite

Uriah was not the only foreign soldier working for David, because in his flight from Absalom we are also introduced to Ittai the Gittite (2 Sam. 15:18-23; 18:1-5).[19] Although not as important as Uriah, he too was a

---

19. An unnamed Cushite was also a member of David's army (2 Sam. 18:19-32), though since Joab apparently regarded him as disposable he was not of a significant rank. Unfortunately, space prohibits a treatment of him here.

significant figure within David's army. Because he receives less narrative space, less attention is given to his characterization. However, like Uriah he becomes a figure through whom readers are able to assess David, though in his case he functions to provide a positive paradigm of what was possible for David even as he fled from Absalom. We can observe similar patterns to Uriah in his characterization.

Ittai's introduction immediately marks him out as a foreign soldier. In this case, he is first characterized through identification and group membership—David's servants, the Cherethites, Pelethites, and six hundred Gittites have passed before him before Ittai is introduced in the first of a series of five encounters David has through to 2 Sam. 16:14. The Cherethites and Pelethites (first mentioned in 2 Sam. 8:18) are probably foreign mercenaries loyal to David,[20] as are the six hundred Gittites who would more specifically have come from Gath. Although Ittai's[21] name could be Semitic, that he is called a "Gittite" indicates that he too comes from Gath. However, within the structure of Samuel the status of these Gittites is less clear than that of the Cherethites and Pelethites since we know that they serve within David's household in some way, whereas these Gittites have not previously been mentioned, creating a degree of ambiguity about them that can be explored in the subsequent narration.

His status as a foreigner is then made explicit by David's speech in vv. 19-20 where David encourages him to return to the king since he is a foreigner (נכרי) and an exile (גלה). The speech not only provides explicit characterization of Ittai as someone who does not receive the formal protection given to the resident foreigner (the גר) under Israel's law, it also shows David at his lowest point since he effectively indicates that Absalom is now king. As an exile from Gath, Ittai's best option would thus be to align himself with Absalom. David's speech, however, reintroduces Yahweh into the narrative as he expresses the wish that Yahweh show חסד ואמת to Ittai.[22] Apart from the rather staged references to God by the wise woman from Tekoa (2 Sam. 14:11-20), God has been notably

---

20. Their names would suggest that they were respectively from Crete and Philistia, but are never explained.

21. Francis Landy, "David and Ittai," in *The Fate of King David: The Past and Present of a Biblical Icon*, ed. Tod Linafelt, Timothy Beal, and Claudia V. Camp, LHBOTS 500 (London: T&T Clark, 2010), 21, notes that his name could be a pun on "with us" and "you," both of which are significant for the narrative. See also Jacob Wright, *David, King of Israel, and Caleb in Biblical Memory* (Cambridge: Cambridge University Press, 2014), 102.

22. Admittedly, reference to Yahweh is missing from the MT, but can reasonably be restored on the basis of the LXX.

absent from the narrative since Solomon's renaming (2 Sam. 12:24). David's speech, however, mentions Yahweh in a more or less conventional sense. But this is turned around by Ittai as his speech in v. 21 also characterizes him further as he swears an oath in Yahweh's name. His speech is important because it is the first point at which anything other than victory by Absalom is suggested. Ittai indeed joins both Yahweh and David in the oath, committing himself to serve David whom he explicitly identifies as king. David, not Absalom is king in spite of the fact that Absalom holds Jerusalem, and this is tied to an expression of faith in Yahweh. Ittai's speech thus characterizes him as someone who sees what Yahweh is doing through David at a point where David does not. His speech is also an action since it commits him to going with David, showing that he too is a loyal soldier.

Ittai's characterization is thus important because we see him through identification and group membership as a foreign soldier, and specifically a foreigner who has no direct claim on many features of Israel's laws. However, through him the narrative also introduces a key upturn in David's fortunes. Yahweh continues to be active, and it is Ittai who effectively reminds him of that through his words and actions. Ittai functions here as a contrast to David, the one through whom a different interpretation of events becomes possible.

Ittai appears again in the preparation for the battle in which Absalom is killed (1 Sam. 18:1-12), though he is not mentioned after this, suggesting his contribution to the plot is complete.[23] His characterization here is rather limited in comparison to his initial appearance. However, there are developments which are indicated through group membership and actions—though in the latter case it is what he is *not* reported as doing.

In preparation for the battle, David had divided his forces into three main groups, with one third under Ittai's command. His foreign status is also emphasized in the initial statement about this (2 Sam. 18:2) in that he is again called "the Gittite," though this term is dropped in the other two references to him (2 Sam. 18:5, 12). He is thus not only someone loyal to David, but also a significant military commander who could be expected to lead a significant portion of David's forces. Beyond this, in both vv. 5 and 12 it is noted that he was one of those who was given the command to deal gently with Absalom for David's sake. In v. 5 this is narrated directly so there can be no doubt that he heard it, while in v. 12 it is mentioned by the soldier Joab believed should have killed Absalom when he found

---

23. Another Ittai is mentioned in 2 Sam. 23:29, but his patronym and indication of his home town and tribe make clear that this is a different person.

him in the forest when explaining why he would not do this. Ittai is not mentioned again, but can at least be included in the summary statement of v. 7 which includes him among "David's servants" in contrast to "the men of Israel," terminology which perhaps implicitly notes that David's forces were not all Israelite. In light of his earlier characterization there is at least the suggestion that he would not have acted as Joab did with Absalom. That is, he did not disobey David even if his initial response to David in 2 Sam. 15:21 is a form of disobedience in order to reframe David's perspective. Although muted, there is thus a hint here that Ittai functions as a contrast to Joab in that his disobedience helps David to see what Yahweh is doing whereas Joab's is purely political. Even if this suggestion is not accepted, Ittai, like Uriah, is a foreign figure who provides a contrast to the Israelites and is faithful to Yahweh in ways Israel's own leaders are not.

Hushai the Archite

A final foreigner to note within David's court is Hushai the Archite.[24] Like Ittai the Gittite he is introduced as one of David's encounters in his flight up the Mount of Olives, in this case just below the summit (2 Sam. 15:32-37). As the third encounter he also represents the mid-point in this sequence, with the final two (Ziba, 2 Sam. 16:1-4, and Shimei, 2 Sam. 16:5-14) both presented more ambiguously since after the encounter with Hushai David begins to demonstrate more confidence in Yahweh.

As with the other foreigners, Hushai is immediately characterized through identification, though in his case his appearance is also shown before any speech. By naming him as an "Archite" he is connected with a Canaanite group mentioned in Josh. 16:2. Their mention there immediately marks them out as distinctive from other groups in that the boundary lines in Joshua run from town to town except for this one point, where the boundary for Joseph runs to the territory of the Archites, implying that this group would continue to exist within Israel, and that they are perhaps not included within the other continuing Canaanites listed for Ephraim (Josh. 16:10). Even if this interpretation is not accepted, the label clearly marks him out as someone of Canaanite descent. That he meets David at the summit of the mountain, a place noted as a shrine,

---

24. One could also mention Araunah the Jebusite (2 Sam. 24:18-25), but although he was resident in Jerusalem after David had captured the city, it is not clear that he had a formal relationship to the court. His characterization, however, is broadly similar to those noted in this essay.

is potentially significant. David had prayed in the preceding verse that Yahweh would thwart Ahithophel's counsel, and at a shrine he then encounters Hushai. Hushai's commitment to David is also characterized through his appearance, and in a contrast to members of David's family who are routinely noted for their beauty, Hushai is instead presented as someone in mourning, something marked by his torn coat and the dirt on his head. Hushai's introduction is, however, highly ambiguous in that readers are not told why he is mourning, and as a Canaanite he might be considered suspect.

In this instance, Hushai is further characterized through David's speech in vv. 33-37. It is clear that as he fled, David needed to travel fast, and by coming Hushai would be a burden (משׂא). How he would be a burden is never made clear, and at this point it is not clear if this is because, as a foreigner, he may in some way be suspect or if he simply could not travel quickly. The rest of David's speech at least partly resolves this because David expresses trust in Hushai, asking him to act as his agent in Absalom's court along with Zadok and Abiathar and their sons. This is a dangerous mission, and that David asks him to undertake it along with the others shows great trust in him, something consistent with the renewal in David's faith that began in his encounter with Ittai. Only at the end of this, as Hushai returns to Jerusalem just as Absalom arrives (and is thus characterized by action which will become a dominant feature) are we informed that he is "David's friend." Exactly what this means is uncertain, though there may be a parallel in the case of Jonadab who was Amnon's friend (2 Sam. 13:3) and acted as a counsellor to him, though perhaps as a private confidant as opposed to the more public role that Ahithophel played.

Within the narrative structure of David's flight, Absalom's entry nto Jerusalem is left aside until 2 Sam. 16:15 in order to recount David's final encounters. At this point, the narrative returns to Absalom, preparing for an encounter between Hushai and Ahithophel through whom the conflict between David and Absalom is initially played out (2 Sam. 16:15–2 Sam. 17:16). The relationship between the counsellors is highlighted from this point as Hushai had to integrate himself into Absalom's court. However, even as he is reintroduced to the narrative there is no doubt where his loyalties lie as he is once again called "David's friend." This means that even as he speaks to Absalom and says "Long live the king" readers know that his speech is double-voiced. Absalom is intended to hear it as a reference to himself, whilst Hushai can actually refer to David. Indeed, a striking feature of his dialogue with Absalom in vv. 15-19 is that he never lies directly, portraying himself to Absalom as someone loyal to the throne itself rather than any one person who held it even as his statements can only mean that he is actually loyal to David. Thus, he finally offers only to serve before (לפני) Absalom, even though Absalom is able to hear it as a pledge of loyalty to him. Hushai's speech, which is also marked by a degree of prolixity that will develop further in his next speech so that he is also characterized through this,[25] shows that he is both shrewd and loyal to David, thus preparing for his conflict with Ahithophel.

The various elements of Hushai's characterization developed to this point then come together in his conflict with Ahithophel (2 Sam. 17:1-14) and his subsequent advice to David. As David's friend, he is a counsellor of some sort, but so too is Ahithophel, and readers have been told that his advice was "as if one consulted the word of God" (2 Sam. 16:23).[26] Hushai's counsel is thus set in contrast to that of Ahithophel, because although readers know him to be a counsellor (something Absalom explicitly recognizes as he asks him to comment on Ahithophel's proposed strike against David [2 Sam. 17:1-6]), no guidance has been given on what this means. As someone not present for the initial discussion, Hushai has to think on his feet, demonstrating a quick-witted ability to respond without preparation. The loquaciousness that was hinted at in his initial encounter with Absalom along with his ability speak in a double-voiced manner comes to full flower here, though in part it also further characterizes him through speech as he uses his speech to play for time. The speech itself breaks into two main sections—in vv. 7-10, Hushai simply proposes that Ahithophel's advice is not good, though without any real proof and in spite of the fact that everyone else had thought it was right (ישר). In the second section (vv. 11-13), he proposes an extensive military campaign which is long on bombast and short on military detail. Indeed, while claiming to have offered Absalom good advice, what he has really done is delay any activity long enough for him to send word to David to encourage him to flee across the Jordan (2 Sam. 17:15-16). But in characterizing Hushai, the narrator is clear that Ahithophel was the one who gave the good advice, and this was defeated only by the command of Yahweh, answering David's earlier prayer. Still, it was a foreigner, not an Israelite, through whom Yahweh achieved his purpose. In doing this, Hushai serves as a figure through whom readers are to assess David, Absalom, and Ahithophel, demonstrating that Yahweh's purposes are not only achieved through Israelites, but also through faithful foreigners.

---

25. For which reason, the longer reading where he says "Long live the king" twice should be retained precisely because it is an essential element of his characterization. Cf. Firth, *1, 2 Samuel*, 463.

26. Here following *Qere* and many mss.

Conclusion

The model of characterization suggested by de Temmeran from classical sources is also useful for understanding characters in Samuel. Although each of the foreigners examined here can rightly be called a minor character, it is through them that readers are given a means of assessing the major characters, something that is largely distinctive to Samuel within the Former Prophets. Both Uriah the Hittite and Ittai the Gittite enable readers to evaluate David, whilst Ittai and Hushai the Archite provide guidance on what Yahweh is doing in ways that Israelites do not see. This enables us to go beyond the more impressionistic model of Simon, and indeed to critique him at one key point. Commenting on Doeg the Edomite killing the priests at Nob (1 Sam. 22:16-19), he claims that Samuel's readers shared the belief that "foreigners have no fear of God and hence no hesitation in committing sins."[27] If that was a shared belief, then a key goal of Samuel's characterization of foreigners in David's court is to undermine it. Rather, Yahweh works through all people since even the greatest of Israelites can do evil. But in David's case, even as he is punished for his sin in 2 Samuel 11, it is through foreigners that readers see both the grievousness of his actions and the processes by which he can be restored. A reader who might have started with the belief that foreigners have no hesitation in committing sin must now view them and Israelites differently. Rather, we are to judge characters in part through the company that they keep. Saul's failures are seen emblematically through Doeg, but while David's worst is seen through Uriah the possibilities for his future are made clear through Ittai and Hushai. Canaanites and a Philistine, not Israelites, point the way forward in David's court.

---

27. Simon, "Minor Characters," 17.

Chapter 16

ABSALOM: A WARRIOR FOR JUSTICE—A LIFE STORY IN SEVEN STAGES

Yairah Amit

Introduction and Background

In Jewish and Christian tradition, David, the father of future Messiah, was considered the almost perfect king;[1] and in the Jewish tradition the borders of his kingdom are both a divine promise and an achievable ideal.[2] Usually the important source for information about David's life and his kingdom and the basis for admiring him is not the book of

---

1. The word "almost" shows that readers usually accept the poetics of biblical narrative, according to which no human being is perfect. The exceptional case of Job is exaggerated for the needs of the story. No wonder the Sages had said: "Job never existed, but was a parable" (*b. Bab. Bat.* 15a). Moreover, even God may be presented as imperfect, which is again prominent in the case of Job; see Yairah Amit, "The Protest in the Story of Job—Form and Content," in *Theodicy and Protest: Jewish and Christian Perspectives*, ed. B. Ego et al. (Leipzig: Evangelische Verlagsanstalt, 2018), 17–27.

2. The archeological-historical possibility that David's kingdom was not an empire is an issue a scholarly issue debated to this very day, e.g., Israel Finkelstein and N. A. Silberman: *David and Solomon: In Search of the Bible's Sacred Kings and the Roots of the Western Tradition* (New York: Free Press, 2006); Israel Finkelstein, "A Great United Monarchy? Archaeological and Historical Perspectives," in *One God—One Cult—One Nation*, ed. R. G. Kratz and H. Spieckermann, BZAW 405 (Berlin: de Gruyter, 2010), 3–28. See lately Nadav Na'aman, "Game of Thrones: Solomon's 'Succession Narrative' and Esarhaddon's Accession to the Throne," *Tel Aviv* 45 (2018): 89–94.

Chronicles,[3] but the stories in the books of Samuel in particular and the Deuteronomistic History in general, which also influenced the editing of the book of Psalms.[4] Thus, even the story about Bathsheba and the murder of Uriah, not even mentioned in Chronicles, is considered a weakness of a great king who was no more than human, and was punished for his misdeeds.[5] With that, including the story about Bathsheba and Uriah is an opportunity to praise biblical authors and editors for not censoring this event and its results as they did in Chronicles. No wonder that in this ambivalent atmosphere of admiration and measured criticism, most readers considered Absalom negatively and perceived him as the bad son, with an endless lust to rule. However, when acquainted with biblical research, one understands that precisely the differences between Chronicles and the Deuteronomistic History provide and enrich the reader with more sophisticated tools to criticize what is told about David's time and to look differently on the characters that surrounded him. In other words, one learns that the books of Samuel contain a quantity of anti-Davidic materials, and therefore did not satisfy the later generations, who needed to reshape David's image as the almost perfect king we find in Chronicles.[6] A quick synchronic reckoning shows that the description of David's empire gets only five chapters in Samuel's detailed description (2 Sam. 5–8; 10), and by contrast fifteen chapters are witness to a different David with his weaknesses exposed, that is, negative criticism. These texts include the civil strife in his time, whether the struggle for kingship

---

3. Unexpectedly the book of Chronicles, a paean of praise to David, founder of the kingdom and planner of the Temple, was a secondary player in the admiration for David. On the one hand, the interpretative tradition was not interested in this book with its many discrepancies and contradictions. It is accepted that even Rashi's commentary to Chronicles is only attributed to Rashi. On the other hand, until the second half of the twentieth-century scholars were not really interested in this book, because they assumed that compared to the Deuteronomistic History, Chronicles was not of reliable historical value. See Sara Japhet, "The Historical Reliability of Chronicles—The History of the Problem and Its Place in Biblical Research," *JSOT* 33 (1985): 83–107; reprinted in *The Historical Books*, ed. J. C. Exum, Sheffield Reader Series (Sheffield: Sheffield Academic, 1997), 258–81.

4. See the progressive intention to attribute the psalms to David: from 73 Psalms in the Masoretic text to 3,600 psalms and 450 songs in Qumran (11QPSa 27:5-6, 9-10).

5. According to Steven McKenzie (*King David: A Biography* [New York: Oxford University Press, 2000], 189): "Apology Worked. It altered David's historical image by legitimating his deeds."

6. Even in Chronicles, the "almost" is valid; see e.g. 1 Chron. 21:1-17.

after Saul's death (chs. 1–4) or Absalom's rebellion (11–19) including the reasons behind it. Absalom's rebellion begins with the Bathsheba–Uriah episode and its outcome, ends with the rebellion of Sheba son of Bichri (ch. 20), and includes the way David treated the descendants of the house of Saul (ch. 9; 19:25-31; 21:1-14). All this material shows why most of Israel was willing to depose David and crown Absalom as their ruler. In contrast to the books of Samuel, the whole first part of Chronicles, eighteen chapters (chs. 12–29), are dedicated to David's empire and the way he organized it in his time and for the future. Absalom is not mentioned there even once.[7]

All this leads to the questions: Who was Absalom according to biblical narrative?[8] Was he a rebel interested only in kingship, a negative personality ready to do everything to achieve his ambitions, or was he a warrior for justice? In this essay, I will continue my efforts to soften the negative criticism against Absalom and to clarify that Absalom was first and foremost motivated by the feeling that justice has to be done and seen.[9]

Stage One—Absalom's Birth

Our first meeting with Absalom is in the report about the sons born to David while he ruled the house of Judah in Hebron (2 Sam. 3:1-5 // 1 Chron. 3:1-4). It was during a long war between the house of Saul and the house of David, and before David was crowned king of all Israel (2 Sam. 5:1-6 // 1 Chron. 11:1-3). When David came to Hebron he already

---

7. Absalom is mentioned in 1 Chron. 3:2 among the other sons of David. He appears again in Chronicles as the father of Maacah in the description of Rehoboam's family (2 Chron. 11:20-21); see Stage Seven below.

8. I leave questions of historical reliability to historians and archeologists and focus on the way later Judahite historians (authors and editors) preferred to depict their past. In my view those historians who are responsible for the base of the books of Judges and Samuel were pre-Deuteronomistic, meaning from the end of the eighth to the end of the seventh centuries BCE. See Yairah Amit, *History and Ideology: An Introduction to Historiography in the Hebrew Bible* (Sheffield: Sheffield Academic, 1999), 31–3 (briefly), 20–81 (at length). Nevertheless I adopt McKenzie's conclusion that the "overall portrait of David, when read critically in the light of ancient Middle Eastern culture, is not unreasonable" (*King David*, 151).

9. My efforts began in 1983 when my essay "The Story of Amnon and Tamar: A Reservoir of Sympathy for Absalom" was published in Hebrew. After 25 years it was translated into English with a retrospective; see Amit, "The Story of Amnon and Tamar: Reservoir of Sympathy for Absalom," in *In Praise of Editing in the Hebrew Bible: Collected Essays in Retrospect* (Sheffield: Sheffield Phoenix, 2012), 203–19.

had two wives: Ahinoam of Jezreel and Abigail of Carmel (2 Sam. 2:2).[10] It seems that while David was in Hebron, after being appointed the king of Judah he was interested in strengthening his political status and power, and he did so not only by marrying four more wives, but by choosing to marry a foreign woman, Maacah, described as a princess, the daughter of King Talmai of Geshur.[11] The fruit of this marriage was Absalom, David's third son.

Stage Two—The Rape of Tamar

Our second meeting with Absalom is in the story of Tamar's rape, when he was an adult prince. It seems that the special connection between Absalom and Tamar is based on blood ties, as they have the same mother and so are full brother and sister, and perhaps had a common childhood.[12] Absalom saw Tamar just after she was raped by their half-brother Amnon.

---

10. See 1 Sam. 25:42-43. The two wives belong to the region of Hebron; see 1 Sam. 25:2-3; Josh. 15:55-56 and Shimon Bar-Efrat, "First and Second Samuel: Introduction and Annotations," in *The Jewish Study Bible*, ed. A. Berlin and M. Z. Brettler (New York: Oxford University Press, 2004), 621.

11. On Geshur and Maacah as different geographical entities, see Na'aman who concludes (p. 97): "What was unclear to the Jerusalemite scribes is the geographical reality in the far north. Hence, they integrated Geshur (and Maacah) in an inaccurate geographical manner" (Nadav Na'aman, "The Kingdom of Geshur in History and Memory," *SJOT* 26 [2012]: 97). See also recently O. Sergi, "The United Monarchy and the Kingdom of Jeroboam II in the Story of Absalom and Sheba's Revolts (2 Samuel 15–20)," in *Hebrew Bible and Ancient Israel*. Vol. 6, *Jeroboam* (Mohr Siebeck: Tübingen, 2017), 337–9; and on the identification of the kingdom of Geshur see O. Sergi and A. Kleiman, "The Kingdom of Geshur and the Expansion of Aram-Damascus into the Northern Jordan Valley: Archaeological and Historical Perspectives," *BASOR* 379 (2018): 1–18.

12. Tamar, who probably was also Maacah's daughter, is not mentioned because this list ignores daughters, but see 2 Chron. 3:9. According to the Chronicler, she was born later in Jerusalem. In 2 Sam. 13:1 Tamar is presented as Absalom's sister and not as Amnon's sister or as David's daughter, while Absalom and Amnon are mentioned as David's sons. Also, Amnon calls Tamar "the sister of my brother Absalom" (v. 4) and not: my sister. Therefore Josephus (*Ant*. 7.162) and most scholars are convinced that she was Absalom's full sister and their common mother was Maacah. See, for example, Charles Conroy, *1–2 Samuel, 1–2 Kings: With an Excursus on Davidic Dynasty and Holy City Zion* (Wilmington: Michael Glazier, 1983), 118; P. Kyle McCarter, Jr., *2 Samuel*, AB 9 (Garden City: Doubleday, 1984), 320; Shimon Bar-Efrat, *Narrative Art in the Bible* (New York: T&T Clark, 2008), 241; idem, "First and Second Samuel," 640: "Tamar was Absalom's full sister and Amnon's half-sister."

When Absalom encountered Tamar after the rape, probably near Amnon's house, he immediately knew what had happened, because Tamar had torn the royal virgin's robe she was wearing, had put ashes on her head, and was crying loudly, mourning as she went. Absalom's first reaction was the question he phrased most gently: "Has Amnon your brother been [not: lain] with you?" (v. 20).[13] His second immediate reaction is strange because it was hardly consoling: "For the present, sister, keep quiet about it; he is your brother. Don't brood over the matter" (v. 20). But how could she keep quiet and not "brood over the matter" that determined her fate? To me this reaction seems to reflect his wrath, his inability to find words of comfort, and also his confusion, because his thoughts were engaged at that very moment in seeking a way to avenge her violated honor too, and his silence may have covered up his plans of revenge.[14] Sensitive Absalom, who understood her new situation, immediately granted her his protection and took her into his house.

More than 2,500 years have passed since the story of the rape of Tamar was written, and only in recent years has Western society begun to understand what was so clear to Absalom: that rapists should not go unpunished, and that in the woman raped, something has been killed, and hence women like Tamar remain desolate and need a big enveloping hug and protection. Hence the idea that Amnon must be punished was clear and justified to Absalom. He expected his father to do justice and to avenge the desecrated honor of Tamar. From now on, Absalom and the reader are waiting to see David's reaction and decision, and the question is how long this expectation will last.

Tamar's story could have ended differently, if, for instance, Amnon had married her, in the spirit of the law in Deut. 22:28-29, instead of sending her away.[15] The text indicates that Tamar would have accepted such a

---

13. In this essay and elsewhere I usually use the JPS translation, but in this case I prefer the refined NRSV translation, not the JPS: "Was it your brother Amnon who did this to you." In the MT his name appears here as Aminon, and see McCarter, *2 Samuel*, 319.

14. For a different interpretation that connects Absalom's reaction with political ambitions, see e.g. A. A. Anderson, *2 Samuel*, WBC 11 (Waco: Word, 1989), 172–3, 177; T. Frymer-Kensky, *Reading the Women of the Bible* (New York: Schocken, 2002), 168, 190; E. A. Davies, *The Dissenting Reader: Feminist Approaches to the Hebrew Bible* (Burlington: Ashgate, 2003), 60; A. Ashman, *The Story of Eve: Daughters, Mothers and Strange Women in the Bible* (Tel Aviv: Miskal/Yedioth Ahronoth Books and Chemed Books, 2008), 167–84 (Hebrew) and more bibliography there.

15. The law in Deuteronomy does not reflect a late reality; as Bernard Levinson writes: "The seizure and rape of a virgin who is not engaged, the enforced marriage,

solution, as she said before the rape: "[...]Please, speak to the king; he will not refuse me to you" (vv. 12-13).[16] Moreover, even after the rape she was ready to accept the solution of marriage, as she pleaded with Amnon: "Please don't commit this wrong; to send me away would be even worse than the first wrong you committed against me" (v. 16).[17] In other words, Tamar saw Amnon's refusal to marry her, expressed by her expulsion, as an even greater evil than the rape itself.

By sharp contrast to Absalom's behavior, David's indifference over the rape is shocking, a situation of absent law and absent judge. It was David who was responsible for sending Tamar to Amnon (v. 7), and he was also the highest judge in the kingdom, responsible for the execution of "true justice among all his people" (8:15). When David "heard about all this, he was greatly upset" (v. 21), yet he did not say or do a thing, and did not even order Amnon to marry Tamar and so rescue her. Thus, Amnon could continue to live his usual life as the potential heir and be very close to his father. Indeed, in some versions we find a completion that explains the reason for David's behavior: "But he did not rebuke his son Amnon, for he favored him, since he was his first-born."[18] The result was that only

---

and the prohibition of divorce correspond to Middle Assyrian Laws §A 55" ("Deuteronomy: Introduction and Annotations," in Berlin and Brettler, eds, *The Jewish Study Bible*, 397). He argues that the use in Deuteronomy of the Hebrew verb תפש and not חזק may show that "the degree of physical force is more ambiguous." However, in our story there is no ambiguity—the narrator twice uses the verb ח.ז.ק in Hiphil: "he caught hold of her...he overpowered her and lay with her by force" (vv. 11, 14).

16. For the de-legitimization of brother and sister marriage, see Lev. 18:9, 11; 20:17 and Deut. 27:22; but see Gen. 20:12. Therefore modern commentators think that Tamar's solution reflects an early social convention. See for example Bar-Efrat, *Narrative Art*, 239–40; Anderson, *2 Samuel*, 172. McCarter (*2 Samuel*, 323–4) brings three more options confirming that David could have been willing to permit the marriage.

17. Although the MT version of this verse is faulty, the interpreters accept the meaning of the ancient versions like the LXX and *Targum Jonathan* on a par with the English translation quoted here.

18. This completion is a homoioteleuton in the transition from v. 21 to v. 22 based on the LXX version and accepted by Josephus (*Ant.* 7.173) and by critical commentators, for example S. R. Driver, who, following others, accepts it "as part of the original text" (*Notes on the Hebrew Text and the Topography of the Books of Samuel*, 2nd ed. [Oxford: Clarendon, 1913], 301). See also 4QSam[a] and what is said about the relations of David and his son Adonijah in 1 Kgs 1:5-6. The translation of the Greek is taken from the Jewish Study Bible of the 2004 JPS translation.

Absalom protected Tamar. David the king and the highest judge did not act according to the principle of justice. This violation of basic justice explains the subsequent behavior of Absalom, namely his anger towards and criticism of his father, who acted neither as a father nor an honest and righteous judge should.

The story of the rape is also the most extreme indictment against Amnon. Immediately after v. 1, which opens the story's exposition[19] and depicts Amnon as a brother who loves his beautiful sister, comes v. 2, the second part of the exposition, which destroys that vision with its unexpected phrasing. Suddenly we learn that Tamar was a virgin and Amnon was engaged with the impossibility "to do anything to her."[20] Thus the exposition takes the reader from Amnon's love (v. 1) to an affair of lust (v. 2).[21] Most of the story's continuation is dedicated to the detailed description of how Amnon fulfilled his lust. In the first scene (vv. 3-5) Amnon meets wise Jonadab who gives him advice about how to meet Tamar.[22] In the second (vv. 6-7) he follows Jonadab's advice and gets his father's agreement to Tamar's visit. In these two scenes, Amnon appears as a liar and a deceiver. He deceives Jonadab about his feelings for Tamar in order to get his wise advice, and pretends to be sick to get his father's agreement to Tamar's visit. In the third long and detailed scene (vv. 8-18), we meet Amnon as a manipulative and cruel personality who is controlled by his sex drive. A most outrageous passage in the story is the description of Amnon ordering his servant to drive Tamar out of his house: "get that woman out of my presence, and bar the door behind her" (2 Sam. 13:17).[23] Again, note the phrasing. In the MT Amnon uses a courteous form to address the servant (שלחו-נא), but calls Tamar "that woman,"

---

19. My approach to the story structure from the exposition, through its scenes, to its closure is described in Amit, "The Story of Amnon and Tamar," 208–10, and more bibliography there.

20. For more hints based on the choice of words, grammar, and syntax of v. 2, see Bar-Efrat, *Narrative Art*, 240–5; Amit, "The Story of Amnon and Tamar," 210–11 and the bibliography there.

21. For a different interpretation that connects Amnon's behavior with the political purpose of preventing Absalom from being a candidate for kingship, see n. 14 above.

22. The Sages (*b. Sanh.* 21a) and many traditional commentators raise the possibility that Jonadab was cunning and capable of evil-doing. See Jer. 4:22; Isa. 31:2 and see also McCarter, *2 Samuel*, 321. But according to 2 Sam. 13:32-33 he is intelligent and wise of mind.

23. See G. Ridout, "The Rape of Tamar: A Rhetorical Analysis of 2 Sm 13:1-22," in *Rhetorical Criticism: Essays in Honor of James Muilenburg*, ed. J. J Jackson and M. Kessler (Pittsburgh: Pickwick, 1974), 75–84 (77).

not even mentioning her name as he orders the door barred behind her. Amnon's extreme callousness appears here as the antithesis of Absalom's sensitivity.

If one asks the following questions—Why did the narrator dedicate half of this story (11 verses in a story of 22 verses), meaning half of its time of narration,[24] to the rape, and five more verses (two scenes vv. 3-7) to its planning? Why was he interested in describing the victim's hopeless and desperate attempts to prevent the rape? Why did he decide to describe Tamar's expulsion in detail?—the answer is unequivocal: The narrator is interested in the negative characterization of Prince Amnon.[25] The result is that the more Amnon is negative, the more Absalom is positive, and the story becomes a reservoir of sympathy for Absalom who does not accept the injustice that the accused will not be punished.

This second stage in our drama ends with the words: "Absalom didn't utter a word to Amnon, good or bad; but Absalom hated Amnon because he had violated his sister Tamar" (13:22). The narrator, who reflects the truth of the story,[26] does not permit us to think that Absalom hated Amnon because he was the heir to the throne. These are the thoughts of those who wish to blame Absalom. According to the narrator, the only reason for Absalom's hatred is the rape of his sister Tamar.[27] But the narrator wants us to understand that the silence of Absalom is only temporary, therefore he adds this information about Absalom's feelings, and we the readers are left with the question of how long this silence will last.

---

24. On the use of time in biblical narrative and its two aspects—time of narration and narrated time—see Yairah Amit, *Reading Biblical Narratives: Literary Criticism and the Hebrew Bible* (Minneapolis: Fortress, 2001), and additional bibliography there.

25. See ibid., 88–91. See also Amit, "The Story of Amnon and Tamar," 218–19, who aimed to show that the story's components lead to this conclusion, against, e.g., Bar-Efrat, *Narrative Art*, 282; idem, "First and Second Samuel," 640; A. Deem, "'Cupboard Love': The Story of Amnon and Tamar," *Hasifrut/Literature* 28 (1979): 100–107 (Hebrew); Anderson, *2 Samuel*, 172–3, 177.

26. See the chapter: "Whom to Believe?" in Amit, *Reading Biblical Narratives*, 93–102.

27. Conroy states that "there is no indication that Absalom hated Amnon as a rival for the throne; his hatred and the subsequent fratricide were clearly motivated by a desire to avenge the wrong done to Tamar (13:22, 32)" (*1–2 Samuel*, 121). In his view: "Political consequences should not be confused with political motivation." He therefore concludes that this case is a "personal, non-political matter" (*Absalom, Absalom! Narrative and Language in 2 Sam 13–20* [Rome: Biblical Institute, 1978], 102–3).

Stage Three—The Murder of Amnon

Absalom's decision to take the law into his own hands and avenge Tamar's rape was not hasty. Our next meeting with Absalom is two years later (v. 23). He waited this long to see how his father would act and if Amnon would be punished. At the same time, every day of these two years he saw his desolate, depressed, and lost sister. But life continued for Amnon and David as if nothing had happened. Therefore Absalom decided to take justice into his own hands and to be both judge and executioner. The claim of some scholars that Absalom murdered Amnon to dispose of an heir to the throne never convinced this writer, for Amnon too knew that a murder on his CV would distance him from the crown. I understood Absalom as someone whose disapproval and anger towards his father only increased during the two years preceding the murder. Jonadab, that very wise and clever man, also understood that Absalom killed Amnon because of the rape and not because of political machinations, and he confirmed it by saying: "Only Amnon is dead; for this has been 'decided by' Absalom ever since his sister Tamar was violated" (v. 32). From Absalom's point of view, the murder of Amnon was fighting for and doing justice, even if he had to leave his country and distance himself from the Jerusalem court.

Stage Four—A Time of Disregard

Our fourth meeting with Absalom is three years later. Again, the narrator wants his readers to be familiar with the timescale. After the murder, Absalom fled to his maternal grandfather, Talmai king of Geshur, and there he stayed three whole years. But after three years Joab saw that David was consoled over the death of Amnon and missed Absalom, hence he convinced David to bring Absalom back. After three years, then, Absalom left his place of exile and returned to Jerusalem. But did he meet or see his father? The answer is NO! David ordered Joab: "Let him go directly to his house and not present himself to me" (14:24). This situation of disregard lasted two more years and ended only by force. Absalom met Joab and demanded that he arrange a meeting with his father, but it happened only after three attempts, which ended with setting fire to Joab's field. Only then did Joab raise the case of Absalom before the king, and David agreed to meet Absalom.

In the context of these two years of Absalom's disappointment, the editor combines two interesting remarks. The first is connected to Absalom's appearance: "No one in all Israel was so admired for his beauty as Absalom…" (14:25-26). References to the handsome looks of leaders are found as well in the cases of Saul (1 Sam. 9:2) and David (1 Sam. 16:12, 18). In other words, this information about Absalom may allude to his suitability for leadership.[28] The second remark tells us that Absalom's daughter's name was Tamar and she too, like Absalom's sister, was a beautiful woman (14:27).[29] By including this remark the writer informs his readers of the strong ties between Absalom and his sister Tamar, his deep sensitivity to her bitter fate, and his pain undiminished by the passing years. Thus the narrator wants us to understand that Absalom's life was interwoven with the pain of Tamar and the injustice of their father: injustice that began with the rape and continued with David's relation to Absalom.

The issue of the narrated time is interesting and unique to the life story of Absalom. The narrator wants his readers to know that the total number of years that passed from the rape to Absalom's decision to rebel against his father was seven years, and that of the five years following the murder, three of them were spent in exile and for two of them being he was being ignored by his father after coming back to Jerusalem. Throughout those years, when Tamar stayed in his house as one dead, reminding him of Amnon's guilt, Absalom felt that he had been right in the case of Amnon who had brought this on his sister, and he developed severe criticism of his father both as father and as a judge, because he did not protect Tamar when obliged to do so, and ignored him, Absalom, for so many years. I emphasize the issue of time because the writer did so by repeating the exact number of years over and over, and if such emphases are found, it demands that we pay attention and ask why. In this way the narrator wanted us, the readers, to understand that the dimension of time is meaningful and has an accumulated psychological influence.

---

28. See Conroy (*1–2 Samuel*, 120) who states: "At this point the narrative is interrupted by a very positive description of Absalom (vv. 25-27), which emphasizes his handsome appearance and lack of physical blemish—qualities that are most appropriate for a king." See also Michael Avioz, "We find, in several places, that one of the traits attributed to the king is his beauty (Ps. 45:3-4)" ("The Motif of Beauty in the Books of Samuel and Kings," *VT* 59 [2009]: 346, and n. 27 there). M. Eilat, *Samuel and the Foundation of Kingship in Ancient Israel* (Jerusalem: Magnes, 1997 [Hebrew]), 104–5, emphasizes that good looks are not a condition of being a king, though it was considered a positive attribute. However, according to Keith Bodner this description of Absalom's appearance is "a physical description fit for a king" (*The Rebellion of Absalom* [New York: Routledge, 2014], 102).

29. Avioz ("Motif of Beauty," 351) notes that "by calling his daughter 'Tamar,' Absalom creates a memorial for his sister."

Absalom's sense that he has done justice and he is not afraid of a trial is shown when he tells Joab: "Now let me appear before the king, and if I am guilty of anything, let him put me to death" (14:32). Absalom is convinced that killing Amnon was the right thing to do, a just punishment. Thus, by an act of violence and a call for justice, Absalom succeeded in meeting his father and in breaking the terrible long silence of the last two years in Jerusalem, when they were physically so close to each other but at the same time so far apart, with a mediator between them and no direct connection. So, did they speak to each other at this meeting? We do not know because we are not told. We only know that Absalom "came to the king and flung himself face down to the ground before the king. And the king kissed Absalom" (v. 33). But does this kiss symbolize a new beginning in their relationship? Bar-Efrat thinks that "Though the kiss signifies forgiveness, it should be noted that the verse repeatedly uses the designation *the king* instead of 'David' or 'his father.' In addition, there is no mention of any verbal exchange between father and son—after five years of separation! This suggests that the enforced reconciliation is purely formal."[30]

Now, is the king's kiss a sufficient reason to forget the past? Or maybe the last seven years are sufficient reason to despair of his father and to think about a different kind of rule, a rule in which justice is its visible guiding principle.

Stage Five—The Rebellion

The kiss confirmed for Absalom that from now on he was formally an integral part of the royal court, and he began to behave appropriately. Not only did he "provide himself with a chariot, horses, and fifty out-runners" (15:1), he also began to promote himself by criticizing his father as judge and presenting himself as the one who would uphold the people's rights. But the main question is, what is the reason for this behavior? Was it only because he wanted to be the ruler, or was it because he deeply and truly believed that he could be a better king and a better judge, and to achieve the aim of replacing his father he had to adopt the look and the rhetoric that influences most people? The writer tells us that "Absalom won away

---

30. Bar-Efrat, "First and Second Samuel," 644. Conroy adds: "It is strange that after the reconciliation scene of 14:33 is presented without any dialogue (though the narrator is clearly a master of dialogue!)…; the reader is left with a certain feeling of unease that the reconciliation is not a whole-hearted one on Absalom's side or at least leaves something to be desired. What follows will make that suspicion a solid certainty" (*1–2 Samuel*, 121).

the hearts of the men of Israel" (v. 6).³¹ According to my interpretation Absalom did not lie, he expressed his truth, his personal experience and mounting protest, but to gather supporters he used demagogic means and generalizations, techniques that work on crowds. Using these techniques caused the narrator to use the verb ג.נ.ב, but one knows that to create a change Absalom had to adopt those means, that serve every candidate in the race to rule, as the French slogan says "À la guerre comme à la guerre."

After four years of preparations³² Absalom appointed himself king: "The conspiracy gained strength, and the people supported Absalom in increasing numbers" (v. 12). The messenger who came to inform David told him: "The loyalty of the men of Israel has veered toward Absalom" (v. 13),³³ meaning that the army of the tribes of Israel had shifted their allegiance to Absalom. This may teach us about the disappointment in David, about his status as a king among most of his people, and about the people's wish to change their king.³⁴

As to the rebellion itself, as long as Absalom followed Ahithophel's advice he had the upper hand, but when Hushai the Archite with his psychological ploys convinced Absalom to adopt his counsel, Absalom joined what could be likened to Barbara Tuchman's *The March of Folly from Troy to Vietnam*. Absalom's human fault fits the world of biblical thought, where the possibility of dual causality exists.³⁵ Absalom's failure

31. The MT uses the verb ג.נ.ב ("to steal"), which may be interpreted very negatively as, for instance, in Exod. 20:15; 21:16; and less negatively as in Jer. 23:30; Job 4:12. The NRSV translation prefers "to steal."

32. According to the MT, these preparations took 40 years, which is unreasonable, even impossible. We should prefer the LXX^L, the Pesh. Vulg. versions, and Josephus, *Ant.* 7.196, which mention only four years; see also Driver, *Samuel*, 311; McCarter, *2 Samuel*, 355, and many others.

33. The combination "The men of Israel" (in Hebrew the word "men" is singular: איש) relates to the army combined of different tribes (*terminus technicus*). If the text relates to the army of a specific tribe, then the name of this tribe appears; e.g. "The men of Judah" (2 Sam. 19:15, 17) is the army of the tribe of Judah. For more examples see Amit, *In Praise of Editing*, 122–30.

34. Although Conroy (*1–2 Samuel*, 121–2) notes that "The anti-Absalom slant of the text here makes it questionable whether vv. 3-6 can be used to show that there actually were serious shortcomings in the administration of justice at Jerusalem," he emphasizes that "the fact that Absalom gained widespread support from both Israelites and Judaeans (cf. 19:9-15) shows that there was much popular discontent with David's reign, probably for a whole variety of reasons."

35. See Amit, *In Praise of Editing*, 105–21 and the bibliography there. See also Jonathan Grossman, "The Design of the 'Dual Causality' Principle in the Narrative of

is a typical case of dual causality. At first it seems that a chain of plausible circumstances caused the rebellion and its results, but the reader who takes into account 2 Samuel 12, knows that what happened to Absalom was part of God's plan to punish David for his crimes of adultery with Bathsheba and Uriah's murder: "Therefore the sword shall never depart from your House…; I will make a calamity rise against you from within your own house…" (vv. 10-11). Absalom chose the advice which he saw as convincing and realistic, and it caused him to fail. He did not know that the reason for this preference was God's will: "The Lord had decreed that Ahithophel's sound advice be nullified, in order that the Lord might bring ruin upon Absalom" (17:14). Many readers accept the rabbinic approach (*b. Sotah* 9b) and connect Absalom's death with the description of his hair (14:45-26), which got caught in the terebinth (18:9). However, the Hebrew version mentions head, not hair.[36] God's ruin even reached as far as Absalom's burial. Instead of being buried under the monument he had prepared for himself, he had a humiliating burial—Absalom was thrown into a great pit in the forest and a great heap of stones was raised over it (18:17-18).[37] The narrator does not want the reader to think that the building of this monument hints at hubris, and he therefore explains that it was because Absalom had no son to keep his name (18:18). Indeed, Absalom was not conscious that he was simply a victim of God's plan, but we the readers have to remember it.[38]

Stage Six—Mourning and Apathy

The civil war and David's deep mourning following the death of Absalom made him apathetic and he lost his desire to rule. However, the call of Sheba son of Bichri the Benjaminite—"We have no portion in David, No share in Jesse's son! Every man to his tent, O Israel" (20:1)—caused "all the men of Israel," meaning the troops of the northern tribes, to leave David and to follow the new rebel.[39] Dissatisfaction with David as

---

Absalom's Rebellion," *Bib* 88 (2007): 558–66, esp. 558 and nn. 1-3 there.

36. See Bodner (*Rebellion of Absalom*, 94–5) who prefers the hair factor and finds irony in the moment of Absalom's hanging.

37. According to 2 Sam. 14:27 Absalom had three sons. Radak assumes that they had died earlier.

38. Conroy (*1–2 Samuel*, 122; and *Absalom, Absalom! Narrative and Language in 2 Sam 13–20* [Rome: Biblical Institute, 1978], 98), like many others, does not ignore God's plan, but ignores its meaning and the conclusion that Absalom is a victim.

39. According to Sergi, "United Monarchy," 352: "The literary shape of the story of Absalom and Sheba's revolts presupposes the power, extent and geo-political

king was common to most Israelites, so they had joined Absalom who had represented social justice. Thanks to Joab, the kingship of David continued, but after Absalom death, David, tired and depressed, lost his desire to rule along with his royal aura. But is that the end of Absalom, the warrior for justice in his family and in his society?

Stage Seven—A Descendant of Absalom on David's Throne

Absalom died in his youth, but according to Chronicles a certain justice was done to him, and his grandson Abijah, son of Maacah, Absalom's daughter (named after Absalom's mother Maacah) was designated "as chief and leader among his brothers, for he intended him to be his successor" (2 Chron. 11:18-23).[40] It is interesting that according to the Chronicler too, Absalom does not forget those who were close to him, in this case his mother Maacah. He names his daughter after her, similar to the case of Tamar in the book of Samuel.[41] Moreover, Abijah was appointed by his father to reign over Judah, even though Abijah was

---

settings of the kingdom of Israel under the reign of Jeroboam II in the first half of the 8th century b.c.e., but ascribes it to David's rule."

40. In 1 Kgs 14:31; 15:1-9 Rehoboam's son is called Abijam, and his mother, Maacah daughter of Abishalom (1 Kgs 15:2), was also the mother of Asa (vv. 10, 13; see also 2 Chron. 15:16). Moreover, in 2 Chron. 13:2 the name of Abijah's mother is: Micaiah daughter of Uriel of Gibeah. According to Japhet, "This creates a famous crux, for which several solutions have been suggested… no one solution can encompass all the evidence" (*1 and 2 Chronicles: A Commentary*, OTL [Louisville: Westminster John Knox, 1993], 670–1). However, she emphasizes that "It is quite probable (although impossible to prove) that 'Absalom', Maacah's father, is the famous son of David." For E. L. Curtis and A. A. Madsen it is clear that Maacah is connected to Absalom son of David (*The Books of Chronicles*, ICC [Edinburgh: T. & T. Clark, 1910], 369, 374). According to M. Kochman, "It is accepted by most interpreters that the text related to Absalom son of David, Rehoboam's uncle" ("II Chronicles chapters 10–27," in *The Book of II Chronicles*, ed. B. Oded [Tel Aviv: Davidzon-Itai, 1995], 89 [Hebrew]). He suggests that David's name as Absalom's father is not mentioned, because Absalom is known as the murderer of his brother and the rebel against his father. According to Ralph W. Klein, "If Maacah's father is the son of David who revolted against the king, she would be a granddaughter of David and a first cousin of her husband Rehoboam" (*Chronicles: A Commentary*, Hermeneia [Minneapolis: Fortress, 2012], 177).

41. According to 2 Sam. 14:27: "Absalom had three sons and a daughter whose name was Tamar." For Josephus (*Ant.* 8.249) Maacah was the daughter of Tamar (Thamare), Absalom's daughter. See R. B. Dillard, *2 Chronicles*, WBC 15 (Dallas: Word, 1987), 99, and Klein, *2 Chronicles*, 177 n. 59. Japhet also suggests "that

not his firstborn, because Rehoboam loved Maacah more than his other wives and concubines, similar to a certain extent to the case of Solomon and his mother Bathsheba. Abijah too is depicted as one of Judah's best kings, the appropriate successor of the house of David. The use of motifs similar to those found in the Succession Narrative[42] strengthens the possibility that the Chronicler was pointing to Absalom son of David. Thus, unexpectedly, the Chronicler does justice to Absalom by telling us that his grandson is not only a great warrior on the battlefield, but that he also transmits the expected legacy of the house of David.

Conclusion

Absalom's rebellion cannot be explained as the war of a handsome, corrupt, and power hungry youth against an aged and helpless father. The reader who examines David's conduct toward his sons, his total dependence on Joab, along with his loss of ability to judge and act, is now in a position to better understand the drastic circumstances that led to a son rising up against his father. Absalom's rebellion changes from a simplistic matter of a young man who wants to inherit his father's throne to a complicated affair involving different levels of justice, with both personal and national elements, from past and present, from emotions and from the force of circumstances. The books of Samuel show that Absalom was a positive, sensitive, and righteous person, and that the dispute between Amnon and Absalom is not about inheriting the crown but about a violation of family honor, for which Amnon bears the guilt with David supporting him. The reader who follows the text from the rape of Tamar to the description of Absalom winning the people's hearts (2 Sam. 15:6) learns that Absalom's struggle against his father is accompanied by feelings of revenge, grievance, unjust discrimination, and injustice. However, in a world designed by dual causality, a warrior of justice too

---

Maacah was not actually Absalom's daughter but his granddaughter, through Tamar and her husband 'Uriel of Gibeah'—Maacah's father" (*1 and 2 Chronicles*, 671).

42. This title usually includes 2 Sam. 9–20 and 1 Kgs 1–2; see e.g. R. N. Whybray, *The Succession Narrative: A Study of II Samuel 9–20; 1 Kings 1 and 2* (London: SCM, 1968), and the bibliography there. On the contrary see David M. Gunn: "this is above all else a story about David and not any successor..." (*The Story of King David: Genre and Interpretation*, JSOTSup 6 [Sheffield: JSOT Press, 1978], 83). For a different viewpoint see also Na'aman who "re-examines the vast literature that has grown around the work that Leonhard Rost called 'the succession to the throne of David'" ("Game of Thrones," 94–7).

becomes a victim of plans from above. Hence Absalom's fight for justice becomes no more than the dance of a marionette in the theater of God.

I will finish by expressing gratitude and esteem to our Sages, who also functioned as editors, for including Chronicles and Samuel side by side in our biblical canon, and for not censoring and excluding one book because it contradicted the other. Thus we learn that David was not the ideal model of a person, a father, and a king, and that Absalom was motivated by his wish for justice, which his grandson would go on to implement.

Chapter 17

NATHAN: THE UNEXPECTED GIFT OF A PROPHET

James E. Patrick

Nathan is the first prophet in monarchic traditions to be labelled exclusively as a "prophet" and not also a "seer."[1] His characterization in Samuel-Kings therefore seems to be conveying something about the distinctive role and activity of the prophet as this phenomenon crystallized in early Israel. David's reign was profoundly influenced by the repeatedly unexpected input of Nathan at key junctures: his adultery with Bathsheba, the start of preparations for the temple, the birth of Solomon, and David's choice of a successor. One might say, without Nathan, there would be no Davidic dynasty; the kingdom was built on the foundation of the prophets.

There have been various important recent studies about Nathan, both diachronic and synchronic,[2] and there is insufficient space here to interact

---

1. Even if the dynastic oracle is said to be a "vision" (2 Sam. 7:17). 1 Sam. 9:9 indicates that prophets used to be known as "seers," whether *ro'ĕh* (Samuel, 1 Sam. 9:11-18; Hanani, 2 Chron. 16:7-10) or *ḥōzēh* (Gad, 2 Sam. 24:11; Iddo, 2 Chron. 9:29; Jehu, 2 Chron. 19:2; cf. Amos 7:12; also three musical patriarchs, 1 Chron. 25:5; 2 Chron. 29:30; 35:13).

2. Ilse von Löwenclau, "Der Prophet Nathan im Zwielicht von theologischer Deutung und Historie," in *Werden und Wirken des Alten Testaments: FS Westermann*, ed. Rainer Albertz et al. (Göttingen: Vandenhoeck & Ruprecht, 1980), 202–15; Gwilym H. Jones, *The Nathan Narratives*, JSOTSup 80 (Sheffield: Sheffield Academic, 1990); Keith Bodner, "Nathan: Prophet, Politician and Novelist?" *JSOT* 95 (2001): 43–54; updated as "Nathan: Prophet, Politician, and Playwright," in *David Observed: A King in the Eyes of his Court* (Sheffield: Sheffield Phoenix, 2005), 67–76; Wolfgang Oswald, *Nathan der Prophet: Ein Untersuchung zu 2 Samuel 7 und*

properly with the diverse views presented, let alone with the voluminous scholarly literature on the chapters in which he plays a role. However, reflecting both diachronic interest in the compositional history of the text as well as synchronic interest in the resulting narrative, this chapter utilizes literary structure and editorial rhetorical intent to shed new light on the presentation of Nathan throughout 2 Samuel 7 to 1 Kings 4. This chapter will therefore seek to piece together the assumed chronology of the narrative against which the abrupt actions of Nathan are meant to be viewed. The reconstructed story can then reveal the strictly principled yet kindly character whose powerful prophecies could never once have been foretold by those to whom he was sent.

Potential Obstacles for Analyzing Nathan's Story-arc in 2 Samuel 7–24 and 1 Kings 1–4

Biblical passages mentioning Nathan the prophet include 2 Sam. 7:1-17 (dynastic oracle), 12:1-15 (indictment of David), 12:24-25 (renaming of Solomon), 1 Kings 1 (succession of Solomon), and presumably 1 Kgs 4:5 (sons of Nathan). Despite the popularity of the so-called "Succession Narrative" (2 Sam. 9–20; 1 Kgs 1–2) ever since it was proposed by Leonhard Rost in 1926, serious objections have been raised both to this designation and to treating 1 Kings 1–2 as part of the same literary composition as 2 Samuel 9–20.[3] Similarly, despite the common scholarly exclusion of 2 Samuel 7 or parts thereof from its surrounding narrative, on the grounds of its ostensibly Deuteronomistic features,[4] there are good reasons to see it as a compositional unity, and an integral part of the wider composition of 2 Samuel.[5] Prominent among these is the editorial

---

12 und 1 Könige 1, AThANT 94 (Zürich: Theologischer Verlag, 2008); Ionel Ababi, *Natan et la succession de David: Une étude synchronique de 2 Samuel 7 et 12 et 1 Rois 1*, BTS 32 (Leuven: Peeters, 2017).

3. Leonhard Rost, *Die Überlieferung von der Thronnachfolge Davids* (Stuttgart: Kohlhammer, 1926). Contrast variously: Gillian Keys, *The Wages of Sin: A Reappraisal of the "Succession Narrative,"* JSOTSup 221 (Sheffield: Sheffield Academic, 1996), 54–70; Serge Frolov, "Succession Narrative: A Document or a Phantom?" *JBL* 121 (2002): 81–124; Walter Dietrich, *The Early Monarchy in Israel: The Tenth Century B.C.E*, trans. Joachim Vette, BibEncycl 3 (Atlanta: SBL, 2007), 228–40.

4. E.g. Omer Sergi, "The Composition of Nathan's Oracle to David (2 Samuel 7:1-17) as a Reflection of Royal Judahite Ideology," *JBL* 129, no. 2 (2010): 261–79.

5. On the most commonly identified "Deuteronomistic insertion," 7:13, see Lyle Eslinger, *House of God or House of David: The Rhetoric of 2 Samuel 7*, JSOTSup 164 (Sheffield: Sheffield Academic, 1994), 49–57.

arrangement of the book's episodes, the careful literary structure that incorporates all episodes from 2 Samuel 7 through 24. By identifying the rhetorical purposes of this structure, its constituent narratives can then be put back into their most likely simple chronological sequence, as a backstory that best accounts for the logic of cause and effect in these narrated events as well as those in 1 Kings 1.[6] This chapter will therefore proceed on the premises that (1) 2 Samuel 7–24 and 1 Kings 1 belong to separate literary compositions, and yet (2) the events in both, whether narrated or reported, do constitute a coherent metanarrative in the mind of the author(s)/editor(s).

It is self-evident that character is manifested through life events, and therefore a character study depends on having an agreed sequential story-arc from which to draw conclusions about the person. In the case of Nathan the prophet, it makes a big difference whether his indictment of David preceded or followed his dynastic oracle. Did he approach David with harsh words of judgement having confidence that David already favored him due to the dynastic oracle, or alternatively, was he perhaps wanting to improve his relationship with David after the indictment, and David's temple query was a good opportunity? Our search for the intended characterization of Nathan in Samuel-Kings has been complicated by the deliberate dischronologization of the narrative,[7] hinted at in the peacetime setting of 2 Sam. 7:1 but wartime setting of 2 Samuel 11–12. Dischronologization was necessary to create the balanced literary structure by which the author's rhetorical messages could be conveyed. Yet with his primary rhetorical purpose being about David, the story of Nathan was evidently secondary, and hence the correct chronological sequence of episodes about Nathan was sacrificed. To ask questions of the narrative which it was not directly trying to answer, in this case about Nathan's story-arc and character, we must analyze our source material in stages: First, we need to recognize the book's literary structure, involving both sequential and dislocated sections. Only then can we reconstruct the

---

6. Recent study of the narrative blocks in Samuel concludes that they "share plots, narratives, and ideological motives that were set against the same historical and chronological background," such that we might speak of a unified (pre-Deuteronomistic) narrative about "the history of the early monarchy" (Sergi, "Composition," 265), necessarily underpinned by a coherent authorial metanarrative. The author of 1 Kgs 1–2 (or else of its source material, cf. 11:41), most likely shared that metanarrative, knowing the story or even text of 2 Sam. 7–24, and composing his own narrative as a satisfying conclusion to the open-ended story of David's reign.

7. See David G. Firth, *1 and 2 Samuel: A Kingdom Comes*, Phoenix Old Testament Guides 9 (Sheffield: Sheffield Phoenix, 2013), 67–79.

metanarrative within which all its episodes find their actual chronological order. And finally, we may interrogate the episodes specifically involving Nathan.

1. *Literary Structure of 2 Samuel 7–24*

The author's doctoral thesis, now being prepared for publication, presents a rhetorical structure that accounts for every episode within 2 Samuel 7–24. This begins with the widespread recognition that the episodes in 2 Samuel 21–24 are disconnected chronologically from each other and from preceding (and following) chapters, and should not therefore be seen as consecutive. In their current location, they are evidently arranged thematically so as to create a balanced inverted parallel structure of A-B-C-C'-B'-A'. Three years of famine punishing Saul's sin (21:1-14) parallels three days of plague punishing David's sin (24:1-25). David's mighty men killing giants (21:15-22) parallels other exploits of David's mighty men (23:8-39). And David's song of deliverance from Saul (22:1-51) parallels David's oracle about kingship (23:1-7). But prior to this so-called "appendix" of disconnected episodes, the David-and-Bathsheba story (2 Sam. 10–12) and the Absalom story (2 Sam. 13–20) do constitute coherent chronological narratives, which also combine to form a chronological pair of Cause and Effect stories.[8] The two judgements pronounced by Nathan at the climax of the David-and-Bathsheba story (12:7-12) are then fulfilled in the twin climaxes of the Absalom story (16:22-23; 18:15-18). David's sin was thus the ultimate cause of Absalom's rebellion and death.

(a) *2 Samuel 7–9 as a Chronological "Intermission"*

As for the chapters before the David-and-Bathsheba story, many scholars have recognized another thematically arranged cluster of episodes, differing as to its extent.[9] I suggest chronological disconnection might better define its limits. 2 Samuel 6 is chronologically linked to what precedes it, completing the narrative arc of the Ark of the Covenant that began in 1 Samuel 4, as well as the narrative arc of Saul's replacement by

---

8. Keys, *Wages*, 123–55.
9. Most commonly chs. 5–8. See especially: Walter Brueggemann, *Power, Providence, and Personality: Biblical Insight into Life and Ministry* (Louisville: Westminster John Knox, 1990), 86–115, at 89–90; Herbert H. Klement, *II Samuel 21–24: Context, Structure and Meaning in the Samuel Conclusion*, EUS XXIII/682 (Frankfurt am Main: Lang, 2000); David G. Firth, "Shining the Lamp: The Rhetoric of 2 Samuel 5–24," *TynBul* 52 (2001): 203–24; Firth, *Kingdom Comes*, 22–3, 44, 47.

David (2 Sam. 6:21) that began in 1 Sam. 13:14.[10] At a more immediate level, this story of the Ark's arrival in "the City of David" also follows on chronologically as the first official act of David's new rule over all Israel from Jerusalem (6:1 alluding to 5:6, as 1 Chron. 11–12 elaborates), after having to repel two Philistine attempts to crush Israel's renewed political unity (5:17-25). The Philistine incursions themselves are said to have been a response to news of David's anointing over Israel (5:17), and their battle locations in the valley of Rephaim both times (5:18, 22) indicates that the newly conquered capital city of Jerusalem (i.e. "the stronghold"—5:9, 17) was their military objective.[11] Chapter 6 therefore rounds off the continuous story begun in 5:1-3, 6-10, and concludes what appears to have been a complete book comprising broadly 1 Samuel 4 through 2 Samuel 6.[12]

Episodes in 2 Samuel 7–9, on the other hand, appear to have been deliberately disconnected and re-ordered so as to create a chronological pause in the story, an "intermission" to balance the "appendix" of chs. 20–24. Scholars have often noted that if 2 Samuel was meant to be a royal chronicle of King David, comparable to the records of later rulers in 1–2 Kings, it does a poor job of chronicling his reign in order. Having arrived in Jerusalem and brought in the Ark in the eighth year of his reign, the story of David never properly resumes. It is not a straightforward task to match up the events of the longer narratives in chs. 10–12 and 13–20 with the timing of those in either previous or subsequent episodes. Although Mephibosheth's introduction in ch. 9 precedes and informs the Absalom narrative (chs. 13–20), so do the list of David's sons (3:2-5) and the Ark's relocation to Jerusalem (ch. 6). Despite ch. 9's story-world links to following chapters, it is not causally connected to them, making chs. 10–12 a discrete unit.[13] As dischronologized clusters of episodes,

---

10. These two narrative arcs are also connected; unlike Saul, David shared God's heart and desired to restore the Ark of His presence into the center of His people. The Chronicler attests this interpretation when he records David's motivation for bringing the Ark into Jerusalem, something not mentioned in 2 Sam. 6: "Let us bring back the ark of our God to us, for we did not seek it in the days of Saul" (1 Chron. 13:3).

11. 5:5 confirms that Jerusalem was conquered at the very start of David's reign "over all Israel and Judah."

12. Further elaboration must await publication of my thesis.

13. Keys, *Wages*, 74–81. Serge Frolov ("Succession Narrative," 95) likewise includes ch. 9 within the "first intermezzo" (5:4–9:13), which collectively balances the second (20:23–24:25). *Pace* Richard G. Smith, *The Fate of Justice and Righteousness during David's Reign: Rereading the Court History and Its Ethics according to 2 Samuel 8:15b–20:26*, LHBOTS 508 (New York: T&T Clark, 2009), 65–73. Smith

therefore, the "intermission" and "appendix" in chs. 7–9 and 21–24 form a thematic frame around the properly chronological core of Cause and Effect stories, chs. 10–20.

(b) *Inverted Parallelism in 2 Samuel 7–9 and 20:23–24:25*

Furthermore, the thematic sequences of episodes in the "intermission" and "appendix" are deliberately inverted parallels of one another. Scholars have long suggested that the two poems by David in 22:1-51 and 23:1-7 were secondary insertions,[14] perhaps balancing the song of Hannah at the start of 1 Samuel so as to bookend the complete book of 1–2 Samuel. Although secondary, they do appear to have been inserted by the same author/editor who composed the whole of 2 Samuel 7–24, to conclude his book with this easily recognizable bow-structure (A-B-C-C'-B'-A').[15] When the poems are removed from the primary structure, the two clusters of stories about David's mighty men lock together once again as a single episode (21:15-22 + 23:8-39), confirmed by the number "thirty-seven" (23:39).[16] On either side of this are episodes that were evidently composed to parallel each other here in the "appendix" as well as paralleling their counterparts over in the "intermission." Three years of famine punishing Saul's sin (21:1-14) parallels three days of plague punishing David's sin (24:1-25). But equally, 21:1-14 can be seen as David avoiding the perfect opportunity to execute the heir to Saul's throne, Mephibosheth, out of loyalty to Jonathan. This parallels the kindness shown to Mephibosheth back in ch. 9. Then the re-united episodes about David's mighty men (21:15-22 + 23:8-39) parallel the list of David's wars in ch. 8. Finally, 24:1-25 can be seen as an account of the prophetic oracle from Gad instructing David to build an altar above Jerusalem to avert the divine plague. This parallels the prophetic oracle from Nathan promising David that the temple would be built, back in ch. 7. The temple and its altar are

---

cannot appeal to the first words of 10:1 to justify its chronological link to ch. 9, if he allows the same phrase in 8:1 to be part of a "dischronologized" narrative (68 n. 14). As for thematic parallels with ch. 10, these do not prove causal links.

14. R. A. Carlson, *David, the Chosen King*, trans. Eric J. Sharpe and Stanley Rudman (Stockholm: Almqvist & Wiksell, 1964), 194–259, esp. 197; P. Kyle McCarter, Jr., *II Samuel*, AB 9 (Garden City: Doubleday, 1984), 16–19.

15. Instead of the anachronistic and ambiguous term *chiasmus*, I prefer *qešet* (longbow), drawn from 2 Sam. 1:18.

16. "Thirty-one" listed in 23:24-39 (including Shammah [23:33 = 23:11-12] and Jonathan [23:32 = 21:21]), plus Benaiah and Abishai (23:18-23; cf. 21:17), Eleazar and Josheb-basshebeth (23:8-10), Elhanan ben Jaare-oregim and Sibbecai (21:18-19).

therefore placed at the outermost edges of the whole structure, just as the Ark of the Covenant bookended the preceding composition of 1 Samuel 4 to 2 Samuel 6.

But there is still one obvious discrepancy in the structure, namely the relative positions of the two lists of David's chief ministers. Based on the current position of the first list (2 Sam. 8:15-18), we can hypothesize that the parallel list in 20:23-26 originally preceded the episode about David's mighty men (21:15-22 + 23:8-39). This original position is then confirmed by the resulting improved balance in the secondary bow-structure, where the list of chief ministers now parallels the list of thirty-one mighty men, and as an extra level of paired episodes, the stories of five giant-killers (including David) neatly parallel stories about five other heroes.[17] Hence the following structure:

(c) *Graphical Representation of 2 Samuel 7–24*

1 Nathan's oracle about the temple (2 Sam. 7:1-29)
  2 David's wars against enemies (8:1-14)
    3 David's list of chief ministers (8:15-18)
      4 Kindness to Mephibosheth (9:1-13)
        5 David and Bathsheba/Uriah = *Cause* (10:1–12:31)

        5' Absalom and his mutiny = *Effect* (13:1–20:22)
      4' Mercy on Mephibosheth, when atoning for Saul's sin (21:1-14)
    3' **David's list of chief ministers (20:23-26)**
  2' David's honored military: giant-killers, heroes, list of mighty men (21:15-22 + 23:8-39)
1' Gad's oracle about the altar, when atoning for David's sin (24:1-25)

The insertion of two poems into the center of the "appendix" then created a secondary bow-structure, as follows:

---

17. The reason for deliberately marring the otherwise perfect structure by dislocating the list of chief ministers (20:23-26) was evidently to distance Joab from the following list of David's honored warriors. Many scholars note the strange absence of Joab from the list of mighty men, despite his two brothers being named (23:18-19, 24; cf. 23:37). But David's deep antipathy towards Joab is well known (3:26-29; 1 Kgs 2:5-6). The rhetorical effect of this dislocation relies on our assumption of perfect balance, hence the exception that proves the rule.

4'=**A**   Mercy on Mephibosheth, when atoning for Saul's sin (2 Sam. 21:1-14)
  3'=**B**   **David's list of chief ministers (20:23-26)**
    2'=**C**   (a) David's fellow giant-killers (21:15-22)
        >> **D**   David's song of salvation from Saul (22:1-51)

        >> **D'**   David's oracle about kingship (23:1-7)
    2'=**C'**   (b) David's honored heroes (23:8-23)
  2'=**B'**   (c) David's list of honored mighty men (23:24-39)
1'=**A'**   Gad's oracle about the altar, when atoning for David's sin (24:1-25)

2. Metanarrative Implications from the Structure of 2 Samuel 7–24

Having demonstrated the careful structural arrangement of episodes in 2 Samuel 7–24, we can return to consider a few implications of this structure that pertain to Nathan the prophet, in particular the relative chronological sequence of episodes in chs. 7, 12, and 24. Only by reconstructing the metanarrative that underpins all the episodes, despite their rearrangement for rhetorical purposes in the book of Samuel, will we be able to track Nathan's involvement in the flow of events.

(a) *Relative Chronology of 2 Samuel 7 and 12*

First, the dischronologized placement of Nathan's dynastic oracle to David in ch. 7 allows for the possibility that its true chronological position, within the metanarrative assumed by the overall story, is actually after Nathan's indictment of David in ch. 12 rather than before. This is then confirmed by the introduction to ch. 7, which explicitly situates its chronological position later than the events of chs. 10–12. Chapter 7 came at a time "when…the LORD had given him rest on every side from all his enemies" (7:1; cf. 7:9-11), whereas the following ch. 8 lists half a dozen different wars that David won against enemy countries on every side. 2 Samuel 8:3-8 itself clearly refers to the events later reported in more detail in 10:6-19, and chs. 10–12 contextualize David's sins against Uriah amidst Israel's battles with the Ammonites and Arameans. Thus, Nathan's indictment of David's sin, during the Ammonite war, must logically precede his dynastic oracle, delivered to David after peace had been achieved with all his enemies on every side. The mention of enemies "on every side" in 7:1 must refer to at least the majority of the wars listed retrospectively in ch. 8, unless we are to imagine numerous unreported wars prior to ch. 7 with Israel's eastern neighbors, not just with the Philistines to the west.[18] Henceforth we will work on the assumption that Nathan's dynastic oracle to David in ch. 7 was chronologically later than his indictment of David in ch. 12.

(b) *Relative Chronology of 2 Samuel 7 and 24*

A second implication of the literary structure also makes a significant contribution to understanding the implied metanarrative behind events to do with Solomon, in which Nathan plays a key role. In a forthcoming article entitled "David's Census as a Response to Nathan's Prophecy (2 Samuel 7 and 24)," I have set out detailed reasons for connecting the census in 2 Samuel 24 with Nathan's temple prophecy in ch. 7, on the level of narrative as well as of thematic juxtaposition. Nathan's oracle to David gave two main promises: (i) secure land-settlement for Israel (7:10-11a), and (ii) a future temple-builder (7:11b-16). In addition to his prayer of thanksgiving, it would have been natural for David to want to do something in response to the prophetic word. Looking back for guidance at the traditions of Israel's early history (as mentioned within the oracle itself, 7:6; cf. also 11:20-21), he would have recalled that Moses had taken two censuses, both at the beginning and end of the wilderness wandering. The reasons for each of these happened to correspond closely to the two promises given to David. The first census had accumulated silver from every family in Israel, which was used in the construction of the Tabernacle (Exod. 30:11-16; 38:25-28). The second census had calculated the relative sizes of each tribe in the new generation, so that after military conquest of Canaan had restored the land to peace, territory might be assigned to each tribe in proportion to its size (Num. 26:52-56). It would have been entirely logical, therefore, for David to conclude that the precedent of Moses himself was sufficient religious justification for him to take a census of Israel also, even if he could not undertake the actual building of the temple.

Despite his godly intentions, though, David realized his error after the "nine months and twenty days" of the census (2 Sam. 24:8), and this again links back to the prophecy of Nathan. The specified period was

---

18. Although 8:1 begins with "Now it came about after this that...," this is conventional language typically used as a resumption of the narrative after a significant break (perhaps harking back to 5:25?), and, as such, its purpose here seems to be for rhetorical effect, more to emphasize discontinuity than continuity. See Robert Alter, *The David Story* (New York/London: W. W. Norton, 1999), 236.

apparently indicating that the census had taken long enough for a child to be conceived and born and named at circumcision on the eighth day, all before David discovered his mistake. Nathan's prophecy had referred to David's successor as one "who will proceed from your inward parts" (7:12). This might have led David to expect that a son not yet born would be his successor, rather than a son born in Hebron (3:2-5). The list of David's Jerusalem-born sons in 2 Sam. 5:13-16 was copied fairly closely in 1 Chron. 14:4-7, but an alternative version in 1 Chron. 3:5-9 incorporated some extra information, drawn either from other ancient sources or merely from close reading of 2 Samuel. In either case, we have reason to take seriously what it says about Solomon's siblings and birth order.

1 Chronicles 3:5 records that Bath-shua daughter of Ammiel bore four sons to David in Jerusalem: Shimea, Shobab, Nathan, and Solomon. 2 Samuel 11:3 gives Bathsheba's father as Eliam (cf. 23:34), and it was not unknown for Israelites to vary the position of the theophoric element in their name (cf. Jehoahaz/Ahaziah in 2 Chron. 21:17; 22:1). The Chronicler omitted the stories of both Tamar and Bathsheba from his source material in 2 Samuel, but since Tamar is also mentioned in 1 Chron. 3:9, it is quite clear that Bath-shua in v. 5 must be an alternative name for Bathsheba. Yet the impression given by 2 Sam. 12:23-25 is that Solomon was born as a direct result of David comforting Bathsheba for the loss of her first son with him (though compare 11:26), so why does the Chronicler list Solomon as Bathsheba's fourth son?

(c) *The Naming of "Solomon" (2 Samuel 12:24-25) in the Context of 2 Samuel 7 and 24*

The answer would seem to be found in 2 Sam. 12:6, where David passed judgement in court that the rich man who had stolen the poor man's lamb must make fourfold restitution.[19] When Nathan identified the rich man as David himself, David's own judgement would be binding upon himself— "in speaking this word the king is as one who is guilty" (14:13). David could not pay back four wives to Uriah who was now dead. But biblical law would support the equivalent idea of raising up four sons to preserve Uriah's name (cf. Gen. 38:8-10; Deut. 25:5-10).[20] The name "Solomon" in 2 Sam. 12:24 could therefore be interpreted in connection with the words

---

19. "Sevenfold" in the LXX may have been changed under the influence of Prov. 6:24-31, to denigrate Bathsheba.

20. Note, David's ruling calls for four of the rich man's flock to be paid to the poor man, not killed; this therefore undermines the common and ancient suggestion that four of David's sons died as punishment for killing Uriah.

šālēm, "complete" (cf. Gen. 15:16), or *šillēm*, "restitution" (cf. Exod. 22:1-15 [MT 21:37–22:14]—the same passage where the legal ruling of fourfold restitution for stolen sheep is taught), not just with *šālôm*, "peace." In fact, the idea of completed restitution makes far better sense within the immediate narrative context of 2 Samuel 10–12, focused as it is on God's legal acceptance of the union of David and Bathsheba.[21]

This then raises the question of the "peaceful" interpretation of Solomon's name that is repeatedly mentioned in narratives later than 2 Samuel. It is implied in Solomon's description of the dynastic oracle in 1 Kgs 5:2-5 [MT vv. 16-19] (cf. 8:15-21), and explicitly connected to Solomon's name in other Davidic traditions incorporated by the Chronicler (1 Chron. 22:7-10; 28:2-7; cf. 17:1-15). Certain details associated with Nathan's dynastic oracle even in the earliest traditions are absent from the version of the oracle preserved in 2 Samuel 7. These include (i) bloodshed or warfare as the reason for David not being permitted to build the temple; (ii) the expectation that David's heir would be a man of rest, at peace with neighboring countries; and (iii) the condition that David's heirs must walk in the LORD's ways as David did (cf. 1 Kgs 2:3-4; 6:11-13; 8:25; 9:4-5; Ps. 132:11-12; Ps. 89:19-37 conforms more closely to 2 Sam. 7). All three of these can be seen as reasonable deductions from a careful reading of 2 Samuel 7. The only additional detail that cannot be deduced from 2 Samuel 7 is the surprisingly explicit and direct naming of the successor: "his name shall be Solomon" (1 Chron. 22:9), or "Your son Solomon is the one who shall build my house and my courts; for I have chosen him to be a son to me, and I will be a father to him" (1 Chron. 28:5-6). So was Solomon himself actually identified directly in Nathan's dynastic oracle? If so, this would explain why in 1 Kings 1, Nathan, Bathsheba, and David all know of a time when David swore to Bathsheba that "Solomon your son shall be king after me" (1 Kgs 1:13, 17, 30).

This brings us back to David's census in 2 Samuel 24, and its connection with 2 Samuel 7. If David had commanded Joab to take the census soon after receiving the dynastic oracle from Nathan, he would also be anticipating the birth of a new son who would succeed him and build the temple. As a thought experiment, let us assume that the original oracle included at least a reference to the name of his (future) son as "Solomon." According to the Chronicler's understanding, David had been

---

21. Scholars including Jones (*Nathan Narratives*, 113; citing J. J. Stamm, "Der Name des Königs Salomo," *ThZ* 16 [1960]: 285–97, at 296) have suggested the name might mean "replacement" for Bathsheba's first son, but this is less likely both semantically (how is this "restitution"?) and theologically (why would he need replacing?).

giving son after son to Bathsheba as restitution to Uriah, and after three sons, he might reasonably have planned to name the fourth and final son "Solomon," "Paid in Full." Three sons might well take us from the time of the Ammonite war in 2 Samuel 10–12 through the remaining wars of David with enemies such as Edom (8:13-14), and into the time of peace referred to in 7:1. If David received an oracle that explicitly named his peacetime successor "Solomon," it would seem obvious that God was identifying the anticipated fourth son of Bathsheba, the completion of his payment for adultery, as the same son who would become his successor and build the temple. It would therefore be entirely logical for David to swear to Bathsheba that her next and final son, "Paid in Full," would also become "Peaceful," his successor on the throne according to God's direct prophetic word.[22] A son conceived shortly after David received the dynastic oracle would therefore have been born, and named one week later at his circumcision, within the "nine months and twenty days" of the census.

Yet when Solomon was born, Nathan was sent to David with another command from the LORD, naming Bathsheba's new son "Jedidiah" for the LORD's sake (2 Sam. 12:24-25). For David, though, this ostensibly reassuring re-naming would instead have thrown him into confusion about the interpretation of the dynastic oracle. Clearly this fourth son of Bathsheba should henceforth be known as "Jedidiah" not "Solomon," but in that case David had completely misunderstood who God was identifying as his successor. Looking around for alternatives, his eye would immediately alight upon Ab-salom, "father of peace." This much older son was already handsome, popular, and a born leader, and David might be forgiven for concluding that Nathan's oracle must have been identifying Absalom as his crown prince. It is perhaps not coincidental that the story of 2 Samuel shifts quite suddenly from the re-named baby "Jedidiah" to "Absalom the son of David" (13:1), who thereafter is treated by David as his sole heir (hence 14:7, 13; 16:18). As "my son who came out from my inward parts" (16:11, a direct allusion to 7:12), Absalom was allowed to assume control of Jerusalem and the Ark of the Covenant without the slightest resistance from David, and remained untouchable even after having slept with his father's concubines and contemplated how best to kill his father.

---

22. As such, there is no need to treat Nathan and Bathsheba's actions in 1 Kgs 1 as a "conspiracy," fabricating the alleged promise to hoodwink a senile David and secure their own position. Cf. Matthew Newkirk, "Reconsidering the Role of Deception in Solomon's Ascent to the Throne," *JETS* 57, no. 4 (2014): 703–13.

As for the freshly completed census, though, David would have realized that a mistake in naming Solomon might also suggest other mistaken interpretations. God had not explicitly commanded David to take a census, in which case David had been presumptuous in treating his Moses-inspired deductions as if they were a divine command. This would therefore explain David's personal recognition of fault in taking the census, without needing any prophet to confront him for his sin (24:10). A plague followed the census, and events with Absalom gradually spiraled out of control, until Absalom's body lay under a heap of stones in the forest, and David's hopes for a dynasty and a temple lay there with him. Absalom's offence against his father's concubines, and his death in civil war, had both been prophesied by Nathan (12:7-12), so David would have seen himself to blame for God's withdrawal of the dynastic oracle, much as Eli's covenant had been withdrawn for similar reasons also after a forty-year reign (1 Sam. 2:27-36; 4:18; cf. 2 Sam. 5:4-5; 15:7). Being under God's judgement, he could not presume to appoint another son as his new successor, hence his sorry situation at the start of 1 Kings 1.

Yet Nathan had brought the dynastic oracle after the indictment for David's sins, not before it, offering reasons for continued hope. Likewise, Gad's oracle about the altar (for the new temple), coming after Gad's declaration of punishments for the census, would have communicated to David that the temple was still part of God's plan. It is not coincidental that the detailed narratives of Sin and Punishment, Cause and Effect (2 Sam. 10–20) are framed by the two prophetic oracles that spoke positively of God's desire for a temple, and thus also a temple-builder.

One might object that all of this depends on a conjecture about the name "Solomon" having been in the original form of Nathan's dynastic oracle. Yet viewed another way, this becomes a neat solution that accounts for many confusing details in the narrative, such as David's exclusive preferral of Absalom even after his death, the wise woman of Tekoa's assumption that Absalom is David's sole heir, the restitution of "four sheep" and the Chronicler's reference to "four" sons, the missing oath to Bathsheba about Solomon, and the reason for David's unprompted repentance after the census of "nine months and twenty days." Perhaps the Chronicler did know an earlier form of the oracle?

3. *Nathan's Story, According to the Chronology Underlying 2 Samuel 7–24 and 1 Kings 1–4*

The first chronological event in which Nathan features is evidently the indictment of David in **2 Sam. 12:1-15** (hereafter bold text will be used to highlight principal texts). Although the audience of 2 Samuel is already aware from ch. 7 that Nathan is a prophet, they might recognize from the war backdrop to ch. 12 that at this point David is still dangerously ignorant of Nathan's divine gift. This is reinforced by the plain designation "Nathan" throughout 12:1-15, never "the prophet." Had David already known Nathan to be a prophet, it is likely that his conscience might have made him more sensitive to what a man of God might be trying to get at with his legal case. But Nathan appears simply as a "gift," without even a theophoric ending to his name to indicate that he was a gift sent by God. David must open the present to discover the utterly unexpected gift inside.

As to his character, Nathan is clearly portrayed as a man of great conviction and courage, so confident in the accuracy of his prophetic knowledge that he was prepared to confront the king in person, presumably seated as judge on his throne to hear complex legal cases (cf. 14:4-22; 15:2; 1 Kgs 3:16-28). David would undoubtedly have been surrounded by armed guards (8:18), so a man accusing the king of vile crimes must have been prepared for David to respond rather more defensively than he did (cf. 1 Sam. 20:27-33; 1 Kgs 13:1-4). Nevertheless, Nathan fearlessly delivered the parable,[23] and then God's devastating indictment, perhaps even including a personal comment in v. 9a, speaking of God in the third person. Since "the word of the LORD" that David had despised cannot refer to Nathan's own oracle in ch. 7, it presumably refers to revealed laws such as those alluded to in 12:6;[24] Nathan is depicted honoring both immediate and traditional divine revelation. After an absolution in response to David's contrition, and a brief word of explanation about the imminent death of Bathsheba's son, he simply "went to his house" (12:15), not necessarily nearby (cf. 17:23). He may have been glad to escape with his life, but on the other hand, neither did he linger to advise the king on appropriate responses, which might have led to an official court position appropriate to one so gifted in divine sight.

Moving on several years later, if we are correct in interpreting **2 Sam. 5:14** according to 1 Chron. 3:5 (four sons of Bathsheba), and interpreting the start of the census and conception of Solomon as direct responses to Nathan's dynastic oracle, this would imply that Solomon's three older

---

23. God is presented elsewhere as a master of creative dissimulation, instructing His prophets how to trick kings (1 Sam. 16:1-5; 1 Kgs 20:35-43), so although 2 Sam. 12:1-4 is silent as to the parable's creative origin, we can assume that the prophet speaks as directed by God (cf. 14:1-3, 19-20), *pace* Bodner, "Playwright," 71–2.

24. Cf. John Goldingay, *1 and 2 Samuel for Everyone* (Louisville: Westminster John Knox, 2011), 146.

brothers had already been born before the census. In that case, we find an interesting detail in **5:14**, where Bathsheba's third son is named "Nathan." This was undoubtedly a common name in ancient Israel, but in the context of this narrative and its named characters, it would not be unreasonable to conclude that Bathsheba might have named this son after the prophet Nathan. This may have been an expression of gratitude for the one whose courageous indictment, comparing David to a sheep thief, had led to David favoring Bathsheba with his company often enough to give her four sons; other wives in 3:2-5 had only one each!

By the time we next encounter Nathan directly in 2 Sam. 7:1-3, he is not only known as "the prophet," but he is near enough to the king that David need not even summon him into his presence to speak with him (7:2—"the king said to Nathan"; contrast 1 Kgs 1:22-23, 28, 32). Nathan has also now become favorably disposed towards David, knowing that "the LORD is with you" (7:3), and is therefore sufficiently confident that God will look kindly upon whatever David wishes to do. There is no indication that Nathan had to travel a great distance after having spoken with the king, or when he returned to the king with the words and vision he had received from God "in the same night" (7:4, 17). This would all be consistent with Nathan having now been designated as "the prophet" at court, a personal adviser to the king, and presumably having a house or lodgings in Jerusalem. The prophet had apparently become close to the king, and perhaps also to his family.

Initially in 7:1-3, Nathan seems to be functioning as, or perhaps merely treated as, a "seer" (equivalent to a diviner in neighboring cultures, cf. Num. 24:1-4; Deut. 18:9-15), available to be consulted by the king on various matters of state (24:11; 1 Chron. 25:5). Prophet-seers may be sought out as oracles, for guidance about what to do in certain situations (cf. 1 Sam. 28:6, 15-16), or else just as spiritually sensitive individuals, who might know how God was feeling about something (cf. 2 Sam. 11:27–12:1), as in this case with David's desire to honor God with a temple. Nathan has received no special revelation yet about David's request, so he does not imply that he has. He gives both his counsel, "Go, do all that is in your mind," and his simple theological justification for saying this, "for the LORD is with you." Mere observation of David's prosperity and power would be enough to conclude that God was with him (5:10-12), and humbly Nathan admitted to David that this was all the insight he had. Having formerly received a divine message of breathtaking accuracy (ch. 12), he was secure enough in his role as God's messenger that when he had heard nothing from God, he did not need to pretend he had. Yet equally, when the word of the LORD then came to Nathan some hours later, giving a completely opposite response to David's query, Nathan was humble enough to return and convey the word to David, an admission that despite being David's trusted counsellor, his own earlier reasoning had been entirely unreliable.

The precise way in which Nathan delivered the prophetic word in **7:4-17** is also significant. He reported to David not only the words he was instructed by God to speak, beginning with the traditional formal introduction "Thus says the LORD…" (as in 12:7-12), but also what God actually spoke to Nathan himself (7:5, 8). Both times, he preserves for David the particular expression that God had used to refer to David, "my servant" (cf. 7:20). Yet this exactitude is contrasted with v. 11, where Nathan seems to put it into his own words, "The LORD also declares to you that the LORD will make a house for you," before returning to first-person divine speech from v. 12 onwards. Since this comes immediately after the reference to "I will give you rest from all your enemies," with echoes of the meaning of the name "Solomon" (cf. 1 Chron. 22:9), maybe the shift to the third person here should not be interpreted as a fault on the part of Nathan himself. Perhaps it is instead an indication that the author/editor of the overall composition has substituted a more vague summary here for the precise wording of this particular detail of the oracle, which now seemed too confusing in light of Solomon's re-naming in 12:24-25.[25] This is exactly where one might have expected some reference to "You shall therefore name your son Solomon, for I will make a house for you," as discussed above.

Having delivered his history-changing oracle, Nathan simply steps away again. He knew he was not to be a mediator between David and God, and David's reaction was not via Nathan but spoken directly and intimately in the presence of (the Ark of?) the LORD (7:17-18). Nathan may be God's ambassador, but he also knew God listens to all His servants personally. This is perhaps made even more significant if the sons of "Nathan" in 1 Kgs 4:5 were sons of Nathan the prophet. The syntax there suggests that both "a priest" and "the king's friend" are official roles played by Zabud son of Nathan; if "Nathan <u>the</u> priest" had been intended to distinguish this individual from "Nathan the prophet," the definite article would have been used (cf. 1 Sam. 1:9). Consequently, "Nathan" without any other identification clearly implies that this is the same Nathan who featured earlier at Solomon's birth and coronation. If that is so, "Nathan the prophet" was in fact a priest also, like his son, but functioned only as a prophet at court (like Jeremiah later). When serving

---

25. Sergi ("Composition," 263–4) sees 7:11 as part of an earlier editorial layer, but also mentions synchronic explanations.

as a prophet, he would not allow himself to slip into a priestly mediator role; he knew his boundaries.

After approximately nine and a half months, Nathan was sent once again to communicate to David the strong emotions he was sensing in the LORD Himself, albeit opposite emotions to when he and David first met. Admittedly, we do not have in **12:24-25** the precise words used by Nathan, but it is reasonable to assume that the statement that "the LORD loved him [the baby Solomon]" is as much part of the word God sent to David through his messenger Nathan, as is the name "Jedidiah," "Beloved of Yah." It also appears that Nathan himself named Solomon "Jedidiah" on behalf of the LORD, as if he himself were acting as the boy's father or mother. Solomon had been named in the previous verse by either his father or mother, ambiguity reflected in the *Kethib* and *Qere* readings of "he" or "she" respectively. This re-naming was presumably unnecessary for the prophet himself to implement, perhaps therefore conveying an increasing personal affection for Bathsheba's household. We are given no indication of whether Nathan was aware that this newborn had been named "Solomon" already, based on his own previous oracle. Regardless, he had a message to pass on, and he was never one to wait around afterwards and offer advice on how to interpret or apply what had been spoken.

Having re-named Solomon, and unwittingly averted David's attention from the boy almost completely,[26] the story of Nathan goes quiet for the entire period from the plague at the end of the census, through the rise and fall of David's new crown prince Absalom, and into the dark years between the end of the narrative in 2 Sam. 20:22 and 1 Kgs 1:1, represented structurally by the dechronologized "appendix" of 2 Sam. 20:23–24:25. Presumably priestly duties kept him busy, as did the upbringing of at least two sons, most likely in Jerusalem and in regular contact with at least Bathsheba's household. According to **1 Kgs 4:5**, Nathan's son Zabud later became the new king Solomon's most trusted counsellor, "the king's friend," as Hushai had been for King David (2 Sam. 15:32-37; 16:16–17:16; 1 Kgs 1:8—"Rei" = "my friend"). As a priest too, Zabud may have been honored with the additional role of royal chaplain, as Ira the Jairite had been in David's latter years (2 Sam. 20:26). Nathan's other son Azariah was also later appointed by the new king Solomon "over the deputies," making him in effect the Lord High Treasurer, managing the economy of the royal household and therefore of the state (1 Kgs 4:7-19;

---

26. An arranged marriage is all we know of before Solomon's coronation (cf. 1 Kgs 14:21 with 11:42), perhaps negotiated at Mahanaim (2 Sam. 17:27-29; cf. 10:1-5; 12:30).

cf. 1 Chron. 27:25-31). Since education of children was primarily the responsibility of parents (cf. Prov. 1:1-9; 4:1-9; 1 Chron. 27:32), Nathan must receive at least some credit for raising two of the most powerful men in Solomon's kingdom.

Even so, **1 Kgs 1:8-12** makes it clear that Nathan's closeness to Bathsheba's family had not won him any favors following the birth of Solomon/Jedidiah, when David's attention turned instead to Absalom. His public indictment of David at court (2 Sam. 12) would have tarnished Bathsheba irredeemably in the minds of the rest of the royal family, the military, and others. And this would have only caused greater resentment when David then counter-intuitively favored "the wife of Uriah the Hittite" above his other wives by giving her four sons. Doubtless their resentment peaked with the king's excitement during the census, while he anticipated the birth of Bathsheba's fourth son, his divinely chosen heir "Solomon." Most would have breathed a sigh of relief after his birth when David's preference was abruptly given instead to Absalom. But even two decades later when Adonijah invited all the royal family, court officials, and tribal leaders to his coronation feast, it was not just David's private bodyguard and chosen warriors who were left at home to guard the old king (1 Kgs 1:5-10). Bathsheba and her son Jedidiah were notably absent from the guest list, presumably because apart from the grief-stricken David, few had forgotten that this young man's birth had briefly threatened the royal succession of his much older half-brothers including Adonijah. Soon he and his scandalous mother would be removed from the scene for good (1:12). Jedidiah is of course called "Solomon" throughout 1 Kings 1, presumably opting for audience familiarity with the king's regnal name instead of a concern for strict historical veracity which might cause confusion.

A prophet of Nathan's caliber might have been quite desirable for Adonijah's party, but he remained loyal to his friend Bathsheba and her children, regardless of the political ramifications. With no further messages from God for David, he had never had reason to approach the king or query his preference for Absalom. It was only when the lives of the young man "Beloved of Yah" and his mother were directly threatened that he suggest she go to David and remind him of his solemn oath about her son (**1:11-31**). He may have feared for his job prospects under Adonijah, but hardly for his own life, given his powerful gift and famous oracle about the Davidic dynasty. Having advised Bathsheba to mention David's oath (1:11-14), Nathan then chose to "fill up" her words rhetorically simply by reiterating her report of Adonijah's coronation feast to which he and other royal servants had likewise not been invited (1:24-27). It would seem

Nathan had not been present when David named Solomon with an oath, being "sent" by the LORD soon afterwards with the new name (2 Sam. 12:24-25), so Nathan could not now testify to it despite knowing it had happened. Furthermore, even mentioning it might have had the effect of adding his own prophetic authority to David's original interpretation of the dynastic oracle, whereas Nathan knew he had no responsibility whatsoever for interpreting the divine messages he delivered. Nevertheless, Nathan's accompaniment of Bathsheba was evidently enough for the old king to conclude that God was not unfavorable to that original interpretation of the oracle, and David sprang into action.[27]

The final action (or non-action) of Nathan himself in the narrative (**1:32-48**) is again a mark of his humble character. King David commanded that both Zadok the priest and Nathan the prophet anoint Solomon as king over Israel at Gihon (1 Kgs 1:34), this being also in Jonathan's official report to Adonijah about the event (1:45). Yet in the narrated version of the anointing, Zadok the priest took the horn of oil from the tent and anointed Solomon alone (1:39). David had been anointed by the prophet Samuel, as had Saul before him, hence David's command regarding Solomon, yet this time it was not God's command. Perhaps Nathan deferred to the superior authority of the high priest, being a priest himself, but more likely he deferred to the ultimate authority of the One who sent him. Prophets would later continue to anoint new kings (2 Kgs 9:1-10; cf. 1 Kgs 11:29-39), but Nathan had done enough already for Solomon, with every divine oracle he had delivered to David. Through His gift of a prophet, the LORD's words had anticipated four sons being born to Bathsheba (2 Sam. 12:6-7) and promised the dynasty to a future son of David (7:12; probably also naming him "Solomon"—"Restitution"/"Peaceful"), only to abruptly re-name the newborn boy "Beloved of Yah" (12:25), which enabled him to grow to maturity out of the public spotlight as far as possible for a royal prince. Never once had David expected to hear what the prophet came to tell him, so he could hardly expect Nathan to be predictable at the coronation.

True to character, Nathan left the actions to others and stepped back into the background, simply letting the word of God, faithfully delivered, continue to accomplish its mighty effects.

---

27. Bodner advocates the common insinuation that Nathan invented the oath ("Playwright," 73–6; again, Bodner, *David Observed*, 155–9), but this fits less straightforwardly with the narrative of a private oath to Bathsheba (1 Kgs 1:20), and a king who, though elderly, is far from forgetful (2:1-9).

AFTERWORD

We have now spent several hundred pages journeying through the Book of Samuel by focusing on a selection of characters. Benjamin Johnson has highlighted the complexity of characters in Samuel and the fact that the characterization of one is often contingent on the characterization of another. Jan Fokkelman has highlighted some of the key structural and compositional features that frame the narrative in which these characters live. Stephen Chapman has offered a reading of the character of God that is both a character like any other, but also decidedly more. Jenni Williams has highlighted that Hannah can be read as a fascinating and interesting character in her own right and not just a functional type for the author's bigger purposes. Marvin Sweeney has shown us Eli's incompetencies that led to his downfall. J. Richard Middleton has taken a deep dive into the characterization of Samuel in 1 Samuel 12 and suggested that not only he is a character with ulterior motives but he is a character with questionable theology as well. Paul Evans has suggested that Saul's character can be understood by viewing him as one who tends toward low self-esteem and addictive behavior. David Gunn has offered a survey of trends in the study of David across the years which highlights the complexity of this central figure. Diana Abernethy has shown the way that Jonathan's positive characterization fits into the author's overall theological portrayal of the narrative. Jonathan Jacobs has demonstrated the effectiveness of reading characters analogously, especially in the case of the two children of Saul. Philip Esler has shown how attending to a character's social context can enlighten the significance of that character. Barbara Green has highlighted the complexity of the characterization of Joab. David Shepherd has highlighted the characterization of Abner and asked the question whether or not he can really be known while highlighting the significance of the theme of knowing throughout the narrative. Michael Avioz studied the character of Ishbosheth and argued that he failed to become a character in his own right and how that was significant for the narrator. David Firth studied the minor characters of Uriah, Ittai, and Hushai and highlighted how attending to the characterization of minor characters influences the characterization of major characters. Yairah Amit attempted to recognize the positive characterization of Absalom so that a more complete picture of this important character could be seen. Finally, James Patrick has highlighted the significance of the character Nathan within the overarching structure of the narrative in Samuel through 1 Kings 2.

The studies offered in this volume have provided fascinating, significant, and sometimes surprising insights into the characters in the Book of Samuel. Even a volume such as this, however, can only but scratch the surface of what a book like Samuel has to offer. Hopefully, this volume is but a contribution to a conversation about characters that will continue.

Keith Bodner
Benjamin J. M. Johnson

Bibliography

Ababi, Ionel. *Natan et la succession de David: Une étude synchronique de 2 Samuel 7 et et 12 et 1 Rois 1*. BTS 32. Leuven: Peeters, 2017.
Ackerman, Angela and Becca Puglisi. *The Negative Trait Thesaurus: A Writer's Guide to Character Flaws*. 1st print ed. Writers Helping Writers. [S.l.]: JADD Publishing, 2013.
Ackroyd, Peter R. *The Second Book of Samuel*. Cambridge: Cambridge University Press, 1977.
Alter, Robert. *The Art of Biblical Narrative*. New York: Basic Books, 1981.
Alter, Robert. *The Art of Biblical Narrative*. Rev. ed. New York: Basic Books, 2011.
Alter, Robert. *The Book of Psalms: A Translation with Commentary*. New York: W. W. Norton, 2007.
Alter, Robert. *The David Story: A Translation with Commentary of 1 and 2 Samuel*. New York: W. W. Norton, 2000.
Amit, Yairah. "'Am I Not More Devoted to You than Ten Sons?' (1 Samuel 1.8): Male and Female Interpretations." In *A Feminist Companion to Samuel and Kings*, edited by Athalya Brenner, 68–76. Sheffield: Sheffield Academic, 1994.
Amit, Yairah. "Dual Causality." In *In Praise of Editing in the Hebrew Bible: Collected Essays in Retrospect*, 105–21. Sheffield: Sheffield Phoenix, 2012.
Amit, Yairah. "'The Glory of Israel does not deceive or change his mind': On the Reliability of Narrator and Speakers in Biblical Narrative." *Prooftexts* 12 (1992): 201–12.
Amit, Yairah. *History and Ideology: An Introduction to Historiography in the Hebrew Bible*. Sheffield: Sheffield Academic, 1999.
Amit, Yairah. "The 'Men of Israel' and Gideon's Refusal to Reign." In *In Praise of Editing in the Hebrew Bible: Collected Essays in Retrospect*, 122–30. Sheffield: Sheffield Phoenix, 2012.
Amit, Yairah. "The Protest in the Story of Job—Form and Content." In *Theodicy and Protest*, edited by B. Ego et al., 17–27. Leipzig: Evangelische Verlagsanstalt, 2018.
Amit, Yairah. *Reading Biblical Narratives: Literary Criticism and the Hebrew Bible*. Minneapolis: Fortress, 2001.
Amit, Yairah. "The Story of Amnon and Tamar: Reservoir of Sympathy for Absalom." In *In Praise of Editing in the Hebrew Bible: Collected Essays in Retrospect*, 203–19. Sheffield: Sheffield Phoenix, 2012.
Anderson, A. A. *2 Samuel*. WBC 11. Waco: Word, 1989.
Andersson, Greger. *Untamable Texts: Literary Studies and Narrative Theory in the Books of Samuel*. LHBOTS 514. New York: T&T Clark, 2009.
Arnold, Bill T. "A Pre-Deuteronomistic Bicolon in 1 Samuel 12:21?" *JBL* 123 (2004): 137–42.

Ashman, A. *The Story of Eve: Daughters, Mothers and Strange Women in the Bible*. Tel Aviv: Miskal/Yedioth Ahronoth Books and Chemed Books, 2008 (Hebrew).
Athas, George. "'A Man After God's Own Heart': David and the Rhetoric of Election to Kingship." *JESOT* 2, no. 2 (2013): 191–8.
Auerbach, Eric. "Odysseus' Scar." In *Mimesis: The Representation of Reality in Western Thought*, 3–24. Princeton, NY: Princeton University Press, 2003.
Auld, A. Graeme. *Kings without Privilege: David and Moses in the Story of the Bible's Kings*. Edinburgh: T. & T. Clark, 1994.
Auld, A. Graeme. *1 and 2 Samuel: A Commentary*. OTL. Louisville: Westminster John Knox, 2008.
Avioz, Michael. "The Motif of Beauty in the Books of Samuel and Kings." *VT* 59 (2009): 341–59.
Avioz, Michael. "The Names of Mephibosheth and Ishbosheth Reconsidered." *JANES* 32 (2011): 11–20.
Avraham, Nahum. "The Nature of David and Jonathan's Relationship." *Beit Mikra* 174 (2003): 215–22 (Hebrew).
Bach, Alice. "The Pleasure of Her Text." In *A Feminist Companion to Samuel–Kings*, edited by Athalya Brenner, 110–28. Sheffield: Sheffield Academic, 1994.
Baden, Joel. *King David: The Real Life of an Invented Hero*. San Francisco: Harper One, 2013.
Bailey, Randall C. "The Redemption of YHWH: A Literary Critical Function of the Songs of Hannah and David." *BibInt* 3 (1995): 213–31.
Bakhtin, Mikhail M. "Discourse in the Novel." In *The Dialogical Imagination: Four Essays by M. M. Bakhtin*, edited by Michael Holquist, translated by Caryl Emerson and Michael Holquist, 259–422. Austin: University of Texas Press, 1981.
Baldwin, Joyce G. *1 and 2 Samuel*. TOTC. Downers Grove: InterVarsity, 1988.
Bar-Efrat, Shimon. *1 Samuel*. Mikra Leyisra'el. Tel Aviv: Am Oved, 1996 (Hebrew).
Bar-Efrat, Shimon. "First and Second Samuel: Introduction and Annotations." In *The Jewish Study Bible*, edited by A. Berlin and M. Z. Brettler, 558–667. New York: Oxford University Press, 2004.
Bar-Efrat, Shimon. *Narrative Art in the Bible*. New York: T&T Clark, 2008.
Batten, Loring. "Helkath Hazzurim, 2 Samuel 2,12-16." *ZAW* 26 (1906): 90–4.
Bellis, Alice O. *Helpmates, Harlots and Heroes: Women's Stories in the Hebrew Bible*. Louisville: Westminster John Knox, 1994.
Ben-Ayun, Chaya Shraga. *David's Wives—Michal, Abigail, Batsheba*. Israel: Levinsky, 2005 (Hebrew).
Ben Zvi, Ehud. *The Signs of Jonah: Reading and Rereading in Ancient Yehud*. JSOTSup 367. Sheffield: Sheffield Academic, 2003.
Bergen, Robert D. *1, 2 Samuel*. NAC 7. Nashville: Broadman & Holman, 1996.
Berger, Yitzhak. "Ruth and Inner-Biblical Allusion: The Case of 1 Samuel 25." *JBL* 128 (2009): 253–72.
Berlin, Adele. "Characterization in Biblical Narrative: David's Wives." *JSOT* 23 (1982): 69–85.
Berlin, Adele. *Poetics and Interpretation of Biblical Narrative*. Sheffield: The Almond Press, 1983.
Biddle, Mark. "Ancestral Motifs in 1 Samuel 25: Intertextuality and Characterization." *JBL* 121 (2002): 617–38.
Birch, Bruce C. *The First and Second Books of Samuel*. The New Interpreter's Bible. Nashville: Abingdon, 1998.

Bloch-Smith, Elizabeth. *Judahite Burial Practices and Beliefs about the Dead.* JSOTSup 123. Sheffield: JSOT Press, 1992.

Boda, Mark J. "Gazing through the Cloud of Incense: Davidic Dynasty and Temple Community in the Chronicler's Perspective." In *Chronicling the Chronicler: The Book of Chronicles and Early Second Temple Historiography*, edited by Tyler F. Williams and Paul S. Evans, 215–45. Winona Lake: Eisenbrauns, 2013.

Bodi, Daniel. "David as an 'Apiru in 1 Samuel 25 and the Pattern of Seizing Power in the Ancient Near East." In *Abigail, Wife of David, and Other Ancient Oriental Women*, edited by Daniel Bodi, 24–59. HBM 60. Sheffield: Sheffield Phoenix, 2013.

Bodi, Daniel. "Was Abigail a Scarlet Woman? A Point of Rabbinic Exegesis in Light of Comparative Material." In *Abigail, Wife of David, and Other Ancient Oriental Women*, edited by Daniel Bodi, 79–95. HBM 60. Sheffield: Sheffield Phoenix, 2013.

Bodner, Keith. *1 Samuel: A Narrative Commentary.* HBM 19. Sheffield: Sheffield Phoenix, 2009.

Bodner, Keith. "Crime Scene Investigation: A Text Critical Mystery and the Strange Death of Ishbosheth." *JHS* 7 (2007), article 13, www.arts.ualberta.ca/JHS/Articles/article_74. pdf. Repr. in idem, *The Artistic Dimension: Literary Explorations of the Hebrew Bible*, 15–35. LHBOTS 590. New York/London: Bloomsbury, 2013.

Bodner, Keith. *David Observed: A King in the Eyes of His Court.* HBM 5. Sheffield: Sheffield Phoenix, 2005.

Bodner, Keith. "Nathan: Prophet, Politician, and Novelist?" *JSOT* 26 (2001): 43–54.

Bodner, Keith. *The Rebellion of Absalom.* New York: Routledge, 2014.

Bodner, Keith and Benjamin J. M. Johnson, eds. *Characters and Characterization in the Book of Kings.* LHBOTS 670. London: Bloomsbury T&T Clark, 2020.

Borgman, Paul. *David, Saul, & God: Rediscovering an Ancient Story.* New York: Oxford University Press, 2008.

Bourdieu, Pierre. "The Sentiment of Honour in Kabyle Society." In *Honour and Shame: The Values of Mediterranean Society*, edited by J. G. Peristiany, 191–241. London: Weidenfeld & Nicolson, 1965.

Bovati, Pietro. *Re-Establishing Justice: Legal Terms, Concepts and Procedures in the Hebrew Bible.* JSOTSup 105. Sheffield: JSOT Press, 1994.

Brenner, Athalya. *The Israelite Woman: Social Role and Literary Type in Biblical Narrative.* Sheffield: JSOT Press, 1985.

Brettler, Marc Zvi. *The Creation of History in Ancient Israel.* London/New York: Routledge, 1995.

Brueggemann, Walter. "1 Samuel 1: A Sense of a Beginning." *ZAW* 102 (1990): 33–48.

Brueggemann, Walter. *David's Truth in Israel's Imagination and Memory.* Minneapolis: Fortress, 1985.

Brueggemann, Walter. *First and Second Samuel.* Interpretation. Louisville: John Knox, 1990.

Brueggemann, Walter. *Power, Providence, and Personality: Biblical Insight into Life and Ministry.* Louisville: Westminster John Knox, 1990.

Buber, Martin. "Autobiographical Fragments." In *The Philosophy of Martin Buber*, edited by Paul Arthur Schilpp and Maurice Friedman. La Salle, IL: Open Court, 1967.

Buchanan, John M. "Editor's Desk: The Bible's Violent God." *Christian Century* (April 17, 2013): 3.

Buracker, William. "Abner Son of Ner: Characterization and Contribution of Saul's Chief General." PhD diss., Catholic University of America, 2017.

Burnside, Jonathan. "Flight of the Fugitive: Rethinking the Relationship between Biblical Law (Exodus 21:12-14) and the Davidic Succession Narrative (1 Kings 1–2)." *JBL* 129, no. 3 (2010): 418–32.
Carasik, Michael. "The Limits of Omniscience," *JBL* 119 (2000): 221–32.
Campbell, Antony F., S.J. *1 Samuel*. FOTL 7. Grand Rapids: Eerdmans, 2003.
Campbell, Antony F., S.J. *2 Samuel*. FOTL 8. Grand Rapids: Eerdmans, 2005.
Campbell, Antony F., S.J. *The Ark Narrative (1 Sam 4–6; 2 Sam 6): A Form-Critical and Traditio-Historical Study*. SBLDS 16. Missoula, MT: Scholars Press, 1975.
Campbell, Antony F., S.J. *Of Prophets and Kings: A Late-Ninth Century Document (1 Samuel 1–2 Kings 10)*. CBQMS 17. Washington, DC: Catholic University of America, 1986.
Campbell, Antony F., S.J., and Mark A. O'Brien. *Unfolding the Deuteronomistic History: Origins, Upgrades, Present Text*. Minneapolis: Fortress, 2000.
Campbell, J. K. *Honour, Family and Patronage: A Study of Institutions and Moral Values in a Greek Mountain Community*. New York: Oxford University Press, 1964.
Carlson, R. A. *David, the Chosen King*, translated by Eric J. Sharpe and Stanley Rudman. Stockholm: Almqvist & Wiksell, 1964.
Cartledge, Tony W. *1 & 2 Samuel*. Smyth & Helwys Bible Commentary. Macon, GA: Smyth & Helwys, 2001.
Chapman, Stephen B. *1 Samuel as Christian Scripture: A Theological Commentary*. Grand Rapids: Eerdmans, 2016.
Chapman, Stephen B. "Martial Memory, Peaceable Vision: Divine War in the Old Testament." In *Holy War in the Bible: Christian Morality and an Old Testament Problem*, edited by Heath A. Thomas, Jeremy Evans, and Paul Copan, 47–67. Downers Grove: InterVarsity, 2013.
Chatman, Seymour. *Story and Discourse: Narrative Structure in Fiction and Film*. Ithaca: Cornell University Press, 1978.
Childs, Brevard S. *Introduction to the Old Testament as Scripture*. Philadelphia: Fortress, 1979.
Childs, Brevard S. "Psalm Titles and Midrashic Exegesis." *JSS* 16 (1971): 137–50.
Chun, S. Min. *Ethics and Biblical Narrative: A Literary and Discourse-Analytical Approach to the Story of Josiah*. Oxford Theology and Religion Monographs. Oxford: Oxford University Press, 2014.
Clines, David J. A. "Michal Observed: An Introduction." In *Telling Queen Michal's Story: An Experiment in Comparative Interpretation*, edited by David J. A. Clines and Tamara C. Eskenazi, 24–63. Sheffield: Sheffield Academic, 1991.
Clines, David J. A. *On the Way to the Postmodern: Old Testament Essays 1967–1998, Vol. 1*. JSOTSup 292. Sheffield: Sheffield Academic, 1998.
Clines, David J. A. "X, X ben Y: Personal Names in Hebrew Narrative Style." *VT* 22 (1972): 266–87.
Clines, David J. A. and T. C. Eskenazi, eds. *Telling Queen Michal's Story: An Experiment in Comparative Interpretation*. Sheffield: Sheffield Academic, 1991.
Conroy, Charles. *1–2 Samuel, 1–2 Kings: With an Excursus on Davidic Dynasty and Holy City Zion*. Wilmington: Michael Glazier, 1983.
Conroy, Charles. *Absalom, Absalom! Narrative and Language in 2 Sam 13–20*. Rome: Biblical Institute Press, 1978.
Conway, Colleen M. "Speaking through Ambiguity: Minor Characters in the Fourth Gospel." *BibInt* 10, no. 3 (2002): 324–41.

Copan, Paul and Matthew Flannagan. *Did God Really Command Genocide? Coming to Terms with the Justice of God.* Grand Rapids: Baker Books, 2014.
Curtis, E. L. and A. A. Madsen. *The Books of Chronicles.* ICC. Edinburgh: T. & T. Clark, 1910.
Czövek, Tamás. *Three Seasons of Charismatic Leadership: A Literary-Critical and Theological Interpretation of the Narrative of Saul, David and Solomon.* Regnum Studies in Mission. Milton Keynes: Paternoster, 2006.
Davies, E. A. *The Dissenting Reader, Feminist Approaches to the Hebrew Bible.* Burlington: Ashgate, 2003.
Davies, Philip R. *In Search of "Ancient Israel": A Study in Biblical Origins.* Sheffield: Sheffield Academic, 1992.
Day, John. *Psalms.* Old Testament Guides. Sheffield: JSOT Press, 1992.
De Temmerman, Koen. "Ancient Rhetoric as a Hermeneutical Tool for the Analysis of Characterization in Narrative Literature." *Rhetorica* 28 (2010): 23–51.
De Vaux, Roland. *Ancient Israel: Its Life and Institutions*, translated by J. McHugh. London: Darton, Longman & Todd, 1961.
Deem, A. "'Cupboard Love': The Story of Amnon and Tamar." *Hasifrut/Literature* 28 (1979): 100–107 (Hebrew).
DeRouchie, Jason S. "The Heart of Yhwh and His Chosen One in 1 Samuel 13:14." *BBR* 24, no. 4 (2014): 467–89.
Dicken, Frank and Julia Snyder. *Characters and Characterization in Luke-Acts.* LNTS 548. New York: T&T Clark, 2016.
Dietrich, Walter. *The Early Monarchy in Israel: The Tenth Century B.C.E.*, translated by Joachim Vette. BibEncycl 3. Atlanta: SBL, 2007.
Dietrich, Walter. "Die Erzählung von David und Goliath in 1 Sam 17." *ZAW* 108 (1996): 180–94.
Dietrich, Walter. *Samuel.* BKAT VIII/1–4. Neukirchen-Vluyn: Neukirchener Verlag, 2003–2007.
Dillard, R. B. *2 Chronicles.* WBC 15. Dallas: Word, 1987.
Docherty, Thomas. *Reading (Absent) Character: Towards a Theory of Characterization in Fiction.* Oxford: Clarendon, 1983.
Donald, David Herbert. *Lincoln.* New York: Simon & Schuster, 1996.
Driver, S. R. *Notes on the Hebrew Text and the Topography of the Books of Samuel.* 2nd ed. Oxford: Clarendon, 1913.
Eco, Umberto. *The Open Work.* Cambridge, MA: Harvard University Press, 1989.
Edelman, Diana V. *King Saul in the Historiography of Judah.* JSOTSup 121. Sheffield: Sheffield Academic, 1991.
Edelman, Diana V. "Ner." *ABD* 4:1073–4.
Eilat, M. *Samuel and the Foundation of Kingship in Ancient Israel.* Jerusalem: Magnes, 1997 (Hebrew).
Elwood, Maren. *Characters Make Your Story.* Boston: The Writer, 1966.
Emmott, Catherin and Marc Alexander. "Schemata." In *The Living Handbook of Narratology*, edited by Peter Hühn et al. Hamburg: Interdisciplinary Center for Narratology, Hamburg University Press. http://www.lhn.uni-hamburg.de/article/schemata. Online article revised 22 September 2014.
Eschelbach, Michael A. *Has Joab Foiled David? A Literary Study of the Importance of Joab's Character in Relation to David.* Studies in Biblical Literature 76. New York: Peter Lang, 2005.

Esler, Philip F. *Babatha's Orchard: The Yadin Papyri and An Ancient Jewish Family Tale Retold.* Oxford: Oxford University Press, 2017.
Esler, Philip F. *Sex, Wives, and Warriors: Reading Old Testament Narrative with Its Ancient Audience.* Eugene: Cascade, 2011.
Eslinger, Lyle. "A Change of Heart: 1 Samuel 16." In *Ascribe to the Lord: Biblical and Other Studies in Memory of Peter C. Craigie*, edited by Lyle M. Eslinger and J. Glen Taylor, 341–61. Sheffield: JSOT Press, 1988.
Eslinger, Lyle. *House of God or House of David: The Rhetoric of 2 Samuel 7.* JSOTSup 164. Sheffield: Sheffield Academic, 1994.
Eslinger, Lyle. "Viewpoints and Point of View in 1 Samuel 8–12." *JSOT* 26 (1983): 61–76.
Evans, Mary J. *1 and 2 Samuel.* NIC. Peabody: Hendrickson, 2000.
Evans, Paul S. *1–2 Samuel.* SOG. Grand Rapids: Zondervan, 2018.
Even, Josef. *Character in Narrative.* Tel Aviv: Hapoalim, 1993 (Hebrew).
Exum, J. Cheryl. "Michal: The Whole Story." In *Fragmented Women: Feminist (Sub)versions of Biblical Narratives*, 42–60. Sheffield: A. & C. Black, 1993.
Exum, J. Cheryl. *Tragedy and Biblical Narrative: Arrows of the Almighty.* Cambridge: Cambridge University Press, 1992.
Fensham, F. C. "Battle between the Men of Joab and Abner as a Possible Ordeal by Battle." *VT* 20 (1970): 356–7.
Fidler, Ruth. "A Wife's Vow—the Husband's Woe? The Case of Hannah and Elkanah." *ZAW* 118 (2006): 374–88.
Finkelstein, I. "A Great United Monarchy? Archaeological and Historical Perspectives." In *One God—One Cult—One Nation*, edited by R. G. Kratz and H. Spieckermann, 3–28. BZAW 405. Berlin: de Gruyter, 2010.
Finkelstein, I. and N. A. Silberman. *David and Solomon: In Search of the Bible's Sacred Kings and the Roots of the Western Tradition.* New York: Free Press, 2006.
Firth, David G. *1 & 2 Samuel.* AOTC. Downers Grove: InterVarsity, 2009.
Firth, David G. *1 & 2 Samuel: A Kingdom Comes.* London: T&T Clark, 2017.
Firth, David G. "David and Uriah with an Occasional Appearance by Uriah's Wife: Reading and Re-Reading 2 Samuel 11." *OTE* 21, no. 2 (2008): 210–28.
Firth, David G. "Shining the Lamp: The Rhetoric of 2 Samuel 5–24." *TynBul* 52 (2001): 203–24.
Fischer, Alexander A. *Von Hebron nach Jerusalem: Eine redaktionsgeschichtliche Studie zur Erzählung von König David in II Sam 1–5.* BZAW 335. Berlin: de Gruyter, 2004.
Flanagan, James W. "Chiefs in Israel." *JSOT* 20 (1981): 47–73.
Fleming, Erin E. "Political Favoritism in Saul's Court: חפץ, נעם, and the Relationship between David and Jonathan." *JBL* 135 (2016): 19–34.
Fokkelman, J. P. *The Crossing Fates.* Vol. 2 of *Narrative Art and Poetry in the Books of Samuel.* Studia Semitica Neerlandica. Assen: van Gorcum, 1986.
Fokkelman, J. P. *King David.* Vol. 1 of *Narrative Art and Poetry in the Books of Samuel.* Studia Semitica Neerlandica. Assen: van Gorcum, 1981.
Fokkelman, J. P. *Major Poems of the Hebrew Bible.* 4 vols. Studia Semitica Neerlandica. Assen: van Gorcum, 1981–96.
Fokkelman, J. P. *Reading Biblical Narrative: An Introductory Guide.* Louisville: Westminster John Knox, 1999.
Fokkelman, J. P. "The Samuel Composition as a Book of Life and Death: Structural, Generic and Numerical Forms of Perfection." In *For and Against David: Story and History in the Books of Samuel*, edited by A. G. Auld and E. Eynikel, 15–46. BETL 232. Leuven: Peeters, 2010.

Fokkelman, J. P. "Structural Reading on the Fracture between Synchrony and Diachrony." *JEOL* 30 (1987–88): 123–36.

Fokkelman, J. P. *Throne and City*. Vol. 3 of *Narrative Art and Poetry in the Books of Samuel*. Studia Semitica Neerlandica. Assen: van Gorcum, 1990.

Fokkelman, J. P. *Vow and Desire*. Vol. 4 of *Narrative Art and Poetry in the Books of Samuel*. Studia Semitica Neerlandica. Assen: van Gorcum, 1993.

Forster, E. M. *Aspects of the Novel*. London: Edwin Arnold, 1949.

Frolov, Serge. "Succession Narrative: A Document or a Phantom?" *JBL* 121 (2002): 81–124.

Frolov, Serge. "Bedan: A Riddle in Context," *JBL* 126 (2007): 164–7.

Frolov, Serge. *The Turn of the Cycle: 1 Samuel 1–8 in Synchronic and Diachronic Perspectives*. BZAW 342. Berlin: de Gruyter, 2004.

Frontain, Raymond-Jean and Jan Wojcik, "Introduction: Transformations of the Myth of David." In *The David Myth in Western Literature*, edited by Raymond-Jean Frontain and Jan Wojcik, 1–10. West Lafayette: Purdue University Press, 1980.

Frontain, Raymond-Jean and Jan Wojcik, eds. *The David Myth in Western Literature*. West Lafayette: Purdue University Press, 1980.

Frymer-Kensky, T. *Reading the Women of the Bible*. New York: Schocken, 2002.

Garsiel, Moshe. *Biblical Names: A Literary Study of Midrashic Derivations and Puns*, translated by P. Hackett. Ramat Gan: Bar-Ilan University Press, 1991.

Garsiel, Moshe. *The First Book of Samuel: A Literary Study of Comparative Structures, Analogies and Parallels*. Ramat-Gan, Israel: Revivim, 1985.

Garsiel, Moshe. "The Relationship between David and Michal, Daughter of King Saul." *Studies in Bible and Exegesis* 10 (2011): 117–33 (Hebrew).

Gerke, Jeff. *Plot Versus Character*. Cincinnati: Writer's Digest Books, 2010.

Gnuse, Robert Karl. *The Dream Theophany of Samuel: Its Structure in Relation to Ancient Near Eastern Dreams and its Theological Significance*. Lanham: University Press of America, 1984.

Goldingay, John. *1 and 2 Samuel for Everyone*. Louisville: Westminster John Knox, 2011.

Goldingay, John. *Biblical Theology: The God of the Christian Scriptures*. Downers Grove: InterVarsity, 2016.

Goldingay, John. *Psalms*. Vol. 2, *Psalms 42–89*. BCOTWP. Grand Rapids: Baker, 2007.

Golub, M. "The Distribution of Personal Names in the Land of Israel and Transjordan during the Iron II Period." *JAOS* 134 (2014): 621–42.

Good, Edwin M. *Irony in the Old Testament*. Philadelphia: Westminster, 1965.

Gordon, Robert. *1 & 2 Samuel: A Commentary*. Exeter: Paternoster, 1986.

Goslinga, C. J. *Het tweede boek Samuel*. Commentaar op het Oude Testament. Kampen: Kok, 1962.

Green, Barbara. *David's Capacity for Compassion: A Literary-Hermeneutical Study of 1–2 Samuel*. London: Bloomsbury T&T Clark, 2017.

Green, Barbara. "Enacting Imaginatively the Unthinkable: 1 Samuel 25 and the Story of Saul." *BibInt* 11 (2003): 1–23.

Green, Barbara. *How Are the Mighty Fallen? A Dialogical Study of King Saul in 1 Samuel*. JSOTSup 365. Sheffield: Sheffield Academic, 2003.

Greenspahn, Frederik E. *When Brothers Dwell Together: The Preeminence of Younger Siblings in the Hebrew Bible*. Oxford: Oxford University Press, 1994.

Grossman, Jonathan. "The Design of the 'Dual Causality' Principle in the Narrative of Absalom's Rebellion." *Bib* 88 (2007): 558–66.

Grossman, Jonathan. *Text and Subtext: On Exploring Biblical Narrative Design*. Tel Aviv: Tvunot, 2015 (Hebrew).

Gunn, David M. *The Fate of King Saul: An Interpretation of a Biblical Story*. JSOTSup 14. Sheffield: JSOT Press, 1980.

Gunn, David M. "Right Reading: Reliable and Omniscient Narrator, Omniscient God, and Foolproof Composition in the Hebrew Bible." In *The Bible in Three Dimensions: Essays in Celebration of Forty Years of Biblical Studies in the University of Sheffield*, edited by David J. A. Clines, Stephen E. Fowl, and Stanley E. Porter, 53–64. JSOTSup 87. Sheffield: Sheffield Academic, 1990.

Gunn, David M. *The Story of King David: Genre and Interpretation*. JSOTSup 6. Sheffield: JSOT Press, 1978.

Gunn, David M. and Danna Nolan Fewell. *Narrative Art in the Hebrew Bible*. The Oxford Bible Series. Oxford: Oxford University Press, 1993.

Hackett, Jo Ann. "1 and 2 Samuel." In *The Women's Bible Commentary*, edited by C. A. Newsom, S. H. Ringe, and J. E. Lapsley, 95. Louisville: Westminster John Knox, 1998.

Halpern, Baruch. *David's Secret Demons: Messiah, Murderer, Traitor, King*. Grand Rapids: Eerdmans, 2003.

Handy, Lowell. K. "The Characters of Heirs Apparent in the Book of Samuel." *BR* 38 (1993): 5–22.

Harding, James E. *The Love of David and Jonathan: Ideology, Text, and Reception*. Sheffield: Equinox, 2013.

Hardy, Donald. *Narrating Knowledge in Flannery O'Connor's Fiction*. Columbia: University of South Carolina Press, 2003.

Haupt, Paul. "Heb. *mardût*, Chastisement and Chastity." *JBL* 39 (1920): 156–8.

Hawkins, Ralph K. "The First Glimpse of Saul and His Subsequent Transformation." *BBR* 22 (2012): 353–62.

Heard, R. Christopher. "Penitent to a Fault: The Characterization of David in Psalm 51." In *The Fate of King David: The Past and Present of a Biblical Icon*, edited by Tod Linafelt, Claudia V. Camp, and Timothy Beal, 163–74. LHBOTS 500. London: T&T Clark, 2010.

Henry, Caleb. "Joab: A Biblical Critique of Machiavellian Tactics." *Westminster Theological Journal* 69 (2007): 327–43.

Herman, David. "Cognitive Narratology." In *The Living Handbook of Narratology*, edited by Peter Hühn et al. Hamburg: Interdisciplinary Center for Narratology, Hamburg University Press, http://www.lhn.uni-hamburg.de/article/cognitive-narratology-revised-version-uploaded-22-september-2013. Online article revised 22 September 2013.

Herman, David. *Storytelling and the Sciences of the Mind*. Cambridge, MA: MIT, 2013.

Herndon, William H. and Jesse W. Weik. *Herndon's Lincoln: The True Story of a Great Life*. Chicago: Belford, Clarke, & Co., 1889.

Hertzberg, Hans Wilhelm. *I & II Samuel: A Commentary*. Philadelphia: Westminster, 1964.

Hildebrandt, Samuel. "The Servants of Saul: 'Minor' Characters and Royal Commentary in 1 Samuel 9–31." *JSOT* 40 (2015): 179–200.

Heschel, Abraham. *The Prophets*. Perennial Classics. New York: Harper & Row, 1962, 2001.

Hoskisson, Paul Y. and Grant M. Boswell. "Neo-Assyrian Rhetoric: The Example of the Third Campaign of Sennacherib (704–681 BC)." In *Rhetoric before and beyond the Greeks*, edited by C. S. Lipson and R. A. Binkley, 65–78. Albany: SUNY Press, 2004.

Hugo, Philippe and Adrian Schenker, eds. *Archaeology of the Books of Samuel: The Entangling of the Textual and Literary History*. Leiden: Brill, 2010.

Humphreys, W. Lee. "The Tragedy of King Saul: A Study of the Structure of 1 Samuel 9–31." *JSOT* 6 (1978): 18–27.

Hutton, Jeremy M. *The Transjordanian Palimpsest: The Overwritten Texts of Personal Exile and Transformation in the Deuteronomistic History*. BZAW 396. Berlin: de Gruyter, 2009.

Iser, Wolfgang. *The Act of Reading: A Theory of Aesthetic Response*. Baltimore: Johns Hopkins University Press, 1978.

Jacobsen, Thorkild. *Toward the Image of Tammuz*. Cambridge, MA: Harvard University Press, 1970.

Janzen, J. Gerald. "Prayer and/as Self-Address: The Case of Hannah." In *A God So Near: Essays on Old Testament Theology in Honor of Patrick D. Miller*, edited by Brent A. Strawn and Nancy R. Bowen, 113–27. Winona Lake: Eisenbrauns, 2003.

Japhet, Sara. *1 and 2 Chronicles: A Commentary*. OTL. Louisville: Westminster John Knox, 1993.

Japhet, Sara. "The Historical Reliability of Chronicles—The History of the Problem and Its Place in Biblical Research." *JSOT* 33 (1985): 83–107.

Jarick, John. *1 Chronicles*. Readings. London: Sheffield Academic, 2002.

Jepsen, A. "*ḥāzâ*." *TDOT* 4:280–90.

Jero, Christopher. "Mother-Child Narratives and the Kingdom of God: Authorial Use of Typology as an Interpretive Device in Samuel–Kings." *BBR* 25, no. 2 (2015): 155–69.

Jobling, David. *1 Samuel*. Berit Olam. Collegeville: Liturgical Press, 1998.

Jobling, David. "Jonathan: A Structural Study in 1 Samuel." *Society of Biblical Literature: Seminar Papers* 10 (1976): 15–32.

Jobling, David. *The Sense of Biblical Narrative I: Structural Analyses in the Hebrew Bible*. JSOTSup 7. Sheffield: JSOT Press, 1986.

Johnson, Benjamin J. M. "Characterizing Chiastic Contradiction: Literary Structure, Divine Repentance, and Dialogical Biblical Theology in 1 Samuel 15:10–35." In *Theology of the Hebrew Bible*. Vol. 1, *Methodological Studies*, edited by Marvin A. Sweeney, 185–211. Atlanta: SBL, 2019.

Johnson, Benjamin J. M. *David: A Man after God's Own Heart*. Cascade Companions. Eugene: Cascade, forthcoming.

Johnson, Benjamin J. M. "David Then and Now: Double-Voiced Discourse in 1 Samuel 16:14-23." *JSOT* 38, no. 2 (2013): 201–15.

Johnson, Benjamin J. M. "The Heart of YHWH's Chosen One in 1 Samuel." *JBL* 131, no. 3 (2012): 455–66.

Johnson, Benjamin J. M. *Reading David and Goliath in Greek and Hebrew: A Literary Approach*. FAT 2. Tübingen: Mohr Siebeck, 2015.

Johnson, Benjamin J. M. "Israel at the Time of the United Monarchy: David and Solomon." In *The Biblical World*, edited by Katharine Dell. Oxford: Routledge, forthcoming.

Johnson, Vivian L. *David in Distress: His Portrait through the Historical Psalms*. LHBOTS 505. New York: T&T Clark, 2009.

Jones, Gwilym H. *The Nathan Narratives*. JSOTSup 80; Sheffield: Sheffield Academic, 1990.

Joseph, Alison L. *Portrait of the Kings: The Davidic Prototype in Deuteronomistic Poetics*. Minneapolis: Fortress, 2015.

Kawashima, Robert S. *Biblical Narrative and the Death of the Rhapsode*. Bloomington: Indiana University Press, 2004.

Kawashima, Robert S. "Biblical Narrative and the Birth of Prose Literature." In *The Oxford Handbook of Biblical Narrative*, edited by Danna Nolan Fewell, 51–60. Oxford: Oxford University Press, 2016.
Keil, C. F. and K. Delitzsch. *Biblical Commentary on the Books of Samuel*. Edinburgh: T. & T. Clark, 1876.
Keren, Orly. "David and Jonathan: A Case of Unconditional Love?" *JSOT* 37, no. 1 (2012): 3–23.
Keren, Orly. "Saul's Son Jonathan: Light and Dark in His Character." *Beit Mikra* 53 (2008): 124–44 (Hebrew).
Keys, Gillian. *The Wages of Sin: A Reappraisal of the "Succession Narrative."* JSOTSup 232. Sheffield: Sheffield Academic, 1996.
Kipfer, Sara. *Der bedrohte David: Eine exegetische und rezeptionsgeschichtliche Studie zu 1Sam 16 – 1 Kön 2*. SBR. Berlin: de Gruyter, 2015.
Klein, Ralph W. *1 Chronicles*. Hermeneia. Minneapolis: Fortress, 2006.
Klein, Ralph W. *1 Samuel*. WBC 10. Waco: Word, 1983.
Klein, Ralph W. *2 Chronicles: A Commentary*. Hermeneia. Minneapolis: Fortress, 2012.
Klein, Ralph W. "David: Sinner and Saint in Samuel and Chronicles." *CTM* 31, no. 4 (2004): 274–81.
Klement, Herbert H. *II Samuel 21–24: Context, Structure and Meaning in the Samuel Conclusion*. European University Studies Series. New York: Peter Lang, 2000.
Knapp, Andrew. *Royal Apologetic in the Ancient Near East*. Writings From the Ancient World. Atlanta: SBL, 2015.
Knoppers, Gary N. "Images of David in Early Judaism: David as Repentant Sinner in Chronicles." *Bib* 76 (1995): 449–70.
Knoppers, Gary N. *1 Chronicles 1–9*. AB 12. New York: Doubleday, 2003.
Kochman, M., "II Chronicles Chapters 10–27." In *The Book of II Chronicles*, edited by B. Oded, 72–212. Tel Aviv: Davidzon-Itai, 1995 (Hebrew).
Kugel, James. "On the Bible and Literary Criticism." *Prooftexts* 1, no. 3 (1981): 217–36.
Landy, Francis. "David and Ittai." In *The Fate of King David: The Past and Present of a Biblical Icon*, edited by Tod Linafelt, Timothy Beal and Claudia V. Camp, 20–3. LHBOTS 500. London: T&T Clark, 2010.
Lapsley, Jacqueline E. "Feeling Our Way: Love for God in Deuteronomy." *CBQ* 65 (2003): 350–69.
Lawton, R. B. "Saul, Jonathan and the 'Son of Jesse'." *JSOT* 58 (1993): 35–46.
Leithart, Peter J. "Nabal and His Wine." *JBL* 120 (2001): 525–7.
Lemche, Niels Peter. "David's Rise." *JSOT* 10 (1979): 2–25.
Levenson, Jon D. "1 Samuel 25 as Literature and as History." *CBQ* 40, no. 1 (1978): 11–28.
Levenson, Jon D. and Baruch Halpern. "The Political Import of David's Marriages." *JBL* 99 (1980): 507–51.
Levinson, Bernard M. "Deuteronomy: Introduction and Annotations." *The Jewish Study Bible*, edited by A. Berlin and M. Z. Brettler, 339–428. New York: Oxford University Press, 2014.
Linafelt, Tod, Timothy K. Beal, and Claudia V. Camp, eds. *The Fate of King David: The Past and Present of a Biblical Icon*. LHBOTS 500. London: T&T Clark, 2010.
Lind, Millard C. *Yahweh Is a Warrior: The Theology of Warfare in Ancient Israel*. Scottdale: Herald, 1980.

Long, D. Stephen. "God Is Not Nice." In *God Is Not...Religious, Nice, "One of Us," an American, a Capitalist*, edited by D. Brent Laytham, 39–54. Grand Rapids: Brazos, 2004.
Long, V. Philips. *The Reign and Rejection of King Saul: A Case for Literary and Theological Coherence*. SBLDS 118. Atlanta: Scholars Press, 1989.
Löwenclau, Ilse von. "Der Prophet Nathan im Zwielicht von theologischer Deutung und Historie." In *Werden und Wirken des Alten Testaments: FS Westermann*, edited by Rainer Albertz et al., 202–15. Göttingen: Vandenhoeck & Ruprecht, 1980.
Lowenstamm, Samuel E. "Baana." In *Encyclopaedia Biblica, Vol. 2*, 301–2. Jerusalem: Bialik Institute, 1981 (Hebrew).
Lyke, Larry L. *King David with the Wise Woman of Tekoa: The Resonance of Tradition in Parabolic Narrative*. Sheffield: JSOT Press, 1997.
Mabee, Charles. "David's Judicial Exoneration." *ZAW* 92 (1980): 89–107.
Maccini, Robert G. *Her Testimony Is True: Women as Witnesses According to John*. JSNTSup 125. Sheffield Academic, 1996.
Malamat, A. "King Lists of the Old Babylonian Period and Biblical Genealogies." *JAOS* 88 (1968): 163–73.
Malina, Bruce J. *The New Testament World: Insights from Cultural Anthropology. Third Edition Revised and Expanded*. Louisville: Westminster John Knox, 2001.
Marböck, J. "*nāḇāl*." *TDOT* 9:158–71.
Mauchline, John. *1 and 2 Samuel*. NCBC. London: Oliphants, 1971.
Mays, James Luther. "The David of the Psalms." *Int* 40 (1986): 143–55.
McCann, J. Clinton, Jr. "The Book of Psalms: Introduction, Commentary, and Reflections." In vol. 4 of *The New Interpreter's Bible*, 639–1280. Nashville, TN: Abingdon, 1996.
McCarter, P. Kyle, Jr. *1 Samuel*. AB 8. Garden City: Doubleday, 1980.
McCarter, P. Kyle, Jr. *2 Samuel*. AB 9. Garden City: Doubleday, 1984.
McCarter, P. Kyle, Jr. "The Apology of David." *JBL* 99, no. 4 (1980): 489–504.
McCarter, P. Kyle, Jr. "The Historical David." *Int* 40, no. 2 (1986): 117–29.
McKane, W. *I & II Samuel: The Way to the Throne*. London: SCM, 1963.
McKenzie, Steven L. *1–2 Chronicles*. AOTC. Nashville: Abingdon, 2004.
McKenzie, Steven L. *King David: A Biography*. New York: Oxford University Press, 2000.
McKenzie, Steven L. "Saul in the Deuteronomistic History." In *Saul in Story and Tradition*, edited by Carl S. Ehrlich and M. C. White, 59–70. FAT 47. Tübingen: Mohr, 2006.
Meyers, Carol. "The Hannah Narrative in Feminist Perspective." In *"Go to the Land I Will Show You": Studies in Honor of Dwight W. Young*, edited by Joseph E. Coleson and Victor H. Matthews, 117–26. Winona Lake: Eisenbrauns, 1996.
Meyers, Carol. *Rediscovering Eve: Ancient Israelite Women in Context*. Oxford: Oxford University Press.
Middleton, J. Richard. "The Battle Belongs to the Word: The Role of Theological Discourse in David's Victory over Saul and Goliath in 1 Samuel 17." In *The Hermeneutics of Charity: Interpretation, Selfhood, and Postmodern Faith*, edited by James K. A. Smith and Henry Isaac Venema, 109–31. Grand Rapids: Brazos, 2004.
Middleton, J. Richard. "God's Loyal Opposition: Psalmic and Prophetic Protest as a Paradigm for Faithfulness in the Hebrew Bible." *Canadian-American Theological Review* 5, no. 1 (2016): 51–65.
Middleton, J. Richard. *The Liberating Image: The* Imago Dei *in Genesis 1*. Grand Rapids: Brazos, 2005.

Middleton, J. Richard. "A Psalm against David? A Canonical Reading of Psalm 51 as a Critique of David's Inadequate Repentance in 2 Samuel 12." In *Explorations in Interdisciplinary Reading: Theological, Exegetical, and Reception-Historical Perspectives*, edited by Robbie Castleman, Darian Lockett, and Stephen Presley, 26–45. Eugene: Pickwick, 2017.

Middleton, J. Richard. "Samuel Agonistes: A Conflicted Prophet's Resistance to God and Contribution to the Failure of Israel's First King." In *Prophets, Prophecy, and Ancient Israelite Historiography*, edited by Mark J. Boda and Lissa M. Wray Beal, 69–91. Winona Lake: Eisenbrauns, 2013.

Miller, Patrick D. *The Way of the Lord: Essays in Old Testament Theology*. Grand Rapids: Eerdmans, 2007.

Miscall, Peter D. *1 Samuel: A Literary Reading*. Indiana Studies in Biblical Literature; Bloomington: Indiana University Press, 1986.

Moberly, R. W. L. "To Hear the Master's Voice: Revelation and Spiritual Discernment in the Call of Samuel." *SJT* 48, no. 4 (1995): 443–68.

Mobley, Gregory. "Glimpses of the Heroic Saul." In *Saul in Story and Tradition*, edited by Carl S. Ehrlich and M. C. White, 80–7. FAT 47. Tübingen: Mohr, 2006.

Moore, Stephen D. "Biblical Narrative Analysis from the New Criticism to the New Narratology." In *The Oxford Handbook of Biblical Narrative*, edited by Danna Nolan Fewell, 27–50. Oxford: Oxford University Press, 2016.

Moran, William L. "The Ancient Near Eastern Background of the Love of God in Deuteronomy." *CBQ* 25, no. 1 (1963): 77–87.

Morgan, Robert with John Barton. *Biblical Interpretation*. Oxford Bible Series. Oxford: Oxford University Press, 1988.

Morrison, Craig E. *2 Samuel*. Berit Olam. Collegeville: Liturgical Press, 2013.

Murphy, Francesca Aran. *1 Samuel*. BTCB. Grand Rapids: Brazos, 2010.

Myers, Alicia D. "The Ambiguous Character of Johannine Characterization: An Overview of Recent Contributions and a Proposal." *Perspectives in Religious Studies* 39, no. 3 (2012): 289–98.

Na'aman, Nadav. "Game of Thrones: Solomon's 'Succession Narrative' and Esarhaddon's Accession to the Throne." *Tel Aviv* 45 (2018): 89–113.

Na'aman, Nadav. "The Kingdom of Geshur in History and Memory." *SJOT* 26 (2012): 88–101.

Na'aman, Nadav. "The Kingdom of Ishbaal." *BN* 54 (1990): 33–7.

Nelson, Richard D. "*Ḥērem* and the Deuteronomic Social Conscience." In *Deuteronomy and Deuteronomic Literature*, edited by M. Vervenne and J. Lust, 36–54. BETL 133. Leuven: Leuven University Press, 1997.

Newkirk, Matthew. *Just Deceivers: An Exploration of the Motif of Deception in the Books of Samuel*. Eugene: Pickwick, 2015.

Newkirk, Matthew. "Reconsidering the Role of Deception in Solomon's Ascent to the Throne." *JETS* 57, no. 4 (2014): 703–13.

Newman, John Henry. *Parochial and Plain Sermons*. San Francisco: Ignatius, 1997.

Nichol, George. "The Wisdom of Joab and the Wise Woman of Tekoa." *Studia Theologica* 36 (1982): 97–104.

Nigosian, Solomon. *Magic and Divination in the Old Testament*. Brighton: Sussex Academic, 2008.

Noegel, Scott B. "The Shame of Ba'al: The Mnemonics of Odium." *JNSL* 41 (2015): 69–94.

Noll, K. L. *The Faces of David*. Sheffield: Sheffield Academic, 1997.

Noll, K. L. "Is There a Text in This Tradition? Readers' Response and the Taming of Samuel's God." *JSOT* 83 (1999): 31–51.
Oatley, Keith. "On Truth and Fiction." In *Cognitive Literary Science: Dialogues Between Literature and Cognition*, edited by Michael Burke and Emily T. Troscianko, 259–78. Cognition and Poetics. New York: Oxford University Press, 2016.
Olyan, Saul M. "Some Neglected Aspects of Israelite Interment Ideology." *JBL* 124 (2005): 601–6.
Oswald, Wolfgang. *Nathan der Prophet: Ein Untersuchung zu 2 Samuel 7 und 12 und 1 Könige 1*. AThANT 94. Zurich: Theologischer Verlag, 2008.
Person, Raymond F. Jr. *The Deuteronomistic History and the Book of Chronicles: Scribal Works in an Oral World*. AIL 6. Atlanta: SBL, 2010.
Peterson, Brian Neil. *The Authors of the Deuteronomistic History: Locating a Tradition in Ancient Israel*. Minneapolis: Fortress, 2014.
Pettie, George. *A petite pallace of Pettie his pleasure contaynyng many pretie hystories by him set foorth in comely colours, and most delightfully discoursed*. R. Watkins, 1576.
Polzin, Robert. *David and the Deuteronomist: A Literary Study of the Deuteronomic History: Part 3: 2 Samuel*. Bloomington: Indiana University Press, 1993.
Polzin, Robert. *Samuel and the Deuteronomist: A Literary Study of the Deuteronomistic History*. Part 2: *1 Samuel*. Bloomington: Indiana University Press, 1993.
Pritchard, James B. *Ancient Near Eastern Texts Relating to the Old Testament*. Princeton: Princeton University Press, 1969.
Prouser, Ora Horn. "Suited to the Throne: The Symbolic Use of Clothing in the David and Saul Narratives." *JSOT* 71 (1996): 27–37.
Provan, Iain, V. Philips Long, and Tremper Longman III. *A Biblical History of Israel*. Louisville: Westminster John Knox, 2015.
Pyper, Hugh. *David As Reader: 2 Samuel 12:1–15 and the Poetics of Fatherhood*. Leiden: Brill, 1996.
Rad, Gerhard von. *Holy War in Ancient Israel*, translated and edited by Marva J. Dawn. Grand Rapids: Eerdmans, 1991.
Ramsey, George W. "Speech-Forms in Hebrew Law and Prophetic Oracles." *JBL* 96 (1977): 45–58.
Redfield, James Adam. "Behind Auerbach's 'Background': Five Ways to Read What Biblical Narratives Don't Say." *AJSR* 39, no. 1 (2015): 121–50.
Reimer, David J. "An Overlooked Term in Old Testament Theology—Perhaps." In *Covenant in Context: Essays in Honour of E. W. Nicholson*, edited by A. D. H. Mayes and R. B. Salters, 325–46. Oxford: Oxford University Press, 2003.
Rendsburg, Gary A. "'Confused Language as a Deliberate Literary Device in Biblical Hebrew Narrative" *JHS* 2 (1999).
Rendtorff, Rolf. "The Psalms of David: David in the Psalms." In *The Book of Psalms: Composition and Reception*, edited by Peter W. Flint and Patrick D. Miller, Jr., with the assistance of Aaron Brunell and Ryan Roberts, 53–64. Leiden: Brill, 2005.
Ridout, G. "The Rape of Tamar: A Rhetorical Analysis of 2 Sm 13:1-22." In *Rhetorical Criticism: Essays in Honor of James Muilenburg*, edited by J. J. Jackson and M. Kessler, 75–84. Pittsburgh: Pickwick, 1974.
Rimmon-Kenan, Shlomit. *The Concept of Ambiguity—the Example of James*. Chicago: University of Chicago Press, 1977.
Rost, Leonhard. *The Succession to the Throne of David*. Sheffield: Almond, 1982. German original, 1926.

Rowe, C. Kavin. *Early Narrative Christology: The Lord in the Gospel of Luke.* Grand Rapids: Baker Academic, 2006.

Rowe, Jonathan Y. *Sons or Lovers: An Interpretation of David and Jonathan's Friendship.* LHBOTS 533. New York: Bloomsbury T&T Clark, 2012.

Ryan, Marie-Laure. "Space." In *The Living Handbook of Narratology*, edited by Peter Hühn et al. Hamburg: Interdisciplinary Center for Narratology, Hamburg University Press, http://www.lhn.uni-hamburg.de/article/space. Online article revised 22 April 2014.

Schipper, Jeremy. *Disability Studies and the Hebrew Bible: Figuring Mephibosheth in the David Story.* LHBOTS 441. New York: T&T Clark, 2006.

Scurlock, Jo Ann. "Death and the Afterlife in Ancient Mesopotamian Thought." In *Civilizations of the Ancient Near East.* New York: Charles Scribner's Sons, 1995. 1883–93.

Seeman, D. "The Wacher at the Window: Cultural Poetics of a Biblical Motif." *Prooftexts* 24 (2004): 1–50.

Segal, M. Z. *The Books of Samuel.* Jerusalem: Qirayat Sepher, 1956 (Hebrew).

Seibert, Eric. *Disturbing Divine Behavior: Troubling Old Testament Images of God.* Minneapolis: Fortress, 2009.

Sergi, O. "The Composition of Nathan's Oracle to David (2 Samuel 7:1–17) as a Reflection of Royal Judahite Ideology." *JBL* 129, no. 2 (2010): 261–79.

Sergi, O. "The United Monarchy and the Kingdom of Jeroboam II in the Story of Absalom and Sheba's Revolts (2 Samuel 15–20)." In *Hebrew Bible and Ancient Israel*, Vol. 6, *Jeroboam*, 329–53. Mohr Siebeck: Tübingen, 2017.

Sergi, O. and A. Kleiman. "The Kingdom of Geshur and the Expansion of Aram-Damascus into the Northern Jordan Valley: Archaeological and Historical Perspectives." *BASOR* 379 (2018): 1–18.

Short, J. Randall. *The Surprising Election and Confirmation of King David.* HTS 63. Cambridge, MA: Harvard University Press, 2010.

Simon, Uriel. "Minor Characters in Biblical Narrative." *JSOT* 46 (1990): 11–19.

Simon, Uriel. *Reading Prophetic Narratives.* Trans. Lenn J. Schramm. Indiana: Indiana University Press, 1997.

Skinner, Christopher W. ed. *Characters and Characterization in the Gospel of John.* LNTS 461. New York: Bloomsbury T&T Clark, 2013.

Skinner, Christopher W. and Matthew Ryan Hauge, eds. *Character Studies and the Gospel of Mark.* LNTS 483. London: Bloomsbury, 2014.

Slomonovic, Elieser. "Toward an Understanding of the Formation of the Historical Titles in the Book of Psalms." *ZAW* 91 (1979): 350–80.

Small, Brian C. *The Characterization of Jesus in the Book of Hebrews.* Leiden: Brill, 2014.

Smith, Henry Preserved. *A Critical and Exegetical Commentary on the Book of Samuel.* ICC. Edinburgh: T. & T. Clark, 1899.

Smith, Mark S. *Poetic Heroes: Literary Commemorations of Warriors and Warrior Culture in the Early Biblical World.* Grand Rapids: Eerdmans, 2014.

Smith, Richard G. *The Fate of Justice and Righteousness During David's Reign: Rereading the Court History and Its Ethics according to 2 Samuel 8:15b–20:26.* LHBOTS 508. New York/London: T&T Clark, 2009.

Soggin, J. A. *Old Testament and Oriental Studies.* Rome: Pontifical Biblical Institute, 1975.

Soggin, J. A. "The Reign of 'Eshba'al, Son of Saul." In *Old Testament and Oriental Studies*, 31–49. BibOr 29. Rome: Biblical Institute Press, 1975.

Speiser, Ephraim A. *Genesis*. AB 1. Garden City: Doubleday, 1964.
Stamm, J. J. "Der Name des Königs Salomo." *ThZ* 16 (1960): 285–97.
Sternberg, Meir. *Expositional Modes and Temporal Ordering in Fiction*. Baltimore: John Hopkins University Press, 1978.
Sternberg, Meir. *The Poetics of Biblical Narrative: Ideological Literature and the Drama of Reading*. Bloomington: Indiana University Press, 1985.
Sternberg, Meir. "Universals of Narrative and Their Cognitivist Fortunes (I)." *Poetics Today* 24, no. 2 (2003): 297–5.
Sternberg, Meir. "Universals of Narrative and Their Cognitive Fortunes (II)." *Poetics Today* 24, no. 3 (2003): 517–638.
Steussy, Marti J. *David: Biblical Portraits of Power*. Columbia, SC: University of South Carolina Press, 1999.
Steussy, Marti J. "The Problematic God of Samuel." In *Shall Not the Judge of All the Earth Do What Is Right? Studies on the Nature of God in Tribute to James L. Crenshaw*, edited by David Penchansky and Paul L. Redditt, 127–61. Winona Lake: Eisenbrauns, 2000.
Steussy, Marti J. *Samuel and His God*. Studies on Personalities of the Old Testament. Columbia, SC: University of South Carolina Press, 2010.
Stoebe, H. J. *Das Erste Buch Samuelis*. Gütersloh: Gütersloher Verlagshaus Gerd Mohn, 1973.
Stoebe, H. J. *Das Zweite Buch Samuelis*. Gütersloh: Gütersloher Verlagshaus Gerd Mohn, 1994.
Stone, Ken. *Sex, Honor, and Power in the Deuteronomistic History*. JSOTSup 234. Sheffield: Sheffield Academic, 1996.
Sweeney, Marvin A. "Samuel's Institutional Identity in the Deuteronomistic History." In *Constructs of Prophecy in the Former and Latter Prophets and Other Texts*, edited by L. L. Grabbe and M. Nissinen, 165–74. ANEM 4. Atlanta: SBL, 2011.
Sweeney, Marvin A. "Israelite and Judean Religions." In *The Cambridge History of Religions in the Ancient World*. Vol. 1, *From the Bronze Age through the Hellenistic Age*, edited by M. Salzman and M. A. Sweeney, 151–73. Cambridge: Cambridge University Press, 2013.
Sweeney, Marvin A. *The Pentateuch*. CBS. Nashville: Abingdon, 2017.
Sweeney, Marvin A. "Prophets and Priests in the Deuteronomistic History: Elijah and Elisha." In *Israelite Prophecy and the Deuteronomistic History: Portrait, Reality, and the Formation of History*, edited by M. R. Jacobs and R. F. Person Jr., 35–49. AIL 14. Atlanta: SBL, 2013.
Taylor, Bernard A. "The Kaige Text of Reigns." In *New English Translation of the Septuagint*, edited by Albert Pietersma and Benjamin G. Wright. Oxford: Oxford University Press, 2007.
Thomason, Alison K. *Luxury and Legitimation: Royal Collecting in Ancient Mesopotamia*. Aldershot: Ashgate, 2005.
Thompson, J. A. "The Significance of the Verb *Love* in the David–Jonathan Narratives in 1 Samuel." *VT* 24, no. 3 (1974): 334–8.
Tigay, Jeffrey E. *Deuteronomy, with Introduction and Commentary*. 2 vols. Mikra Le-Yisrael. Tel Aviv: Am Oved and Jerusalem: Magnes, 2016 (Hebrew).
Tolkien, J. R. R. "Foreword to the Second Edition." In *The Lord of the Rings*, xxii–xxv. 50th Anniversary Edition. New York: Houghton Mifflin, 2004.
Tushima, Cephas T. A. *The Fate of Saul's Progeny in the Reign of David*. Cambridge: James Clarke, 2012.

Tsumura, David. *The First Book of Samuel*. NICOT. Grand Rapids: Eerdmans, 2007.
Ulrich, Eugine. *The Biblical Qumran Scrolls: Transcriptions and Textual Variants*. VTSup 134. Leiden: Brill, 2010.
Uspensky, Boris. *A Poetics of Composition: The Structure of the Artistic Text and Typology of a Compositional Form*, translated by V. Zavarin and S. Wittig. Berkeley: University of California Press, 1973.
Van Seters, John. *The Biblical Saga of King David*. Winona Lake: Eisenbrauns, 2009.
Van Seters, John. *In Search of History: Historiography in the Ancient World and the Origins of Biblical History*. New Haven: Yale University Press, 1983.
VanderKam, James C. "Davidic Complicity in the Deaths of Abner and Eshbaal: A Historical and Redactional Study." *JBL* 99, no. 4 (1980): 521–39.
Vanhoozer, Kevin J. *Is There a Meaning in This Text? The Bible, the Reader, and the Morality of Literary Knowledge*. Grand Rapids: Zondervan, 1998.
Vannoy, J. Robert. *Covenant Renewal at Gilgal: A Study of 1 Samuel 11:14–12:25*. Eugene: Wipf & Stock, 2008. Reprint 1978.
Veijola, T. *Die ewige Dynastie: David und die Entstehung seiner Dynastie nach der deuteronomistischen Darstellung*. AASF Series B 193. Helsinki: Suomalainen Tiedeakatemia, 1975.
Veijola, T. *Das Königtum in der Beurteilung der deuteronomistischen Historiographie: Eine redaktionsgeschichtliche Untersuchung*. AASF B 198. Helsinki: Suomalainen Tiedeakatemia, 1977.
Vette, Joachim. "Samuel's 'Farewell Speech': Theme and Variation in 1 Samuel 12, Josephus, and Pseudo-Philo." In *Literary Construction of Identity in the Ancient World*, edited by Hanna Liss and Manfred Oeming, 325–39. Winona Lake: Eisenbrauns, 2010.
Walsh, Jerome T. *Old Testament Narrative: A Guide to Interpretation*. Louisville: Westminster John Knox, 2009.
Waltke, Bruce K. and M. O'Connor. *An Introduction to Biblical Hebrew Syntax*. Winona Lake: Eisenbrauns, 1990.
Walton, John H. and J. Harvey Walton. *The Lost World of the Israelite Conquest: Covenant, Retribution, and the Fate of the Canaanites*. Downers Grove: InterVarsity, 2017.
Weiland, K. M. *Creating Character Arcs: The Masterful Author's Guide to Uniting Story Structure, Plot, and Character Development*. EBL ed. PenForASword Publishing, 2016.
Weitzman, Steven. "David's Lament and the Poetics of Grief in 2 Samuel." *JQR* 85 (1995): 341–60.
Weitzman, Steven. "King David's Spin Doctors." *Prooftexts* 23, no. 3 (2003): 365–76.
Wellhausen, Julius. *Prolegomena to the History of Israel*, translated by J. S. Black and A. Menzies. Edinburgh: A. & C. Black, 1885.
Wenham, Gordon J. *Psalms as Torah: Reading Biblical Song Ethically*. Studies in Theological Interpretation. Grand Rapids: Baker Academic, 2012.
Westbrook, April D. *"And He Will Take Your Daughters…" Woman Story and the Ethical Evaluation of Monarchy in the David Narrative*. London/New York: Bloomsbury T&T Clark, 2015.
White, Ellen. "Michal the Misinterpreted." *JSOT* 31 (2007): 451–64.
Whybray, R. N. *The Succession Narrative: A Study of II Samuel 9–20; I Kings 1 and 2*. London: SCM, 1968.
Widmer, Michael. *Standing in the Breach: An Old Testament Theology and Spirituality of Intercessory Prayer*. Siphrut 13. Winona Lake: Eisenbrauns, 2015.

Williams, James G. "The Beautiful and the Barren: Conventions in Biblical Type-Scenes." *JSOT* 5 (1980): 48–55.

Willis, John T. "Function of Comprehensive Anticipatory Redactional Joints in 1 Samuel 16–18." *ZAW* 85 (1973): 294–314.

Wimsatt, William K. *The Verbal Icon: Studies in the Meaning of Poetry*. London: Noonday, 1970.

Wolde, Ellen van. "A Leader Led by a Lady: David and Abigail in 1 Samuel 25." *ZAW* 114 (2002): 355–75.

Wright, Jacob L. *David, King of Israel, and Caleb in Biblical Memory*. Cambridge: Cambridge University Press, 2014.

Wright, Jacob L. "Making a Name for Oneself: Martial Valor, Heroic Death, and Procreation in the Hebrew Bible." *JSOT* 36 (2011): 131–62.

Yee, Gale A. "'Fraught with Background': Literary Ambiguity in II Samuel 11." *Int* 42, no. 3 (1988): 240–53.

Yoon, Sung-Hee. *The Question of the Beginning and the Ending of the So-Called History of David's Rise: A Methodological Reflection and Its Implications*. BZAW 642. Berlin: de Gruyter, 2014.

Zakovitch, Yair. *From Shepherd to Messiah*. Jerusalem: Yad Ben-Tsvi, 1995.

Ziegler, Yael. *Promises to Keep: The Oath in Biblical Narrative*. VTSup 120. Leiden: Brill, 2008.

Index of References

Old Testament/ Hebrew Bible

Genesis
1	15
2	15
2:16	110
2:17	110
4:9	207
10:15	244
12:11	169
15:16	281
16	63–5
17	46
19	104
20:12	260
21	63, 65
24	170
24:53	170
24:61	170
27:18	213
27:32	213
29–30	64, 65
29:1-12	106
29:2	106
29:10	106
29:11	106
29:17	169
30:1	46, 55
30:14	55
31	63
35	63
38:8-10	280

Exodus
2	106
2:17	107
17:8-16	37
20:15	266
20:20	97
21:16	266
21:37– 22:14 MT	281
22:1-15	281
22:21-23	232
29	71
30:11-16	279
34:19-20	65
38:35-28	279

Leviticus
4	68
8	71
10:10-11	69
18:9	260
18:11	260
20:17	260

Numbers
3	64
8	64, 71
16:15	83
24:1-4	285
24:11	285
26:52-56	279

Deuteronomy
6:12	87
8:11	87
8:14	87
8:16	32
8:19	87
18:9-15	285
20:1-4	74
22:28-29	259
23:10	246
23:11 ET	246
24:6	229
25:5-10	280
25:17-19	37
27:22	260
28:25-26	236
28:33	86
32:18	87
34:1-5	87

Joshua
1:1-2	87
15:55-56	258
16:2	251
16:10	251
18:21-22	105
18:25	104
24	86

Judges
2:4	87
3–16	88, 89
3	89
3:7	87
3:8	87
3:9	87
3:13	36
4–5	89
4:2	87
6–9	89
6:3-5	36
6:33	36
7:12	36
8:23	39
10–11	89
10:7	87
10:10	87, 90
10:12	36
13–16	89

Judges (cont.)

16:25	217	1:23	57	4–6	73		
16:27	217	1:24-28	17	4	61, 62, 73, 74, 274, 275, 277		
17:1	31	1:26-28	31				
18:1	31	1:26	56, 209, 210	4:1-22	72, 73		
18:5	211	1:27-28	31, 32, 49	4:1	70		
19–21	104, 105	1:27	16	4:16-17	243		
19	104	1:28	78	4:18	283		
19:1	31	2	18, 33, 48, 62, 95	7–16	78		
				7	74, 85, 92, 100, 104		

1 Samuel

		2:1-10	17, 33, 43		
1–16	62	2:3	33	7:3-6	92
1–15	77	2:5	58	7:3	85, 228
1–3	61, 62, 69, 70, 74, 77	2:6	18, 33	7:4	85, 228
		2:7-8	32	7:6	92
1	17, 62, 63, 158, 240	2:9	33	7:7-12	92
		2:10	33, 95	7:15-17	92
1:1–4:1	62	2:12-36	67	7:16	104
1:1–2:11	62, 64	2:12-26	66	7:17	104
1:1-13	15, 17	2:12-17	50, 67, 68	8	53, 84, 91, 92, 94
1:1-2	17	2:12	55		
1:1	31	2:17-21	67	8:1-22	102
1:2	54	2:18-21	67	8:1-2	82
1:3-8	17	2:18	66	8:3	82
1:5-6	30, 32, 54	2:22-36	67	8:4	91
1:5	35, 53	2:22-26	67	8:5	49
1:8	54	2:22	66	8:7	35, 39, 84, 91
1:9-11	17	2:23-25	68		
1:9	55, 286	2:24	154	8:9	39
1:10-12	31	2:25	28, 35	8:10-18	35
1:10	31	2:27-36	17, 66, 68, 283	8:11-17	83
1:11	31, 56			8:18	92
1:12-18	17	2:29	49	8:19	90, 91
1:12-16	31	2:30	35	8:22	39, 84, 85, 91
1:13	34	2:31-34	35		
1:14-26	15	2:35	95	9–15	83
1:15-16	15	3	78	9–10	83
1:15	31	3:1–4:1	67, 70–2	9	39, 91, 94, 103, 230
1:16-17	55	3:1	66		
1:17	15, 31, 32, 46, 57	3:2	71	9:1–10:6	102
		3:3-9	71	9:1-14	240
1:18	56	3:10	71	9:1	108
1:19-20	17	3:11-14	35	9:2	104, 264
1:19	30, 56	3:17–4:1	70	9:3	105
1:20	31, 78	3:19-20	95	9:4	154
1:21-23	17	3:19	95	9:5	105
1:22	31, 57	4–7	49, 88	9:6-10	109

Ref	Page	Ref	Page	Ref	Page
9:6	105	11:1	91	12:16	94
9:7	105	11:5	109, 113	12:17-18	95
9:9	271	11:6	39, 109, 115	12:17	84, 94
9:10	105			12:18	94, 96–8
9:11-18	271	11:7	98	12:19	78, 84, 95
9:11	106	11:12-13	116	12:20-25	68, 97, 98
9:13	107	11:12	109	12:20-22	78
9:14	107	11:13	109	12:20-21	95
9:15-17	87, 91	11:14-15	104	12:20	96–8
9:15-16	34	11:14	86	12:21	109, 115
9:16-17	39, 91, 96	11:15	85	12:22	97
9:16	91, 144, 147	12	76–8, 80, 83, 85–7, 91–5, 98, 100, 109, 290	12:23	98, 100
				12:24-25	78
9:18	107			12:24	84, 96
9:20	39, 107			12:25	97, 109
9:21	107			13–14	70, 111, 146
9:22	83, 103	12:1-25	102		
9:26–10:1	91	12:1-5	78, 81, 85	13	39, 77, 98, 141, 222
9:27	154	12:1	84, 85, 109		
10	94, 230	12:2	81, 82, 86, 109	13:2	142
10:1-14	248			13:3-14	102
10:1-8	39	12:3	81, 82, 84, 86	13:5	110
10:1-6	108			13:6	146
10:2-6	91	12:4	83, 84	13:7	98, 154
10:7	91, 110	12:5	84	13:8-15	36
10:8	91, 104, 110, 140	12:6-15	78	13:8-9	140
		12:6-13	78, 79, 85, 93	13:8	110
10:9-21	108			13:11	111
10:9	39	12:6-8	86, 87	13:12	110
10:10-13	39	12:6	86, 87	13:13-14	140, 146
10:10	105	12:7	85, 86	13:14	39, 124, 126, 140, 143, 275
10:15-16	108	12:8	87		
10:17-27	102	12:9-11	86, 87, 89		
10:17-23	92	12:9	87, 88	13:16	142
10:17	104	12:10	87, 90, 94	13:19-22	147
10:22	108	12:11	88, 89, 92	13:22	147
10:23	83, 103, 120	12:12-13	86, 90	14	139, 140, 146–8, 153–6
		12:12	84, 90, 91, 94		
10:24	87, 108				
10:26	104	12:13	84, 87, 109	14:1-23	140, 142, 144, 145, 155
10:27	108, 109	12:14-25	78, 79		
11	77, 85, 91, 94, 119, 144	12:14-15	39, 93		
		12:14	84, 92, 93, 96	14:1-8	153
				14:1	154
11:1-15	102	12:15	93	14:2	111
11:1-11	109	12:15 LXX	84	14:3	64, 111
11:1-5	90	12:16-19	94	14:4	154

1 Samuel (cont.)

14:6	142, 154	15:2	39	17–18	145
14:7	142, 143	15:3	35, 113, 114, 116	17	115, 146–8, 156, 208, 210, 216, 218
14:8-12	143	15:6	113		
14:8	154	15:8-9	35		
14:10	143	15:8	113	17:1–18:4	11
14:12	143, 144	15:9	36, 113, 114	17:4-7	243
14:13-14	147			17:5-7	147
14:14-20	147	15:10-11	40	17:11	146
14:14-15	144	15:11	35	17:24	146
14:14	112	15:12	114, 154	17:25	209
14:15	112, 144	15:13	117	17:26	105, 125, 181
14:18	112	15:15	39, 99		
14:19	112	15:17	103, 114	17:32	125, 126
14:20	147	15:18	36	17:37	147
14:23	143, 144, 154	15:20-21	39	17:38-39	147
		15:21	99	17:43-47	147
14:24-46	140, 145, 154	15:22-23	114	17:46	147
		15:22	39	17:47	147
14:24	112, 145	15:23	109	17:50-51	147
14:27	145	15:24	36, 114, 154	17:55-58	208, 212, 213, 215
14:29-30	154				
14:32-33	112	15:26-28	36	17:55	209, 210
14:35	112	15:26	39	17:56	210, 211
14:36	113	15:28	39, 103, 115, 146	18–20	152, 160
14:37	113			18	134, 161, 164, 209
14:38-46	146	15:29	40		
14:39	18, 21, 22, 113, 145	15:30	99, 114	18:1-5	149
		15:32-33	36	18:1-4	148, 150, 151
14:40	113, 154	15:33	37		
14:41	113	15:35	40, 115, 117	18:1	148, 150, 161
14:43	145				
14:44	113, 145	16–17	146	18:3	149, 150, 152, 161
14:45	18, 21, 22, 113, 116, 145	16	11, 40, 61, 230		
				18:6	11
		16:1-5	284	18:7	115
14:46	113	16:7	126, 181	18:8	115
14:47-48	144	16:8	154	18:11	115, 151
14:48	36	16:9	154	18:13	115
14:49	226	16:10	154	18:17	116
14:50-52	208	16:12	146, 155, 243, 264	18:20	161
14:50	116			18:25	116, 170
14:52	83, 144	16:14	115, 209	18:27	161
15–17	146, 148	16:18-19	208	19–20	135, 153
15	34–40, 99, 100, 103, 113, 114	16:18	210, 211, 243, 264	19	150, 161, 164
		16:23	115		

19:1-7	150, 151, 154, 161–3	20:27-33	284	24:4-5	7
19:1-2	161	20:27	154	24:5	126, 135
19:1	150, 154, 163	20:28-42	152	24:5 MT	134, 135
		20:28-29	151	24:6	166, 214
19:2-3	150, 154, 163	20:28	154	24:6 MT	135
		20:30	116, 151, 154, 228	24:7	214
19:2	161, 163	20:31	18, 21, 214	24:8 EVV	213
19:4-5	116, 151	20:32	154	24:9	213
19:4	154	20:33-34	154	24:10	214
19:5	163	20:33	116, 151, 154	24:11	214
19:6	18, 21, 22, 151, 161			24:16	117, 213
		20:36	154	24:17	209
19:8-10	161	20:41	153, 165	24:19	135
19:10	151	20:42	152	24:20 MT	135
19:11-17	161, 162	21:5 ET	246	25	5, 8, 123, 167, 214, 215, 222
19:11	161, 163	21:6	246		
19:12	165	21:8	239	25:1–28:2	11
19:13-14	163	22	62	25:1	169, 247
19:15-17	163	22:2	135	25:2-3	172, 258
19:17	161, 163	22:6-23	11, 239	25:3	7, 181
19:18– 21:10	11	22:8	112, 116	25:4	171
		22:13	116	25:5-8	172
20	139, 150–2, 155, 164	22:14	235	25:6-8	172
		22:16-19	254	25:7-8	172
20:1-23	154	22:18	116	25:8	172
20:1-4	151	22:19	116	25:9	7
20:1	154	22:20	64	25:10	7
20:2	154	23	150	25:11	7
20:3	18, 21, 154	23:3-5	240	25:13	135, 169, 173
20:5-8	151	23:6-14	11		
20:6	154	23:7	117	25:14-16	173
20:8	151, 152, 154	23:9	112	25:15-16	172
		23:13	135	25:15	6
20:9	154	23:16-17	155	25:16	182
20:10	154	23:17	152, 206	25:17	173
20:12-17	155	23:18	152, 153	25:18	7, 175
20:12-16	155	23:19-24	11	25:19	154, 175
20:12	154	23:21	112	25:20	175
20:13	154	23:28	117	25:21-22	7, 176
20:14-16	151	24	21, 117, 134–6, 166, 212	25:22	173, 181
20:14	18			25:23-31	7
20:16	152			25:23	7, 176
20:18-23	155	24:2	117	25:24-31	171, 176
20:21	21	24:3	134	25:24-25	176
20:25	154, 212	24:4	134, 135	25:24	176
20:26	154	24:4 MT	134	25:25	169, 177

Index of References

1 Samuel (cont.)		26:16	18, 21, 22, 214	*2 Samuel*	
25:26	8, 21, 178			1–4	257
25:27	175, 180	26:17-20	213	1	17, 20, 21, 23
25:28	7, 8, 180, 218	26:17	209, 213, 215	1:1	11
25:29	180	26:21	117	1:3-16	11
25:30	181	26:22	154	1:5-10	11
25:31	8, 126	26:25	117	1:8	213
25:32	181	27–31	17, 20	1:10	18, 21
25:33-34	181	27	23, 36	1:17-27	133, 247
25:33	169	27:1	34	1:18	276
25:34	21, 173, 181, 214	27:2	135, 154	1:22-27	153
		27:3	116	1:23	18, 19, 21, 153, 154
25:35	175, 181, 218	27:4	117		
		28	23, 78	1:26-27	153
25:36-37	182	28:2	235	1:26	153
25:36	7	28:3-25	247	2–4	226, 237
25:37	181	28:3	118	2–3	185, 187
25:38	35, 182	28:6	118, 285	2	9, 21, 215, 220
25:39-42	182	28:9-10	18, 21		
25:39	182	28:14	107	2:1-11	239
25:41	178	28:15-16	285	2:2	11, 116, 258
25:42-43	258	28:16-19	154		
25:42	170, 171, 178, 179	28:16	117	2:4–4:12	11
		28:20	118	2:4-11	215
25:43-44	151	28:22	118	2:4-7	247
25:43	116	28:23	118	2:8	226, 229
25:44	229	29–31	139	2:9	230
26	21, 117, 159, 188, 212, 217, 223, 225, 235	29	23	2:15-22	276
		29:1–30:31	11	2:17	187, 217
		29:2	154	2:18-23	9
		29:6	21	2:21	217
		30	23, 36	2:22	9, 217, 223
26:2	117	30:5	116	2:23	187
26:5	212	30:9	135	2:24	218, 220
26:6-12	212	30:10	135, 154	2:25	218
26:6	185	30:21	135	2:26-27	187
26:7	212	31	17, 20, 23, 145, 226, 234	2:26	219
26:9-11	7			2:27	219
26:9	166			2:28	220
26:10	18, 21, 22	31:2	155, 226	2:30-31	220
26:11	214	31:4	118, 119	2:30	220
26:12	205, 214	31:7	154	3	9, 125, 188, 218, 220, 224
26:13	154	31:8	118		
26:14	212, 213	31:9-10	119		
26:15-16	213	31:9	120	3:1-5	257
26:15	214			3:1	9, 220, 221

3:2-5	275, 280, 285	5:1-3	275	7:10-11	279	
		5:3	11	7:11-16	279	
3:2	116	5:4–9:13	275	7:11	286	
3:3	171	5:4-5	283	7:12	280, 282, 286, 289	
3:6	9, 221	5:5	11, 275			
3:7-11	230	5:6-10	275	7:17-18	286	
3:7-8	220, 222	5:6	131, 275	7:17	271, 285	
3:7	9, 10, 229, 230, 232	5:9	275	7:18-29	133	
		5:10-12	285	7:20	286	
3:8	229	5:13-16	11, 280	7:27	127	
3:11	229	5:14	284, 285	8	61, 276, 278, 279	
3:12	10, 220	5:17-25	275			
3:13-16	220	5:17	275	8:1-14	277	
3:14-15	233	5:18	275	8:1	276, 279	
3:14	229	5:22	275	8:2	18	
3:15	229	5:25	279	8:3-12	248	
3:20-21	220	6	73, 274, 275, 277	8:3-8	278	
3:20	10			8:13-14	282	
3:21	10	6:1	11, 275	8:15-18	277	
3:22	220	6:3-4	11	8:15	260	
3:23	10, 221	6:5-11	246	8:16-18	11	
3:24-25	188	6:6-14	11	8:16	185	
3:24	221	6:7	35	8:18	249, 284	
3:25	221	6:10-12	243	9–24	61, 75	
3:26-39	277	6:16	34	9–20	269, 272	
3:26	10, 207, 221	6:20-23	11	9	11, 159, 257, 275, 276	
		6:21	275			
3:27	188, 218, 221, 223	7–24	272–4, 276–8, 283	9:1–20:26	11	
3:28-39	189	7–9	274–6	9:1-13	277	
3:30	221	7	7, 202, 272, 273, 276, 278–81, 284	9:2	159	
3:31-39	125			9:9-10	159	
3:34	221			9:9	159	
3:37	125			9:12	159	
4–5	224	7:1-29	277	9:23	185	
4	224, 234	7:1-17	272	10–20	276, 283	
4:1	229	7:1-3	285	10–12	190, 274, 275, 278, 281, 282	
4:2-3	239	7:1	239, 273, 278, 282			
4:4	234, 242			10	256, 276	
4:9-10	18	7:2	285	10:1–12:31	277	
4:10	21	7:3	127, 285	10:1-5	287	
4:11	237	7:4-17	286	10:1	276	
4:12	234	7:4	285	10:6-19	278	
5–24	239	7:5	286	10:11-12	190	
5–8	256, 274	7:6	279	11–20	243	
5	11, 230	7:8	286	11–19	257	
5:1-6	257	7:9-11	278			

2 Samuel (cont.)

11–12	76, 211, 273	12:15-23	240	14:19-20	284
		12:15	284	14:19	209, 210
		12:18	18	14:20	27
11	131, 243, 244, 247, 248, 254	12:21	18	14:21	194
		12:22-23	18	14:22	194
		12:23-25	280	14:24	263
11:1	245	12:24-25	272, 280, 282, 286, 287, 289	14:25-27	264
11:2	169			14:25-26	263
11:3	244, 245, 248, 280			14:25	242
		12:24	245, 250, 280	14:27	169, 264, 267, 268
11:4	180				
11:6	245	12:25	289	14:32	265
11:11	93, 245, 246	12:26-31	192	14:33	265
		12:30	287	14:45-46	267
11:14-25	190	13–20	274, 275	15–19	195
11:15	190	13–19	192	15:1	265
11:16-17	190	13:1–20:22	277	15:2	284
11:18	190	13:1	169, 258, 261, 282	15:3-6	266
11:19-21	191			15:6	266
11:20-21	279	13:2	261	15:7	283
11:22-24	191	13:3-7	262	15:12	248, 266
11:25	191	13:3-5	261	15:13– 17:29	196
11:26	280	13:3	252		
11:27–12:1	285	13:4	258	15:13	266
11:27	34	13:6-7	261	15:18-23	248
11:36	248	13:7	260	15:18-22	22
11:37	248	13:8-18	261	15:19-20	249
11:38	248	13:11	260	15:21	18, 21, 250, 251
11:41	273	13:12-13	260		
12–29	257	13:14	260	15:32-37	251, 287
12	22, 267, 278, 279, 284, 285, 288	13:16	260	15:33-37	252
		13:17	261	16:1-4	160, 251
		13:20	259	16:5-14	251
		13:21	260	16:10	185
12:1-15	272, 283, 284	13:22	260, 262	16:11	282
		13:23	263	16:14	249
12:1-4	284	13:30-36	240	16:15	252
12:5-23	22	13:32-33	261	16:18	282
12:5	18, 21, 242	13:32	263	16:22-23	274
12:6-7	289	13:39	193	16:23	253
12:6	280, 284	14	192, 193	17:1-14	253
12:7-12	274, 283, 286	14:1-3	284	17:1-6	253
		14:1	193	17:7-10	253
12:7-8	116	14:4-22	284	17:11-13	253
12:9	284	14:7	282	17:14	28, 41, 267
12:10-11	267	14:11-20	249	17:15-19	252
12:13	136	14:13	280, 282	17:15-16	253

17:16	252	20:23–24:25	275, 276	24:3	195	
17:23	284	20:23-26	277, 278	24:8	279	
17:24	234	20:23	200	24:10	126, 132,	
17:27-29	287	20:26	287		283	
17:27	234	21–24	132, 137,	24:11	271	
18	211		195, 248,	24:18-25	251	
18:1-12	250		274, 276	26	166	
18:1-5	248	21:1-14	257, 274,			
18:2	196, 250		276–8	*1 Kings*		
18:5	196, 250	21:15-22	274, 276–8	1–4	272, 283	
18:6-8	196	21:17	276	1–2	14, 17, 21,	
18:7	251	21:18-19	276		22, 69, 74,	
18:8	243	21:21	276		185, 200,	
18:9	267	22	14, 18, 19,		269, 272,	
18:10-17	196		33		273	
18:11-13	196	22:1-52	278	1	272, 273,	
18:12	250	22:1-51	48, 274,		282, 283,	
18:14-15	18, 197		276		288	
18:15-18	274	22:2	131	1:1-52	11	
18:17-18	267	22:4	34	1:1	287	
18:18	267	23:1-7	133, 274,	1:3	169	
18:19-32	248		276, 278	1:5-10	288	
18:19-20	197	23:8-39	247, 274,	1:5-8	201	
18:21	197		276, 277	1:5-6	260	
18:22-23	197	23:8-23	278	1:8-12	288	
18:28-30	197	23:8-10	276	1:8	287	
18:29	198, 207	23:11-12	276	1:9-53	201	
18:31-33	198	23:18-29	277	1:11-31	288	
19:2	198	23:18-23	276	1:11-14	288	
19:5-7	198	23:18	185, 186	1:11	206	
19:7	18	23:23	235	1:12	288	
19:9-15	266	23:24-39	276, 278	1:13	281	
19:14	199	23:24	185, 186,	1:17	281	
19:15	104, 266		277	1:20	289	
19:17	266	23:29	250	1:22-23	285	
19:25-31	257	23:32	276	1:24-27	288	
19:31	160	23:33	276	1:28	285	
20–24	275	23:34	247, 280	1:30	281	
20	11, 257	23:37	185, 186,	1:32-48	289	
20:1	267		277	1:32	285	
20:3	18	23:39	243, 247,	1:34	289	
20:8-10	200		276	1:39	289	
20:11	200	24	131, 195,	1:45	289	
20:13	200		243, 273,	2	21, 22, 62,	
20:15	200		278–81		69, 71, 72,	
20:16-21	200	24:1-25	274, 276–8		137, 291	
20:22	287	24:1	243	2:1-9	289	

2 Samuel (cont.)

2:3-4	281
2:5-9	11
2:5-6	202, 277
2:13-46	11
2:22	22
2:24	18, 21
2:27-39	69
2:27	69
2:28-34	224
2:28-30	202
2:30-36	69
2:32	206
3	22
3:5-13	23
3:10-13	23
3:16-28	284
4	272
4:5	272, 286, 287
4:7-19	287
5:2-5	281
5:16-19 MT	281
6:11-13	281
8	66
8:15-21	281
8:25	281
9:4-5	281
11	185
11:29-39	289
11:42	287
13:1-4	284
13:22	236
14:10-11	236
14:10	173
14:21	287
14:31	268
15:1-9	268
15:2	268
15:4-5	243
15:5	68
15:10	268
15:13	268
16:11	173
17	69, 216
20:35-43	284
21:21	173

2 Kings

9:1-10	289
9:8	173
13	69
22–23	185

1 Chronicles

1:12	131
1:14	131
3:1-4	257
3:1	171
3:2	257
3:5-9	280
3:5	280, 284
3:9	280
4:43	36
6:1-15	63
7:17	88
8:33	226, 228
9	63
9:39	226, 228
10:7	131
11–12	275
11:1-3	257
11:4	131
13:3	275
14:4-7	280
17:1-15	281
21	131
21:1-17	256
22:5	130
22:7-10	281
22:9	281, 286
24:1-3	64
25:5	271, 285
27:25-31	288
27:32	288
28:2-7	281
28:5-6	281

2 Chronicles

3:9	258
9:29	271
11:18-23	268
11:20-21	257
13:2	268
15:16	268
16:7-10	271
19:2	271
21:17	280
22:1	280
29:30	271
35:13	271

Esther

1:10-11	169
2:7	169
3:1	36

Job

1:3	169
4:12	266
12:12	171
32:8-9	171
42:15	169

Psalms

18	19, 20
18:5-7	20
18:8-20	20
18:17-20	20
18:21-29	20
18:26-27	19
18:26	19
18:27	19
18:30-46	20
45:3-4	264
45:11	169
51	136, 137
89:19-37	281
93:1	39
106:23	99
119:100	171
132:11-12	281
142	134–6
142:3	135, 136
142:4	135
142:4 MT	135, 136
142:5 MT	135
142:6	135, 136
142:7 MT	135, 136

Index of References

Proverbs
1:1-9	288
4:1-9	288
6:24-31	280
11:22	169

Song of Songs
1:5	169
3:7	236

Isaiah
5:15	86
6:5	39
31:2	261
41:29	95
44:9	95
44:10	96
57:12	96

Jeremiah
2:8	96
4:22	261
16:4	236
16:19	96
23:30	266
28:2	35
28:10	35

Ezekiel
16:4-8	168

Hosea
5:11	86

Amos
3:6	32
4:1	86
7:12	271

Jonah
1:12	207

Micah
6	86
6:1-5	86
6:3	86
6:4	86
6:5	86

Zephaniah
3:15	39

New Testament

Matthew
1:6	245

Luke
18:1-8	31

John
18:12-27	235
11:32	137

Pseudepigrapha
Liber Antiquitatum Biblicarum
57	86

Qumran
11QPSa
27:5-6	256
27:9-10	256

Babylonian Talmud
Baba Batra
15a	255

Rosh Hashanah
25a	88

Sanhedrin
21a	261

Midrash
Midrash on Psalms
32:1	161

Josephus
Antiquities
6.68-71	91
6.83	77
6.86-94	86
6.86	77
7.48	235
7.162	258
7.173	260
7.196	266

Index of Authors

Abadi, I. 272
Ackerman, A. 111, 112, 116, 118
Ackroyd, P. R. 246
Alexander, M. 80
Alter, R. 4, 9, 11, 44, 45, 60, 82, 105–7, 117, 121, 125, 126, 140, 149, 152, 154, 159, 160, 196, 223, 232, 233, 235, 279
Amit, Y. 4, 40, 54, 255, 257, 261, 262, 266
Anderson, A. A. 9, 220, 237, 259, 260, 262
Andersson, G. 79, 138
Arnold, B. 96
Ashman, A. 259
Athas, G. 124
Auerbach, E. 2, 12
Auld, A. G. 59, 86, 130, 209, 210, 222
Aune, D. 12
Avioz, M. 104, 106, 228, 264
Avraham, N. 161

Bach, A. 175, 177
Baden, J. 60, 123
Bailey, R. C. 33, 35, 48
Bakhtin, M. M. 78
Baldwin, J. G. 163, 170
Bar-Efrat, S. 4, 41, 106, 157, 158, 160, 206, 207, 229, 232, 258, 260–2, 265
Barton, J. 122
Batten, L. 216
Beal, T. K. 137
Bellis, A. O. 231
Ben Zvi, E. 80
Ben-Ayun, C. S. 160, 165
Bergen, R. D. 77, 84, 87, 90
Berger, Y. 8, 179
Berlin, A. 4, 5, 160, 232
Biddle, M. 6
Birch, B. C. 161
Bloch-Smith, E. 236

Boda, M. J. 130
Bodi, D. 7, 172
Bodner, K. 8, 77, 99, 104–7, 110, 125, 129, 141, 145, 150, 151, 154, 183, 187, 192, 193, 196, 199, 209, 227, 235, 245, 264, 267, 271, 284, 289
Borgman, P. 126
Boswell, G. M. 232
Bourdieu, P. 168
Bovati, P. 231
Breen 82
Brenner, A. 46, 47
Brettler, M. Z. 237
Brueggemann, W. 33, 129, 137, 163, 218, 220, 231, 274
Buber, M. 37
Buchanan, J. M. 37
Buracker, W. 208, 209, 211–13, 215, 217, 218, 220, 222, 230, 231, 234, 236
Burnside, J. 202

Camp, C. V. 137
Campbell, A. F., S.J. 60, 62, 66, 68, 70, 73
Campbell, J. K. 170
Carasik, M. 28
Carlson, R. A. 276
Cartledge, T. W. 89
Chapman, S. B. 38, 111, 126, 141–4, 147, 152
Chatman, S. 1, 2, 140, 227
Childs, B. S. 33, 133
Chun, S. M. 185
Clines, D. J. A. 160, 163, 229, 239
Conroy, C. 258, 262, 264–7
Conway, C. M. 13
Copan, P. 36, 37
Curtis, E. L. 268
Czövek, T. 77, 97, 99

Index of Authors

Davies, E. A. 123, 259
Davies, P. R. 999
Day, J. 133
De Temmerman, K. 241-3
De Vaux, R. 233
DeRouchie, J. S. 124
Deem, A. 262
Delitzsch, K. 219
Dietrich, W. 59, 208, 272
Dillard, R. B. 268
Docherty, T. 227
Donald, D. H. 60
Driver, S. R. 260, 266

Eco, U. 13
Edelman, D. V. 102, 141, 142, 144, 145, 154, 161, 164, 165
Eilat, M. 264
Elser, P. 999
Elwood, M. 232
Emmott, C. 999
Eschelbach, M. A. 201, 232
Eskenazi, T. C. 160, 239
Esler, P. F. 5, 51, 168, 180
Eslinger, L. 78, 103, 272
Evans, M. J. 170, 174
Evans, P. S. 111
Even, J. 157
Exum, J. C. 102, 110, 113, 114, 160, 165, 233, 236

Fensham, F. C. 216
Fewell, D. N. 4, 122, 207
Fidler, R. 57
Finkelstein, I. 255
Firth, D. G. 10, 48, 86, 87, 93, 140, 141, 143, 144, 151, 152, 154, 213, 216, 217, 219-22, 224, 230, 243, 244, 253, 273, 274
Fischer, A. A. 226
Flanagan, J. W. 999
Flannagan, M. 36, 37
Fleming, E. E. 149, 150, 153
Fokkelman, J. P. 4, 14, 15, 17-19, 21, 23, 59, 95, 142, 144, 145, 147, 148, 150-2, 154, 160, 161, 163, 164, 195, 196, 202, 209, 211, 212, 214, 216, 217, 219, 221, 222, 230, 235, 236
Forster, E. M. 41, 157
Frolov, S. 60, 88, 92, 272, 275

Frontain, R.-J. 121, 137
Frymer-Kensky, T. 259

Garsiel, M. 104, 163, 228
Gerke, J. 101, 120
Gnuse, R. K. 70
Goldingay, J. 32, 137, 284
Golub, M. 228
Good, E. M. 119
Gordon, R. P. 178, 208, 216, 221, 222, 235
Goslinga, C. J. 219
Green, B. 6, 8, 9, 127, 137, 145, 183-5
Greenspahn, F. E. 226
Grossman, J. 164, 266
Gunn, D. M. 4, 5, 27, 28, 59, 102, 110, 117, 122, 124, 125, 150, 163, 207, 236, 269

Hackett, J. A. 58
Halpern, B. 59, 116, 121, 123, 139, 207
Handy, L. K. 238
Harding, J. E. 149
Hardy, D. 205
Haupt, P. 151
Hawkins, R. K. 102
Heard, R. C. 136
Henry, C. 189
Herman, D. 79-81, 184
Herndon, W. H. 61
Hertzberg, H. W. 40, 169, 170, 182, 235
Heschel, A. 99
Hildebrandt, S. 118
Hoskisson, P. Y. 232
Hugo, P. 4
Humphreys, W. L. 102, 104, 118
Hutton, J. M. 128, 226, 227, 234

Iser, W. 231

Jacobsen, T. 233
Janzen, J. G. 34
Japhet, S. 63, 130, 256, 268, 269
Jarick, J. 131
Jepsen, A. 71
Jero, C. 49, 50
Jobling, D. 60, 141, 151, 154, 160, 209
Johnson, B. J. M. 6, 35, 40, 79, 122, 124, 126, 134, 135, 141, 143, 208, 210
Johnson, V. L. 999

Jones, G. H. 271, 281
Joseph, A. L. 137

Kawashima, R. S. 4, 232
Keil, C. F. 219
Keren, O. 153, 155, 160
Keys, G. 227, 272, 274, 275
Kipfer, S. 137
Kleiman, A. 258
Klein, R. W. 63, 89, 93, 108, 115, 131, 161, 175, 176, 178, 181, 209, 268
Klement, H. H. 132, 137, 195, 274
Knapp, A. 123
Knoppers, G. N. 63, 132
Kochman, M. 268
Kotter, W. R. 104
Kugel, J. 3

Landy, F. 249
Lapsley, J. E. 34
Lauton, R. B. 999
Lawton, R. B. 160
Leithart, P. J. 182
Lemche, N. P. 123
Levenson, J. D. 7, 116, 179
Levinson, B. M. 259, 260
Linafelt, T. 137
Lind, M. C. 144
Löwenclau, I. von 271
Long, D. S. 37, 114
Long, V. P. 123, 143, 144, 147
Longman, T. III 123
Lowenstamm, S. E. 229
Lyke, L. L. 193

Mabee, C. 237
Maccini, R. G. 235
Madsen, A. A. 268
Malamat, A. 999
Malina, B. J. 168, 172
Marböck, J. 222
Mauchline, J. 117
Mays, J. L. 134
McCann, J. C., Jr 260
McCarter, P. K., Jr 59, 78, 93, 108, 123, 141, 143, 161, 178, 216, 223, 231, 235, 237, 258, 259, 261, 266, 276
McKane, W. 217
McKenzie, S. L. 8, 59, 123, 124, 131, 139, 170, 179, 207, 256, 257

Meyers, C. 31, 168
Middleton, J. R. 35, 76, 77, 80, 83, 95, 100
Miller, P. D. 55
Miscall, P. D. 93, 96
Moberly, G. 999
Moberly, R. W. L. 72
Mobley, G. 102
Moore, S. D. 124
Moran, W. L. 149
Morgan, R. 122
Morrison, C. E. 231
Murphy, F. A. 119
Myers, A. D. 13

Na'aman, N. 226, 255, 258, 269
Nelson, R. D. 38
Newkirk, M. 235, 282
Newman, J. H. 111
Nichol, G. 193
Nigosian, S. 143
Noegel, S. B. 228
Noll, K. L. 35, 60, 128

O'Brien, M. A. 68
O'Connor, M. 144
Oatley, K. 81
Olyan, S. M. 236
Oswald, W. 271

Person, R. F., Jr 130
Peterson, B. N. 11
Pettie, G. 205
Polzin, R. 50, 60, 85, 104, 110, 119, 125, 141, 142, 154, 161, 209
Pritchard, J. B. 65
Prouser, O. H. 150
Provan, I. 123
Puglisi, B. 111, 112, 116, 118
Pyper, H. 208, 214

Rad, G. von 144
Ramsey, G. W. 231
Redfield, J. A. 2, 12
Reimer, D. J. 142
Rendsburg, G. A. 106
Rendtorff, R. 133
Ridout, G. 261
Rimmon-Kenan, S. 206
Rost, L. 73, 272

Rowe, C. K. 231
Rowe, J. Y. 148, 151
Ryan, M. L. 80

Schenker, A. 4
Schipper, J. 235
Scurlock, J. A. 119
Seeman, D. 163
Segal, M. Z. 235
Seibert, E. 37
Sergi, O. 258, 267, 272, 286
Shepherd, D. 9, 218
Short, J. R. 123
Silberman, N. A. 255
Simon, U. 157, 240, 254
Skinner, C. W. 12
Slomonovic, E. 134
Small, B. C. 227
Smith, H. P. 164
Smith, M. S. 149, 152, 153
Smith, R. G. 275
Soggin, J. A. 224, 226, 231
Speiser, E. A. 65
Stamm, J. J. 281
Sternberg, M. 3, 4, 7, 25–7, 52, 59, 205–7, 231, 241
Steussy, M. J. 27–32, 77, 125, 137
Stoebe, H. J. 215, 216, 219, 221, 222
Stone, K. 231
Sweeney, M. A. 63–5, 68, 75

Taylor, B. A. 235
Thomason, A. K. 233
Thompson, J. A. 149
Tigay, J. E. 229
Tolkein, J. R. R. 42
Tsumura, D. 59, 112
Tushima, C. T. A. 129, 229, 230

Ulrich, E. 230
Uspensky, B. 227

Van Seters, J. 4, 11, 102, 119, 128
VanderKam, J. C. 10
Vanhoozer, K. J. 122
Vannoy, J. R. 86
Vannoy, R. 999
Veijola, T. 5, 127
Vette, J. 86, 99

Walsh, J. T. 6, 202, 241
Waltke, B. K. 144
Walton, J. Harvey 38
Walton, John H. 38
Weik, J. W. 61
Weiland, K. M. 103
Weitzman, S. 123, 153
Wellhausen, J. 130
Wenham, G. J. 999
Westbrook, A. D. 129, 137, 231
White, E. 160
Whybray, R. N. 269
Widmer, M. 99, 100
Williams, J. G. 45, 52
Willis, J. T. 208
Wimsatt, W. K. 157
Wojcik, J. 121, 137
Wolde, E. van 6, 8
Wright, J. L. 59, 233, 249

Yee, G. A. 245
Yoon, S.-H. 227

Zakovitch, Y. 135
Ziegler, Y. 210

www.ingramcontent.com/pod-product-compliance
Lightning Source LLC
Chambersburg PA
CBHW070013010526
44117CB00011B/1549